xho

Beverley Kirsch

Silvia Skorge

with Sindiwe Magona

TEACH YOURSELF BOOKS

For UK order queries: please contact Bookpoint Ltd, 39 Milton Park, Abingdon, Oxon OX14 4TD. Telephone: (44) 01235 400414, Fax: (44) 01235 400454. Lines are open from 9.00–6.00, Monday to Saturday, with a 24-hour message answering service. Email address: orders@bookpoint.co.uk

For U.S.A. & Canada order queries: please contact NTC/Contemporary Publishing, 4255 West Touhy Avenue, Lincolnwood, Illinois 60646–1975, U.S.A. Telephone: (847) 679 5500, Fax: (847) 679 2494.

Long renowned as the authoritative source for self-guided learning – with more than 30 million copies sold worldwide – the *Teach Yourself* series includes over 200 titles in the fields of languages, crafts, hobbies, and other leisure activities.

British Library Cataloguing in Publication Data
A catalogue entry for this title is available from The British Library.

Library of Congress Catalog Card Number: On file.

First published in UK 1999 by Hodder Headline Plc, 338 Euston Road, London, NW1 3BH.

First published in US 1999 by NTC/Contemporary Publishing, 4255 West Touhy Avenue, Lincolnwood (Chicago), Illinois 60646–1975, U.S.A.

Typeset by Transet Limited, Coventry, England.
Printed in Great Britain for Hodder & Stoughton Educational, a division of Hodder Headline Plc, 338 Euston Road, London NW1 3BH by Cox & Wyman Ltd, Reading, Berkshire.

Impression number   10 9 8 7 6 5 4 3 2 1
Year   2004 2003 2002 2001 2000 1999

Contents

Acknowledgements

It is impossible to quantify Ralph Kirsch's part in helping us to bring this book to fruition. His interest, support, technical advice and especially his generosity of spirit are unfailing.

We would also like to thank Ms Theresa Soci for her help with proof reading and for the many useful suggestions she made.

We are grateful to the following copyright owners for permission to reproduce texts and photographs:

David Philip Publishers (Pty) Ltd, Cape Town
Fort Hare University, Alice, Eastern Cape
John Murray, London
Witwatersrand University Press, Johannesburg
Heinemann Publishers (Pty) Ltd, Johannesburg
Sunday Independent, Johannesburg
Maskew Miller Longman, Cape Town
Little, Brown, UK
Educum Publishers, Halfway House
Bona, Durban

Photographs

TV Bulpin, Muizenberg, Cape Town
Independent Newspapers, Cape Town
National Botanical Institute, Kirstenbosch, Cape Town
Department of Water Affairs, Pretoria
United Cricket Board of South Africa, Northlands, Johannesburg
Bona, Durban
MacGregor Museum, Kimberley
National Gallery, Cape Town
Mayibuye Centre, University of the Western Cape
Touchline Photo
Lorton Communications
Fair Lady, Cape Town
Internet
Imvo
SA Garden & Home

Introduction

About Xhosa

The word **Xhosa** comes from the name of a legendary chief. In addition to English and Afrikaans, there are nine official languages in South Africa. These nine belong to the Sub-Saharan *Bantu* or *Sintu*[1] family of languages.

Xhosa, Zulu, Ndebele and Swati constitute the Nguni group, Southern Sotho, Pedi (Northern Sotho) and Tswana constitute the Sotho group. Venda and Tsonga (Shangaan) do not belong to either the Nguni or the Sotho group.

Xhosa, President Mandela's mother tongue, is the southernmost of the nine African languages and together with Zulu, the most widely spoken language in South Africa, is spoken by approximately 18 per cent of South Africans, the vast majority of whom live in the Eastern and Western Cape Provinces.

'... history has proved that the Xhosa language is one of the tenaciously enduring elements of Xhosa culture for it has maintained a firm foothold on Southern African soil, growing like an evergreen, deep-rooted tree, and has manifested itself as a dynamic, vibrant, virile language adaptable to, and developing in harmony with, the changing environment in that it sprouts new words and expressions to accommodate new concepts and cultural items and, to an even greater extent, absorbs and xhosaizes foreign words and terms. This it did originally from the Khoisan languages, thus extending and enriching its vocabulary and speech sound system, and for the past hundred years has been doing [so] from Dutch and Afrikaans and in this century especially from English with which the amaXhosa came into close contact through the schools that were established by the missionaries of various denominations ...'

[1] *Si*ntu is used by Pahl in his dictionary as a variant of *Ba*ntu. In Xhosa *isi*Ntu denotes the language or anything characteristic, e.g. dress, custom of the *aba*Ntu or the *aba*kwaNtu, in the descendants of **Ntu**, their legendary progenitor. Pahl, H.W. (ed.) *The Greater Dictionary of Xhosa*, vol. 3. Alice: University of Fort Hare, 1989.

It was the Scottish missionary John Bennie of Lovedale who first recorded the **Xhosa** language and produced the first written texts using the Latin alphabet with the letters **c**, **q**, **x** representing the three click sounds. The clicks and sounds such as 'rh' (pronounced like the Afrikaans initial 'g' in 'goed' or the German 'ch' in 'nach') testify to the influence of the **Khoi** and **San** languages spoken by the indigenous herders and hunters of Southern Africa with whom the various **Xhosa** tribes had early and intimate contact.

This influence is also reflected in some geographical names e.g. *Keiskamma* (great water). Another manifestation of this influence is in the coexistence of synonyms taken from the **Khoi** language, for example:

*u*tyani / *i*ngca (grass)
*im*vu / *i*gusha (sheep)
*um*thakathi / *i*gqwira (sorcerer)

In more recent years many English and Afrikaans words have been 'xhosalised', for example:

*isi*kolo (school)
*i*bhokisi (box)
*u*matshini (machine)

Xhosa is a heterogeneous and complex language originating from a large and diversified group with many chiefs and clans. Until the mid-1950s the **Xhosa** spoken by *ama*Gcaleka and *ama*Rharhabe (also known as *ama*Ngqika or **Tshiwo Xhosa**)[2] was regarded as standard literary **Xhosa** – 'isi**Xhosa** esithethwa ngama**Ngqika** omgquba' – but nowadays the variations of the dialects of the other groups further north, namely *aba*Mbo or **Fingoes**, *aba*Thembu, *ama*Bomvana, *ama*Mpondo and *ama*Mpondomise, are also accepted in the written language. Like all languages, everyday colloquial **Xhosa** differs from that found in 'authoritative' grammars. Similarly, language usage often differs not only from region to region, but also from generation to generation, and you may encounter these differences when conversing with Xhosa speakers.

---

[2] *Ama*Gcaleka and *ama*Rharhabe were named after the two brothers, chief **Gcaleka** and chief **Rharhabe**. **Ngqika** was **Rharhabe**'s grandson.

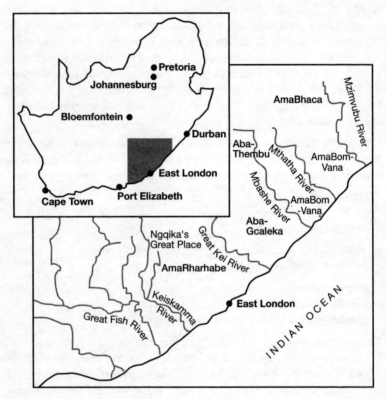

About this book

Teach Yourself Xhosa is intended for all who are interested in learning one of the most widely spoken African languages in South Africa.

It is aimed at both South Africans and visitors to South Africa, and at those who are learning Xhosa from scratch as well as those who would like to brush up their existing skills. As such, it should benefit students at high school and university level, as well as those involved in adult education.

Wherever possible, the communicative aspect of the language has been emphasised which has hopefully resulted in a course which is useful and practical. Cultural background and information forms an integral part of the course.

The book is divided into 16 units which range from basic functions and language usage in the initial units to more varied and complex usage in the later units. The inclusion of material from Xhosa literature and magazines is aimed at encouraging further reading.

Each unit consists of:

- a list of functions
- a dialogue (*in***coko**) 🔊 setting out the situation and functions
- a vocabulary (*isi***gama**) box 🔊 with all new words and expressions
- a 'How to ...' section ❓ which summarises and expands upon the functions dealt with in the conversation
- a 'How it works' section 🔧 which explains the grammatical structures as they occur in the conversations and exercises
- a 'How to apply it' section ✅ comprising a number of exercises to help you to evaluate your progress and your ability to apply the new vocabulary and structures you have learnt.

In the initial units, useful idiomatic expressions and phrases which crop up in the conversations are highlighted in a 'Try to memorise' box. You will understand their grammatical structure as you progress through the course.

Cultural information and songs are included throughout the course. Translations of the dialogues of each unit and the key to exercises are found after the last unit followed by a Xhosa–English vocabulary, an index and a bibliography.

The use of contrasting typefaces

One of the most striking features of **Xhosa** is the combination of different parts of speech into a 'single' word. Thus the equivalent of 'I *am* **Jenny**' is 'Ndi*ngu***Jenny**'. We have used contrasting typefaces to identify the components of **Xhosa** words and sentences as illustrated here. In order to establish this usage, these are used in all components of Units 1–3. In Units 4–16 contrasting typefaces have only been used in certain sections where they are useful in explaining grammar. English translations are in the same typefaces as the corresponding **Xhosa**, and therefore almost always self-explanatory.

Key to the use of typefaces:

To find examples consult the index.

Italics:

noun prefixes
object concords, *subject concords* of vowel verbs
negative subject concords and final *-i*
adjectival, relative, possessive concords and *suffix '-yo'*
recent past tense suffixes '-ile' and *'-e'*
-ni in instructions
emphatic pronouns preceded by **na-**, **ku-**, **nga-** and followed
by -**na**
locative prefixes and *suffixes*
■ *palatalised forms* of the *passive, locative* and *diminutive*
ideophones and *idioms*.

Bold:

stems of **nouns, verbs, adjectives, relatives**
interrogatives
possessive adjectives
■ final -**e** of **subjunctive**
negative infixes
elements with shortened emphatic pronoun **na-**, **ku-**, etc.

Italicised bold:

copulatives
two juxtaposed components.

<u>Underlining</u>:

added emphasis.

Worth knowing before embarking on this course

Before you start this course, it would be useful to make yourselves aware of some of the striking characteristics of the **Xhosa** language.

The lacing of words

One of the most striking differences between Xhosa and English sentence constructions is that Xhosa 'laces' words together where English has mostly separate words:

Ndi*ngu*Jenny	one word
I *am* **Jenny**	three words
Ndiya**vuya** uku*kw*azi	two words
I am **glad** to **know** *you* (lit. … you know)	six words

All nouns consist of two parts

Every noun in **Xhosa** consists of two parts, namely, a **prefix** and a **stem**. The **prefix** indicates whether a noun is **singular** or **plural** – unlike in English where, in most cases, the addition of 's' makes a noun plural. The **stem** carries the **meaning** and does not change:

*um*ntu	one person
*aba*ntu	people

Noun stems can occur with different prefixes thereby altering the meaning:

*um*ntu	one **person**	*um*Xhosa	a Xhosa **person**
*aba*ntu	**people**	*ama*Xhosa	Xhosa **people**
*isi*ntu	dress, language, custom of *aba*Ntu	*isi*Xhosa	Xhosa **language**
*ulu*ntu	**human**kind		
*ubu*ntu	common **human** decency	*ubu*Xhosa	'Xhosaness'

It is very important to be able to identify this division between prefix and stem as nouns are listed in dictionaries according to their stem.

The division of nouns into groups or classes

Another characteristic of **Xhosa**, as with most of the indigenous languages spoken south of the Sahara, is the **division of nouns** into different **groups** or **noun classes**. The **prefix** of the noun **determines** the **class** to which a particular noun belongs.

No article

Unlike English, there is no definite (the) or indefinite (a /an) article in **Xhosa**. Context indicates whether the meaning of, for example, '*um*ntu' is '*the* person' or '*a* person'.

No gender

Like English (but unlike many other languages such as French, German, Italian, etc.) there are no masculine, feminine or neuter nouns in **Xhosa**:

*um***numzana**	(a / the gentleman)
*um***fazi**	(a / the woman)
*um***ntwana**	(a / the child)

The equivalent of English pronouns are called subject concords

Subject concords (SC) are always attached, i.e. they never stand alone as is the case with English pronouns:

Ndihlala eKapa   **I** stay in Cape Town

Verb endings are the same for all persons, singular and plural

Ndiyavuya	**I** am glad
Siyavuya	**We** are glad
Ùyavuya	**You** (s.) are glad
Niyavuya	**You** (pl.) are glad
Úyavuya	**He/she** is glad
Bayavuya	**They** are glad

Verb endings remain the same not only for all persons, whether singular or plural, but also in all tenses.

Note: he **and** she = **ú**-. Note also a **tone difference** distinguishes **ù**- = you (s.) from **ú**- = he / she.

Word order

Question words (interrogatives) usually **follow the verb** (or predicate):

Ùphila **njani?**	**How** are you?
	(lit. You live **how**?)
Ùhlala **phi?**	**Where** do you live?
	(lit. You live **where**?)

Similarly, **descriptive words** such as adjectives, numerals and possessives, are usually placed **after the word they describe**:

*um*ntu *om*tsha	a **young** person
	(lit. a person *who* is **young**)
*um*ntu *om*nye	**one** person
	(lit. a person *who* is **one**)
*um*ntwana *wa*m	**my** child (lit. child *of* **mine**)

Another interesting difference between English and **Xhosa** word order is that **Xhosa** often starts a sentence with the predicate (verb):

Li**hle** *iz*ulu namhlanje.	lit. It is **beautiful** the **weather** today

---

Symbols and abbreviations

📼 recorded cassette

→ cf. / see **Unit** ...

SC	subject concord
OC	object concord
AC	adjectival concord
RC	relative concord
s.	singular
pl.	plural
adj.	adjective
lit.	literally

Preceding an element, e.g. '-na', means something must be attached before. Following an element, e.g. 'na-', means something must follow. On either side of an element, e.g. '-ng-', means something must precede and follow.

Pronunciation guide

It goes without saying that a written guide to pronunciation can at best only give an approximation of sounds. Therefore, to 'tune in' to the language try, as much as possible, to listen to mother-tongue speakers (radio and television are excellent resources) and to the cassette that accompanies this book.

Tone

Xhosa is a **tone language**. Its range of **tones** makes Xhosa the beautiful, musical language that it is. The **three** tonal distinctions are:

| high ´ tone | falling ^ tone | low tone ` |

Examples of some tonal patterns are:

high / falling / low	**ékhâyà**	at home
high / high / low	**ábántù**	people
high / low / low	**ízòlò**	yesterday
high / low	**mólò**	hello
low / high	**èwé**	yes

This difference in tone can change the meaning of two words or elements that are written identically, e.g.:

| **ùnjani?** How are **you**? (s.) | **úlùsú** *skin* | **íthàngá** thigh |
| **únjani?** How is **he/she**? | **úlúsù** *intestine* | **íthàngà** pumpkin |

Notwithstanding these differences in tone, learners should not allow concern regarding the use of 'the correct tone' to inhibit their efforts to speak, especially as a word may have different tone patterns in different dialects of Xhosa. As is the case with all languages, the context will, in most cases, help the listener to understand the intended meaning.

Stress

The penultimate syllable of most Xhosa words is **lengthened** (stressed):

| nam**hla**nje today | ibho**to**lo butter |
| um**hlo**bo friend | kulun**gile** all right |

The penultimate syllable in a sentence structure is often lengthened beyond the single word limit:

Ùve**la** phi?	Where do you come from?
Hayi, akukh**o n**to.	No, there is nothing bad.
	i.e. I'm fine.

A working guide to Xhosa pronunciation

Vowels

Letter	Approximate sound		Example	
a	English	fast	lala	(sleep)
e (open)	English	egg	ewe	(yes)
e (closed)	English	e(i)ght	iveki	(week)
i	English	be	nini	(when?)
o (open)	English	law	izolo	(yesterday)
o (closed)	English	own	ngoku	(now)
u	English	rule	umntu	(person)

In Xhosa, two vowels never follow one another within a word. Double vowels only occur in the **plural prefixes**, *oo-* and *ii-*:

   *oo***mama** (mothers)   *ii***veki** (weeks)

Double vowels also occur in some **demonstratives**:

   l**oo** nto (**that** thing)   ab**aa** bantu (**those** people over there)

In words adopted from English and Afrikaans, vowels are often separated by a hyphen:

   *i-*eropleni (aeroplane)   *i-*ofisi (office)

Xhosa speakers tend not to pronounce the final vowel of a word, especially when the following word starts with a vowel:

Yiz' apha	instead of	Yiza apha (Come here)
Ùlind' ithuba		Ùlinde ithuba! (Wait your chance!)
Enkos' kakhulu		Enkosi kakhulu (Many thanks)

Consonants

Single consonants similar to English in pronunciation are:

d	f	g
h	j	l
n	s	v
w	y	z

The Xhosa consonants **b**, **k**, **p**, **t** are very interesting. Followed by '*h*' (aspirated) they are pronounced as they are in English, i.e. that is accompanied by a puff of air:

> **B***h*ala! (Write!)
> **K***h*ap*h*a! (Go with!)
> **P***h*ap*h*a! (Be alert!)
> **T***h*at*h*a! (Take!)

However, when they are not followed by '*h*', air is drawn into the mouth. Compare the following:

B*h*ala! (Write!)	**B**ala (Count!)
K*h*ap*h*a! (Go with!)	i**K**a**p**a (Cape Town)
P*h*ap*h*a! (Be alert!)	i**pap**a (porridge)
T*h*at*h*a! (Take!)	u**tat**a (father)

In order to ascertain whether you are pronouncing:

> **b** or **b***h*   **k** or **k***h*   **p** or **p***h*   **t** or **t***h*

you might find it helpful, in the beginning, to hold your hand in front of your mouth when pronouncing these consonants. If you feel a puff of air, you will be pronouncing an aspirated consonant and vice versa.

m, when not followed by a vowel or the consonants b / v, is pronounced as a syllable:

> ú / **m** /ntù (person)   3 syllables
> ú / **m** / fu / ndi (student, pupil)   4 syllables

As **p***h* represents an aspirated 'p' and is **not** pronounced like the English '**f**', similarly, **t***h* represents an aspirated '**t**' **not English** 'th' as in 'thing'.

Some consonant combinations similar to English

ng	i**ng**oma (song) pronounced like English	'**ng**' in si**ng**
sh	i**shish**ini (factory)	'**sh**' in **sh**ine
tsh	ikhi**tsh**i (kitchen)	'**tch**' in ki**tch**en
ntsh	i**ntsh**onalanga (west)	'**nch**' in i**nch**
ny	u**ny**ana (son)	'**ny**' in ca**ny**on
ths	**ths**u (pitch-black)	'**ts**' in i**ts**

Consonant combinations with no English equivalents

Because there are no English equivalents of the following consonant combinations it might take you a little longer to master them:

dl	um**dl**alo (game, play)	
hl	**hl**ala (sit, stay (as in reside))	(cf. Zulu '**Hl**uh**l**uwe' or Welsh **Ll**andudno. Don't insert an 's' making it sound like 'shl')
ntl	i**ntl**anzi (fish)	
dy	-**dy**u**dy**uza (pour with rain)	
ty	uku**ty**a (to eat)	(cf. 'Cape' Afrikaans '**tjie**')
ts	iin**ts**apho (families)	('t' is not aspirated)
rh	i**Rh**awuti (Johannesburg)	(< Afrikaans 'goud' = gold; cf. <u>G</u>auteng (Sotho); Scottish 'lo<u>ch</u>')
kr	-**kr**ele**kr**ele (sharp < i**kr**ele = sword)	

<u>**kr**</u> as well as <u>**rh**</u> and the **clicks** are sounds taken over from the Khoi and San languages.

The clicks

The **three clicks** are represented by the letters:

c   q   x

When Xhosa became a written language in the 1800s, these three letters were chosen to represent the three click sounds because the letter **k** could replace each one:

c**at**	could be written **k**at
queen	could be written **k**ween
a**x**e	could be written a**k**s

C – the '*what a pity*' click

This is a **dental click** produced by pressing the **tip** of the **tongue** against the **upper front teeth** where these meet the gum and rapidly pulling it away with a '*tut-tutting*' sound.

Q – the 'champagne cork popping' click

This is a **palatal click** produced by pressing the **front part of the tongue** against the **hard palate behind the front teeth** and rapidly pulling it away with a '*popping*' sound.

X – the 'cantering horse' click

This is a **lateral click** produced by placing the **side of the tongue** against the **upper side teeth** and rapidly pulling it away with a '*clucking*' sound.

Clicks may also be aspirated, i.e. followed by '*h*':

c*h* -*ch*ach*a* (recuperate)	c -caca (be clear)
q*h* -q*h*uba (drive)	q -qubha (swim)
x*h* -x*h*ox*h*a (mash)	x -xoxa (discuss)

Remember that '*ch*' is not pronounced like the English 'ch' therefore '*ch*ach*a*' = 'recuperate' is not pronounced like the Latin American dance!

Non-aspirated clicks can be preceded by the following consonants and consonant combinations:

*g*c (voiced)	*n*c (nasalised)	*ng*c (nasalised voiced)	*nk*c*
c um*gc*a (row)	u*n*cedo (help)	ii*ngc*ango (doors)	i*nk*citho (expenditure)

*g*q	*n*q	*ng*q	*nk*q
q u*gq*irha (doctor)	i*n*qwelo-moya (aeroplane)	i*ngq*ondo (intelligence)	*nkq*o*nkq*oza (knock)

*g*x	*n*x	*ng*x	*nk*x
x i*gx*alaba (shoulder)	u*n*xano (thirst)	i*ngx*oxo (discussion)	i*nkx*aso (support)

*In these nasalised voiceless sounds 'k' is not pronounced.

 Practise the **q** clicks by listening to the first few lines of the '*Click Song*' made famous by **Miriam Makeba**. Try singing along:

'I*g*qirha lendlela ngu*q*o*ng*qothwane,
Ebeqabel' e*g*qith' apha uqo*ng*qothwane!'

Here are some phrases or words you'll come across in this course. Take special note of the implosives **b**, **t**, **k**, the **consonant combinations** with no English equivalents and the **clicks**:

Sobonana!	*We'll see each other!*
Bekumnandi ukudibana nawe	*It was nice to meet you*
Hamba kakuhle!	*Go well!*
Namkelekile eKapa	*Welcome to Cape Town*
Siza kufika eKapa kamsinyane	*We'll arrive in Cape Town shortly*
Kulungile	*All right*
Molo tata!	*Hello, father!*
Ndisatotoba	*I'm well (I'm still tottering along)*
Siphi isibhedlele?	*Where's the hospital?*
Abadlali badlala umdlalo	*The players are playing a game*
Masihlale ngaphandle namhlanje	*Let's sit outside today*
Mhlawumbi, yonke imihla	*Perhaps, every day*
Intle le ntlanzi	*It's beautiful, this fish*
Intle intlakohlaza	*It's beautiful, spring*
Tyala ezi zityalo ehlotyeni	*Plant these plants in summer*
Ikomityi enye kuphela	*One cup only*
Nantsi ikofu!	*Here's the coffee!*
Ukrelekrele gqitha	*He's very sharp*
Uhlala eRhawutini	*He lives in Johannesburg*
Ndingakuncedisa?	*Can I help you?*
Zincede	*Help yourself*
Uchan' ucwethe!	*You're spot on!*
Cheba ingca!	*Cut the grass!*
Ndigqibile!	*I've finished!*
Ekugqibeleni!	*At last!*
Qhuba kuQoboqobo	*Drive to Keiskammahoek*
Masiqabule unxano	*Let's quench the thirst*
Ndinxaniwe	*I'm thirsty*
Uxolo!	*Sorry! (lit. peace)*

1 | Ukwazana *kwi-***eropleni*** *Getting acquainted on an aeroplane*

In this Unit you will learn how to:

- exchange greetings
- welcome a group
- ask how someone is and respond to being asked how you are
- introduce yourself and respond to an introduction
- ask where someone lives and respond to being asked where you live
- say goodbye to a group and individuals

Incoko (*Dialogue*)

Thandi Thamsanqa and Jenny Murray are seated next to each other on a flight from Port Elizabeth. The stewardess greets the passengers.

Umququzelelikazi	Molweni *ma*nene n*ama*nenekazi!
	Namkelek*ile ku*flight 301 *o*ya *e***Kapa**!
UThandi	Molo **sisi**, ù**njani** namhlanje?
UJenny	Ewe **sisi**, si**khona**!
UThandi	Oo! Ù*si***thetha** kakuhle *isi***Xhosa**, sisi!
	Ndi*ngu***Thandi** Thamsanqa.
UJenny	Ndi*ngu***Jenny** Murray. Ndiya**vuya** uku*kw***azi**,
	Thandi. Wena, u**phila njani**?
UThandi	Hayi, si**phil***ile* enkosi. Nam, ndiya**vuya** uku*kw***azi**,
	Jenny.
UJenny	Ù**hlala** *e***Kapa**, **Thandi**?
UThandi	Ewe, si**hlala** *e***Pinelands**.

*Anglicised version of the much more picturesque '*in*qwelo-moya' (lit. wagon (of the) air).

UJenny	Oo! Nam ndi**hlala** *e***Pinelands**!
UThandi	Ndawoni kanye?
UJenny	Ngase**Forest Drive**. Wena u**hlala ndawo***ni*?
UThandi	Ngase**Pinelands** High School.

For the duration of the flight Thandi and Jenny get to know each other and agree to make contact again soon.

Umququzelelikazi	*U***xolo**, *ma***nene** n*ama***nenekazi**. **Qhobosha***ni* *ama***bhanti**. Siza ku**fika** *e***Kapa** kamsinya. Enkosi kakhulu ngoku**khetha** i-*Rainbow Airlines*. Ndiya**themba** so**bonana** kwakhona kamsinyane! **Namkelek***ile* *e***Kapa**! **Hamba***ni* kakuhle!
UJenny	**Hamba** kakuhle Thandi. Beku**mnandi** kakhulu uku**thetha** nawe.
UThandi	So**bonana** sisi, beku**mnandi** uku**dibana** nawe!

Isigama (*Vocabulary*)

*um*ququzelelikazi	**stewardess**	ndi-	I
Molweni	good day / hello (pl.)	*-ng-*	*am*
*ma*nene	**gentlemen** (direct address)	*u*Thandi	**Thandi**
na*ma*nenekazi	and **ladies**	-vuya	**glad**
namkelek*ile*	(you (pl.) are) **welcome**	ndiyavuya	I am **glad**
*ku*flight	*on* (*board*) flight	uku-	to
*o*ya *e*Kapa	*which* is *going*	*-kw-*	*you* (s.) (object)
	to **Cape Town**	-azi	**know**
molo	hello (to one person)	uku*kw*azi	to **know** *you*
sisi (< *u*sisi)	**sister** (direct address)	wena	as for you (s.)
ù-	you (s.) (subject)	-phila	**be well, alive**
njani?	**how?**	hayi	no
ù**njani?**	**how** are you?	si**phil***ile*	we are **well**
namhlanje	today	enkosi	thank you
ewe	yes	nam	me too, I also
si-	we	-hlala	stay, live (also sit)
-**khona**	(be) present / here	*e***Pinelands**	in **Pinelands**
si**khona**	we are **here** i.e. well	ndawoni kanye?	where abouts exactly?
-si-	it (referring to *isi*Xhosa)	ngase-	near / in the vicinity
-**thetha**	**speak**	*u*xolo	excuse me (lit. peace)
kakuhle	well	**qhobosha***ni*	**fasten** (pl.)
*isi*Xhosa	**Xhosa**	*ama***bhanti**	(seat) **belts**

siza kufika	we will **arrive**	hamba*ni*	**go** (pl.)
kamsinya(ne)	shortly, soon	**hamba**	**go** (s.)
ngoku**khetha**	for **choosing**	beku**mnandi**	it was **nice**
-**themba**	**hope**	kakhulu	very
so**bonana**	we'll **see each other**	na*we*	**with** *you*
kwakhona	again	uku**dibana**	to **meet**

Try to memorise

Namkelekile!	Welcome! (pl.)
Ndiyavuya uku*kwazi*	I am glad to know *you* (s.)
Ndawoni?	Where abouts exactly?
Sobonana	We shall see each other
Bekumnandi ukudibana nawe	It was nice to meet (with) you (s.)
Bekumnandi ukuthetha nawe	It was nice to talk with you (s.)

? *How to ...*

Exchange greetings

With **one person**:

> Mol<u>o</u> sisi!
> Mol<u>o</u> *n*kosikazi!

With *more than* one person:

> Mol<u>weni</u> *ma*nene n*ama*nenekazi!

A guide to help you greet appropriately in Xhosa

1 An older man of your father's generation:

Molo tata! (affectionate)	Hello father!
Molo bawo! (more respectful)	Hello my father!
Molo mnumzana!	Hello sir! (lit. owner of homestead/s = um**zi** / imi**zi**)
Molo mhlekazi! (formal)	Hello sir! (lit. handsome big one)

2 An older man of your grandfather's generation:

Molo tat'omkhulu! Hello grandfather!

3 A woman of your mother's generation:

Molo mama! Hello mother!

4 A woman of your grandmother's generation:

Molo makhulu! Hello grandmother!

5 A married woman of your age or younger:

Molo nkosikazi! Hello madam!
(cf. Afrikaans *mevrou*,
French *madame*)

6 An unmarried lady or a young girl:

Molo nkosazana! Hello miss! (cf. Afrikaans
mejuffrou, French
mademoiselle)

(The literal meaning of in**kosazana** is a little chieftainess
i.e. princess.)

7 A person of approximately the same age as yourself:

Molo mfondini! Hello my fellow!
(< *umfo* = fellow) + -*ndini* is used as a term of affection
between male equals)

Molo bhuti! Hello brother!

Molo sisi! Hello sister!

Molo mhlobo wam! Hello my friend!

8 A young man:

Molo mfana! Hello young man!
(A young man after circumcision is referred to as *um***fana**.)

9 A young girl (also daughter):

Molo ntombi! Hello young lady!

10 A little girl:

Molo ntombazana! Hello little girl!

11 A little boy:

Molo nkwenkwe!	Hello little boy!
Molo nkwenkwana!	Hello little boy!
Molo kwedini!	Hello little chap!

(**kwedini** < in**kwenkwe** + -*ndini* expresses affection, intimacy between an older and younger man / boy)

12 A child:

Molo mntwan'am!	Hello my child!

→ See cultural background.

Welcome a group

Namkelek*ile* (lit. You (pl.) are **welcome**)
Note: W̲amkelek*ile* (lit. You (s.) are **welcome**)

Ask how someone is

Singular	Plural
Ùnjani?	Ninjani?
Ùphila njani?	Niphila njani?

Respond to being asked how you are

Singular	Plural
Hayi, ndiphil*ile*.	Hayi, siphil*ile*.
Ndikhona.	Sikhona.

In Xhosa, unlike in English, there is a distinction in form between the **second person singular** and **plural** '*you*' (cf. Afrikaans *jy*; *julle*, French *tu; vous*). It is common practice in Xhosa to use the plural form '*Ni-*' instead of the singular form '*Ù-*' when enquiring after someone's health, thereby showing an interest in the well-being not only of the person being directly addressed, but also in that of the immediate family. Similarly, the response, more often than not, will be in the plural form '*Si-*' (= '*we*') even though only one person is responding.

Xhosa speakers often preface '**Hayi**' (= '**no**') when responding positively to the question 'How are you?':

Hayi, siphil*ile*.   **No**, we are well.
(cf. Afrikaans **Nee**, dit gaan goed. **No**, it's going well.)

A positive response will often also be qualified by a complaint of sorts,
e.g. about the weather, work, fatigue, etc.:

Ndiphilile **ngaphandle**   I'm fine **except for**
  kobu bushushu.   this heat.

→ See **Unit 7** for other ways of asking after someone's health and
responding.

Introduce yourself

Ndi*ngu*Jenny Murray
Ndi*ngu*Nkosikazi Thamsanqa

Note: *in*kosikazi   = lady, madam
   *u*N**kosikazi** + surname   = Mrs

Respond to an introduction

Ndiya**vuya** uku*kw*a**zi**.

Ask where someone lives

Singular	Plural
Ùhlala phi?	Nihlala phi?

Respond to being asked where you live

Singular	Plural
Ndi**hlala** *e***Kapa**.	Si**hlala** *e***Kapa**.

Say goodbye

Singular	Plural
Hamba kakuhle!	**Hamba**ni kakuhle!

So**bonana**!

Note: **Sala** kakuhle! (s.) **Sala**ni kakuhle! (pl.) = '**Stay well!**' is said by the
party who is leaving to the party who is staying.

Cultural background

'**Greetings** are the key to almost everything among Xhosa speakers in particular, and among Africans in general. We do not only get surprised but also are somewhat disturbed when someone walks past without saying hello.'

(Chapole, S. *Course Notes in Conversational Xhosa.* (Summer School) Department of Adult Education and Extra-Mural Studies University of Cape Town, 1988.)

The various stages from babyhood to old age are of great importance in Xhosa society. This is mirrored in how people of various age groups address each other. It is important for us, as learners of Xhosa, to be aware of this etiquette when greeting Xhosa speakers.

Molo/Molweni is used to greet at any time of day. It is followed by the name or title of the person/s being addressed and is the usual way of initiating a conversation with anyone, irrespective of age. Usually the person who is arriving greets first. However, a younger person should always be the first to address an older person, whatever the circumstances. The greeting includes questions about state of health, current affairs, the weather, etc.

In an article in the *Sunday Independent* (23/11/1997, p.10) entitled *Urban Youth don't know what it means to be African*, journalist **Lungile Madywabe** describes the puzzlement of his 23-year-old nephew when he discovers that his urban way of greeting an older man meets with indignation. 'He is used to meeting and greeting a lot of people in Johannesburg, but no one has told him before that merely saying "*Molo, kunjani ndikhona*" (*Hi, how are you, I am fine*) is inadequate, at least in the subtle terms of traditional Xhosa etiquette.' The young man didn't realise that 'greeting in an African culture is more than just uttering the words.' A detailed explanation of who he was and where he came from had been expected.

Madywabe goes on to reflect on 'how important a role the rural setting plays in the development of our minds. Those of us who grew up in urban areas when the influence of Western cultures was still minimal, and where elderly people counselled us a lot, are fortunate to have had access to the experiences and insight that have made us understand certain indigenous practices. Although certain things may not have made sense then because we were young, it is somehow strangely ironic how they now fit into place as we travel through adulthood.'

How it works

1 The Xhosa equivalent of English pronouns 'I,' 'we', 'you' (s. & pl.)

Ndi-	I
Si-	We
Ù-	You (s.)
Ni-	You (pl.)

The Xhosa equivalents of English pronouns **never stand alone**. They are therefore known as **subject concords** (SC):

Ndiyavuya	**I** am glad
Siyavuya	**We** are glad
Ùyavuya?	**You** (s.) are glad?
Niyavuya?	**You** (pl.) are glad?

2 Proper names

You will have noticed **proper names** are **prefixed** by *u-* which is omitted in direct address:

*u***Jenny**   *u***Thandi**   **Molo Jenny / Thandi**

Xhosa first names ending in **-a** or **-e** are not necessarily feminine and those ending in **-o** are not necessarily masculine as is the case in many Romance languages:

uThemba̱ (promise)   uSipho̱ (gift)   masculine
uThembeka̱ (reliable)   uNomvuyo̱ (mother of joy) feminine

3 Giving instructions

Giving instructions in Xhosa is easy. When instructing one person simply
use the verb stem.* To give instructions to more than one person simply
suffix '-ni':

Singular	**Plural**
Hamba kakuhle!	**Hamba**ni kakuhle!
Sala kakuhle!	**Sala**ni kakuhle!
Thetha isiXhosa!	**Thetha**ni isiXhosa!
Hlala phantsi!	**Hlala**ni phantsi! (Sit down!)
Qhobosha ibhanti!	**Qhobosha**ni amabhanti!

*Verb stems prefix 'uku-' = 'to', and thereby form the **infinitive**. In **Xhosa**
the infinitive is also a noun and as such is listed in dictionaries under the stem.

4 Making statements

The Xhosa statements that you have come across so far have a similar
pattern to their English equivalent:

NdinguJenny.   I *am* **Jenny**.
Sihlala ePinelands.   We **live** *in* **Pinelands**.

5 Asking questions

As in English, there are two types of question: The first type requires a
'yes'/'no' answer. In Xhosa only **intonation** distinguishes statements and
questions:

Ùthetha isiXhosa kakuhle.   You **speak** Xhosa well.
Ùthetha isiXhosa kakuhle (na)?   Do you **speak** Xhosa well?

To make this distinction clearer, **na** is often added.

The second type of question requires **specific answers. Question words**
(interrogatives) usually follow **the verb** (or **predicate**) and **do not occur
at the beginning of a question** as is the case in English:

Ùphila **njani**?   **How** are you? (lit. You are
                                                     alive **how**?)
Ùhlala **phi**?   **Where** do you **stay**?

→ See **Unit 2** and **Unit 8** for more about **interrogatives**.

6 Some Xhosa equivalents of English prepositions

In Xhosa, there are several ways in which the equivalent of English prepositions (*in, on, at, to, from*, etc.) can be expressed, two of which are illustrated in this unit:

Ukwazana _kwi_-eropleni.	Getting **acquainted** _on_ the **aeroplane**.
Ùhlala _e_Kapa?	Do you **stay** _in_ **Cape Town**?
Namkelek_ile_ _e_Kapa!	**Welcome** _to_ **Cape Town**!

Note: The **context** denotes translation of the preposition.

→ See **Unit 4** for more examples.

Cultural background

In Xhosa society a great deal of significance is attached to the name given to a new-born baby. The name often reflects the hopes, aspirations, emotions, special qualities, historical events and even family circumstances at the time of birth, e.g. a boy called **Kwanele** (< *ukw*anela = to become enough) indicates that the family now considers itself complete!

Natural occurrences at the time of the birth also influence a choice of name: a girl named **Nomakhwezi** (< *ama*khwezi = stars) was probably born on a clear night while a girl named **Nomvula** (< *im*vula = rain) was probably born when it was raining!

No- meaning '**mother of**' is often prefixed to a masculine name to form the feminine equivalent while *-kazi / -wa / -eka* are feminine suffixes. The suffix *-iwe* indicates either a girl's or boy's name.

Boys	Girls	Meaning	Derivation
Sipho	**Sipho**_kazi_	**gift**	(< *isi*pho = a **gift**)
Siph_iwe_	_No_zi**pho**		
Vuyo	**Vuyo**_kazi_	**gladness, joy**	(< *uku*vuya = *to* be **glad**)
Vuyani	_No_m**vuyo**		
Mandla	_No_**mandla**	**strength**	(< *ama*ndla = **strength**)
Khaya	_No_**khaya**	**home**	(< *i*khaya = **home**)
Mpumelelo	_No_**mpumelelo**	**success**	(< *uku*phumelela = *to* **succeed**)
Mbulelo	**Bulel**_wa_	**gratitude** (< *uku*bulela = *to* **thank**)	

Xola	Xoliswa	pacifier	(< ukuxola = to calm down)
Bongani	Bongiwe	praise, be praised	(< ukubonga = to praise)
Linda	Lindiwe	wait, awaited	(< ukulinda = to wait)
Thando	Thandiwe	love, loved	(< ukuthanda = to love)
	Thandeka	loveable	
Themba	Thembeka	trust, trustworthy	(< ukuthemba = to hope)

Song
Molweni Nonke!

Molweni nonke, niphila njani?	Hello all of you, how are you?
Sisaphil' enkosi.	We are still well thank you.
Kunjani kuwe?	How are you?

How to apply it

1 Greetings and introductions

(a) How would you greet Thandi?

(b) How would you greet an older lady?

(c) How would you greet an older gentleman?

(d) How would you greet a female friend?

(e) How would you greet a male friend?

(f) How would you greet a married lady?

(g) How would you greet a gentleman?

(h) How would you greet an unmarried lady?

(i) How would you greet a child?

(j) How would an air hostess greet passengers?

(k) How would you introduce yourself?

(l) How would you respond to an introduction?

2 Ask one person

(a) How are you?

(b) Do you live in Cape Town?

(c) Whereabouts exactly?

3 Say

(a) Welcome to Cape Town
     ladies and gentlemen!
(b) I am well, thank you.
(c) I am glad to meet you.
(d) I live in Cape Town.
(e) It was nice to talk with you!
(f) It was nice to meet you!
(g) We shall see each other soon again!
(h) Goodbye when leaving a friend.
(i) Goodbye when leaving a group.
(j) Goodbye when a friend is leaving.
(k) Goodbye when a group is leaving.

4 What questions would you ask to obtain the following answers?

(a) Sikhona.
(b) Ndihlala eKapa.
(c) NgaseForest Drive.

5 Re-write the following putting in the appropriate word breaks

NamndiyavuyaukukwaziJenny.

6 Do you recognise the following Xhosa words which are in everyday use?

fundi
indaba
ingozi
ithuba
zama

7 Listen to the following Xhosa words adopted from English and write down their meanings in the order in which you hear them.

(a) _____   (h) _____   (o) _____
(b) _____   (i) _____   (p) _____
(c) _____   (j) _____   (q) _____
(d) _____   (k) _____   (r) _____
(e) _____   (l) _____   (s) _____
(f) _____   (m) _____   (t) _____
(g) _____   (n) _____

2 | Ukudibana kwakhona kwaMurray
Meeting again at the Murrays' home

In this Unit you will learn how to:

■ invite guests into your home
■ express pleasure at meeting
■ make introductions (using kinship terms)
■ ask what someone's name is
■ offer refreshments
■ ask someone what they want to do
■ ask someone what they prefer to do
■ suggest doing something
■ offer help

Incoko

Thandi and Themba Thamsanqa visit Jenny and Peter Murray.

UJenny	Molweni! **Ngena***ni*!
UThandi	Ewe, ni**njani**?
UJenny	Hayi, si**khona**. Kumnandi kakhulu uku**ni**bona!
UThandi	*Ngum***yeni** wam, *u***Themba** lo.
UJenny	Molo Themba, ndiya**vuya** kakhulu uku**kw**azi. Lo *ngum***yeni** wam, *u***Peter**.
UThemba	Ndiya**vuya** uku**n**azi.
UPeter	**Na***thi* siya**vuya** uku**n**azi. **Namkelek***ile* e**khay***eni* lethu!

David, Jenny and Peter's son, comes in.

	Lo *ngu***nyana** wethu.
UThandi	Molo *m***ntwan'**am. *Ng*ubani *i***gama** lakho?
UDavid	Ndi*ngu***David**.
UThemba	Ù**yafunda**,* David?
UDavid	Ewe, ndi**funda** *e***Grove**.
UThandi	Ù**funda phi** uku**thetha** *isi***Xhosa**?

UDavid   Ndi*si*fund=a *esi*kol*weni*, **Nkosikazi**.

Peter asks about Themba and Thandi's children.

UPeter   Nina, nina*ba*ntwana?
UThemba   Ewe sina*bo*, *u*nyana nentombazana.
UPeter   Baya**funda**?*
UThemba   Ewe, baya**funda**. Ba**funda** *e*Westerford.
UJenny   **Kunjani** ngoku**phunga**? Ni**khetha** *i*ti okanye *i*kofu
                    okanye *i*nto *e*banda*yo* yoku**sela**?
OoThamsanqa   Nokuba yintoni. Ewe, nokuba yintoni.
UPeter   Ni**funa** *uku*hlala ngaphakathi okanye ngaphandle?
UThandi   Masihlal*eni* ngaphandle. **Lihle** namhlanje! Ndinga*ku*-
                    ncedisa, Jenny?
UJenny   Enkosi **sisi**. **Peter** no**Themba**, ninga**ncokola**!
UPeter   **Kulung**i*le*!

*Lit. Are you learning? i.e. Are you at school? Are they learning?
i.e. Are they at school?

Isigama

kwa-	at the home of	sina*bo*	we **have** *them*
ngenani!	**come in** (pl.)	nentombazana	and a **daughter**
ni-	you (subject) (pl.)	ba-	they
ku**mnandi**	it's **nice**	**kunjani** ngoku-	how about
-*ni*-	you (object) (pl.)	-**phunga**	**drink** (hot liquid)
-**bona**	see	-**khetha**	**prefer**
*u*m**yeni** wam	my **husband**	*i*ti	**tea**
lo	this	okanye	or
-n- (< -*ni*-)	you (object) (pl.)	*i*kofu	**coffee**
na*thi*	and *us*	*i*nto *e*banda*yo*	something **cold**
ekhay*eni* lethu	*to* our **home**	yoku**sela**	(of) to **drink**
*u*nyana wethu	our **son**	*oo*Thamsanqa	the **Thamsanqa**s
mntwan'am	my **child**	nokuba yintoni	whatever
(< *um*ntwana wam)		-**funa**	**want**
*n*gubani *i*gama	**what** *is* your **name**?	ngaphakathi	inside
lakho?		ngaphandle	outside
-**funda**	**learn/study/read**	masihlal*eni*	**let's sit**
phi?	**where**?	**lihle**	it's **beautiful**
*esi*kol*weni* (< *isi*kolo)	at **school**	-*nga*-	may/can
uku**thetha**	to **speak**	-**ncedisa**	**help** <u>someone with</u>
nina	as for you (pl.)	-**ncokola**	**chat**
nina*ba*ntwana?	do you have **children**?	kulungile	it's all right / fine
*aba*ntwana	**children**		

Try to memorise	
Namkelekile ekhayeni lethu!	Welcome to our home!
Kunjani ngokuphunga?	How about something warm to drink?
Nikhetha into yokusela?	Do you prefer something cold to drink?
Nokuba yintoni	Whatever
Masihlaleni ngaphakathi / ngaphandle	Let's sit inside / outside
Lihle namhlanje!	It is beautiful (weather) today!

? *How to ...*

Invite guests into your home

Singular	Plural
Ngena!	Ngena*ni*!

Express pleasure at meeting (again)

Kumnandi kakhulu uku*ku*bona (kwakhona) (to one person)
Kumnandi kakhulu uku*ni*bona (kwakhona) (to more than one person)

Make introductions

Jenny noPeter, lo *ngum*yeni wam, *u*Themba
Ndinga*nazisa umy*eni wam, *u*Themba

Ask what someone's name and surname is

*Ng*ubani *i*gama lakho?
*Ng*ubani *i*fani yakho? (*i*fani < Afrikaans *van*) (What is your surname?)

Note: When you can't recall the name of someone whom you've met before:

Ndiza kuthi u*ng*ubani kanene? (lit. I am going to say who are you, by the way, i.e. just remind me)

See Cultural background.

Offer refreshments

Kunjani ngoku**phunga**/ngoku**sela**?

Singular	Plural
Ù**funa** *into* yoku**phunga**?	Ni**funa** *into* yoku**phunga**?
Ù**funa** *into* yoku**sela**?	Ni**funa** *into* yoku**sela**?

Ask what someone wants/prefers to do

Ù**funa** uku**hlala** ngaphakathi okanye ngaphandle?
Ù**khetha** uku**hlala** ngaphakathi okanye ngaphandle?

Suggest doing something

Masi**ncokole**!   Masi**phunge** *i***kofu**!   Masi**hlale** ngaphandle!

Note: These forms already incorporate a plural marker, i.e. '-si-' = 'us'. However, the addition of the plural suffix '-**ni**' can be heard in everyday speech when addressing a group.

Masi**hlale***ni* phantsi!   Masi**thethe***ni* *isi***Xhosa**!   Masi**hambe***ni*!

Offer to help with a specific activity

Ndinga*ku***ncedisa**?

cf. uku**nceda** = to **help someone by doing something <u>for them</u>** not together with them.

Cultural background

When Xhosa speakers meet for the first time, it is customary to find out each others **clan names** by saying:

Ù**ngumni**? (to a male) Ù**ngumamni**? (to a female) or
Khawuzibonge! / **Khawuzithuthe**! Please praise *yourself*!

A **clan** is a conceptual kinship group. Members trace their kinship to a common male ancestor. The name of this male ancestor is the clan name – **isiduko** – and members are usually called by this name. Mentioning the **clan** name(s) of someone you wish to thank or sing the praises (**izibongo**) of, starting with the main clan name and then continuing with the sub-clan names, is the ultimate way of showing respect used among family and friends, e.g.:

Tolo, Zulu, Mchenge, Mabhanekazi

The response to this is *Utsho kum kanye!* or *Ndim kanye lowo!* A man and woman of the same clan name can never marry as they are considered to be related to one another. A woman always keeps her clan name which is prefixed by *Ma-*. Children take their father's clan name.

Dlamini, Gambu, Jwarha, Jili, Mbanjwa, Mnguni, Mpinga, Tolo and *Tshawe* (**royal** *clan name*) are but a few of the many clan names.

Do you know which famous South African has the clan name *Madiba*?

Find out the clan names of your Xhosa friends and acquaintances.

How it works

1 The Xhosa equivalent of English 3rd person pronouns 'he', 'she', 'they'

You have already learnt how to say '**I**', '**we**' and '**you**' (s. & pl.) in Xhosa. In English, the pronouns for the **3rd** person '**he**' / '**she**' / '**it**' tell us whether the noun we are referring to is masculine, feminine or neuter. This gender distinction does not exist in Xhosa. Instead, **subject concords** are used. These subject concords are **derived** from **noun prefixes** and are **attached** to the **verbal form**, e.g.:

*Um*ntwana úya*kw*azi ukuthetha *isi*Xhosa?	Does the **child** (he / she) **speak** Xhosa? (lit. He / she **knows how** to **speak** Xhosa?)

*Aba*ntwana <u>ba</u>funda *isi*Xhosa.   The **children** (they) **learn** Xhosa.

Note: The use of both noun and subject concord in Xhosa explains why some Xhosa speakers, when speaking English, will say, for example:

The **children** <u>**they**</u> are learning.

Similarly, the fact that 'ú-' = 'he' / 'she' explains why some Xhosa speakers are inclined to use 'he' / 'she' interchangeably in English.

'ú-' = 'he' / 'she' has a **higher tone** while 'ù-' = 'you' (s.) is pronounced with a **low tone**.

To ensure that you are not misunderstood, you can use the so-called **emphatic pronoun** '*we***na**' = '**as for** *you*' (cf. French '*toi*'), as well as the **subject concord** 'ù-':*

_We_na, ùphila njani?

→ *See **Unit 3** for a complete list of noun classes and their corresponding **subject concords**.

2 The present tense – positive

In the present tense (as well as in all other tenses) verb endings are the same for all persons, masculine and feminine, singular and plural.

In the **present tense** the verb ends in -**a**. The subject concord (SC) is the only indicator of person and number.

Ndiyafunda	**I** am learning
Siyafunda	**We** are learning
Ùyafunda	**You** are learning
Niyafunda	**You** are learning
Úyafunda	**He/She** is learning
Bayafunda	**They** are learning

The **infix** -**ya**-, inserted between SC and verb, only occurs in the **present tense positive** and simply denotes the **long form** of this tense.

However, if an **object** (noun) or an **adverb** (e.g. 'kakhulu' = 'a lot/much') follows the verb, -**ya**- is usually **omitted**. This is known as the **short form** of the present tense:

Ndifunda **kakhulu**.	I read **a lot**.
Ùfunda _eyunivesithi_?	Do you study _at_ **the university**?
Úfunda _esikolweni_.	He/she learns _at_ **school**.
Sifunda **namhlanje**.	We are studying **today**.
Nifunda **phi** ukuthetha isiXhosa?*	**Where** are you learning to speak Xhosa?
Bafunda _ekhaya_.	They are studying _at_ **home**.

Note: * '-ya-' is **never** used in a sentence **with a question word**:

_Aba_ntwana ba_ya_funda.
Bafunda **phi**? **Ba**funda _esikolweni_. **Ba**funda **kakhulu**.

3 Infixes '-nga-' = 'may', 'can' and '-sa-' = 'still'

Unlike the infix '-ya-' '-nga-' and '-sa-' have a specific meaning:

Ndinga_kun_ceda?	**May** I help _you_?
Ningancokola.	You **may** chat.

Ndingangena?	**May** I come in?
Sisaphil' enkosi.	We are **still** well, thanks.

4 The infinitive

Nearly all **verbs** in the **infinitive**, like the forms in the present tense positive, also end in '-**a**':

uku**thetha**	uku**phunga**	uku**sela**
uku**fika**	uku**dibana**	uku**hlala**

There are only **three exceptions**:

uk**w**azi*	to **know**	Ndiy**azi**.	I **know**.
uku**thi**	to **say**	Ùth**ini**?	What do you **say**?
uku**tsho**	to **say so**	Útsh**o**.	He / she **says so**.

Note: '-**thi**' and '-**tsho**' never occur with infix '-**ya**-'.

* As it is not possible to have two different vowels following one another in the same word in Xhosa, **sound changes** must take place, i.e. **u** > **w**: uku- + -**azi** > uk**w**azi.

5 The Xhosa equivalent of English 'am', 'is', 'are'

With **nouns beginning with '_u_-' and '_um_-'**

Ndi**ngu**Jenny.	I **am** Jenny.
Lo **ngu**nyana wam.	This **is** my son.
Lo **ngum**yeni wam.	This **is** my husband.
Lo **ngum**ntwana wam.	This **is** my child.

Note: Idiomatic expression: **Ng**ubani **i**gama lakho? What **is** your **name**? (lit. It **is** who **name** of yours?)

Where '**am**', '**is**', '**are**' is understood

Ùnjani?	**How** (**are**) you?
Ndi**khona**.	I (am) **well**. (lit. I am **here**)
Si**khona**.	We (are) **well** (lit. We are **here**)

6 The Xhosa equivalent of English 'me', 'us', 'you' (s. and pl.) called object concords

-ndi-	me	-si-	us
-ku-	you (s.)	-ni-	you (pl.)

The form of the **object concord** is **identical** to that of the **subject concord** except where the subject concord is a vowel only:

ù- (SC) > _ku-_ (OC)

In this case -_k_- is inserted to separate two vowels.

Object concords are always placed **directly before the verb**:

Ndiya_ku_**thanda**.	I **love** _you_. (lit. I _you_ **love**.)

Position of subject and object concord

Ndiyabona.	I see.	Uya_ndi_**bona**?	Do you **see** _me_?
Siyabona.	We see.	Uya_si_**bona**?	Do you **see** _us_?
Ndiyafundisa.	I teach.	Ndiya_ku_**fundisa**.	I **teach** _you_.
Siyafundisa.	We teach.	Siya_ni_**fundisa**.	We **teach** _you_.

The '-_i_-' of -_ndi_-, -_si_-, -_ni_- is dropped before a vowel verb:

Ùya_nd_**azi**?	Do you **know** _me_?
Niya_s_**azi**?	Do you **know** _us_?
Ndiya**vuya** uku_n_**azi**.	I am **glad** to **know**, i.e. meet _you_.

Note: In the present tense positive -ya- is usually omitted when some other word follows the verb (predicate), e.g.:

Ndiy**a**funda.	BUT	Ndi**funda** _isi_**Xhosa**.

This is also the case when there is an object concord involved:

Ndiy**a**_si_**funda**.*	BUT	Ndi_si_**funda** _esi_kol_weni_.

*-_si_- = '_it_' refers to _isi_**Xhosa**.

7 Interrogatives

You are already familiar with the interrogative -**phi**? = '**where**?':

Uhlala **phi**?	**Where** do you live/stay?
Ufunda **phi** isiXhosa?	**Where** do you learn Xhosa?

You have also come across **njani**? = '**how**?':

Uphila **njani**?	**How** are you?
Ku**njani** ngokuphunga?	**How** about (something hot) to drink?

Another important question word is -**bani**? = '**who**?':

_Ng_ubani?	**Who** is it?
_Ng_ubani igama lakho?	**What** is your name? (lit. It is **who** ...)

8 Possessive adjectives – 'my', 'our', 'your' (s. & pl.)

In Xhosa, unlike in English, **possessive adjectives** e.g. '**my**'; '**our**'; '**your**'; etc., follow the noun:

Lo *ngu*mntwana *wa*m.	This *is* **my** child. (lit. This is child *of* **mine**)
Lo *ngu*mntwana *wa*kho?	*Is* this **your** (s.) child?
Lo *ngu*nyana *we*thu.	This *is* **our** son.
*Ngu*bani *i*gama *la*kho?	What *is* **your** name?
*I*gama *la*m *ngu*David.	**My** name is David.

From these examples you can see that Xhosa **possessive adjectives** consist of **two parts**. The **first part**, e.g. '*wa-*' '*la-*' = '*of*', **changes** according to the noun in question, while the **second part**, representing '**mine**', '**yours**', '**ours**', **does not change**.

→ See **Unit 14.4**, for more **possessive adjectives**.

9 Na = 'and', 'with' as well as 'have', 'has'

Before a noun '**na-**' = '**and**' (as well as '**with**', '**also**', '**even**'):

na- + *a-* = **na-**

Manene **na**manenekazi, namkelekile eKapa!

na- + *i-* = **ne-**

Sinabo abantwana, unyana **ne**ntombazana.

na- + *u-* = **no-**

Ndifuna ukudibana **no**Peter **no**Themba. (i.e. **with** Peter **and** Themba)

When two dissimilar vowels follow one another in the same word, to avoid an inharmonious sound, yet another **sound change** occurs.

Between a subject concord and a noun '**-na-**' = '**have**', '**has**':

Ni**na**ba**ntwana**?	(Do you **have** children?)	(lit. You **with** children?)
Ewe, si**na**ba**ntwana**.	(Yes, we **have** children.)	(lit. We **with** children.)
or: Ewe, si**na**bo.*	(Yes, we **have** *them*.)	(lit. Yes, we **with** *them*.)

* -*bo* shortened form of emphatic pronoun '*bo*na' 'as for *them*'.

Some kinship terms and relationships

- **Parents –** *Abazali*
  mother **umama**   father   u**tata**
- **Children –** *Abantwana*
  daughter   in**tombi**   son   u**nyana**
- **Grandparents –** *Oomawokhulu*
  grandmother u**makhulu**   grandfather   u**tat'omkhulu**
- **Grandchild(ren) –** *Umzukulwana* (*aba-*)
- **Aunts**
  maternal   u**makazi**   paternal   u**dad'obawo**
- **Uncles**
  maternal   u**malume**   paternal   u**tat'omkhulu**
                                           (older)
                                    u**tat'omncinci**
                                           (younger)

- **Cousins –** *Abazala*
  parents are **brother** and **sister**   u**mza** / u**mzala**
  fathers are **brothers**   u**kayise**
  mothers are **sisters**   u**kanina**
- **Nieces and Nephews –** *Abatshana*
- **Kinship terms between siblings**
  u**mnta**kwethu   my / our **brother**
  u**dade**wethu   my / our **sister**
  u**mafungwashe**   eldest **sister** (lit. by whom one takes an oath)
  aba**nta**kwethu   my / our **siblings** (lit. of our **home**)
  aba**nta**kwenu   your (s./pl.) **siblings** (lit. of your **home**)
  aba**nta**kwabo   his / her / their **siblings** (lit. of their **home**)
  oo**dade**wethu   my / our **sisters**

Brothers refer to one another as:
  um**khuluwa** = **older brother**
  um**ninawa** = **younger brother**

When talking **about** a **third person's brother** or **sister**:
  u**mna**kwabo (his / her / their **brother**)
  u**dade**wabo (his / her / their **sister**)

When talking **to** a 2nd person about a:

sister	u**dade**wenu	your (s./pl.) **sister**
brother	u**mna**kwenu	your **brother**

☑ *How to apply it*

1 Ask the appropriate question for the following answers

    (a) NdinguDavid.
    (b) Hayi, sikhona.
    (c) Ewe, ndifunda eGrove.
    (d) Ndi*si*funda esikolweni.

2 Complete appropriately

UThandi Uphi umyeni _____, Jenny?
UJenny Lo ngumyeni _____, uPeter.
UThandi Lo ngumntwana _____, Jenny?
UJenny Ewe, lo ngunyana _____, uDavid.

3 Being hospitable

    (a) Invite someone into your home: _____
    (b) Express pleasure at meeting: _____
    (c) Ask him / her to sit down (phantsi): _____
    (d) Offer refreshment: _____
    (e) Say goodbye (to someone leaving): _____

4 Ask a guest what he/she wants

    (a) Do you want coffee?
    (b) Do you want tea?
    (c) Do you want to meet (with) Peter?
    (d) Do you want to speak with Themba?
    (e) Do you want to speak Xhosa?
    (f) Do you want to sit outside?
    (g) Do you want to sit inside?
    (h) Do you want go now (ngoku)?

5 Ask guests what they want

    (a) Do you want to drink coffee?
    (b) Do you want to drink tea?
    (c) Do you want to meet (with) Peter?
    (d) Do you want to speak with Themba?
    (e) Do you want to speak Xhosa?

(f) Do you want to sit outside?
(g) Do you want to sit inside?
(h) Do you want go now?

6 Ask what your guest prefers

(a) Do you prefer tea or coffee?
(b) Do you prefer to sit inside or outside?
(c) Do you prefer to speak Xhosa or English (isiNgesi)?

7 Suggest to your friend

(a) Let's go in!
(b) Let's sit down
(c) Let's speak Xhosa!
(d) Let's drink coffee!
(e) Let's drink tea!
(f) Let's drink something cold!
(g) Let's sit outside!
(h) Let's chat!
(i) Let's stay!
(j) Let's go!

8 Ask where and give the answer

(a) ____hlala phi uThandi noThemba?
(b) ____funda phi ukusithetha isiXhosa, uDavid?
(c) ____funda phi ukusithetha isiXhosa, David?
(d) ____hlala phi ooThamsanqa nooMurray?

9 Complete the questions and answer them

(a) Ngu_____ igama lakho?
(b) Ùhlala _____?
(c) Ùphila _____ namhlanje?

10 Listen to the dialogue and say whether the statements are correct or not

(a)	Thandi visits Jenny.	yes	no
(b)	Thandi wants a cool drink.	yes	no
(c)	Thandi wants to sit inside .	yes	no
(d)	Jenny accepts Thandi's help.	yes	no

3 | Ukwazi ukuthetha isiXhosa
Knowing how to speak Xhosa

In this Unit you will learn how to:

■ discuss your ability with regard to speaking and understanding Xhosa
■ make comparisons
■ make polite requests

Incoko

Peter and Themba continue with their conversation.

UThemba	*We*na Peter, ù*si*thetha kakuhle *isi*Xhosa! *Ndi*xelel*e*, wa**funda phi** uku*si*thetha kakuhle kangaka?
UPeter	Nda**khulela** *e*fama nga*se*Rhini. Ndaqhuba ke ngoku*si*funda *esi*kolweni. Ngelishwa ndi**libele** *in*to eninzi. *E*nye *in*to, ndiy**azi** ukuba ndisa**phazama** kakhulu kodwa ndiy**azama** noko!
UThemba	Ayinamsebenzi loo *n*to yoku**phazama**. *In*to e**balulekile**yo kukuba ù**zam***e* uku*si*thetha yonke *imi*hla!
UPeter	Ù**nyanis***ile*. Ku**funeka** ù*ndi*xelel*e* xa ndi**phazama**.
UThemba	Kulungile, kodwa ke ù**yalandela**.
UPeter	Ewe, ukuba *um***ntu** úya**cothisisa**!
UThemba	Heke, **nam** ndiza ku**zama** uku**zekelela**.
UPeter	Enkosi kuba *a*ndi**thethi** kakuhle njengoJenny. **Na**ye wa**khulela** *e*fama *e*Mpuma-Koloni. *Ye*na wa*si*funda *esi*kolweni na*se*yunivesithi. Ú*si*thetha njengo*m*Xhosa kangangokuba uya*si*fundisa ngoku!
UThemba	Intle loo *n*to! Uy**azi** ba**thi** *aba*ntu ba*se*Holani: *'So veel tale as jij kan, so veel male is jij man'* (lit. As many languages as you can, so much more are you a person!).
UPeter	Y*in*yaniso leyo!

Isigama

*Ndi*xelel*e*	tell *me*	xa	whenever
wa**funda**	you **learnt**	-**landela**	**follow**
kangaka	so	ukuba	if
nda**khulela**	I **grew up**	*um*ntu	a **person**
*e***fama**	*on* a **farm**	-**cothisisa**	**speak slowly**
nga*se***Rhini**	near **Grahamstown**	heke	well then
nda**qhuba**	I **continued**	na*m*	I **too**
ke	then	ndiza ku**zama**	I will **try**
ngelishwa	unfortunately	uku**zekelela**	to **speak slowly**
-**libele**	forgotten	*a*ndi**theth***i*	I **don't** speak
*in*to *e***ninzi**	a lot	njengoJenny	as Jenny
enye *in*to	another **thing**	na*ye*	she **also**
ukuba	that	*e*M**puma-Koloni**	**Eastern Cape**
ndi*sa***phazama**	I still **make mistakes**	yena	as for her
kodwa	but	wa*si***funda**	she **studied** *it*
ndi**yazama**	I am **trying**	na*se***yunivesithi**	and *at* **university**
noko*	in a small way	njengo*m***Xhosa**	like a **Xhosa**
ayinamsebenzi	it doesn't matter	kangangokuba	so much so
loo *n*to	that (thing)	-**fundisa**	**teach**
yoku**phazama**	of **making mistakes**	ngoku	now
*in*to	the **thing**	intle loo *n*to!	that's lovely!
*e***balulekile***yo*	which is important	*a*ba**ntu**	Dutch (lit. the people
kukuba	is that	ba*se***Holani**	of Holland)
yonke *imi***hla**	every **day**	y*in***yaniso** leyo	that's the **truth**
*ù*nyanis*ile*	you are **right**		
ku**funeka**	you must (lit. it's **necessary**)		

*There is no exact equivalent in English for '**noko**'. It is a kind of pleading for the listener's sympathy and understanding (cf. Afrikaans 'maar').

Try to memorise

Ngelishwa ndilibele into eninzi	Unfortunately I've forgotten a lot
Ayinamsebenzi loo nto	It doesn't matter
Into ebalulekileyo kukuba	The important thing is that
uzame	you try
Unyanisile	You are right
Intle loo nto!	That's lovely!
Yinyaniso leyo	That's the truth

? *How to ...*

Discuss your ability with regard to speaking and understanding Xhosa

Ndiya*kw*azi uku**thetha** *isi***Xhosa**.	I know (how) to **speak** Xhosa.
Andi<u>kw</u>**azi**.	I do *not* **know** (how).
U**xolo**, *a*ndi*si***thethi** kakuhle.	I'm sorry, I do*n't* **speak** *it* well.
Ndi*si***thetha** kancinci nje.	I **speak** *it* just a little.
Ndisa**funda**.	I am still **learning**.
Ndiya**zama** noko.	I am **trying** in a small way.
Ù**yaqonda**?	Do you **understand**?
Ù**ya***ndi***va**? (lit. Do you **hear** *me*?)	Do you **understand** *me*?
Ù**ya***ndi***landela**?	Do you **follow** *me*?
Ndiya**qonda**.	I **understand**.
*Andi***qond***i*.	I do*n't* **understand**.
Ndi**qonda** kancinci nje.	I **understand** a little.
*Andi***landel***i* kakuhle.	I do*n't* **follow** well.
U**xolo**, ù**th**<u>i</u>**ni**?	**Pardon, what** <u>do</u> **you say**?
U**xolo**, ù**th**<u>e</u>**ni**?	**Pardon, what** <u>did</u> **you say**?
Zekelela! / Nceda ù**zekelel**<u>e</u>!	**Speak slowly**!/**Please speak slowly**!
Cothisisa! / Nceda ù**cothisis**<u>e</u>!	**Speak slowly**!/**Please speak slowly**!
Phinda kwakhona.	**Repeat** (again)!
Nceda ù**phind**<u>e</u> kwakhona.	Please **repeat** (again).
Nceda ù*ndi***xelel**<u>e</u> xa ndi**phazama**.	Please **tell** *me* when I make mistakes.
*Y*intoni le nge*si***Xhosa**?	**What** is this in Xhosa?
*Y*intoni '...' nge*si***Xhosa**?	**What** is '...' in Xhosa?
I**thetha ntoni** le nto nge*si***Xhosa**?	**What** does this (thing) mean in Xhosa?

Make comparisons

*Andi***theth***i* kakuhle **njengo**Jenny.
Yena u*si***thetha** *isi***Xhosa njengo**mXhosa.

How it works

1 Summary of nouns of Units 1–3

To help you understand how **nouns** are **grouped** according to their **prefix**:

um-:				
*um*ntu	*um*ntwana	*um*yeni	*um*hlobo	*um*fana
*um*ququzelelikazi	*um*Xhosa	*um*numzana		*um*hlekazi

u-:					
*u*mama	*u*tata	*u*nyana	*u*bawo	*u*sisi	*u*bhuti
*u*makhulu	*u*tatomkhulu			*u*Nkosikazi Thamsanqa	
*u*Thandi	*u*Jenny	*u*Peter	*u*Themba	*u*David	

aba-:			
*aba*ntu	*aba*ntwana	*aba*hlobo	*aba*fana

um-:
*um*sebenzi

imi-
*imi*hla

i(li)-:	
*i*gama	*i*khaya

ama-:			
*ama*nene	*ama*nenekazi	*ama*Xhosa	*ama*bhanti

isi-:					
*isi*Xhosa	*isi*Ngesi	*isi*Bhulu	*isi*Zulu	*isi*Phutukezi	*isi*kolo	*isi*gama

in- / *i-*:						
*in*coko	*in*kosikazi	*in*kosazana	*in*kwenkwe	*in*tombazana		
*i*kofu	*i*Kapa	*i*-eropleni	*in*qwelo-moya	*i*ti	*in*to	*i*fama
		*i*yunivesithi				

uku- / *ukw-*:				
*uku*vuya	*uku*phila	*uku*funa	*uku*khetha	*uku*hamba
*uku*sala	*uku*dibana	*uku*bona	*uku*thanda	*uku*phunga
*uku*ngena	*uku*funda	*uku*ncokola	*uku*ncedisa	*uku*sela
*uku*qonda	*uku*themba	*uku*xelela	*uku*zekelela	*uku*zama
*uku*thetha	*ukw*amkela	*ukw*azi	*ukw*azisa	*ukw*azana

Noun groups

Class	Prefix	Stem	S.C.	Translation
1	um-	**ntu**	ú-	the person (he/she)
2	aba-	**ntu**	ba-	the people (they)
1a	u-	**Themba**		Themba (he)
	u-	**Thamsanqa**		Thamsanqa (he)
	u-	**mama**	ú-	the mother (she)
	u-	**nyana**		the son (he)
	u-	**loliwe**		the train (it)
2a	oo-	**Sipho**		Sipho and co. (they)
	oo-	**Thamsanqa**		the Thamsanqas (they)
	oo-	**mama**	ba-	the mothers (they)
	oo-	**nyana**		the sons (they)
	oo-	**loliwe**		the trains (they)
3	um-	**hla**	u-	the day / date (it)
4	imi-	**hla**	i-	the days (they)
5	ili-	**zwe** (one syllable)	li-	the country (it)
	i-	**gama** (two syllables)	li-	the name (it)
6	ama-	**zwe**	a-	the countries (they)
	ama-	**gama**	a-	the names (they)
7	isi-	**kolo**	si-	the school (it)
8	izi-	**kolo**	zi-	the schools (they)
9	in-	**to**		the thing (it)
	in-	**coko**	i-	the conversation (it)
	i-	**fama**		the farm (it)
10	izin-	**to** (one syllable)		the things (they)
	iin-	**coko** (two syllables)	zi-	the conversations (they)
	ii-	**fama**		the farms (they)
11	ulu-	**thi** (one syllable)	lu-	the stick (it)
	u-	**lwimi** (two syllables)	lu-	the tongue / language (it)
10	izin-	**ti** (no 'h')	zi-	the sticks (they)
	ii-	**lwimi**	zi-	the tongues/languages (they)
14	ubu-	**sika**	bu-	the winter (it)
	ubu-	**ntu** *	bu-	human decency (it)
15	uku-	**hamba**		to walk / walking (it)
	ukw-	**azi**	ku-	to know / knowledge (it)
	uk-	**oja**		to roast / roasting (it)

* → See Cultural background.

From these tables you will see that all **nouns** are grouped into **classes according** to their **prefix**.

■ The noun classes are **numbered 1–15**.

  Classes **1, 3, 5, 7, 9** and **11** are **singular** nouns.

  Classes **2, 4, 6, 8** and **10** are the corresponding **plural** nouns.

■ Classes **14** and **15** have **no plural**.

  Classes **12** and **13 are no longer active** in Xhosa.

No hard and fast rules enable one to classify a particular noun into a specific class or group. However a few principles apply. Nouns of:

■ **Classes 1** and **2**: only refer to **people** (but not all nouns referring to people are in this class).

  Classes 1a and **2a**: include all **proper names, kinship terms**, (e.g. mother/s, father/s, uncle/s, aunt/s, sister/s, brother/s), some **professions** (e.g. doctor/s, social worker/s, teacher/s) and **personifications** (e.g. train/s, radio/s, machine/s).

■ **Classes 3** and **4**: many trees and rivers; some parts of the body, e.g. leg/s, mouth/s, finger/s, as well as some abstract nouns, (e.g. miracle/s, anger, contribution/s, organisation/s, law/s, marriage/s).

■ **Classes 5** and **6**: some parts of the body, (e.g. eye/s, breast/s, knee/s, ankle/s, bone/s), nouns describing personal characteristics, (e.g. brave person/s; eloquent speaker/s; skilful person/s; liar/s) and some adopted from English/Afrikaans, (e.g. police, card, wheel, kitchen)

Note: Some nouns of **Classes 1 and 9** have their plural in **Class 6**, e.g.:

*um*Xhosa   *in*doda (man)   *in*kosikazi   *in*kwenkwe   *in*tombazana
*ama*Xhosa   *ama*doda   *ama*k̲hosikazi   *ama*k̲hwenkwe   *ama*n̲tombazana.

  Classes 7 and **8**: all **languages, ordinal numbers** 2–10, (2nd, 3rd, 4th etc.) many **implements**, words adopted from English or Afrikaans beginning with '<u>sc</u>-', <u>st</u>-', '<u>sp</u>-': e.g. *isi*kolo < <u>sc</u>hool, *isi*tovu < <u>st</u>ove, *isi*pili < <u>sp</u>ieël [mirror], as well as many **grammatical terms**.

  Classes 9 and **10**: many **animals**, nouns adopted from English and Afrikaans, (e.g. bus/es, car/s, money, bicycle/s, window/s, phone/s)

  Class 11: many **abstract nouns**. Plural: prefix of Class 10 where applicable.

  Class 14: mainly abstract nouns but also others, (e.g. face, beer, honey, winter, night). **No plural**.

  Class 15: all **infinitives** which can also function as nouns.

2 Emphatic pronouns

Similar to the French '*moi*', *toi*', '*lui*', '*mna*', '*wena*', '*yena*' is used for **emphasis** and **contrast**, and can be used as well as, but **never instead of**, the **subject concord**:

*M*na, **ndi**yahamba ngoku.	**As for** *me*, **I** am going now.
*Thi*na, **si**yahamba ngoku.*	**As for** *us*, **we** are going now.
*We*na, **ù**phila njani?	**As for** *you*, how are **you**?
*Ni*na, ni**na**bo aba**ntwana**?	**As for** *you*, do **you** have children?
*Ye*na, uPeter wa**si**funda isi**Xhosa** esi**kol**weni.	**As for** *him*, Peter, **he** learnt Xhosa *at* **school**.
*Ye*na, u**Jenny** wakhulela e**fama**.	**As for** *her*, Jenny **she** grew up *on* a **farm**.
*Bo*na, aba**ntwana** bakhulela e**Kapa**.	**As for** *them*, the children, **they** grew up *in* **Cape Town**.

*→ see Cultural background.

Note: The function of '**-na**' is simply to avoid a one syllable word to which Xhosa has an aversion! However, when the two elements of the **emphatic pronoun** are **transposed**, '**na-**' carries a **meaning**:

*m*na > **na***m*	and *me* / **with** *me* / *I* **too, also**
*we*na > **na***we*	and *you* / **with** *you* / *you* **too, also**
*thi*na > **na***thi*	and *us* / **with** *us* / *we* **also**
*ye*na > **na***ye*	and *him*, *her* / **with** *him*, *he*r *he*, *she* **too, also**
Na*m*, ndiyavuya uku*kw***azi**.	*Me* **too**, I am pleased to know *you*.
Bekumnandi ukuthetha **na***we*.	It was nice to talk **with** *you*.
Na*thi*, siyavuya uku**na**zi.	*We* **also**, we are pleased to know *you*.

3 Present tense negative

The negative of the present tense is formed by prefixing '*a-*' before the subject concord and changing the final vowel of the verb '*-a*' to '*-i*'. If a noun (object) follows the verb, the initial vowel of the prefix of all subsequent nouns is dropped e.g.:

*Andi*phung*i* <u>k</u>ofu.	I do<u>n't</u> **drink** coffee.
*Andi*fun*i* <u>k</u>uphunga <u>k</u>ofu.	I do<u>n't</u> **want** to drink coffee.

Positive	**Negative**
Ndiya**phunga**.	*Andi***phung***i*.
Siya**phunga**.	*Asi***phung***i*.
Ùya**phunga**?	*Aku***phung***i*? (kofu)
Niya**phunga**?	*Ani***phung***i*?
Úya**phunga**.	*Aka***phung***i*.
Baya**phunga**.	*Aba***phung***i*.

Remember: -ya- only occurs in the present tense **positive** when no object follows the verb.

As you can see, when the subject concord consists of a vowel only, e.g. ù- / ú; -**k**- (or -**w**- in spoken language) is inserted:
a- + ù- > *a*<u>k</u>u- / a*w*u-; **a**- + ú- > *a*<u>k</u>a-.

Note: The negative form of: 'Ndiya**phila**' / 'Ndi**phil***ile*' is *Andi***phil***anga*. See Unit 7.3

4 Remote past tense

One of the past tenses used when talking about past events and actions is the remote or narrative past tense. The subject concord indicates the tense. It is characterised by a long '-**a**-' with a falling tone:

Ndakhulela efama.
Sakhulela efama.
Wakhulela* efama.
Nakhulela efama.
Wakhulela* efama.
Bakhulela efama.

* ù- + **a** = **wa**- and ú- – + **a** = **wa**-.

5 Polite requests

The **tone** used when giving a one-word instruction in Xhosa largely indicates the 'softness' or 'severity' of such an instruction, e.g.:

Hlala phantsi! (s.)   **Hlala***ni* phantsi! (pl.)

However this can easily be changed into a **polite request** by saying:

Ndi**cela u**hlal**e** phantsi.   (lit. I **beg** you (s.) sit down.)
Ndi**cela ni**hlal**e** phantsi.

'Ndicela' can also be said when asking for something:

> Ndicela *amanzi*.   (lit. I **beg** for water.)
> Ndicela *i*kofu.
> Ndicela *into* yokusela.

'Nceda' (lit. help) is the equivalent of the English '**please**' and can also introduce a polite request:

> Nceda uhlale phantsi.
> Nceda*ni* nihlale phantsi.

Note: The verb following 'Ndicela' and '**Nceda**' ends in -**e**.
→ See also **Unit 4.5**.

> Ndicela ùthethe *isi*Ngesi.   **Please** (you) speak English.
>   (lit. I **beg** (that) you
>   speak English.)
> Nceda ùthethe *isi*Xhosa.   **Please** (you) **speak** Xhosa.
> Nceda ùzame ukuthetha *isi*Xhosa. **Please** (you) **try** to speak Xhosa.
> Nceda ùcothisise.   **Please** (you) **speak** slowly.
> Nceda ùkhumbule.   **Please** (you) **remember**.
> Nceda*ni* nithethe *isi*Xhosa.   **Please** (you all) **speak** Xhosa.

6 Impersonal ku- – the equivalent of English 'it'

> **Ku**njani?   How is **it**? (lit. **It** is how?)
> **Ku**funeka ndihambe.   **It** is necessary (that) I go
>   [i.e. I must go]
>
> **Ku**lungile.   **It** is all right.
> **Ku**shushu.   **It** is hot.
> **Ku**thethwa *isi*Ngesi apha.   **It** is spoken (English here).

7 More interrogatives

In **Units 1** and **2** you were introduced to the question words '**phi**?'; '**njani**?' and '**bani**?'. Two other interrogatives which you will need are '**nini**?' = '**when**?' and '**ntoni**?' = '**what**?':

> Wazalwa **nini**?   **When** were you born?
> Ufuna **ntoni**?   **What** do you want?
> Uthi**ni**?   **What** do you say?

Note: with the verb '-**thi**' = '**say**', the shortened form '-**ni**?' (< **ntoni**?) must be used.

8 Conjunctions 'because', 'but', 'if', 'that', 'when'

Like English, Xhosa has **conjunctions to join clauses**:

Ndilandela kakuhle **kuba** uyacothisisa.	I follow well **because** you are speaking slowly.
Ndiyazama ukuthetha isiXhosa, **kodwa** kunzima.	I am trying to speak Xhosa, **but** it is difficult.
Ndiyaqonda **ukuba** umntu úyacothisisa.	I understand **if** a person speaks slowly.
Ndiyazi **ukuba** ndiyaphazama kakhulu.	I know **that** I make a lot of mistakes.
Nceda *ndi*lungise **xa** ndiphazama.	Please **correct** *me* **when** I make a mistake.

Note: A verb **following 'xa'** (= 'when', 'whenever') **never infixes** '-ya-'.
→ See **Unit 12.1**.

Cultural background

The concept of 'Ubuntu'

'*Ubu*ntu' – common human decency, humanism or as defined by the editor of the *S.A. Medical Journal*, Professor Daniel Ncayiyana, in a recent editorial, '*ubu*ntu, the deeper meaning of which cannot be explained in one or two sentences but which can be said to encompass all the attributes of caring' for one's fellow human being. The concept of *ubu*ntu is also closely related to the proverb: '*Um*ntu ng*um*ntu ng*aba*ntu.' (lit. a **person** is a **person** through **other people**.)

Professor Ncayiyana explains the meaning of this proverb as 'attaining the totality of being a fully adjusted member of society only through the support, counselling, love, assistance, shelter, example, etc., of one's fellow human beings'.

Nkosi sikelel' iAfrika,	God bless Africa,
Maluphakanyisw' uphondo lwayo,	Let its horn (i.e. spirit) rise,
Yiva imithandazo yethu,	Hear also our prayers,
Nkosi, sikelela, **thina**,	God bless us,

Lusapho lwayo,	Its (Africa's) family,
Nkosi, sikelela, **thina**,	God bless us,
Lusapho lwayo.	Its family.
Yiza Moya! Sikelela, Nkosi, sikelela,	Come, O Spirit, bless God bless,
Yiza Moya! Sikelela, Nkosi, sikelela,	Come, O Spirit, bless God bless,
Yiza Moya Oyingcwele,	Come, O Holy Spirit,
Nkosi, sikelela, **thina**,	God bless us,
Lusapho lwayo.	Its family.
Nkosi, sikelela, **thina**,	God bless us,
Lusapho lwayo.	Its family.

The first verse of **NKOSI 'SIKELEL' I-AFRIKA** was composed in 1897 by **Enoch Sontonga**, a school teacher from Kliptown, to be sung by school children and church choirs. It was completed by **Samuel E. Mqhayi** (→ see **Unit 16** for more about **Mqhayi**) and later, it was adopted by the African National Congress as the closing hymn at meetings. Other organisations followed this practice and the song became recognised as the people's national anthem. As its dissemination was largely oral, there are a number of versions which often vary from place to place and from occasion to occasion. It is often sung in a combination of Xhosa, Zulu and Sotho, and versions of it are also used as the national anthems in Zambia, Zimbabwe and Tanzania.

☑ *How to apply it*

1   Say (Yithi)

(a)   I want to speak Xhosa.

(b)   May I speak English?

(c)   I like to speak Xhosa.

(d)   I try to speak Xhosa.

(e)   I speak only a little Xhosa.

(f)   I am still learning.

(g)   I still make a lot of mistakes when I speak Xhosa.

(h)   Please correct me.

2 What would you say when you don't understand what someone says?

(a) _____

(b) _____

(c) _____

(d) _____

3 Answer the following questions in the negative

(a) Uyakwazi ukuthetha isiNgesi?   Hayi, _____

(b) Uthetha kakuhle isiXhosa?   Hayi, _____

(c) Uyaqonda?   Hayi, _____

(d) Uyaphila? / Uphilile?   Hayi, _____

(e) Uyakhumbula?   Hayi, _____

(f) Ufuna ikofu?   Hayi, _____

(g) Ufuna amanzi?   Hayi, _____

4 Convert these instructions into polite requests

(a) Thetha isiXhosa.

(b) Zekelela.

(c) Phinda kwakhona.

(d) Zama kwakhona.

(e) Ndixelele.

5 Try to get the gist of the following dialogue

These are the sorts of questions you will find useful should you want to know someone's biographical details:

(a) Wazalwa nini **uMongameli Nelson Mandela**?

(b) Wazalwa nge18 Julayi ngo-l918.

(a) Wakhulela phi?

(b) Wakhulela _e_**Qunu** _e_**Mpuma-Koloni** (Eastern Cape Province).

(a) Wafunda phi?

(b) Waya kwisikolo sama**Wesile** (Wesleyan). Emva koko (after that) waya kufunda eyunivesithi yase**Fort Hare**.

(a) Emva koko wenza ntoni?

(b) Wasebenza njengepolisa lasemgodini (as a mines policeman) kodwa waqhuba ngokufundela (study for) ubugqwetha (legal profession).

6   Use the map on the following page to answer the questions.

Besides English, *isi*Ngesi, and Afrikaans, *isi*Bhulu, South Africa has
nine official languages: **Nguni** group: *isi*Xhosa, *isi*Zulu, *isi*Swati,
*isi*Ndebele; **Sotho** group: *isi*Suthu, *isi*Pedi (North Sotho),
*isi*Tswana. Other groups: *isi*Venda, *isi*Tsonga (or Shangaan).

All languages prefix *isi-*: *isi*Jamani, *isi*Frentshi, *isi*Phutukezi, etc.

(a)   Kuthethwa eziphi iilwimi kakhulu *eN*tshona-Koloni?
(b)   Kuthethwa eziphi iilwimi kakhulu *eM*puma-Koloni?
(c)   Kuthethwa eziphi iilwimi kakhulu *eM*ntla-Koloni?
(d)   Kuthethwa eziphi iilwimi kakhulu *e*Freyistata?
(e)   Kuthethwa eziphi iilwimi kakhulu *e*Gauteng?
(f)   Kuthethwa eziphi iilwimi kakhulu *eM*pumalanga?
(g)   Kuthethwa eziphi iilwimi kakhulu *kwa*Zulu-Natal?
(h)   Kuthethwa eziphi iilwimi kakhulu *eM*ntla-Ntshona?
(i)   Kuthethwa eziphi iilwimi kakhulu *eM*ntla?
(j)   Kuthethwa *isi*Xhosa kakhulu ndawoni *eM*zantsi Afrika?
(k)   Kuthethwa *isi*Zulu kakhulu ndawoni *eM*zantsi Afrika?
(l)   Kuthethwa *isi*Tswana kakhulu ndawoni *eM*zantsi Afrika?
(m) Kuthethwa *isi*Suthu kakhulu ndawoni *eM*zantsi Afrika?

7   Complete according to the example

*Ama*Xhosa a̲thetha *isi*Xhosa.

(a)   *Ama*Zulu _____ .
(b)   *Ama*Swati _____ .
(c)   *Ama*Ndebele _____ .
(d)   *Ama*Bhulu _____ .
(e)   *Ama*Venda _____ .
(f)   *Ama*Ngesi _____ .
(g)   *Ab̲e*Tswana _____ .
(h)   *Ab̲e*Suthu _____ .

kuthethwa	it is spoken	na̲se-	and *in*
u̲lwimi	language (lit. tongue)	*eziphi ii̲*lwimi?	which languages?
ii̲lwimi	languages	zonke ii̲lwimi	all languages

1. *iN*tshona-Koloni   (Western Cape)
2. *uM*ntla-Koloni   (Northern Cape)
3. *iM*puma-Koloni   (Eastern Cape)
4. *i*Freyistata   (Free State)
5. *Kwa*Zulu-Natal

6. *i*Gauteng   (Sotho for 'gold')
7. *uM*ntla-Ntshona   (North West Province)
8. *uM*ntla   (Northern Province)
9. *iM*pumalanga   (Lit. coming out of the sun i.e. the east)

*uM*ntla
(Upper side)

*iN*tshonalanga
(Where the sun disappears)

N

*iM*pumalanga
(Where the sun goes out)

*uM*zantsi
(Lower part)

4 | Ukuthetha ngomsebenzi
Speaking about work

In this Unit you will learn how to:

■ ask what someone does for a living
■ say what your occupation is
■ ask where someone works
■ respond to being asked where you work
■ comment on someone's work

Incoko

Peter and Themba discuss work while waiting for Jenny and Thandi to join them with the coffee, cake and sandwiches.

UPeter	Ndixelele Themba, wenza ntoni ngokomsebenzi?
UThemba	Ndisebenzela inkampani yeenqwelo-moya njengomphathi-basebenzi.
UPeter	Oo, ipersonnel manager ngesiNgesi na?
UThemba	*Uchan' ucwethe!**
UPeter	Uya*k*wazi ke ukusebenza nokuthetha kakuhle nabantu!
UThemba	Ewe, ndiyakuthanda kakhulu ukusebenza nabantu. Uyazi isaci sesiXhosa sithi: *Umntu ngumntu ngabantu*!
UPeter	Unyanisile!
UThemba	Wena, yintoni umsebenzi wakho, Peter?
UPeter	Mna, ndiyingcaphephe yezityalo eKirstenbosch.
UThemba	Mm, yinto enomdla leyo!
UPeter	Ewe, ngumsebenzi onomdla. Kananjalo laa ndawo yindawo entle yokusebenza! UThandi naye uyasebenza?
UThemba	Ewe, naye uthanda ukusebenza nabantu. Ungugqirha. Usebenza kwisibhedlele sabantwana i**Red Cross**. Uya khona kusasa kuphela. Emva kwemini usebenza kwikliniki ye**P**rimary Health Care.

UPeter	Naye usebenza kakhulu!
UThemba	UJenny, ufundisa kwesiphi isikolo?
UPeter	Akafundisi sikolweni. Ufundisa abantu abadala abafuna ukufunda ukuthetha isiXhosa. Uyazi, baninzi kakhulu abantu abafuna ukufunda ukuthetha isiXhosa ngoku ngakumbi oosomashishini nabasebenzi beenkampani, abanikazi-khaya, oogqirha nabongikazi, njalo njalo.
UThemba	Heke, bathini kanene ngesiNgesi? *'Better late than never!'*
UPeter	Ithini loo ntetho ngesiXhosa?
UThemba	Andazi. Lunjalo kaloku ulwimi. Akusoloko kulula ukutolika ngakumbi wakufika kwizaci.

Isigama

wenza	you do	sabantwana	of children
ntoni?	what?	khona	there
ngokomsebenzi	as far as work goes	kusasa	in the morning
-sebenza	work (verb)	kuphela	only
-sebenzela	work for	emva kwemini	in the afternoon
inkampani	company	kwikliniki ye	at a clinic of
umphathi-basebenzi	personnel manager	kwesiphi isikolo?	at which school?
		akafundisi	she doesn't teach?
umsebenzi	worker	abantu abadala	adults
abasebenzi	workers, staff	abafuna	who want
uchan' ucwethe!	you're spot on!	baninzi	they are many
	(lit. you've aimed at (and hit) the shrew)	ngakumbi	especially
		oosomashishini	business people
-thanda	like, love	abanikazi-khaya	housewives
isaci sesiXhosa	Xhosa idiom	abongikazi	nurses
sithi	saying	njalo, njalo	etc. etc.
yintoni?	it is what?	ngesiNgesi	in English
mna	as for me	ithini	what is it?
ingcaphephe		loo ntetho	that saying
yezityalo	horticulturist	kanene	indeed
umdla	interest	ngesiXhosa	in Xhosa
-nomdla	interesting	lunjalo kaloku	it's like that
leyo	that	ulwimi	language
kananjalo	also	akusoloko kulula	it isn't always easy
laa ndawo	that place	ukutolika wakufika	to translate when
yindawo entle	it's a lovely	kwizaci	it comes to idioms
yokusebenza	place to work		
ugqirha	doctor		
isibhedele	hospital		

? *How to ...*

Ask what someone does for a living

Wenza **ntoni** ngokom**sebenzi**?
*Y*intoni *um***sebenzi** wakho?

Say what your occupation is

Ndi*ngu*gqirha
Ndi*ngu*somashishini
Ndi*ngum*phathi-basebenzi
Ndi*ngum*ongikazi
Ndi*ngum*nikazi-khaya
Ndi*li*gqwetha
Ndiyi*ngcaphephe yezityalo* (lit. an expert in plants)
Ndiyi*i*personnel manager
Ndi**sebenza** njengo*m***phathi** weshishini
Ndi**sebenzela** *in*kampani

Ask where someone works

U**sebenza** phi?
U**phangela** phi?

Respond to being asked where you work

	*e*doloph*ini*
	*e*yunivesithi
	*esi*bhedlele
Ndi**sebenza**	*esi*kol*weni*
	e-ofis*ini*
	*e*Kirstenbosch
	*kwi*shishini lee**ncwadi** (publishing house)
	*kwi*shishini lempahla (clothing factory)

Comment on someone's work

*Ngum***sebenzi** *o*nom**dla**
*Yin***dawo** *en***tle** yoku**sebenza**

How it works

1 More about the Xhosa equivalent of English 'am', 'is', 'are' followed by nouns

You already know that '*-ng-*' prefixed to **nouns beginning with** '*um-*' and '*u-*', (Classes 1, 1a and 3 **nouns**) expresses '*am*', '*is*' (→ see **Unit 2.5**):

Ndi*ngu*Jenny.	I *am* Jenny.
Lo *ngu*nyana wam.	This *is* my **son**.
UThandi *ngu*gqirha.	Thandi *is* a **doctor**.
Ndi*ngum*yeni *wakhe*.	I *am* her **husband**.
UDavid *ngum*fundi.	David *is* a **pupil / student**.
UThemba *ngum*phathi.	Themba *is* a **manager**.
*Ngum*sebenzi onomdla.	It *is* interesting **work**.

Similarly, '*ng-*' / '*-ng-*' prefixed to **nouns** beginning with '*aba-*', '*oo-*' and '*ama-*' (Classes 2, 2a, and 6 **nouns** → see **Unit 3.1**):

Aba**ntwana** *ngaba***fundi**.	The **children** *are* **pupils**.
*Ngoo*Thamsanqa aba.	These *are* the **Thamsanqas**.
*Ngoo*Murray aba.	These *are* the **Murrays**.
Ba*ngama*gqwetha.	They *are* **lawyers**.

< *uku*gqwetha = to turn upside down, to be back to front, i.e. everything is the opposite of what it should be.

To express '*am*', '*is*', '*are*' with **Class 5 nouns** prefix '*-l-*':

Ndi*li*gqwetha.	I *am* a **lawyer**.
Ú*li*gqirha.	He *is* a **traditional healer**.
Ú*li*xhwele.	She *is* a **herbalist**.

To express '*am*', '*is*', '*are*' with **Classes 7** and **8 nouns** prefix '*-s-*' and '*-z-*' respectively:

U*sisi*thethi sepalamente.	She *is* the **speaker** of parliament.
Ba*zizi*thethi zepalamente.	They *are* **speakers** of parliament.

To express '*am*', '*is*', '*are*' with **Class 9 nouns** prefix '*-y-*':

Ndi*yi*ngcaphephe yezityalo.	I *am* a **horticulturist**.
Ndi*yi*personnel manager.	I *am* a personnel manager.

Note: <u>ukuba</u> *ngum*phathi / *li*gqwetha / *yi*ngcaphephe yezityalo means <u>to</u> *<u>become</u>* a manager / lawyer / horticulturist.

2 Some occupations

Those derived from verbs prefix *um-* and change the final vowel **-a** to **-e**:

uku**phath**a	to **handle**	>	*um***phath**i	manager
uku**fund**a	to **study**	>	*um***fund**i	student
uk**ongamel**a	to **rule over**	>	*um***ongamel**i	president
uku**phek**a	to **cook**	>	*um***phek**i	cook
uku**qhub**a	to **drive**	>	*um***qhub**i	driver
uku**thung**a	to **sew**	>	*um***thungi**(kazi)	tailor (seamstress)
uku**sebenz**a	to **work**	>	*um***sébenz**i	worker

(cf. *um*sêbenzi Class 3 = work)

Note: uku**theth**a to speak   >   *isi***theth**i   speaker

Those adopted from **English** or **Afrikaans** prefix '*u-*' / '*i-*' or '*in-*':

*u***titshala** / *oo***titshala**(kazi)	teacher/s
*i***titshala** / *ii***titshala**(kazi)	teacher/s
*u***profesa** / *oo***profesa**	professor/s
*u***njingalwazi** / *oo***njingalwazi**	
*i***njingalwazi** / *ii***njingalwazi**	
(< **-jinga** = **wave around**)	professor/s
(< *ulw***azi** = knowledge)	professor/s
*u***mantyi** / *oo***mantyi**	magistrate/s
*i***joni** / *ama***joni** (< English Johnny)	soldier/s
*i***polisa** / *ama***polisa**	policeman/men
*i***toliki** / *ii***toliki** (< Afrikaans vertolk)	interpreter/s
*in***tatheli** / *iin***tatheli** (< -thath<u>ela</u> = to take to)	journalist/s
*im***balisi** / *iim***balisi** (< -balisa = relate)	historian/s

Those incorporating '**-no-**', a contraction of '*u*ni<u>na</u> w<u>o</u>-' = 'mother of' or the male equivalent '**-so-**', a contraction of 'uyi<u>se</u> w<u>o</u>-' = 'father of':

*u***nobhala** / *oo***nobhala** (lit. **mother of** writing)	secretary/ries
*u***nogadi** / *oo***nogadi** (lit. **mother of** guards)	guard/s
*u***noncwadi** / *oo***noncwadi** (lit. **mother of** books)	librarian/s
*u***nondyebo** / *oo***nondyebo** (lit. **mother of** abundance)	treasurer/s
*u***nongendi** / *oo***nongendi** (lit. **mother of** not marrying)	nun/s
*u***nontlalo-ntle** / *oo***nontlalo-ntle** (lit. **mother of** good living)	social worker/s

*u*noposi / *oo*noposi (lit. **mother of** post)	postman/men
unosilarha / *oo*nosilarha (lit. **mother of** slaughtering)	butcher/s
uno**venkile / *oo*no**venkile (lit. **mother of** a shop)	shopkeeper/s
*u*somashishini / *oo*somashishini (lit. **father of** factories)	businessman/men
*u*sompempe / *oo*sompempe (lit. **father of** the whistle)	referee/s

3 Suffixing '-kazi' to a noun

Can make it feminine

inkosi	chief	inkosi**kazi**	chief's wife, lady, wife, madam
utitshala	teacher	utitshala**kazi**	
umongi	nurse	umongi**kazi**	
umnini	owner	umni**kazi**	

Can indicate greatness of size

ilizwe	country	ilizwe**kazi**	continent
umthi	tree	umthi**kazi**	**big** tree
umlambo	river	umlambo**kazi**	**large** river
intaba	mountain	intaba**kazi**	**high** mountain

Can express relationship

uma**kazi**	my mother's sister, i.e. maternal aunt
ubawo**kazi**	my father's brother, i.e. paternal uncle

4 Omission of the initial vowel of the noun

In direct address

If you look again at the explanation of how to greet appropriately in Unit 2, you will see that all nouns following 'Molo / Molweni' have lost their initial vowel:

*u*tata / *u*bawo / *u*mnumzana / *u*mhlekazi
> Molo **t**ata, **b**awo, **m**numzana, **m**hlekazi
*i*nkosikazi / *i*nkosazana / *i*ntombi / *i*ntombazana / *i*nkwenkwe
> Molo **n**kosikazi / **n**kosazana / **n**tombi / **n**tombazana / **n**kwenkwe

After negative forms

> *Andi*thand*i* **k̲ofu**.
> UJenny *aka*fundisi **b̲antwana**.

After demonstratives

> *Ayi*namsebenzi **loo n̲to**.
> Intle **loo n̲to**.

→ see **Unit 9.5** for more about **demonstratives**.

5 When verbs end in '-e' instead of '-a' (subjunctive)

In instructions preceded by an object concord

*Ndi*xelel*e̲*.	**Tell** *me*.
*Si*bonis*e̲*.	**Show** *us*.

After the expressions **kufuneka** (ukuba) = it is **necessary** (that) / **must**, **kubalulek***ile* (ukuba) = it is **important** (that)

Kufuneka ukuba uzam*e̲*	You **must try** to speak
ukuthetha isiXhosa yonke imihla!	Xhosa every day!
Kubalulek*ile* ukuba uzam*e̲*	**It is important** that you **try**
ukuthetha isiXhosa yonke imihla.	to speak Xhosa every day.

After ma- 'let'

Masithethe̲ isiXhosa.	**Let**'s **speak** Xhosa.
Masihlale̲ ngaphandle.	**Let**'s **sit** outside.

After -cela 'ask', 'request', 'beg'

Ndi*cela* uthethe̲ isiXhosa!	I **request** you to **speak** Xhosa.

→ cf. **Unit 3.5**.

6 Verbal extensions '-el-', '-is-', '-an-'

Another interesting feature of Xhosa is the extension of verbs by means of infixes, adding an implicit preposition or even a change of meaning.

'-el-' translates 'for', 'to'

UNomsa u**funda** eyunivesithi.	Nomsa **studies** at the university.
U**fundela** ntoni?	**What** is she **studying for**?

| Ndi**sebenza** njengomphathi. | I **work** as a manager. |
| Ndi**sebenzela** inkampani. | I **work for** a company. |

| **Xela** igama lakho! | **Tell** your name! |
| Ndi**xelele**. | **Tell (for)** me. |

'-is-' translates 'cause to', 'make'

UPeter u**funda** isiXhosa.	Peter **learns** Xhosa.
UJenny u**fundisa** isiXhosa.	Jenny **teaches** Xhosa.
	(lit. causes to learn)

| Ndiya**bona**. | I **see**. |
| Ndi**bonise**. | **Show** me. (lit. **make** me **see**) |

| **Hamba**! | **Go**! |
| **Hambisa**! | **Continue**! (lit. **make go**) |

Ndi**xelele** xa ndi**phazama**.	**Tell** me when I **make a mistake**.
U**xolo** ngoku**kuphazamisa**.	Sorry for **disturbing /**
	interrupting you.

Note: When '-**is**-' is doubled = '-**isis**-' it intensifies the meaning:

Fundisisa	=	**Read carefully**
Cingisisa	=	**Think carefully**
Cothisisa	=	**Speak very slowly**
Qhuqhisisa	=	**Beat very well** (See **Unit 5**)
Xubisisa	=	**Mix very well** (See **Unit 5**)

'-an-' usually indicates reciprocity 'each other'

| Siza ku**bona**. | We'll **see**. |
| Siza ku**bonana** > So**bonana** | We'll **see each other**. |

More than one extension can be used in the same verb: uku**bon / is / an /a** to discuss something (lit. show **each other**):

| Masi**bonisane** ngale nto! | **Let's discuss** that! |

7 Various meanings of the preposition 'nga-'

Indicating place = 'in the vicinity of', 'towards', 'near'

| nga**se**Rhini | **near** Grahamstown |
| nga**se**Forest Drive | **in the vicinity of** Forest Drive |

In connection with 'phandle', 'phakathi'

Nifuna ukuhlala **nga**phakathi
okanye **nga**phandle?

Do you want to sit inside
or outside?

Indicating time = 'at', 'in'

ngeli xesha
ngamanye amaxesha
ngokuhlwa

at this time
sometimes (lit. **at** some times)
in the evening

Translating 'by (means of)', 'with'

ukuhamba **nge**-eropleni
ukuhamba **nge**bhasi / **nge**moto
ukuhlawula **nge**khadi

to go **by** plane
to go **by** bus / car
to pay **by** card

Translating 'about', 'concerning', 'as'

Wenza ntoni **ngoko**msebenzi?

Kunjani **ngo**kuphunga?

What's your line of work?
(lit. What **do** you do **as far as**
work is concerned?)
How **about** (something hot)
to drink?

Forming an adverb

ngelishwa (*ili*shwa = 'misfortune')
ngethamsanqa (*i*thamsanqa = 'luck')

unfortunate**ly**
lucki**ly**

With a language translating 'in'

Yintoni leyo **nge**siNgesi?
Uthini **nge**siXhosa?

What is this **in** English?
What do you say **in** Xhosa?

After 'enkosi' = 'thanks'; 'uxolo' = 'sorry' translating 'for'

Enkosi **nge**nto yonke.
Uxolo **ngoku***ni***lindisa**
ixesha elide.

Thanks **for** everything.
Sorry **for making** *you* **wait**
so long.

ng**a**- + **a**- = ng**a**-   ng**a**-+ **i**- = ng**e**-   ng**a**- + **u**- = ng**o**-
(cf. na- + a- / i- / u- etc. → see **Unit 2.9**).

8 More about the equivalent of English prepositions (known as locatives in Xhosa)

You already know that to express the English prepositions 'at', 'in', 'to', 'from' with **place names**, you change the **initial vowel** of the prefix to 'e-':

Uhlala phi?	Ndi**hlala** _e_**Kapa**, _e_**Pinelands**.
	Ndi**hlala** _e_**fama**.
	Ndi**hlala** _e_**Mzantsi Afrika**.
Uvela phi?	Ndi**vela** _e_**Monti** / _e_**Goli** / _e_**Pitoli** / _e_**Bhayi**.
	Ndi**vela** _e_**Mpuma-Koloni** / _e_**Ntshona-Koloni**.

Eight of the nine provinces of South Africa prefix '_e_-'. Which one doesn't? (→ see map **Unit 3**).

Another verb which is always followed by the locative form of the noun is 'ukuya' = 'to **go to**':

Uya phi?	**Where** are you **going to**?
Ndiya _e_**yunivesithi**.	I am **going** _to_ **university**.
Ndiya _e_si**bhedlele**.	I am **going** _to_ **hospital**.
Ndiya _e_**khaya**.	I am **going** (_to_) **home**.

Note: The verb 'ukuya' = 'to **go to**' is used when a destination, direction is mentioned. '**Uku**hamba' = 'to **go**' in the sense of leave, depart (also walk) **is not used** when a **destination** is mentioned:

| Ndiya**hamba**. | I am **going**. |
| Ndiya _e_**doloph**_ini_. | I am **going** _to_ **town**. |

You have also come across '**ku-**' expressing '**at**', '**in**', '**on**', '**to**', '**from**':

Namkelekile _ku_**flight** 301 oya eKapa.
Usebenza _kwi_**kliniki** yePrimary Health.
Ukwazana _kwi_**-eropleni**.

_ku-_ + _i-_ = _kwi-_ (< _ku-_ + _i_**kliniki**), (< _ku-_ + _i_**-eropleni**).

Note: '_ku-_' is normally used when the noun is followed by a qualifying phrase.

'**kwa-**' as in '**kwaZulu**' and '**kwaLanga**' (the suburb of Cape Town named after the Xhosa chief _u_**Langa**) is always prefixed to **proper names** and translates '_at_ **the place of**, _at_ **the residence of**'.

However, by far the commonest way of expressing prepositions in Xhosa is by changing the **initial vowel** of the noun to '*e-*' and the **final vowel** of the noun as follows:

-a >	-eni:	i**khaya**	>	e**khay**_eni_*	*at / in / from / to* our **home**
-e >	-eni:	i**lizwe**	>	e**lizw**_eni_	*in / from / to* the **country**
-i >	-ini:	um**sebenzi**	>	em**sebenz**_ini_	*at / to / from* **work**
-o >	-weni:	i**sikolo**	>	e**sikol**_weni_	*at / in / from / to* **school**
-u >	-wini:	i**Theku**	>	e**Thek**_wini_	*in / to / from* **Durban**

But -u > -ini after:

f:	i**kofu**	> e**kof**ini	*in* the coffee
ph:	i**doloph**u	> e**doloph**ini	*at / in / from / to* **town**

Note: *e**khaya** > e**khay**eni when followed by a possessive.

☑ *How to apply it*

1 Complete the dialogue

UDavid	Uyafunda, Bongani?
UBongani	Ewe, ndifunda eWesterford. Wena?
UDavid	Ndifunda eGrove. Uya*ba*thanda* (a) __titshala bakho?
UBongani	Abanye (some) (b) ____lungile kakhulu, abanye hayi.
UDavid	Udadewenu wenza (c) _____?
UBongani	(d) ____umfundi eyunivesithi.
UDavid	Ufundela (e) _____?
UBongani	Ufundela ubugqwetha.
	Benza ntoni abazali (f) _____?
UDavid	Utata (g) ____ingcaphephe yezityalo. Usebenza eKirstenbosch. Umama (h) _____utitshalakazi.
UBongani	Ufundisa (i) _____?
UDavid	Ufundisa (j) ____Xhosa (k) n ____Ngesi.
	Benza ntoni (l) _____zali bakho, bona?
UBongani	Utata (m) ___umphathi, umama (n) ____ugqirha. Nam ndifuna ukuba ngugqirha. Wena?
UDavid	Andazi. Mhlawumbi ndiza kuba yinjineli. (engineer)

* -*ba*- = them.

2 Derive the appropriate occupations from the verbs

-akha	build
-bhala	write
-coca	clean
-cula	sing
-fota	to take photos
-guqula	translate
-lawula	direct
-lima	farm
-phatha	manage
-qeqesha	train
-sasaza	broadcast
-thengisa	sell ('-thenga' = 'buy')
-thwala	carry*
-zoba	paint, draw

* What is the English translation of this occupation?

3 You are introduced to a number of people by name and occupation. Write in English who does what

(a) _____ _____   (f) _____ _____

(b) _____ _____   (g) _____ _____

(c) _____ _____   (h) _____ _____

(d) _____ _____   (i) _____ _____

(e) _____ _____   (j) _____ _____

4 You are already able to introduce your husband, son and friend (Ngumyeni wam lo; ngunyana wam; ngumhlobo wam, uThandi, etc.). Now introduce other members of your family (usapho lwakho)

your parents	Ngabazali bam
your children	___abantwana bam
your grandchildren	___abazukulwana bam
your wife	Yinkosikazi yam
your daughter	___intombi yam, uLindi.

Use the list of greetings in **Unit 1** to introduce:

> your father
> your mother
> your grandfather
> your grandmother

5 **You are introduced to someone's relatives. Write down who they are**

(a) _____   (e) _____.
(b) _____   (f) _____.
(c) _____   (g) _____.
(d) _____   (h) _____.

6 **Answer the questions**

(a) Uvela phi uPeter?
(b) Uhlala phi ngoku?
(c) Uya phi yonke imihla?
(d) Uvela phi uJenny?
(e) Ufundisa bani?
(f) Usebenza phi uThandi kusasa?
(g) Uya phi emva kwemini?
(h) Usebenzela bani uThemba?

7 **Say in Xhosa**

(a) Where you come from
(b) Where you live now
(c) What your occupation is
(d) Where you work

8 **Fill in the verbal extension for a meaningful answer**

(a) Wena uyasebenza?
    Ewe, ndisebenz__a inkampani yekhomphyutha.
(b) Intombi yakho uyakwazi ukupheka?
    Ewe, iphek__a usapho.
(c) Uyasifunda isiXhosa?
    Ewe, uJenny uyandifund__a.
(d) UNomsa ufunda eyunivesithi?
    Ewe, ufund__a ubugqwetha.
(e) OoThamsanqa bathanda ooMurray?
    Ewe, bayathand__a!

9 Say to a friend

(a) Let's teach each other!
(b) Let's meet!
(c) Let's help each other!
(d) Let's pull together!
    (i.e. Let's build one another!)

MASAKHANE

IT'S HAPPENING

10 Say that you must

(a) go now   Kufuneka ndi_____.
(b) go to work   Kufuneka ndi _____.
(c) work now   Kufuneka ndi _____.
(d) go to the hospital   Kufuneka ndi _____.
(e) go home (-goduka)   Kufuneka ndi _____.
(f) speak Xhosa every day   Kufuneka ndi _____.
(g) pay by card   Kufuneka ndi _____.

11 Complete appropriately

(a) Ndiya eBhayi ngomso.
    Uhamba __bhasi? Hayi, ndihamba __eropleni.
(b) Uthanda ukuhamba ___eropleni?
    Hayi, ndikhetha ukuhamba ___moto.
(c) Wenza ntoni ___komsebenzi? Ndi___umphathi.
(d) Usebenza __shishini lempahla? Hayi, ndisebenza __-ofisi___.
(e) Usebenza na___kuhlwa? Ewe, ___manye amaxesha.
(f) Hamba kakuhle. Sala kakuhle. Enkosi ___nto yonke.

12 Complete the idioms using the correct form of 'is', 'are'

Ba___umthi nexolo.

They <u>are</u> great friends.
(lit. They <u>are</u> tree and resin.)

Ba___inyoka nesele.

They <u>are</u> great enemies.
(lit. They <u>are</u> snake and frog.)

U___inyoka.

He/she <u>is</u> a treacherous person.

U___umkhombe.

He/she <u>is</u> a very angry person.
(lit. He/she <u>is</u> a rhino.)

U___indlovu.

He/she <u>is</u> a very strong person.
(lit. He/she <u>is</u> an elephant.)

13 Listen to the dialogue and answer the questions

(a) **Who** are talking to each other?

(b) **What** are they talking about?

(c) **Where** are they talking?

umsebenzi omkhulu	huge job	kanjalo	as well
umsebenzi onzima	a hard job	-phumelela	succeed, manage
ndigqibile	I have finished		

5 | Uyithanda njani ikofu yakho?

How do you like your coffee?

In this Unit you will learn how to:

apologise

say you are thirsty / hungry

ask guests how they take their coffee

offer refreshments

accept and decline

express appreciation

remark on a change in the weather

Incoko

Jenny and Thandi arrive with refreshments.

UPeter	Ekugqibeleni. Masiqabuleni unxano!
UJenny	Uxolo ngokunilindisa ixesha elide. Besincokola! Ndiqinisekile ukuba ninxaniwe.
UPeter	Ewe, sinxanwe kakhulu! Silambile kananjalo.
UThemba	Hayi, kulungile, nathi besincokola!
UJenny	Thandi, uyithanda njani ikofu yakho? Ufuna ubisi neswekile?
UThandi	Ubisi *qha*, enkosi sisi.
UJenny	Wena, Themba ufuna ikofu enobisi?
UThemba	Ewe, enkosi neetispuni ezimbini zeswekile.
UJenny	Nantsi iswekile. Zincede.
UPeter	Kunjani ngekeyiki neesengwitshi, Thandi?
UThandi	Enkosi Peter. Ndingafumana isilayi esincinci sekeyiki? Ijongeka intle!
UPeter	Inene, imnandi kakhulu. Nasi isilayi.
UThandi	Enkosi. Mmm! inencasa le keyiki. Jenny, ndingafumana iresiphi?
UJenny	Ngokuqinisekileyo, sisi. Undikhumbuze. Themba, ndingakupha isilayi sekeyiki, nawe?

UThemba	Enkosi, Jenny. Mna, ndizithanda kakhulu izinto ezimnandi!
UJenny	Peter, nceda ugqithisele uThemba ikeyiki ngoku ndigalela ikofu yakho.
UPeter	Kulungile. Thandi, kunjani ngenye ikomityi yekofu?
UThandi	Hayi enkosi. Ikomityi enye yekofu yanele kum!
UPeter	Yho! ilanga lithe *shwaka*. Kuyaphola ngoku. Sifanele ukungena ngaphakathi?
UJenny	Ewe, ngesaquphe kuyabanda. Mna, ndiyagodola. Nina?
UThandi	Ewe, kancinci.
UJenny	Kulungile, masingeneni! Peter, nceda uvale ucango!

After coffee Thandi reminds Jenny about the recipe.

UThandi	Jenny, ungalibali ukundinika iresiphi yekeyiki.
UJenny	Andilibalanga, sisi. Nantsi.

Ukuba ukhetha i chocolate icing, unganyibilikisa icephe lecocoa powder kwicephe lamanzi abilayo, uqhuqhisise kwi-icing.

Isigama

ekugqibeleni	at last	imnandi	it's nice
-qabula	quench	nasi (isilayi)	here it is
unxano	thirst	inencasa	it's delicious
-lindisa	cause to wait	iresiphi	recipe
ixesha elide	a long time	ngokuqinisekileyo	certainly
besincokola	we were chatting	-khumbuza	remind
-qinisekile	(be) certain / sure	-pha	give
-nxaniwe	thirsty	isilayi sekeyiki	a slice of cake
-nxanwe kakhulu	very thirsty	izinto ezimnandi	sweet things
-lambile	hungry	-gqithisela	pass to someone
kananjalo	also	-galela	put in, pour
ubisi	milk	enye ikomityi yekofu	another cup of coffee
iswekile	sugar	ikomityi enye yanele kum	one cup is enough for me
qha	*only*		
enobisi	which has milk	ilanga lithe *shwaka*	the sun's disappeared
neetispuni ezimbini	and 2 teaspoons	kuyaphola	it's getting cool
zeswekile	of sugar	-fanele	ought
zincede	help yourself	kuyabanda	it's cold
ikeyiki	cake	ngesaquphe	suddenly
iisengwitshi	sandwiches	-godola	(be) cold (humans)
-fumana	get, obtain	-vala	close
isilayi esincinci	a small slice	ucango	door
ijongeka intle	it looks lovely	-nika	give
inene	indeed		

Ikeyiki enye eneencasa
EZININZI

IZITHAKO:
4 amaqanda
310ml (1¼ yekomityi) yecastor sugar
*500ml (2 iikomityi) yeSNOWFLAKE
Cake Flour*
15ml (3 iitispuni) yebaking-powder
250ml (ikomityi) yobisi
90g yemagarini OKANYE ibhotolo
7ml (1½ yetispuni) yevanilla essence

INDLELA YOKWENZA:
Ionti yenze shushu kwangaphambili
ifike kwi-180°C. Qhuqha amaqanda
neswekile ndawonye de aqine abe
nombala olubhelu. Sefa **iSNOWFLAKE
Cake Flour** ndawonye nebaking
powder, uxube kumxube
weqanda. Yenza shushu ibisi
nemagarini ndawonye kodwa
ungalubilisi. Umxube wobisi
nevanilla essence wuzamisele
entlameni, galela ngecephe kwiitin
zekeyiki ezingqukuva neziyi-23cm,
bhaka ama-25 ukuya kuma-30
emizuzu.

I-icing Engundoqo
Qhuqha i-500g (ipakethi) yeicing
sugar ne-250g yemagarini okanye
ibhotolo ethambileyo de ibe
khaphukhaphu. Yisebenzise
phakathi koomaleko nakumphezulu
wekeyiki.

icephe (ama-)	spoon	uxube kumxube	fold into egg
-qhuqhisisa	beat well	weqanda	mixture
izithako	ingredients	ungalubilisi	you shouldn't boil *it*
amaqanda	eggs	*wu*zamisele	stir it into the batter
indlela yokwenza	method (lit. way	entlameni	
	of making / doing)	*ezi*ngqukuva	*which* are round
i-onti	oven	i-icing engundoqo	basic icing
yenze	make *it*	*e*thambileyo	*which* is soft
shushu	hot	khaphukhaphu	light and fluffy
kwangaphambili	pre-heat to		*yi*sebenzise use *it*
ifike kwi-180°C	180°C	phakathi	between layers
qhuqha ndawonye	beat together	koomaleko	
de aqine abe	until thick and	nakumphezulu	and on top
nombala olubhelu	yellow in colour		

Try to memorise	
Uxolo ngokunilindisa ixesha elide	Sorry for keeping *you* waiting such a long time
Zincede!	Help yourself!
Ikomityi enye yekofu yanele kum!	One cup of coffee is enough for me!
Ilanga lithe *shwaka!*	The sun has *disappeared!*
Ungalibali!	Don't forget!
Andilibalanga!	I haven't forgotten!

? *How to ...*

Apologise

*U*xolo! (ngoku*ku*lindisa *i*xesha *eli*de)
*U*xolo! (ngoku*ni*lindisa *i*xesha *eli*de)

Say you are thirsty / hungry

Ndi**nxan***iwe.* Ndi**nxan***we* kakhulu.
Ndi**lamb***ile.* Ndi**lamb***e* kakhulu.

Ask how someone takes their coffee / tea

U*yi***thanda njani** *i*kofu / *i*ti yakho?
Ufuna *u*bisi **neswekile** *e*kof*ini* / *e*t*ini*?
Ufuna *i*kofu *e*nobisi?
Ufuna *i*kofu *e*neswekile?

Offer refreshments

Kunjani ngekofu / nge**ti**?
Kunjani ngenye *i***komityi** yekofu / yeti?
Kunjani ngokusela *i*nto *e*banda*yo*?
Kunjani ngewayini? (wine)
Kunjani ngotywala? (beer / alcohol)
Kunjani ngekeyiki?
Kunjani ngeesengwitshi?
Zincede!
Ndinga*ku***pha** *isi*layi se**keyiki**?
Ndinga*ku***pha** *i*sengwitshi?
→ See Cultural background.

Accept and decline

Ewe, enkosi.
Hayi, enkosi.
Ndinga**fumana** isi**layi** esi**ncinci** qha?
Ikomityi enye ye**kofu** yanele ku**m** enkosi.

Express appreciation

Ku**mnandi**!
Ine**ncasa** gqitha!
Imnandi kakhulu!
I**jongeka** intle le **keyiki**!

Remark on a change in the weather

Li**njani** izulu? / Injani imozulu? (lit. **How** is the **weather**?)
Ingathi ilanga lithe shwaka.
Ilanga litshonile (the sun has gone down).
Liya**phola** ngoku.
Kuya**banda** ngesaquphe.

Ideophones (Izifanekisozwi)

An **ideophone** is a part of speech which is a characteristic and distinctive feature of Xhosa. You have already come across two examples in this book: 'qha' and 'shwaka'.

Ideophones are often onomatopoeic, i.e. they suggest the action by their sound, e.g. 'dyumpu', similar to the English 'plop', but they mostly describe manner and are used where English uses adverbs, e.g.:

Hamba ngqo! **Go** straight along.

Ideophones are often introduced by 'uku**thi**' which indicates the tense, mood, person, and class, but can also be used with other verbs, e.g.:

Si**phile** qete! We are completely **well**.

However, because **ideophones** are interjectional in nature, they are often more effective when standing alone, e.g.:

Nkqi ivili! The wheel is stuck fast!

Ideophones are also used to emphasise the intensity of some colours:

Le ntyatyambo i**bomvu** *krwe(e)*.	This flower is *blood* **red**.
Imithi i**luhlaza** *yaka*!	The trees are *grass* **green**.
Iinwele zakhe zi**mnyama** khaca *(thsu)*!	Her hair is *pitch* **black**.
Iinwele zakhe zi**mhlophe** *qhwa*!	Her hair is *snow* **white**.

→ See **Unit 14.6**.

Cultural background

Some traditional brews

Umqombothi: An **alcoholic** drink made from **maize porridge** and **sprouts** which is left until it ferments.

Amarhewu: **Non-alcoholic** maize meal liquid. A small amount is mixed with **flour** and **sugar** (optional). It is then put into the main porridge container until ready.

Ublayi: **Maize porridge** made in a three-legged pot. It is cooked until the bottom of the pot is scalded. This scalded part is then scraped off and mixed with porridge and allowed to ferment.

How it works
1 More object concords

In English, the pronouns '*him*' and '*her*' are the same irrespective of whether you are referring to a student, lawyer or engineer, etc. This is not so in Xhosa where '*him*' and '*her*' are represented by different forms which change according to the *noun* to which they refer. These are known as **object concords** and are derived from the noun prefixes:

Jenny **teaches** *him/her* (the **student**).	UJenny uya**m**fundisa (**um**fundi).
She **teaches** *him/her* (the **lawyer**).	Uya**li**fundisa (**i**gqwetha).
She **teaches** *him/her* (the **engineer**).	Uya**yi**fundisa (**i**njineli).

The plural form '*them*' also has different forms in Xhosa:

She **teaches** *them* (**workers**).	Uya**ba**fundisa (**aba**sebenzi).
She **teaches** *them* (**doctors**).	Uya**ba**fundisa (**oo**gqirha).
She **teaches** *them* (**lawyers**).	Uya**wa**fundisa (**ama**gqwetha).
She **teaches** *them* (**engineers**).	Uya**zi**fundisa (**ii**njineli).

Similarly, there are several Xhosa equivalents for the English pronoun '*it*' and its plural '*them*', which also depend on the noun referred to:

I **ask** for *it* (**work**).	Ndiya*wu*cela (*um*sebenzi).
I **like** *them* (**illustrations**).	Ndiya*yi*thandi (*imi*zobo).
I **like** *it* (the **name**).	Ndiya*li*thandi (*i*gama).
I **like** *them* (the **names**).	Ndiya*wa*thandi (*ama*gama).
I **like** *it* (the **Xhosa language**).	Ndiya*si*thandi (*isi*Xhosa).
How do you **like** *it* (**coffee**)?	U*yi*thandi njani (*i*kofu)?
How do you **like** *them* (**sandwiches**)?	U*zi*thandi njani (*ii*sengwitshi)?
Do*n't* you **like** *it* (the **milk**)?	Aku*lu*thandi (*u*bisi)?
I do*n't* **like** *it* (**winter**).	Andi*bu*thandi (*ubu*sika).
I **like** *it* (**travelling**).	Ndiya*ku*thandi (*uku*hamba).

From the 'at a glance' table you will see that the **object concords** have the same form as the subject concords except where the subject concord is a vowel only. In these cases the subject concord incorporates a consonant to form the **object concord**. Do you remember why? (See **Unit 2.6**):

Subject concords		*Object concords*	
	at a glance		
ndi-	I	-ndi-	me
si-	we	-si-	us
ù-	you (s.)	-ku-	you (s.)
ni-	you (pl.)	-ni-	you (pl.)
ú-	he / she	-m-	him / her
ba-	they	-ba-	them
u-	it	-wu-	it
i-	they	-yi-	them
li-	it / he / she	-li-	it / him / her
a-	it	-wa-	them
si-	it	-si-	them
zi-	them	-zi-	them
i-	it / he / she	-yi-	it / him / her
zi-	them	-zi-	them
lu-	it	-lu-	it
bu-	it	-bu-	it
ku-	it	-ku-	it

2 Possessives

In English, possessive relationship can be expressed by ''*s*' or '*of* ', e.g. 'the **boy**'*s* **name**' or 'the **name** *of* the **boy**'.

In Xhosa, only the '*of* ' construction exists. The two nouns ('name' and 'boy') are **linked** by a **possessive concord** which is characterised by the possessive '*-a*'.

This **link** (representing '*of* ') between the two nouns **changes** according to the prefix of the first noun (possessee) and influences the prefix of the second noun (possessor) resulting in a **sound change**:

*um*sebenzi *wa*-   + *i*nkampani > w*e*nkampani
                                          (employee *of* a company)

*u*somashini *wa*- + *i*nkampani > w*e*nkampani
                                          (businessman *of* a company)

*aba*sebenzi *ba*- + *ii*nkampani > b*ee*nkampani* (staff *of* a company)

*oo*somashini *ba*- + *ii*nkampani > b*ee*nkampani*
                                          (businessmen *of* a company)

*um*xube *wa*-   + *i*qanda   > w*e*qanda (mixture *of* egg)

*imi*zobo *ya*-   + *aba*ntwana   > y*aba*ntwana (paintings *of* the children)

*i*xesha *la*-   + *i*ti   > l*e*ti (time *of* tea i.e. teatime)

*ama*gama *a*-   + *aba*ntwana   > *aba*ntwana (names *of* the children)

*isi*celo *sa*-   + *um*sebenzi   > s*om*sebenzi (application *of* a job)

*izi*celo *za*-   + *um*sebenzi   > z*om*sebenzi (applications *of* jobs)

*i*komityi *ya*-   + *i*kofu   > y*e*kofu (cup *of* coffee)

*ii*tispuni *za*-   + *i*swekile   > z*e*swekile (teaspoons *of* sugar)

*ulu*hlu *lwa*-   + *izi*thako   > lw*ezi*thako (list *of* ingredients)

*ubu*ntu *ba*-   + *aba*ntu   > b*aba*ntu (the humanity *of* the people)

*uku*bhakwa *kwa*-+ *ii*keyiki   > kw*ee*keyiki* (the baking *of* cakes)

*ukw*enziwa *kwa*- + *ubu*si   > k*obu*si† (the making *of* honey)

*ii- > -ee-. †For ease of pronunciation '**w**' is omitted before '**o**'.

3 How to express 'am', 'is', 'are'

With interrogative '-phi?' where *'am'*, *'is'*, *'are'* are understood

U**phi** uDavid?   **Where** (is) David?
Si**phi** isibhedlele?   **Where** (is) the hospital?
I**phi** i-ofisi yakho?   **Where** (is) your office?

→ cf. **Unjani**? = lit. You **how**? (see **Unit 2.5**).

With the adverb 'apha' = 'here'

I-ofisi i*l*apha *e*Kapa.　　　　　　The office *is* here *in* **Cape Town**.

With forms such as 'esikolweni', 'e-ofisini', 'emsebenzini', esibhedlele, eKapa, etc. (known as the locative form)

Ndi*se*khaya.	I *am* *at* **home**.
U*se*-ofis*ini*.	He *is* *in* the **office**.
Ba*se*sikol*weni*.	They *are* *at* **school**.

Note: The locative -s- also separates the two vowels in:

nga*se*-: nga*se*Rhini	**near Grahamstown**
na*se*-: na*se*yunivesithi	**and** *at* the **university**
ba*se*-: *aba*ntu ba*se*Holani	the **people of** (in) **Holland**

4 How to express 'here is', 'here are'

Once again the noun class system in Xhosa necessitates the use of several different forms where only two are used in English:

Nanku *u***Jenny**.	**Here is Jenny**.
Naba *aba***ntwana**.	**Here are** the **children**.
Nanku (or **nangu**) *um***nxeba**.	**Here is** the **phone**.
Nantsi *imi***qamelo**.	**Here are** the **pillows**.
Nali *i***cephe**.	**Here is** the **spoon**.
Nanga *ama***cephe**.	**Here are** the **spoons**.
Nasi *isi***layi** se**keyiki**.	**Here is** a **slice** of **cake**.
Nazi *ezi***nye** *izi***layi**.	**Here are** some **more slices**.
Nantsi *i***kofu**.	**Here is** the **coffee**.
Nazi (or **nanzi**) *ii***tispuni**.	**Here are** the **teaspoons**.
Nalu *u***bisi**.	**Here is** the **milk**.
Nabu* *ubu***si**.	**Here is** the **honey**.
Naku *uku***tya**.	**Here is** the **food**.

* Nabu is seldom used as nouns belonging to Class 14 are nearly all abstract.

5 The equivalent of English 'myself', 'yourself', etc.

At last, here is a case where there is only one form in Xhosa where English has more than one form!

Like the object concord, '-*zi*-' = '*myself*', '*yourself*', '*ourselves*', etc., is placed immediately before the verb:

Ndiya**zidla**. (lit. I am eating *myself*)	I am **proud** of *myself*.
Baya**zidla**.	They are **proud** of *themselves*.
Zi**ncede**.	**Help** *yourself*.

6 *Expressions in Xhosa ending in '-ile'*

These expressions often refer to one's **physical state**. They are verbal forms in Xhosa, but correspond to adjectives in English:

Ndi**phil***ile*.	I am **well**.	Namkelek*ile*!	You're **welcome**!
Ndi**lamb***ile*.	I am **hungry**.	Kubalulek*ile*.	It's **important**.
Ku**lung***ile*.	It is **all right**.	Uxakek*ile*?	Are you **busy**?
Ndi**qinisek***ile*?	I'm **sure**.	Ndi**ngxam***ile*.	I'm in a **hurry**.
Utshat*ile*?	Are you **married**?	Unyanis*ile*.	You're **right**.
Ukhululek*ile*?	Are you **comfortable**?	Kuphol*ile*.	It is **cool**.

Note: Two frequently used expressions which end in '*-iwe*', not '*-ile*':

Ndi**nxan***iwe*.	I am **thirsty**.	Ndi**din***iwe*.	I am **tired**.

7 *'Xhosalised' words*

In Units 1–5 you have come across a number of '**xhosalised**' nouns, i.e. those nouns adopted from **English** and / or **Afrikaans**:

from English		*from Afrikaans*	
*i*bhotolo	butter	*i*bhanti (*ama-*)	band
*i*fama	farm	*i*dolophu	dorp
*in*kampani	company	*i*komityi	koppie
*i*keyiki	cake	*i*swekile	suiker
*i*kliniki	clinic		
*i*kofu	coffee		
*i*majarini	margarine		
i-ofisi	office		
*i*resiphi	recipe		
*i*sengwitshi	sandwich		
*i*ti	tea		
*i*tispuni	teaspoon		
*i*yunivesithi	university		

As you can see, most of these 'adopted words' belong to Classes 9 /10 prefixing *i-/ii-*. However, when the adopted English or Afrikaans word begins with an 's' followed by a consonant, e.g. '**s**chool', '**s**lice', these nouns usually belong to the '*isi-*' class:

*isi***kolo**   <u>s</u>chool   *isi***layi**   <u>s</u>lice

Although the majority of nouns adopted from English or Afrikaans belong to Classes 9 and 10, there are a number of nouns besides '*i***bhanti**' which belong to Classes 5 and 6 and **not** to Classes 9 and 10:

*i***khitshi**	*ama***khitshi** (kitchen/s)	*i***khadi**	*ama***khadi** (card/s)
*i***phepha**	*ama***phepha** (paper/s)	*i***polisa**	*ama***polisa** (police)
*i***tikiti**	*ama***tikiti** (ticket/s)	*i***vili**	*ama***vili** (wheel/s)

Adopted words are often used in everyday speech while the original Xhosa words are preferred in the written language, especially in literature, e.g.:

i-**eropleni**	*in***qwelo**-**moya** (lit. wagon (of the) air)
*i***khitshi**	*i***gumbi** lo*ku***phekela** (lit. room of / for cooking)
*i***flawa**	*um***gubo** (flour)
*i***fowuni**	*um***nxeba** (phone) (lit. a rope)

Note: When English words are used in written or spoken Xhosa they must have a prefix which is usually '*i-*' (Class 9):

*i***personnel manager**
*i***Red Cross Hospital**
*i***Primary Health Care**

⚑ *How to apply it*

1 Ask

    (a)   Where is the sugar?
    (b)   Where is the milk?
    (c)   Where is the cake?
    (d)   Where is a spoon?
    (e)   Where is the coffee?
    (f)   Where is the tea?
    (g)   Where is a teaspoon?

2 Answer

    (a)   Here is the sugar.
    (b)   Here is the milk.

    (c)   Here is the cake.

    (d)   Here is a spoon.

    (e)   Here is the coffee.

    (f)   Here is the tea.

    (g)   Here is a teaspoon.

3 Say that you like *'it'*

    (a)   Ndi___thanda (ikeyiki).

    (b)   Ndi___thanda (amaqanda).

    (c)   Ndi___thanda (izinto ezimnandi).

    (d)   Ndi___thanda (iisengwitshi).

    (e)   Ndi___thanda (ikofu) enganaswekile. (without sugar) (lit. not having sugar)

4 Give the instructions replacing the word in brackets with the appropriate object concord

    (a)   _____zalise (iketile – fill the kettle).

    (b)   _____bilise (amanzi).

    (c)   _____zise (ubisi).

    (d)   _____gqithise (iswekile).

    (e)   _____ncede (yourself).

    (f)   _____vale (ucango).

5 Ask (using *-njani*)

    (a)   How are you today?

    (b)   How are the children?

    (c)   How is your husband?

    (d)   How is your wife?

    (e)   How are your parents?

    (f)   How is work?

    (g)   How is the weather?

    (h)   How is the cake?

    (i)   How are the sandwiches?

6 Look at the recipe Jenny gives Thandi

    (a)   Circle the object concords and the noun to which they refer. (You should find three)

    _____   _____   _____

    (b)   Circle the possessives.

7 Write a list in Xhosa of the things Thandi asks Lindiwe to buy for her

UThandi 'Lindiwe, ndifuna ukubhaka ikeyiki ngomso kusasa kodwa andinaxesha lokuthenga izithako ezifunekayo. Ndicela uye esuphamakete uzithenge. Nalu uluhlu:'

    eggs   _____
    flour   _____
    butter   _____
    sugar   _____
    milk   _____
    margarine   _____
    icing sugar   _____

ULindiwe Kulungile. Ndiza kukwenzela loo nto.

8 Complete the text by filling in

Use 'amanzi', 'ikofu' and 'ubisi'.

A   Ngena sisi, uphumle umzuzwana. Ujongeka udiniwe! Hlala phantsi. Lixesha leti okanye ukhetha _____?

B   Enkosi. Nokuba yintoni.

A   David, layita iketile ubilise _____.

D   Kulungile, mama.

A   Nantsi _____. Ungathanda _____ neswekile?

B   Galela _____ qha, enkosi.

A   David, nceda uzise _____.

D   Luphi _____, mama? Lusefrijini? Andiluboni *tu*!

A   Oo, ndilibele ukuluthenga _____!

-phumla	rest, relax	iketile	kettle
umzuzwana	a little while	-bilisa	boil
-layita	switch on	-zisa	fetch

9 Fill in the missing forms

Use:

(a) ndilambile, (b) kubalulekile, (c) wamkelekile, (d) ndiphilile,
(e) ndingxamile, (f) utshatile, (g) ndinxanwe and (h) kupholile

Molo, (1) _____ ekhayeni lam!
Unjani namhlanje? (2) _____ enkosi.
Ufuna into yokusela? Ewe, (3) ndi _____kakhulu!
Ufuna into yokutya kananjalo? Ewe, (4) _____.
Ndicela uze apha. Ungandincedisa? Hayi, ndilusizi,
(5) _____.
Nceda uzise ijezi yam. Ndiyagodola. (6) _____ngoku.
(7) _____ufowune uThandi.
(8) _____uThemba? Ewe, uThandi yinkosikazi
yakhe.

6 | Nifudumele ngokwaneleyo?
Are you warm enough?

In this Unit you will learn how to:

■ ask whether someone is warm enough
■ discuss the weather
■ express likes / dislikes
■ refer to the days of the week / months / seasons

Incoko

The Murrays and the Thamsanqas move inside and discuss the variable weather.

UPeter	Nifudumele ngokwaneleyo okanye ndilayite isifudumezi?
UThemba	Hayi enkosi, asifuni sifudumezi. Akubandi kangako.
UJenny	Linjalo izulu laseKapa. Umzuzu ilanga liyakhanya, kolandelayo kuyana!
UThandi	Hayi, maan, musa ukubaxa! Yaye ungakhalazi ngezulu laseKapa! Imvula ibhetele kunembalela! Ibe siyayifuna imvula eMzantsi Afrika. Inqabile.
UPeter	Jenny, ufana nabantu abavela eGauteng! Bona, kaloku, abalithandi izulu lethu! Ebusika bakhalaza ngemvula; ehlotyeni ngokuvuthuza komoya!
UThemba	Kodwa masiyivumeni inyani, lihle izulu laseGauteng ebusika. Lomile, alini.
UThandi	Kodwa iindudumo nemibane phaya ehlotyeni!
UJenny	Hayi, masivumeni yonke indawo inezinto ezilungileyo nezinto ezingalunganga!
UThandi	Unyanisile! Umzekelo, eThekwini kumnandi ebusika kodwa ukufuma apho ehlotyeni, *kugqithe emgceni*!!
UJenny	Ewe, kunjalo kanye sisi.

UPeter	Ndiyathemba ukuba liza kuba lihle* ngempela-veki ezayo kuba kukho ukhuphiswano olukhulu lweqakamba eNewlands. Uyakuthanda ukubukela iqakamba, Themba?
UThemba	Kakhulu! Utsho no**Makhaya Ntini** kwiTV: *'I don't like cricket. I love it!'*
UPeter	Heke, ndiza kuya noDavid emdlalweni ngoMgqibelo. Uyafuna ukusikhapha nonyana wakho?
UThemba	Ewe, singavuya kakhulu.
UPeter	Kulungile, ndiza kukufowunela ngoLwesihlanu ukuze sithethe ngexesha nendawo yokudibana.

*In 'liza kuba lihle' 'li-' = 'it' refers to Class 5 noun '*izulu*' = weather.

Isigama

-fudumele	be warm	masiyivumeni inyani	let's admit the truth
ngokwaneleyo	enough	-omile	be dry
-layita	switch on	alini	it doesn't rain
isifudumezi	heater	iindudumo	thunder
kangako	so	imibane	lightning
-njalo	like that	phaya	over there
izulu	weather	yonke indawo	every place
laseKapa	of the Cape	inezinto ezilungileyo	has good things
umzuzu	minute	ezingalunganga	not good (things)
-khanya	shine	umzekelo	for example
kolandelayo	at the next	eThekwini	in Durban
-na	rain (verb)	ukufuma	humidity
musa	don't	apho	there
-baxa	exaggerate	*kugqithe emgceni*	intolerable
yaye	and		lit. beyond the line
ungakhalazi	don't complain	kunjalo kanye	it's exactly like that
imvula	rain (noun)	liza kuba lihle	it will be fine
-bhetele	better	impela-veki ezayo	coming weekend
kunembalela	than drought	ukhuphiswano olukhulu	big match
imbalela	drought	lweqakamba	of cricket
ibe	moreover	iqakamba	cricket
-nqabile	be scarce	-bukela	watch
-fana na-	be like	-tsho	say so
abavela	who come	emdlalweni	to the game
bona, kaloku	as for them	ngoMgqibelo	on Saturday
ebusika	winter	-khapha	accompany
-khalaza nga-	complain about	-fowunela	phone (for)
ehlotyeni	in summer	ngoLwesihlanu	on Friday
-vuthuza komoya	blowing of wind	ukuze	so that

How to ...

Ask whether someone is warm enough/cold

U**fudumele** ngok**waneley**o?
Uya**godola**?

Note: '-**godola**' = 'be **cold**' refers to **humans** while '-**banda**' = 'be **cold**' refers only to **inanimate** objects.

Comment on warm/hot/pleasant weather

Ku**shushu**!	It's **hot**!
*Yi*mini *en*tle!	It *is* a **beautiful day**!
*I*langa liya**khanya**.	The **sun** is **shining**.
*I*langa liya**qaqamb**a (lit. throbbing).	The **sun** is **shining**.
*I*langa liya**tshisa**!	The **sun** is **burning**!
*I*langa li**balele**.	It is **intensely hot**. There is a **drought**.
*Likhupha intlanzi emanzini!**	(It is so hot that) *it takes the fish out of the water!*
*Ligqatse ubhobhoyi!**	(It is so hot that) *it scorches the African hoopoe bird!*
Ku**fudumele**.	It is **warm**.
Ndi**fudumele**.	I am **warm**

→ *See **Unit 10.1** for more about idioms and proverbs.

Comment on cool/cold/less pleasant weather

*I*hlobo *ali***fun***i* kufika.	**Summer** doesn't want to come.
*I*hlobo *ali***vum***i* ukude lingene.	**Summer** is late. (lit. summer does*n't* **agree** (yet) to **come in**.)
*I*hlobo li**phel***ile*.	**Summer** *has* **come to an end**.
Kuya**phola**.	It is becoming **cool**.
Ku**phol***ile*.	It is **cool**.
Kuya**banda** (phandle)!	It is **cold** (outside)!
Beku**banda** izolo.	It was **cold** yesterday.
*Yi*mini *em***bi**!	It is a **terrible day**!
Ku**jongeka** ngathi *i*mini iza kuba *m***bi**!	It **looks as if** it is going to be a **terrible day**!

Izulu limathumb' antaka!*	The weather is rather unsettled. (lit. like the intestines of a bird)
*Ubu*sika *abu*fun*i* ku**mka**.	**Winter** doesn*'t* **want** to **go away**.
*Andi*zi**thandi** *tu* ii**ny**anga zo*bu***sika**!	I do*n't* **like** the **winter months** *at all*!

→ *See **Unit 10.1** for more about idioms and proverbs.

Comment on rainy weather

*I*zulu liye**zisa**.	**Rain** is imminent. (lit. the weather is **bringing** rain)
Kuy**ana**.	It's **raining**.
Ndi**cinga** ukuba kuza ku**netha**!	I think it is going **to rain**!
Ngathi kuza ku**netha**.	It looks like it is going **to rain**.
Ndi**themba** ukuba iza ku**yeka** kamsinya *uku***netha**!	I **hope** that it **stops raining** soon!
Si**fumene** *im***vula** eninzi kutshanje.	We've **had** a lot of **rain** recently.
Nantsi *im***vula**!	Here's the **rain**!
Iya**galela** *im***vula**!	It's **pouring** with **rain**!
*Im***vula** iya**dyudyuza**!	It's **pouring** with **rain**!

Comment on windy/misty/overcast/dry weather

*U***moya** uya**vuthuza**.	It's **very windy**. (lit. it is **blowing**)
*U***moya** uya**bhudla**.	The wind is **blowing hard**.
Kukho *in***kungu**.	It's **misty**.
Ku**sibekele**.	It's **overcast**.
Kom*ile*.	It's **dry**.
Ku**fum***ile*.	It's **humid**.
Ku**zol***ile*.	It's **calm**.

Note: '*in***kungu** ne**langa**' (lit. **mist** and **sun**) is an idiomatic way of saying 'a multitude of people': 'Bekukho *in***kungu** ne**langa**' 'There was a huge crowd.'

Comment on thunder/lightning/hail

Mamela *ii***ndudumo**!	**Listen** to the **thunder**!
Jonga *um***bane**!	**Look** at the **lightning**!
Jonga *isi***chotho**!	**Look** at the **hail**!

Ask what the temperature is

*Yi*ntoni *i***qondo** lo*bu***shushu** namhlanje?	**What's** the **temperature** today? (lit. degree of heat)

Cultural background

Seasons of the year
(*Ama*xesha Lo**nyaka**) (lit. times of the year)

summer	*i*hlobo	(< *um*hlobo = friend (i.e. the friendly season)
spring	*int*lakohlaza	(lit. the points of the green grass)
	*int*wasahlobo	(< -thwasa = become visible, appear
		(lit. the appearance of summer)
autumn	*u*kwindla	(< -dla = eat, i.e. the season of eating) (Class 14!)
winter	*ubu*sika	(< -sika = cut, i.e. the cutting season)

Months of the year
(*lin*yanga Zo**nyaka**)

January	uJanuwari	eyom**Qungu**	(month of the **Tambuki grass**)
February	uFebruwari	eyom**Dumba**	(month of the **swelling grain**)
March	uMatshi	eyo**Kwindla**	(month of the **first fruits**)
April	uApril	eka**Tshaz'iimpuzi**	(month of the **withering pumpkins**)
May	uMeyi	eka**Canzibe**	(month of the **Canopus**)*
June	uJuni	eye**Silimela**	(month of the **Pleiades**)
July	uJulayi	eye**Khala**	(month of the **aloes**)
August	uAgasti	eye**Thupha**	(month of the **buds**)
September	uSeptemba	eyom**Sintsi**	(month of the **coast coral tree**)
October	uOktobha	eye**Dwarha**	(month of the **ragwort**)
November	uNovemba	eye**Nkanga**	(month of the **broad-leaved ragwort**)†
December	uDisemba	eyom**Nga**	(month of the **mimosa thorn tree**)

*Bright star seen before dawn in May. †Tall and smaller yellow daisies respectively.

Note: As can be seen from the explanation in brackets, the Xhosa months were named after plants or flowers flowering in that particular month. The original names of the months are very often used in literature while the Anglicised versions seem to be used in everyday speech especially by the younger generation.

Poem and songs

Imbalela

'Yoo! Yoo!
Siyalila,
Iinkomo zethu zifile,
Iintlanti zikhedamile,
Amasimi axwebile.
Imimango ibharile,
Izityalo zibunile.
Izilwana ziziimpanza,

Amacebo aphelile.'

Drought

Oh! Oh!
We are weeping,
Our cattle are dead,
The cattle *kraals* are bereft,
The fields are cracked like dry skin.
The hillsides are parched,
The plants are withered.
The small wild animals are like a
   broken up, dispersed army,
We don't know what to do.
   (lit. Plans have come to an end.)

(From a poem by **G. Soya Mama**)

Imvula

Imvula, imvula,
Chapha, chapha, chapha,
Imanz' ilokhwe yam,
imanz' ilokhwe yam,
Gqum, gqum, kuyaduduma,
Gqum, gqum, kuyaduduma.
Imanz' ilokhwe yam,
Imanz' ilokhwe yam.

Rain

Rain, rain,
Splash, splash, splash,
My dress is wet,
My dress is wet,
Boom, boom, it is thundering.
Boom, boom, it is thundering.
My dress is wet.
My dress is wet.

Umoya

Khanibone nank ' umoya!
Wu! Wu! Wu!
Ungen' efestileni,
Ucim' isibane sam,
Uyaphuma ndiyasala,
Undishiya emnyameni,
Zuhambe zuhambe (uze uhambe).
Wu! Wu! Wu!

Wind

Please see here is the wind!
Wu! Wu! Wu!
It comes through the window,
It puts out my light.
It goes out and I stay,
It leaves me in the dark.
It should go, it should go.
Wu! Wu! Wu!

How it works

1 The equivalent of English 'every', 'all', 'the whole' = '-onke'

From the following list you can see that '-onke' is preceded by the consonant associated with the noun to which it refers and can precede or follow a noun depending on emphasis:

_w_onke _um_**ntu**	_every_ **person, everyone**
_b_onke _ab_**antu**	_all_ **persons, everybody**
_w_onke _um_**sebenzi**	_all_ **work**
_y_onke _imi_**hla** (lit. all days)	_every_ **day**
_l_onke _ili_**zwe**	the _whole_ **country**
_l_onke _i_**xesha**	_all_ the **time**
onke _ama_**zwe**	_all_ **countries**
onke _ama_**xesha**	_all_ **times**
_s_onke _isi_**kolo**	the _whole_ **school**
_z_onke _izi_**kolo**	_all_ **schools**
_y_onke _in_**to**	_every_**thing**
_z_onke _izin_**to**	_all_ **things**
_l_onke _ulu_**ntu**	_all_ **mankind**
_b_onke _u_**kwindla**	the _whole_ **autumn**
_b_onke _ubu_**sika**	the _whole_ **winter**
_k_onke _uku_**tya**	_all_ the **food**

Remember: in the case of nouns prefixing '_um-_' the associated consonant is 'w-' and in the case of nouns prefixing '_imi-_' / '_i-_' / '_in-_' / '_im-_' the associated consonant is 'y-'.

Note: No concord in Class 6 (_ama-_).

'-onke' can also be used with 'si-' = 'we' and 'ni-' = 'you' (pl.):

Yizani apha _n_onke. *All of you* come here.

2 Adjectives

There are only a few so-called adjectives in Xhosa, several of which you have already come across, but they are frequently used. They include the numerals 1–6 as well as the following adjectival stems:

-nye	= one	**-ne**	= four
-bini	= two	**-hlanu**	= five
-thathu	= three	**-thandathu**	= six

-hle	= beautiful	**-bi**	= bad, ugly
-de	= long, tall, far	**-futshane**	= short
-fuphi	= near	**-tsha**	= young, fresh
-dala	= old, stale	**-ninzi**	= many
-ngaphi?	= how many?	**-ncinane**	= little
-khulu	= big	**-ncinci**	= small

In Xhosa, adjectives follow nouns and to mark the relationship between noun and adjective, an **adjectival concord** (corresponding to 'that', 'which', 'who') is used e.g.:

*um*sebenzi *om*khulu	a **big** job	(lit. a **job** *that* is **big**)
*isi*layi *esi*ncinci	a **small** slice	(lit. a **slice** *that* is **small**)
*i*komityi *e*nye	**one** cup	(lit. a **cup** *that* is **one**)
(cf. **_enye_** ikomityi yekofu = **another** cup of coffee)		

om-	*um*ntwana	*om*nye	**one** child
aba-	*aba*ntu	*aba*dala	**adults** (lit. old people)
om-	*um*sebenzi	*om*khulu	**big/much** work
emi-	*imi*hla	*emi*de	**long** days
eli-	*i*zulu	*eli*hle	**fine** weather
ama-	*ama*cephe	*ama*khulu	**big** spoons
esi-	*isi*layi	*esi*ncinci	a **small** slice
izi-	*izi*kolo	*ezi*ninzi	**many** schools
en-	*i*keyiki	*en*tle*	a **beautiful** cake
en-	*i*nto	*en*kulu†	a **great** thing
ezin- / *ezim-*	*ii*tispuni	*ezim*bini[a]	**two** teaspoons
olu-	*u*bisi	*olu*tsha	**fresh** milk
obu-	*ubu*sika	*obu*bi	a **bad** winter
oku-	*uku*tya	*oku*dala	**stale** food

* -**hle** > -**tle** before an **n**: i*nto* e*ntle*; *i*keyiki e*ntle*.

† A consonant after **n** is **never aspirated**. [a] **n** > **m** before **b, p, f, v**.

Although there are only a few true adjectives in Xhosa, the Xhosa language is not short of descriptives.

One group includes words referred to in Xhosa grammar books as
'**relatives**', e.g.:

-mnandi	sweet, nice	**-muncu**	sour
-lula	easy, light	**-nzima**	difficult, heavy
-lusizi	sad, sorry	**-bomvu**	red
-mhlophe	white	**-mnyama**	black
-ntsundu	brown	**-blowu**	blue
-luhlaza	green* / blue†	**-lubhelu**	yellow

*Okwe**ngca** = as grass.
†Okwe*si***bhakabhaka** = as the sky.

→ **Unit 8.1** for more **relative stems**.

Other descriptives are **derived from verbs** and suffix -*yo* when no other
word follows:

-balulekile_yo_	important	**-za**_yo_	coming
-landela_yo_	following	**-vela**	coming from
-lungile_yo_	good	**-ya**	going to

Kubaluleki*le*.	It's **important**.
Yinto *e***balulekile**_yo_.	It's an **important** thing.
	(lit. *which* is **important**)

Yet another group uses -**na**- = 'have' / 'has' / 'with' together with an
abstract noun:

-**no***m***dla** (interesting): *um*sebenzi *o***nomdla** (lit. **work** that **has interest**)
-**na***m***andla** (strong): *in*doda *e***namandla** (lit. a **man** who **has strength**)

The **difference** between **adjectives** and **other descriptives** is in their
concord or **link** to the noun in the following noun classes only:

		Adjectives	**Other descriptives**	
Class 1	_um_ntu	_om_hle	_um_ntu	_o_nomdla
Class 3	_um_sebenzi	_om_hle	_um_sebenzi	_o_nomdla
Class 4	_imi_hla	_emi_hle	_imi_hla	_e_mnandi
Class 6	_ama_zwe	_ama_hle	_ama_zwe	_a_mnandi
Class 9	_in_to	_en_tle	_in_to	_e_mnandi
Class 10	_izin_to	_ezin_tle	_izin_to	_ezi_mnandi

Note: A **relative concord** prefixed to a **verb** forms a **relative clause**:

Ufana nabantu _aba_**vela**	You are like people _who_ **come**
eGauteng.	**from** Gauteng.

3 The present tense in the negative

There is no word in Xhosa corresponding to the English 'not'.

Instead, the **negative** form of the subject concord is used and the verb ending changes (cf. **Unit 3.3**). Compare the subject concords of the 3rd person:

Positive	Negative	
ú-	*aka-*	*U*Thandi *aka*thand*i* *n*dudumo namibane.
ba-	*aba-*	*Aba*ntu baseGauteng *aba*l*i*thand*i* *i*zulu laseKapa.
u-	*awu-*	*U*m*o*ya *awu*band*i* namhlanje.
i-	*ayi-*	*I*m*i*sebenzi *ayi*phel*i*. (The tasks have not ended.)
li-	*ali-*	*I*langa *ali*khany*i* namhlanje.
a-	*aka-*	*A*ma*n*zi *aka*band*i*.
si-	*asi-*	*I*s*i*fudumezi *asi*sebenz*i* kakuhle.
zi-	*azi-*	*I*z*i*fudumezi *azi*sebenz*i* kakuhle.
i-	*ayi-*	*I*m**vula *ayi*fun*i* kuma namhlanje.
zi-	*azi-*	*I*im**vula *azi*fun*i* kuma namhlanje.
lu-	*alu-*	*U*lwandle (the sea) *alu*band*i* namhlanje.
bu-	*abu-*	*U*b*u*sika *abu*band*i*.
ku-	*aku-*	*U*k*u*tya *aku*band*i*.

4 The future tense

In **Unit 1** you came across an example of the **future tense**:

Siza **ku**fika eKapa kamsinya.   We **will** arrive in Cape Town soon.

As you can see the future tense is formed in the following way:
SC + '-**za ku-**' (or '-**ya ku-**') + verb stem:

Ndiza **ku**zama.   I'**ll try**.
Ndiza **ku***ku***fowunela**.   I'**ll** phone *you*.
Ndicinga ukuba li**za ku**na.   I think it **will** rain.

Note: the position of the object concord.

The **short** (**contracted**) **form** of the **future tense** is often heard in colloquial speech but can also be found in written texts:

Nd**o**bona, s**o**bona,   I'**ll** see, you'**ll** see,
w**o**bona, n**o**bona, etc.   he'**ll** / she'**ll** see, you'**ll** see, etc.

Remember: So**bonana.**   We'**ll** see each other.

The **negative form**: '-**zi ku-**' (or '-**yi ku-**'):

*Andizi ku**kwenzalisa**.*   I **will** *not* **hurt** *you*.

→ See **Unit 8.**

5 Instruct not to do something

It is very easy to instruct someone **not to do** something. Simply use
'**Musa**' followed by the infinitive when instructing one person and
'**Musani**' when instructing more than one person:

One person	**More than one person**
Musa ukubaxa.	**Musani** ukubaxa.

Don't exaggerate.

Musa ukukhalaza.	**Musani** ukukhalaza.

Don't complain.

Musa ukulibala.	**Musani** ukulibala.

Don't forget.

Musa ukuzikhathaza.	**Musani** ukuzikhathaza.

Don't worry (*yourself*).

In spoken language the shortened forms are preferred:

Sukubaxa.	**Sanuku**baxa.
Sukukhalaza.	**Sanuku**khalaza.
Sukulibala.	**Sanuku**libala.
Sukuzikhathaza.	**Sanuku**zikhathaza.

If you want to express yourself more 'elegantly' you can say:

Unga**khalazi**.	**Ni**nga**khalazi**.	You should**n't** complain.
Unga**libali**.	**Ni**nga**libali**.	You should**n't** forget.
Unga**zikhathazi**.	**Ni**nga**zikhathazi**.	You should**n't** worry.

→ See **Unit 15.2.**

6 Different ways of expressing 'can'

The English translations show that these different ways of expressing
'**can**' are not always interchangeable:

Unoku**za**? (< U**nakho** ukuza?)	**Can** you (are you able to) come?
Ewe, ndi**noku**za.	Yes, I **can** (come).
Hayi, *a*ndi**naku**za.	No, I **can**'*t* (come).

Unga*ndi*nceda?	**Can** you **help** *me*?
Ndi*nga*ngena?	**Can** (may) I come in?
Uya*kw*azi *uku*thetha isiXhosa?	**Can** you (do you know how to) **speak** Xhosa?

7 More Xhosa equivalents of the English prepositions 'in', 'at'

*Times of the day (ama*xesha osuku) (usuku = 24-hour day)*

*e*mini	*in* **daytime**
*e*mini *e*maqanda	*at* **midday**
*ema*langa / emva kwe*mini	*in* the **afternoon**
*ebu*suku	*at* **night**
*ezinzul*wini zobu**suku**	*at* **midnight**
ngorhatya (< *u*rhatya)	**at** dusk
ngokuhlwa (< *uku*hlwa)	**in** the evening

'**Nga-**' is also used with **days** of the **week** – *iin*tsuku zeveki:

Monday	*uM*vulo (< -vula = open)
on Monday	ngo*M*vulo
Tuesday	uLwesibini*
on Tuesday	ngoLwesibini
Wednesday	uLwesithathu*
on Wednesday	ngoLwesithathu
Thursday	uLwesine*
on Thursday	ngoLwesine
Friday	uLwesihlanu*
on Friday	ngoLwesihlanu
Saturday	*uM*gqibelo (< -gqibela = finish)
on Saturday	ngo*M*gqibelo
Sunday	*i*Cawa (cf. *i*cawa = church)
on Sunday	ngeCawa

*cf. **Adjectival stems**.

'**Nga-**' is used also with **months** of the **year** – *iin*yanga zonyaka:

in which **month**?	nge*yiphi in*yanga?
in January	**ngo**Janyuwari
in February	**ngo**Febhuwari

in March	**ngo**Matshi
in April	**ngo**Apreli
in May	**ngo**Meyi

Seasons – *ama*xesha *o*nyaka:

in summer	*e*hlo*ty*eni*	(< *i*hlo<u>b</u>o)
in autumn	*e*kwindla	(< *u*kwindla (Class 14 *ubu-*)
in winter	<u>e</u>bu<u>sika</u>	(< *ubu*sika)
in spring	<u>e</u>ntlakohlaza	(< *in*tlakohlaza)

* '<u>b</u>' followed directly by '<u>w</u>' is not easily pronounceable in Xhosa, therefore '**b**' > '*ty*' before *-eni*.

8 Adverbs

You have already come across some adverbs of time and place:

namhlanje	today	apha	here
ngomso	tomorrow	apho	there
lonke ixesha	always	onke amaxesha	always
phaya	over there	futhi	often

Adverbs can be formed with **ka-**:

kakuhle	well	**ka**kubi	badly
kakhulu	much	**ka**ncinci	a little
kangaka	so much	**ka**njalo	like this
kamnandi	nicely	**ka**msinya(ne)	soon
kanye	once, exactly	**ka**bini	twice
kaninzi	often		

Note: Kahle! = Hold on!

Adverbs can be formed with **ku-**:

kudala	long ago	**ku**phela	only
ku<u>nge</u>**ku**dala	shortly (lit. **it** is **not** long)		

And adverbs can be formed with **nga-**:

ngethamsanqa	luckily	**nge**saquphe	suddenly
ngelishwa	unfortunately	**nga**kumbi	especially
ngokukhawuleza	quickly	**nga**phakathi	inside
ngokwaneleyo	sufficiently	**nga**phandle	outside
ngamanye amaxesha	sometimes		

Others include:

kwakhona	again	*qha*	only
e*ku*gqibel*eni*	at last	*qho*	always

☑ *How to apply it*

1 **Find the contrasting word / expression**

Choose from: (a) Ilanga libalele, (b) Liyabanda kakhulu, (c) Lomile, (d) Kusibekele, (e) Umoya uyavuthuza and (f) Masihlale elangeni.

1   Likhupha intlanzi emanzini.
2   Ilanga liyakhanya.
3   Iyagalela imvula.
4   Kuzolile. / Akukho moya.
5   Lifumile.
6   Masihlale emthunzini. (shade)

2 **Yithi**

(a) I am cold.   It is cold.

_____   _____

(b) I am warm.   It is warm.

_____   _____

(c) It becomes cool.   It is cool.

_____   _____

(d) It will rain tomorrow.   It won't rain today.

_____   _____

3 **Yithi**

(a) It's a nice day.   Yimini _____
(b) It's an awful day.   Yimini _____
(c) It's a cool day.   Yimini _____
(d) It's hot day.   Yimini _____
(e) It's a cool night.   Bubusuku _____

4 **Complete the dialogue with the appropriate subject concord**

A   (a) ____za kuya eRobben Island ngoLwesihlanu, mna nabantwana. (b) ____ngathanda uku*si*khapha, wena nabantwana? (c) ___namanye amatikiti amathathu.

B   Mna (d) ____ngathanda ukunikhapha, kodwa (e) ___xhomekeke
     kwimozulu. Ukuba umoya (f) ____vuthuza gqitha, ulwandle
     (g) ___za kulwa. (h) ____oyika ukuba ndingagula ngenxa
     yokudlokova kwenqanawa!

A   Hayi, (i) ____zi kuya ukuba (j) ____vuthuza gqitha.

B   (k) ____za kuya ukuba (l) ____yanetha?

A   Ewe, mna, (m) ___oyiki mvula.

B   (n) ____za kuya ukuba (o) ____shushu gqitha?

A   Ewe, (p) ____khathazeki bubushushu.

ulwandle	sea	-gula	be sick
-xhomekeke ku-	depend on	ngenxa ya-	because of
-lwa	fight i.e. rough	-dlokova kwenqanawa	rolling of the ship
-oyika	be afraid of	-khathazeka	mind, worry

5 Listen to the weather reports and say which refers to the weather in summer and which to the weather in winter

(a)   _____

(b)   _____

6 Use the appropriate expression in Xhosa for 'can'

(a) Can you speak Xhosa?   No, I can only speak a little Zulu.
(b) Can you speak English?   Yes, I am learning it at school.
(c) Can you please help me?   Of course (kakade), I'll help you.
(d) Can you come on Friday?   I'm sorry, I can't help you.
(e) Can I phone you tomorrow?   I'm sorry. I can't come. I am too busy.
(f) Can I pour you another cup of coffee? No thanks, one cup is enough.
(g) Can I come in?   Yes, please come in.

7 Say what you prefer

(a) Someone says: Ndithanda izinto ezimuncu (sour).
     Say you prefer sweet things.

(b) Someone says: Ndithanda ikofu engenabisi* naswekile.
     Say you prefer coffee with milk and sugar.

(c) Somebody says: Ndithanda ikeyiki.
     Say you prefer sandwiches.

(d) Somebody says: Ndithanda ibhotolo.
    Say you prefer margarine.
(e) Somebody says: Ndithanda iwayini ebomvu.
    Say you prefer white wine.

→ *See **Unit 15.2**.

8 The South African flag (indwe yoMzantsi Afrika). Colour in appropriately and number the colours

iluhlaza
ilubhelu
imnyama
(okwengca)

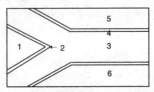

ibomvu
imhlophe
iluhlaza
(okwesibhakabhaka)

9 Read this excerpt from a poem by Minazana Dana

From which climatic region is the poet writing? How do you know?
Complete the missing lines of the translation.

Ihlobo

'Ewe, kambe ihlobo lifikile	Yes, no doubt summer has arrived
Ngubo yehlwempu, mhlaziyi-lizwe	Blanket of the poor, renewer [...]
Kaloku nje sinethemba lempilo,	Now we have hope for health
Kaloku nje sinethemba loxolo	....
Kaloku nje sinethemba lokonwaba	....
Ngokufika kweemvula zehlobo	....
Zithembis' isivuno soxolo	They promise a peaceful harvest
Kuba kambe ihlobo lifikile.'	....

7 UJenny emsebenzini – 'Masithethe isiXhosa'
Jenny at work – 'Let's speak Xhosa'

In this Unit you will learn how to:

■ ask how you may help someone
■ ask how someone is in different ways
■ respond in different ways
■ know what to say when at the garage
■ thank someone in different ways
■ know what to say when giving someone a tip
■ congratulate and express good wishes

Incoko

One of Jenny's groups has come to the end of its module. Jenny puts her students through their paces to see whether they are proficient enough to proceed to the next level.

UJenny	Molweni bafundi! Namhlanje nina niza kuthetha isiXhosa, mna ndiza kuphulaphula! Ngoobani abafuna ukuqala?
UMark noPaul	Siza kuqala Jenny.
UMark	Mna, ndiza kuba ngumthengisi-petroli. Yena, uPaul uza kuba ngumqhubi-wemoto.
UJenny	Kulungile, bafundi, thethani!

Egaraji.

Umthengisi-petroli	Molo mhlekazi. Kunjani? Ndingakunceda ngantoni namhlanje?
Umqhubi wemoto	Molo, mnumzana. Kunjani?
Umthengisi-petroli	Hayi, akukho nto. Ndihamba nazo! Wena?
Umqhubi wemoto	Nam, ndiphilile enkosi.
Umthengisi-petroli	Ndiyizalise itanki namhlanje?

Umqhubi wemoto	Hayi, ndiphe nge-fifty rand *qha* namhlanje.
Umthengisi-petroli	Kulungile mhlekazi. Anjani amavili?
Umqhubi-wemoto	Ingathi ivili lasekunene ngaphambili lifuna umoya. Khawukhangele onke jikelele.
Umthengisi-petroli	Kulungile, mhlekazi. Umoya ungakanani?
Umqhubi wemoto	Wampompe aye ku-210 jikelele. Ndicela ungalibali ukukhangela namanzi ne-oyile.
Umthengisi-petroli	*Utsho endodeni!*

After a few moments.

	Heke, zonke izinto zilungile ngaphambili. Ndisule neefestile?
Umqhubi wemoto	Ungaba undincedile!
Umthengisi-petroli	Heke, ndigqibile, mhlekazi.
Umqhubi-wemoto	Ndiyabulela. Undincedile. Nantsi imali yepetroli. Nali ke icuba.
Umthengisi-petroli	Enkosi. Uhambe kakuhle, mhlekazi.
Umqhubi wemoto	Usale kakuhle, mnumzana. Sobonana!
UJenny	Mark noPaul nenze kakuhle! *Huntshu!*
UJenny	Heke, Val noSally, masiveni eyenu incoko!
OoVal	Kulungile.

Isigama

-phulaphula	listen	*utsho endodeni*	*no sooner*
umthengisi-petroli	petrol attendant		*said than done*
umqhubi wemoto	motorist		(lit. you've
ndihamba nazo	I'm fine		said so to a man!)
ndiyizalise itanki?	should I fill the tank?	-sula	wipe
amavili	tyres, wheels	ifestile	window
ivili lasekunene	the right wheel	ungaba	that would be
ngaphambili	in front	undincedile	helpful
umoya	air	nantsi imali	here is money
khawukhangele	please check	yepetroli	for the petrol
-khangela	check, look at	nali ke icuba	here then is
onke jikelele	all round		(money) for
-ngakanani	how much?		tobacco
-mpompa	pump up	-bulela	to be grateful
aye ku-	up to	*huntshu!*	*well done!*
i-oyile	oil	masiveni	let's hear
		eyenu incoko	your conversation

Incoko

Val accidentally bumps into a lady with her trolley while waiting in the checkout queue and a conversation ensues.

UVal	Uxolo Nkosikazi! Ndikwenzakalisile?
Inkosikazi	Hayi, akukho nto. Oo! uyasithetha isiXhosa?
UVal	Ndiyazama noko!
Inkosikazi	Hayi, akuzami! Uyasithetha! Usazela phi isiXhosa?
UVal	Uxolo, andiva kakuhle. Khawuphinde.
Inkosikazi	Ndithe usifunde phi?
UVal	Heke, ndiyaqonda ngoku! Ndisifunda eklasini yesiXhosa.
Inkosikazi	Ufundiswa ngubani?
UVal	NguNkosikazi Murray. Yena wakhulela emaXhoseni.
Inkosikazi	Nam, ndivela emaXhoseni.
UVal	Liphi ikhaya lakho?
Inkosikazi	LiseCacadu.
UVal	Oo YiLady Frere ngesiNgesi leyo?
Inkosikazi	Yho! Unyanisile. Uyasazi isiXhosa inene!
UVal	Uhlala phi, Nkosikazi?
Inkosikazi	EClaremont. Wena uhlala phi?
UVal	EKenilworth kodwa ndisebenza apha eClaremont.
Inkosikazi	Nam ndisebenza apha eClaremont. Ndinerestyu eFir Avenue ebizwa ngegama elithi *'Ningene'*.
UVal	Inene! Mhlawumbi ndiza kukutyelela apho! Yhoo, ndiphantse ndalibala, igama lam nguVal Todd.
Inkosikazi	Ndiyavuya ukukwazi Val. Mna ndinguXoliswa Silinga.
UVal	Nam ndiyavuya ukukwazi, Xoliswa. Bekumnandi kakhulu ukuthetha nawe. Ndiyathemba ukuba siza kubonana kwakhona. Ndiza kuxelela utitshalakazi wam neklasi yam ngerestyu yakho. Mhlawumbi sonke siza kutyelela irestyu yakho kamsinyane!
UXoliswa	Ingantle loo nto, Val. Uhambe kakuhle.
UVal	Uhambe kakuhle nawe, Xoliswa. Sobonana kwakhona apho erestyu!
UJenny	Nani nenze kakuhle, Val noSally! Ndonwabile! Ndonwabe gqitha ngokuqhubela phambili kwenu! Ndiyavuyisana nani! Ngoku mandininqwenelele iholide emnandi!

Isigama

ndikwenzakalisile?	did I hurt you?	-tyelela	visit
usazela phi?	where do you know it from?	ndiphantse	I nearly
		ingantle loo nto!	that would be lovely!
iklasi	class	ndonwabile	I'm happy
ufundiswa ngubani?	by whom are you taught?	ndonwabe gqitha	I'm very happy
		ngokuqhubela phambili kwenu	with your progress
leyo	that		
irestyu	restaurant	-vuyisana na-	rejoice with, i.e.
ebizwa	which is called		congratulations
ngegama elithi	by the name	mandininqwenelele	let me wish you
mhlawumbi	perhaps	iholide	holiday

? How to ...

Ask how you may help someone

Ndinga*ku*nceda ngantoni?

Ask how someone is in different ways

U**phila** / Ni**phila njani**?
U**phil***ile* / Ni**phil***ile*?
Usa**phila** / Nisa**phila**?
U**njani** / Ku**njani**? / Ni**njani**?

Respond to being asked how you are in different ways

Ndiya**phila**. / Si**phila** kakuhle enkosi.
Ndi**phil***ile*. / Si**phil***ile*.
Ndisa**phila**. / Sisa**phila**.
Ndi**khona**. / Si**khona**.

Idiomatic expressions to ask how someone is

U**vuka njani** / Ni**vuka njani**?	(lit. How do you **wake up**?)
U**vuk***ile* / Ni**vuk***ile*?	(lit. Have you **woken up**?)
Usa**hleli** / Nisa**hleli**?	Are you still **seated**? (implication being that those who are not well would not be sitting up).

Some idiomatic expressions in response

Ndi**hleli**.	I am **seated**.
Si**hleli**.	We are **seated**.
Ndi**hamba na**zo.	I am **going along with** *them*.
Si**hamba na**zo.	We are **going along with** *them*.
	('-zo'refers to '*ii*ng**xaki** =. **problems**)
Ndi**khohlela** ndihamba.	I am '**coughing** along'.
Si**khohlela** sihamba.	We are'**coughing** along'.
Ndisa**totoba**.	I am still **tottering along**.
Sisa**totoba**.	We are still **tottering along**.
Ndi**qhwalela** ndisiya.	I am **limping** going along.
Si**qhwalela** sisiya.	We are **limping** going along.
Nd**onwab**ile.	I am **happy**.
S**onwab**ile (ekhaya).	We are **happy** (at home).
Ndiya**cothoza**.	I am **going along slowly**.
Siya**cothoza**.	We are **going along slowly**.
Aku**kho** nto (*im*bi).	**There is nothing (bad)**.
(shortened to: **Akho***'n***to**)	
Ku**nceda** ntoni uku**khalaza**?	What does it **help** to **complain**?
Aku**ncedi** uku**khalaza**!	It doesn't **help** to **complain**!

Know what to say at the garage

Ndinga**fumana** *i*petroli.
Nceda, **zalisa** *i*tanki.
Nceda y*i***zalis**ẹ.
Galela nge-fifty rand *qha*.
Unga**khangela** *i*-**oyile**, *ama*nzi n*ama***vili**.
Mpompa amavili ngo-1.8.
W*a***mpomp**ẹ ngo-1.8.
Ingathi *i***vili** ngaphambili / ngasemva li**hl***ile* kakhulu.

Thank in different ways

Enkosi kakhulu (nge*n***to** yonke).
U*ndi***nced**ile.

Ungaba un*di*nced*ile*.
Ndiya**bulela**.
→ See cultural background

Know what to say when giving someone a tip

Nali *i*cuba.   (lit. Here is **tobacco**.)
Nazi *ii*lekese.   (lit. Here are **sweets**.)
Ina **tshaya**.   (lit. Take for something to **smoke**.)

Congratulate and express good wishes

Huntshu! / *Halala!*	*Hurray*!
Nantso ke!	*That's it*!
Ndiya**vuyisana na***we*!	Congratulations! (lit. I **rejoice** with *you*)
Ngxatsho ke!	*Well spoken*!
*Maqobokazana phambili!**	Young ladies, well done!
Siya**vuyisana na***we* ngo*ku***nyuselwa** kwakho!	Congratulations on your **promotion**!
Zonwabise! / **Zonwabise***ni*!	**Enjoy** *yourself* / *yourselves*!
Ndi*ku***nqwenelela** *im***pumelelo**!	Good luck! (lit. I **wish** *you* **success**)
Ubhale / **Nibhale** kakuhle!	Good luck for the exams! (lit. **Write** well)
Mini *E***mnandi** (yoku**zalwa**) ku*we*!	Happy Birthday **to** *you*!
*I***Kresmesi** *e***myoli** / *e***mnandi**!	Happy Christmas!
Nyak' *om***tsha** *o***mnandi**! (*o***zele** ng*ama***thamsanqa**!)	Happy New Year! (**filled** with **good luck**)
*N***dlela** *n***tle**!	Have a **good trip**!
Ube / **Nibe** ne**mini** *e***mnandi**!	Have a **nice day**!
Ube / **Nibe** ne*m***pela-veki** *e***mnandi**!	Have a **nice weekend**!
Ube / **Nibe** ne**holide** emnandi!	Have a **nice holiday**!
Njalo naku*we*!	And the same to *you*! (lit. **and** it is like that to *you*)

*An expression of praise for a person or persons who have completed a task efficiently and quickly.

Cultural background

There are several idiomatic ways of saying **thank you** in Xhosa which you may come across.

Nangamso or the full saying *Ungadinwa nangomso* (lit. 'you should not be tired (to do the same) tomorrow') was coined by one of the greatest Xhosa teachers, scholars and writers of our time **A.C. Jordan** whose novel, *Ingqumbo Yeminyanya – The Wrath of the Ancestors*, is considered one of the finest in Xhosa.

Maz' enethole (lit. a female animal and its young, usually cow and calf) is another, the explanation being as follows: As a mother always does things for her young, especially when still suckling, the recipient of a kind gesture feels the kindness that has been bestowed is equivalent only to that which a mother usually bestows on her young.

Ukwanda kwaliwa ngumthakathi (lit. Increase (of prosperity) is opposed by the witch) i.e. there is only one 'person' (the witch) who rejects the kindness, help, etc., shown by one person to another which has led to an increase in happiness and prosperity of the person on whom this kindness has been bestowed.

Ndibamba ngazibini / ngazo zombini (lit. I hold with two / both hands) is usually said when one person receives something concrete from another.

How it works

1 Verb stems beginning with a vowel

You will have observed that most verb stems in Xhosa begin with a consonant. There are, however, a number of verb stems that begin with vowels.

> -**amkela** (welcome)
>   Ni- + **amkelek**ile!   > N**amkelek**ile!   (ni- > n-)
> -**azi** (know)
>   Ndiyavuya uku*ku* + **azi**   > Ndiyavuya uku*kw***azi** (-*ku*- > -*kw*-)
> -**enza** (do, make)
>   U + **enza** ntoni?   > W**enza** ntoni?   (u- > w-)

A verb beginning with a vowel influences a preceding vowel in one of two ways, yet another example of a **sound change** occurring.

2 Verb stems with a latent 'i-'

There are also a few very frequently used **one-syllable verbs** in Xhosa containing a so-called latent **i-**. This latent **i-** influences a preceding 'a'which changes to 'e':

-(i)va (hear, feel)	Ndiya + (i)va	> Ndiyeva	I **hear**, **understand**
	Nda + (i)va	> Ndeva	I **heard**
-(i)za (come)	Ndiya + (i)za	> Ndiyeza	I am **coming**
	Nda + (i)za	> Ndeza	I **came**
-(i)ma (stand, stop)	Ndiya + (i)ma	> Ndiyema	I am **stopping**
	Nda + (i)ma	> Ndema	I **stopped**
-(i)mba (dig)	Ndiya + (i)mba	> Ndiyemba	I am **digging**
	Nda + (i)mba	> Ndemba	I **dug**

Note: When using vowel and one-syllable verbs to give instructions, prefix ' *y- / yi-*' respectively:

*Y*enza ikofu, nceda!	**Make** coffee, please!
*Yi*z' apha	**Come** here!
*Yi*ma!	**Stop!**
*Yi*mba!	**Dig!**
*Y*omba!	**Dig!** (often used in spoken Xhosa)
*Yi*tsho uphinde!	You can **say** that **again!**

3 Tenses denoting past actions and events

The main ways of describing **past actions** and **events** are:

- The **recent** past tense
- The **remote** past tense
- The **continuous** *recent* past tense (see **Unit 12.2**)
- The **continuous** *remote* past tense (see **Unit 12.3**).

The recent past tense

Like the present tense, the **recent past** tense has two forms which correspond to the long and short form of the present tense (cf. **Unit 2.2**).

The **long form** is characterised by suffixing '*-ile*' to the verb when no other word follows, while the **short form** is characterised by suffixing *-e* when another word follows the verb:

Ugqib*ile*?	*Have* you **finish**ed?
Ugqib*e* nini?	When *did* you **finish**?
Abafundi ba**phum***ile*.	The students *have* **left**.
Ba**phum***e* ngokukhawuleza.	They **left** in a hurry.

Note: The following frequently used verbs do not follow this rule. They have **only one written form** with **tone** and **length distinguishing between long and short forms**:

-lib**ala** (forget)	> -lib**ele**	Ndilib**ele** kwakhona.
		I have **forgotten** again.
-l**ala** (sleep)	> -l**ele**	Ul**ele** kakuhle?
		Did you **sleep** well?
-fum**ana** (get, find)	> -fum**ene**	Ufum**ene** incwadi?
		Did you **get** the letter / book?
-dib**ana** (meet)	> -dib**ene**	Udib**ene** nini n**o**Thandi?
		When did you meet
		(with) Thandi?
-ph**atha** (bring)	> -ph**ethe**	Uy*i*ph**ethe** imali?
		Did you **bring** the money?

Remember there are a number of expressions incorporating '-*ile*' (cf. **Unit 5**). These expressions often referring to one's **physical state**, are **present tense in meaning**, even though they have a **past tense form** and are referred to as **stative verbs** in Xhosa grammar books:

S**ithabhathek***ile*.	We *are* **impressed**.
Ndonwabi*le*.	I *am* **happy**.

To form the **negative** of the **recent past tense** (and **stative** verbs) prefix the **negative SC** and suffix '-*anga*':

Abafundi *aba***phum**anga.	The students **have** *not* gone out.
	(**recent past**)
*Andi***phil**anga.	I am *not* **well**. (**stative**)

→ See **Unit 12.2** for the **past tense** of **stative** verbs.

The remote past

This tense is characterised by the long '-**a**' of the subject concord (cf. **Unit 3.4**) and is used extensively in the telling of **folktales**.

→ See **Unit 16**.

ndi-	> **nda**zalwa ngo-1950	si-	> **sa**zalwa ngo-1950 nathi
u-	> **wa**zalwa nini?	ni-	> **na**zalwa nini?
u-	> **wa**zalwa ngo-l955	ba-	> **ba**zalwa ngo-1955 nabo

The subject concords for Classes 3–15 are as follows:

u-	> **wa**-
i-	> **ya**-
li-	> **la**-
a-	> **a**-
si-	> **sa**-
zi-	> **za**-
i-	> **ya**-
zi-	> **za**-
lu-	> **lwa**-
ba-	> **ba**-
ku-	> **kwa**-

To form the **negative** of the **remote past tense** use either the '-*anga*' form of the recent past (e.g. *andi***hamb***anga*) or the auxiliary verb -**zange** (e.g. (andi)**zange** ndihambe.) lit. I **never** went.

4 Kha- = '(would you) please'

Khawulind**e** umzuzwana.   Would you **please** wait a moment.
Khanilind**e** umzuzwana.   Would you (pl.) **please** wait a moment.

Kha-+ u- > **kha**wu-.

→ cf. **Unit 4.5** verb form ending in '-**e**'.

☑ *How to apply it*

1 Say sorry when

(a) you think you may have hurt someone by accident.
(b) you have to interrupt someone.
(c) you are late.
(d) you forgot something.
(e) you've kept someone waiting.
(f) you don't speak Xhosa well.

2 Match verb and noun to give the appropriate instruction

Use: (a) iifestile, (b) i-oyile namanzi, (c) ipetroli, (d) itanki and (e) amavili.

1　Galela
2　Sula
3　Mpompa
4　Khangela
5　Zalisa

3 Give instructions and responses

(a)　Come here.　　　　　OK, I'm coming.
(b)　Stop!　　　　　　　OK, I'm stopping.
(c)　Make the tea now.　　OK, I'll make it now.

4 Complete the dialogue between a petrol attendant and a customer

Umthengisi-petroli	Molo nkosikazi. Ndingakunceda?
Umqhubi	_____
Umthengisi-petroli	Ufuna eyiphi ipetroli? Uthatha u-95 okanye u-97?
Umqhubi	_____
Umthengisi-petroli	Ndiyizalise *qhu* itanki?
Umqhubi	Hayi, _____
Umthengisi-petroli	Kulungile. Ungandipha izitshixo (keys)?
Umqhubi	_____
Umthengisi-petroli	Enkosi. Ndingakhangela i-oyile?
Umqhubi	Hayi, _____
Umthengisi-petroli	Kulungile. Umoya ungakanani?
Umqhubi	_____
Umthengisi-petroli	Amavili ngaphambili ahlile kakhulu. Ndiwampompe ngo-210. Ndisule neefestile?
Umqhubi	Ewe. _____
Umthengisi-petroli	Hayi, amanzi alungile. Ndigqibile nkosikazi.
Umqhubi	_____
Umthengisi-petroli	Enkosi. Hamba kakuhle.

5 Complete the dialogue

Xoliswa and Val meet again. Complete their chat by filling in the missing subject concords:

UVal   Ndiyakhumbula, uthe uvela eCacadu. (a) __zalelwa khona?

UXoliswa   Hayi, (b) ___zalelwa kuKomani, kodwa abazali bam (c) __fudukela eCacadu ndisemncinci. (d) __khulela khona.

UVal   Oo, ndiyabona.

UXoliswa   Wena (e) __zalelwa eKapa?

UVal   Ewe, (f) ___zalelwa eFish Hoek, kodwa (g) ___hlala eminye iminyaka eGoli. (h) __tshatile, Xoliswa?

UXoliswa   Ewe, (i) __sebenza erestyu, mna nomyeni wam. (j) __tshatile wena?

UVal   Hayi, andisatshatanga. Sahlukene.

UXoliswa   Torho! Unabantwana?

UVal   Ewe, (k) __neentombi ezimbini. Wena (l) __ nabantwana?

UXoliswa   Ewe, (m)___nabantwana abathathu, oonyana ababini nentombi. Intombi (n) __sencinci.

UVal   (o)__funeka   ndihambe   ngoku.   (p)___leyithi. (q)____mnandi ukuthetha nawe. Hamba kakuhle, wethu.

UXoliswa   Sobonana.

-fudukela	move to
torho!	shame!
ndisemncinci	while I was <u>still</u> young
andisatshatanga	I am <u>no longer</u> married
sahlukene	we are divorced (lit. we are separated from each other)

6 Wish someone

(a) A nice weekend in Grahamstown.

(b) A good holiday.

(c) Good luck (success) at work.

(d) Good luck for exams.

(e) Happy Christmas and a happy New Year.

(f) Listen to the songs on tape. Can you guess the special occasions on which they are sung?

Min' Emnandi Kuwe   **Thina Sobabini Sovumelana**

Min' emnandi kuwe,   ⌐   Mna nawe,

Min' emnandi kuwe,   Thina sobabini sovumelana
Min' emnandi kuwe, Thandi,   Sovumelana nawe
Min' emnandi kuwe.   Sovumelana

                                      -vumelana = be in harmony

7 Match the English sentence with the correct Xhosa sentence

(a) Please sit down (lit. perch) and make yourself comfortable.
(b) Please repeat, I'm listening (lit. hearing).
(c) Please come in and sit down.
(d) Please talk, I'm listening.
(e) Please help me here.
(f) Please advise (me).
(g) Please check oil and the battery.
(h) Please give me your phone number.
(i) Please wait a few minutes.
(j) Please give me your address.

1   Khawulinde nje imizuzu embalwa.
2   Khawundinike idilesi yakho.
3   Khawuphinde ndive.
4   Khawundinike inombolo yefowuni yakho.
5   Khawukhangele i-oyile nebhetri.
6   Khawuthethe ndive.
7   Khawungene uhlale phantsi.
8   Khawundincede apha.
9   Khawundicebise.
10 Khawuchophe apha ukhululeke.

8 The poet Soya Mama

How would you translate 'igama' in the context in which it is found in the notes of the poet Soya Mama whose poem *Imbalela* appears in Unit 6?

USoya Mama u*li*bone ilanga kwilali yaseNew Brighton eBhayi ngomhla we-11 kweyeNkanga ngonyaka we-1919. Uqale ukuy*i*bonakalisa imibongo kwamanye amaphepha-ndaba. Emva koko wapapasha ingqokelela yemibongo phantsi kwegama elithi *AmaQunube*.

ilali (< Afrikaans 'laager')	settlement	imibongo	poems
-bonakalisa	make appear	ingqokelela	collection
-papasha	publish	amaphepha-ndaba	newspapers
		amaqunube (ama-)	berries

8 | UThandi emsebenzini – 'Ndingugqirha Thamsanqa'
Thandi at work – 'I am Dr Thamsanqa'

In this Unit you will learn how to:

■ comfort / reassure by telling someone not to worry
■ ask what is wrong with someone
■ say what is wrong with you
■ ask someone's age
■ characterise pain

Incoko

A mother brings her small child who complains of a headache to the hospital.

UThandi	Molo Nkosikazi. Molo mntwan 'am. Khaningene. Ndingugqirha Thamsanqa. Hlalani phantsi. Nasi isitulo. Ngubani igama lakho, Nkosikazi?
UMama	NdinguNonceba Majola.
UThandi	Wena, mntwan'am, ngubani igama lakho?
Umntwana	NguLindiwe.
UThandi	Hayi, sukulila mntwan'am. Ungazikhathazi! Andizi kukwenzakalisa! Nanku unopopi. Ufuna ukumphatha? Heke, Nkosikazi, ndixelele, nize kusibona ngantoni apha esibhedlele?
UMama	Hayi, yile ntwazana, gqirha.
UThandi	Itheni?
UMama	Iphethwe yintloko, gqirha. Enye into iyakhohlela. Ikhohlela kakhulu.
UThandi	Mingaphi iminyaka yakhe?
UMama	Mihlanu, gqirha.
UThandi	Uliphethe ikhadi le**Ndlela eya eMpilweni**?
UMama	Ewe, nali.

UThandi	Kulungile. Heke, sana lwam, ndibonise, intloko ibuhlungu phi kanye? Ungandikhombisa na apho ibuhlungu khona intloko?
ULindiwe	Ibuhlungu apha, gqirha.
UThandi	Ubuhlungu umqala?
ULindiwe	Hayi.
UThandi	Zibuhlungu iindlebe?
ULindiwe	Ewe.
UThandi	Uvuza ezindlebeni umntwana wakho, Nkosikazi?
UMama	Ewe, gqirha.
UThandi	Uqale nini ukugula umntwana wakho, Nkosikazi?
UMama	Lusuku lwesithathu olu.
UThandi	Ndixelele, ukhe wamnika into yokudambisa iintlungu?
UMama	Ewe, ndimnike iiPanado kodwa azincedi *tu*.
UThandi	Wakhe wenzakala entloko ngaphambili, umntwana lo?
UMama	Hayi, gqirha.
UThandi	Wakhe wagula kakhulu ngaphambili?
UMama	Hayi, gqirha.
UThandi	Ingaba unazo ezinye iingxaki, lo mntwana?
UMama	Ewe gqirha, akakucacelanga ukutya.
UThandi	Kulungile, Nkosikazi. Ngoku, ndifuna ukumxilonga. Khawumkhulule umlalise apha ebhedini.

Isigama

isitulo	chair	mihlanu	they are five
sukulila	don't cry	uliphethe	did you bring it
ungazikhathazi	don't worry	ikhadi	card
andizi kukwenzakalisa	I won't hurt *you*	**Indlela eya eMpilweni Road to Health**	
unopopi	doll	(u)sana Iwam	my baby
-phatha	hold	-buhlungu	sore, painful
nize	you have come	-khombisa	point
kusibona	to see us	apho … khona	where
ngantoni?	about what?	umqala	throat
yile ntwazana	it is this little one	-vuza	discharge
itheni?	what is it?	iindlebe	ears
-phethwe yintloko	have a headache	-qala	begin
-khohlela	cough	ukhe	did you ever
mingaphi iminyaka	how old is she?	wamnika	give *her*
yakhe	(lit. they are how many her years?)	-dambisa	alleviate

iintlungu	pain	wakhe wagula?	was she ever ill?
azincedi *tu*!	they didn't help	ezinye iingxaki	other problems
	at all!	-cacela ukutya	have interest in food
wakhe wenzakala	did she ever hurt	akakucacelanga	she has no appetite
entloko?	(her) head?	-xilonga	examine
ngaphambili	before	-khulula	undress
lo	this	-lalisa	let someone lie down

? *How to ...*

Reassure someone

Musa uku*zi*khathaza, (andizi ku*kw*enzakalisa).
Suku*zi*khathaza, (andizi ku*kw*enzakalisa).
Unga*zi*khathazi, (andizi ku*kw*enzakalisa).

Ask what's wrong with someone

Unantoni na?
Uphethwe *y*intoni?
Ugula *y*intoni?
Ukhala ngantoni ke?

Say what is wrong with you

Ndiyakhohlela.
Andi*ku*cacel*anga uku*tya.
Ndiya**bhitya** (I'm **getting thin**).

Wonke *um*zimba wam ubuhlungu		My whole **body** is sore.
Ndine*n*tloko.	(lit. I have a **head**) i.e.	I have a **head**ache.
Ndine*n*tamo.	(lit. I have a **neck**) i.e.	I have a sore **neck**.
Ndine*n*dlebe.	(lit. I have an **ear**) i.e.	I have a sore **ear**.
Ndino*m*qala.	(lit. I have a **throat**) i.e.	I have a sore **throat**.
Ndino*m*qolo.	(lit. I have a **spine**) i.e.	I have a sore **back**.
Ndine*l*iso.	(lit. I have an **eye**) i.e.	I have a sore **eye**.
Ndina*mehlo*.	(lit. I have **eyes**) i.e.	I have sore **eyes**.
Ndine*z*inyo.	(lit. I have a **tooth**) i.e.	I have **tooth**ache.
Ndine*s*isu.	(lit. I have a **stomach**) i.e.	I have a sore **stomach**.

Ndine*si*fuba.	(lit. I have a **chest**) i.e.	I have **chest** pain.
Ndine*n*galo.	(lit. I have an **arm**) i.e.	I have a sore **arm**.
Ndinegxalaba.	(lit. I have a **shoulder**) i.e.	I have a sore **shoulder**.
Ndino*m*nwe.	(lit. I have a **finger**) i.e.	I have a sore **finger**.
Ndine*s*andla.	(lit. I have a **hand**) i.e.	I have a sore **hand**.
Ndino*m*lenze.	(lit. I have a **leg**) i.e.	I have a sore **leg**.
Ndino*n*yawo.	(lit. I have a **foot**) i.e.	I have a sore **foot**.
Ndino*z*wane.	(lit. I have a **toe**) i.e.	I have a sore **toe**.
Ndine*n*gqiniba.	(lit. I have an **elbow**) i.e.	I have a sore **elbow**.

Some idiomatic expressions incorporating parts of the body

Une*si***bindi**	He/she is **brave**	(lit. to be with a **liver**)
Une*n***tliziyo**	He/she is **kind**	(lit. to be with a **heart**)
Uno**lwimi**	He/she is a **gossiper**	(lit. to be with a **tongue**)
Une**sandla**	He/she is **skilful**	(lit. to be with a **hand**)
Uno**mlomo**	He/she is a **big talker**	(lit. to be with a **mouth**)
Une*m*i**nwe** *emi***de**	He/she is a **thief**	(lit. to be with long **fingers**)
Uno**mqolo**	He/she is **reliable**	(lit. to be with a **spine**)
Ndi**ph**e*ni* **iindlebe**	Listen carefully	(lit. give *me* your **ears**)
Ndi*cela iz*andla	I need help	(lit. I ask for **hands**)
*Is*andla si**hlamba** esi*nye*	help each other	(lit. one **hand** washes the other)

Ask how old someone is

Une*mi*nyaka *emi*ngaphi (*ubu*dala = **age**)?
*Mi*ngaphi *imi*nyaka yakho?
Wazalwa **nini**?

Characterise pain

Kuyatshisa.	It is **burning**.
Kuya**luma**.	It is **colicky**. (lit. it **bites**)
Kuyaqaqamba.	It is **throbbing**.
Kuyahlaba.	It is **stabbing**.

Song

THULA THUL' THULA BHABHA
HUSH HUSH HUSH BABY
(originally a Zulu song)

Thula thu' thula bhabha,	Hush, hush, hush baby,
thula sana,	Hush baby,
Thul' umam' uzobuya	Hush mother will come back
ekuseni,	in the morning,
Thula thu' thula bhabha,	Hush, hush, hush,
thula sana,	Hush baby,
Uzodlul' entaben'	She will cross the mountain
emathafeni,	and hills,
Kukhw'inkanyezi ekhokhel'	There is a star that leads
ubaba	the father
Emkhanyisela indlel' eziy' ekhaya.	Lighting his path coming home.
Sobe sikhona xa bonke	It will be there when they all
betshoyo,	say so,
Bethi buyela ubuyel'	Saying return, return,
uzekhaya.	and come home.
Thula, thu', thula bhabha	Be quiet, be quiet, be quiet, baby
Ungakhali, thula sana,	Don't cry, be quiet, baby,
Thula, thu' thula, thul' mntwana.	Be quiet, be quiet, be quiet, child
Thula bhabha, thula sana.	Be quiet baby, be quiet baby.

▣ How it works

1 Descriptives used as predicates

Relatives

The most commonly used relative stems are those conveying ideas of taste, degrees of warmth, heaviness, etc., and include the colours (cf. **Unit 6.2**):

Some opposites

easy	**-lula**	difficult	**-nzima**
light	**-lula**	heavy	**-nzima**
expensive	**-dulu**	cheap	**-tshiphu**
bitter	**-krakra**	sweet	**-mnandi**

| blunt/rounded | -ngqukuva | pointed | -tsolo |
| wide | -banzi | narrow | -mxinwa |

Miscellaneous

better	-bhetele / -ngcono	dark	-mdaka
deep	-nzulu	hot	-shushu
innocent	-msulwa	lukewarm	-dikidiki
nice	-mnandi	painful	-buhlungu
sad	-lusizi	sharp	-bukhali

It is very easy to use relatives as predicates. Simply prefix the relevant subject concord to the relative stem:

Ndi**lusizi**.	I am **sorry**. (lit. I **sorry**)
U**lusizi**?	Are you **sad**?
I**buhlungu** intloko?	Is (your) head **sore**?

Adjectives

When adjectives are used as **predicates**, the adjectival concord **minus its initial vowel** is prefixed to the adjectival stem except in Class 9 nouns where the adjectival concord '*en-*' > '*in-*':

AC	AC minus initial vowel	
om-	*M*hle *um*ntwana.	The child *is* **beautiful**.
aba-	*Ba*hle *aba*ntwana.	The children *are* **beautiful**.
om-	*M*khulu *um*sebenzi.	The task *is* **huge**.
emi-	*Mi*khulu *imi*sebenzi.	The tasks *are* **huge**.
eli-	*Li*hle *izulu*.	The weather *is* **beautiful**.
ama-	*Ma*hle *ama*zinyo.	The teeth *are* **beautiful**.
esi-	*Si*ncinci *isa*ndla.	The hand *is* **small**.
ezi-	*Zi*ncinci *iza*ndla.	The hands *are* **small**.
en-	*In*kulu *i*pilisi.	The pill *is* **big**.
ezin-	*Zi*nkulu *ii*pilisi.	The pills *are* **big**.
olu-	*Lu*khulu *u*sana.	The baby *is* **big**.
obu-	*Bu*de *ubu*sika.	The winter *is* **long**.
oku-	*Ku*tsha *uku*tya.	The food *is* **fresh**.

Note: When adjectives are used predicatively the preferred word order seems to be adjective followed by noun.

With the **1st** and **2nd persons** singular and plural (I, we, you), the adjectival concords '-*m*-'and '-*ba*-' are placed between the subject concord and the adjectival stem:

| Ndi*m*dala. | I am **old**. | U*m*tsha | You are **young**. |
| Si*ba*dala. | We are **old**. | Ni*ba*tsha. | You are **young**. |

→ See **Unit 15.5** for **negative** of adjectives and relatives.

In order to express 'still' with descriptives such as relatives and adjectives, '-<u>se</u>-' as opposed to '-sa-' (which is used with verbs) is placed between the subject and adjectival concords:

U<u>se</u>*m*tsha.	You are <u>still</u> **young**.
Lu<u>se</u>*lu*ncinci usana.	The baby is <u>still</u> **small**.
Ba<u>se</u>*ba*hle abafazi.	The women are <u>still</u> **beautiful**.
Ubisi lu<u>se</u>*lu*tsha.	The milk is <u>still</u> **fresh**.

'-<u>Se</u>-' can also be used with other non-verbs:

| U<u>se</u>*sesi*bhedlele umntwana. | The child is <u>still</u> in hospital. |
| U<u>se</u>khona ugqirha. | The doctor is <u>still</u> here. |

In the **negative** '-<u>se</u>-' means '**no longer**':

| Hayi, ugqirha aka<u>se</u>kho. | No, the doctor is <u>no longer</u> there. |

2 Equivalent of 'and' between verbs

In **Unit 2.9**, you learnt that **nouns** are connected by '**na-**':

*aba*zali **na***ba*ntwana: parents **and** children

However, when **two verbal forms** follow one another, the second verb ends in '-<u>e</u>' to indicate consequential action (sequential):

| *M*khulul<u>e</u> u*m*lalis<u>e</u> *e*bhed*ini*. | Undress her **and** lie her down *on* the **bed**. |
| *I*in tlungu zifika zimk<u>e</u>? | Does the **pain** come **and** go? |

Note*: iin*tlungu = physical pain(s) always in the plural form.

3 Equivalent of the English adverbs 'already', 'always', 'ever', 'never', 'nearly', 'usually'

These English adverbs are expressed in Xhosa by so-called **auxiliary** (helping) **verbs**:

'-khe' = 'ever'

Wa**khe** we**nzakala** intloko ngaphambili?	Did she **ever** hurt her head before?
Wa**khe** wa**gula** kakhulu ngaphambili?	Was she **ever** very sick before?
Wa**khe** wa**mbona** ngaphambili?	Have you **ever** seen *him* before?

'-sele(-)', *often shortened to* '-sel / se-'= 'already'

Sekwanele!	It's all over! (lit. It's **already enough**)

'-soloko' = 'always'

Intloko i**soloko** ibuhlungu?	Is your head **always** sore?

'-zange' / '-khange' = 'never'

*Aka***zange** wagula.	She has **never** been sick. (cf. **Unit 7.4**)
*Andi***zange** ndatsho.	I **never** said so.
Zange sabonana.	We've **never** met.
Khange atsho.	He **never** said so.
Khange ndi*ku***bon***e* ixesha elide.	I haven't seen *you* for a long time.

'-soze'= 'shall' / 'will never'

Uxolo, andi**soze** ndi**phinde**.	Sorry, I'**ll never** do it again.
Soze ndisele kwakhona.	I'**ll never** drink (alcohol) again.

'-phantse' = 'nearly'

Yhu, ndi**phantse** ndawa!	Oops, I **nearly** fell!

'-dla ngoku-' = 'usually', 'frequently'

U**dla ngoku**gula ebusika.	He/she is **frequently** ill in winter.

4 Different ways of saying 'why?'

When Thandi asked Mrs Majola **why** she had come to hospital she said:
Nize kusibona **ngantoni** apha esibhedlele? (lit. You have come to see us
for what here at the hospital?). Here are three of the several other ways
of expressing '**why**?' in Xhosa:

'Kutheni'

Unlike other interrogatives **'kutheni'** *introduces* a question:

Kutheni unga*ndi*xelel*anga*?	**Why** did*n't* you **tell** *me*?
Kutheni ufunda isiXhosa?	**Why** are you **learning** Xhosa?

'-elani' / '-eleni' (*lit. 'what for?'*)

U*si***fundelani** isiXhosa?	**Why** <u>do</u> you learn Xhosa?
U*si***fundeleni** isiXhosa?	**Why** <u>did</u> you learn Xhosa?

'ngo(ku)ba'

Ufunda isiXhosa **ngoba**?	**Why** are you learning Xhosa?

5 Another interrogative: '-phi?' = 'which?'

You are already familiar with '**-phi**?' = '**where**?'which is prefixed by the subject concord:

U**phi** *um*ntwana?	**Where** (is) the **child**?
Ba**phi** *aba*ntwana?	**Where** (are) the **children**?

However, '**-phi**?' can also mean '**which**?':

*Wu***phi** *um*ntwana?	*Which* **child**?
*Ba***phi** *aba*ntwana?	*Which* **children**?

In the so-called '**strong**' classes, i.e. where the subject concord consists of a consonant and a vowel (ba-, li-, si-, zi-, lu-, bu-, ku-) **only tone distinguishes the two interrogatives**:

'**where**?' = **high** tone	'**which**?' = **low** tone

Where the subject concord consists of a vowel only (in the so-called '**weak**' classes), '**w-**' or '**-y-**' is prefixed to the subject concord:

U**phi** *um*andlalo?	**Where** is the **bed**?
<u>*Wu*</u>**phi** *um*andlalo?	*Which* **bed**?
I**phi** *im*andlalo?	**Where** are the **beds**?
<u>*Yi*</u>**phi** *im*andlalo?	*Which* **beds**?
A**phi** *ama*yeza?	**Where** are the **medicines**?
<u>*Wa*</u>**phi** *ama*yeza?	*Which* **medicines**?
I**phi** *in*cwadi?	**Where** is the **book**?
<u>*Yi*</u>**phi** *in*cwadi?	*Which* **book**?

Besides this **basic form** there is also a longer, more specific form (prefixing o- / a- / e-), with the meaning '**which** *particular*'. It seems to be preferred in everyday speech, possibly to distinguish between the meaning 'where?' and 'which?':

*Wu*phi *um*ntwana?	*Which* **child**?
*Qwu*phi *um*ntwana?	*Which* ***particular* child**?
*Ba*phi *aba*ntwana?	*Which* **children**?
*Aba*phi *aba*ntwana?	*Which* **children**?
*Wu*phi *um*andlalo?	*Which* **bed**?
*Qwu*phi *um*andlalo?	*Which* **bed**?
*Yi*phi *im*andlalo?	*Which* **beds**?
*Eyi*phi *im*andlalo?	Which **beds**?
*Li*phi *i*khadi?	*Which* **card**?
*Eli*phi *i*khadi?	*Which* **card**?
*Wa*phi *ama*yeza?	*Which* **medicines**?
*Awa*phi *ama*yeza?	*Which* **medicines**?
*Si*phi *isi*bhedlele?	*Which* **hospital**?
*Esi*phi *isi*bhedlele?	*Which* **hospital**?
*Zi*phi *izi*kolo?	*Which* **schools**?
*Ezi*phi *izi*kolo?	*Which* **schools**?
*Yi*phi *i*pilisi?	*Which* **pill**?
*Eyi*phi *i*pilisi?	*Which* **pill**?
*Zi*phi *iin*cwadi?	*Which* **books**?
*Ezi*phi *iin*cwadi?	*Which* **books**?
*Lu*phi *u*siba?	*Which* **pen**?
*Qlu*phi *u*siba?	*Which* **pen**?
*Ku*phi *uku*tya?	*Which* **food**?
*Qku*phi *uku*tya?	*Which* **food**?

When **nga-** / **ku-** / **na-** are prefixed to this form it makes the 'string' even longer.

Wazalwa **ng***owu***phi** *u*nyaka?
Uya **k***we**si***phi** *isi*bhedlele?
Ufuna ukuthetha **n***owu***phi** *u*gqirha?

How to apply it

1   Give the plurals

iliso	umlenze
indlebe	unyawo
ingalo	uzwane
isandla	izinyo
umnwe	idolo (knee)

2   Questions and responses

You meet a friend whose child has been ill. In order to complete the conversation, translate your questions and responses into Xhosa:

(a) *How is your child? Is she still in hospital?*
Hayi, ubhetele kancinci, akasekho sibhedlele.

(b) *I am sorry that she is only a little better, but I am glad that she is at home again.*
Ndikhathazeka kakhulu kuba akakucacelanga ukutya. Ubhityile.

(c) *What did the doctor say?*
Undinike iyeza, kodwa ngelishwa alisebenzi.

(d) *Let's hope she will soon be well again.*
Hayi, sithemba njalo.

3   Read the dialogue and answer the questions

UZodwa	Molo, Nomsa.
UNomsa	Molo sisi. Uphila njani?
UZodwa	Hayi, akukho nto. Wena?
UNomsa	Awu, mna, andiphilanga.
UZodwa	Awu, ukhangeleka ugula ngenene. Ugula yintoni?
UNomsa	Ndineflu. Intloko ibuhlungu. Ndinefiva.
UZodwa	Kufuneka ugoduke uphumle ebhedini. Ubuyile kugqirha?
UNomsa	Ewe, undiphe amayeza. Ndiyathemba ukuba aza kusebenza ngokukhawuleza.
UZodwa	Nam, ndithemba njalo. Ngubani oza kukugcina ekhaya?
UNomsa	Usisi uza kundigcina.
UZodwa	Kulungile. Ndiyathemba ukuba uza kuphila kamsinyane kwakhona. Hamba kakuhle.
UNomsa	Enkosi. Kamnandi.

-buya	return	-gcina	look after

Which of the following Xhosa words can replace the 'xhosalised' English words:

(a) umkhuhlane   can replace   _____
(b) ubushushu   can replace   _____
(c) umandlalo (lit. mat)   can replace   _____
(d) udadewethu   can replace   _____

4 Read the dialogue

UNokhaya	Hi Xoliswa.
UXoliswa	Molo wethu. Ndiyakubona uphilile, Nokhaya. Banjani ekhaya?
UNokhaya	Oo, umama yena akaphilanga *tu*.
UXoliswa	Kwenzekeni?
UNokhaya	Uwile ebesihla iziteps. Ugqirha umthumele esibhedlele kwangoko.
UXoliswa	Oo, nkosi yam! Ndilusizi kakhulu.
UNokhaya	Ewe, waphuka umlenze, usesibhedlele ndithetha nje (as I speak).
UXoliswa	Ndiyathemba ukuba uza kuchacha ngokukhawuleza. Khawundibulisele kumama wakho.
UXoliswa	Enkosi. Hamba kakuhle.

-wa	fall	-aphuka	break
ebesihla	going down	-chacha	recover
iziteps	steps	-khawundibulisele	please greet from me
-thumela	send to		

Imagine you are visiting Nokhaya's mother in hospital. How would you:

(a) greet her (you are younger)?
(b) ask her how she is today?
(c) say you are sorry that she is in hospital and ill?
(d) ask whether you can help her with something?
(e) ask whether she is in pain?
(f) wish her a speedy recovery?
(g) say goodbye?

5   Match the following appropriately

Use these phrases: (a) isifuba sibuhlungu phi kanye?, (b) kuba utya kancinci gqitha, (c) ulale apha ebhedini, (d) xa ukhohlela?, (e) andazi kukwenzakalisa and (f) nasi isitulo.

1	Hlala phantsi	4	Khawukhulule
2	Isifuba sibuhlungu kakhulu	5	Ndicela undibonise
3	Wena uyabhitya	6	Ungazikhathazi

6   Put the sentences in the right sequence

(a) Lifuna ukubona ugqirha kuba linesisu.

(b) Emva koko uthi: Nanzi iipilisi. Zitye kathathu ngemimi emva kokutya.

(c) Ixhegokazi elithile liya ekliniki.

(d) Isisu sibuhlungu kakhulu.

(e) Heke gqirha, Ndiza kuzitya iipilisi, kodwa ngubani oza kundinika ukutya?

(f) Ugqirha uyalixilonga.

kathathu	three times	-thile	certain
emva kokutya	after meals (lit. after eating / food)	ukutya iipilisi	take pills
ixhegokazi	old woman		

7   Say

(a) He is brave.

(b) She is very kind.

(c) They are very reliable.

(d) He is a big talker.

(e) She is very skilful.

8   Give the literal meaning for the idiomatic expressions

(a) Unesandla esibandayo
    (He/she is stingy.)   _____

(b) Unesandla esishushu
    (He/she is generous.)   _____

(c) Unika ngentliziyo entle
    (He/she gives gladly.)   _____

(d) Unentliziyo emhlophe
   (He/she has a kind heart.)   _____

(e) Unamadolo anzima?
   (Are you exhausted?)   _____

9 Translate the following

(a) Intliziyo yam ibuhlungu.   _____
(b) Unentliziyo emdaka/emnyama. _____
(c) Unentliziyo emsulwa.   _____

10 Complete the questions

(a) Wena, uthetha ___phi ulwimi ekhaya?
(b) Ufunde ___phi iilwimi esikolweni?
(c) Ufunde n___nye iilwimi eyunivesithi okanye kw___nye ilizwe?
(d) Ukhetha ukuthetha___phi ulwimi?
(e) Ndixelele, wazalwa ng___phi unyaka?
(f) Wazalwa ng___phi inyanga?
(g) Wazalwa ng___phi imini?
(h) Wazalelwa kw___phi ilizwe?
(i) Wazalelwa kw___phi idolophu?
(j) Ufunde kw___phi isikolo?
(k) Waphuma kw___phi ibanga (standard)?
(l) Ufunde kw___phi iyunivesithi?

9 | UPeter emsebenzini eKirstenbosch

Peter at work at Kirstenbosch

In this Unit you will learn how to:

- introduce someone you work with
- point or single out
- say what a place is famous for
- encourage environmentally friendly practices
- request that appropriate etiquette be observed in public places
- say what the best is

Incoko

Peter introduces his colleague Phumla Bongela to a group of school children who will tell them about two vital projects that Kirstenbosch is involved in.

UPeter   Molweni bafundi. Namkelekile e*Kirstenbosch*! Igama lam nguPeter Murray. Lo nguNkosikazi Phumla Bongela, endisebenza naye. Sobabini siziingcaphephe zezityalo apha e*Kirstenbosch*.

UNkosikazi Bongela uza kunixelela ngeegadi ezinolondolozo-manzi ne*Outreach Gardening Project*. Le nkqubo yaqalwa ukuze sincede izikolo ukuseka iigadi ezifanelekileyo.

Kodwa kuqala ndiza kuthi *gqaba-gqaba* nge*Kirstenbosch*. UNkosikazi Bongela uza kunika umfundi ngamnye imaphu yase*Kirstenbosch*. Le gadi idume kulo lonke ihlabathi ngobuhle. Yasekwa ngo-1913. Ithandeka kakhulu ngenxa yenkitha yezityalo zaseMzantsi Afrika.

Jongani nje lo mfanekiso othathwe e*Chelsea Flower Show* yaseLondon apho i*Kirstenbosch* yazuza izidanga ezininzi khona iminyaka ngeminyaka.

Isigama

endisebenza naye	with whom I work	idume kulo lonke	it is famous all
sobabini	both of us	ihlabathi	over the world
iigadi	gardens	ubuhle	beauty
ezinolondolozo-manzi	which save water	yasekwa	it was established
le nkqubo	this project	-thandeka	be popular
yaqalwa	was started	inkitha yezityalo	collection of plants
ukuseka	to establish	jongani nje	just look at
ezifanelekileyo	suitable	lo mfanekiso	this picture
kuqala	firstly	othathwe	which was taken
gqaba-gqaba	a bit about (lit. here and there)	yazuza	it won
		izidanga	medals
umfundi ngamnye	each pupil	iminyaka	year(s) after
imaphu	map	ngeminyaka	year(s)

Flower muti: Traditional healer, Elliott Ndlovu, from the Drakensberg foothills, brought a little magic to London's world-famous Chelsea Flower Show this week. South Africa's Syfrets-Kirstenbosch exhibit depicted a botanical representation of the R6-million conservatory at Kirstenbosch as well as a traditional healer's hut, with Ndlovu in his traditional attire (which impressed the Queen). The stand won a silver gilt medal for its efforts – its 22nd medal in its 22 years at the show.

Iindlela ezintandathu zokulondoloza amanzi

1

Tyala izityalo ezingafuni manzi maninzi

(Plant plants which do not require a lot of water)

2

Wulungise umhlaba ngokufaka isivundiso ukuze ukwazi ukuwagcina amanzi

(Prepare the soil by putting in compost so that it is able to retain water)

3

Wugqume umhlaba phakathi kwezityalo ngezinto ezigcina ukufuma emhlabeni – umzekelo umgquba
(Cover the soil between plants with material that will keep the moisture in the soil – for example, compost)

4

Zahlule izityalo ngokweemfuno zazo zamanzi

(Group plants according to their watering needs)

5

Yityale ingca kuphela apho kuyimfuneko khona

(Plant grass only where needed)

6

Nkcenkceshela ngokufanelekileyo kunjalo nje xa kuyimfuneko

(Water appropriately according to need only)

Phumla gives each pupil a map of Kirstenbosch and takes them on the tour of the gardens starting with the waterwise garden. She asks them to read the information boards that explain how to establish an environmentally friendly waterwise garden.

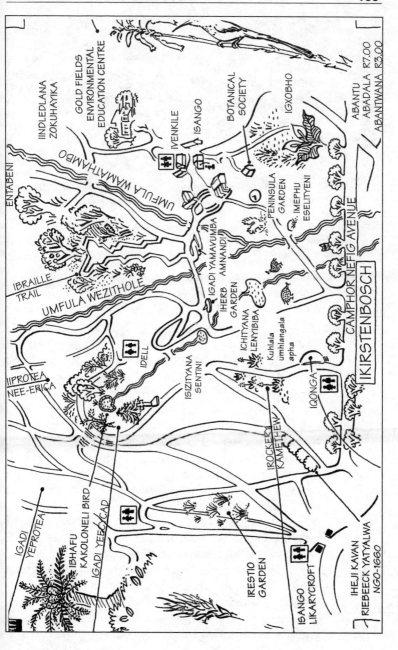

IINDLEDLANA ZOKUHAYIKA

GOLD FIELDS ENVIRONMENTAL EDUCATION CENTRE

IVENKILE

ISANGO

BOTANICAL SOCIETY

IGXOBHO

ABANTU R7.00
ABADALA R3.00
ABANTWANA

ENTABENI

UMFULA WAMATHAMBO

PENINSULA GARDEN

IMEPHU ESELITYENI

IBRAILLE TRAIL

IGADI YAMAVUMBA AMNANDI

IHERB GARDEN

UMFULA WEZITHOLE

ICHITYANA LENYIBIBA

Kuhlala umhlangala apha

CAMPHOR NEFIG AVENUE

IKIRSTENBOSCH

IIPROTEA NEE-ERICA

IDELL

ISIZITYANA SENTINI

IQONGA

IROCKEK KAMETLEW

IGADI YEPROTEA

IBHAFU KAKOLONELI BIRD

IGADI YEE-CYCAD

IRESTIO GARDEN

ISANGO LIKARYCROFT

IHEJI KAVAN RIEBEECK YATYALWA NGO-1660

The Kirstenbosch Outreach Bus sponsored by the Anglo-American and De Beers Chairman's Fund.
(Photographs courtesy National Botanical Gardens, Kirstenbosch)

They go on a tour of the gardens after which Phumla tells the pupils that she will be coming to their school shortly to help them establish their own waterwise garden.

UPhumla	Heke, bafundi, ndiza kunityelela esikolweni ukuze siqale igadi enolondolozo-manzi. Mna, ndiza kuzisa izityalo nezixhobo zegadi, kodwa ndifuna ukuba nina nithabathe inxaxheba kulo msebenzi ngokuzama ukulungisa umhlaba esikolweni.
Abafundi	Siyenza njani, loo nto, Nkosikazi?
UPhumla	Eyona ndlela ilungileyo kukuqala ngokwenza umgquba. Ningaqala ngokuqokelela inkunkuma yekhitshi. Umzekelo, amaxolo emifuno, amaqokobhe amaqanda, amagqabi, amathambo kunye nengca esikiweyo neentyatyambo ezifileyo neentsiba nothuthu lweenkuni. Kodwa ningazifaki iitoti, iplastiki okanye amaphepha.
	Ndiza kutyelela esikolweni senu kwiveki ezayo. Siza kukhetha indawo efanelekileyo senze umgquba kuyo. De kube ngoko, ningafaka yonke into eniyiqokeleleyo kwezi ngxowa.
	Heke, bafundi, ndiyanibulela ngokumamela ngenyameko engaka. Nibe nepikiniki emnandi ke ngoku, kodwa ndicela niyigcine icocekile igadi. Ningalibali ukuchola onke amaphepha phambi kokuba nihambe niwafake emigqomeni yenkunkuma. Hambani kakuhle. Sobonana kwiveki ezayo.

Isigama

-zisa	bring	-faka	put in
izixhobo zegadi	garden implements	iitoti	tins
-thabatha inxaxheba	take part	amaphepha	papers
kulo msebenzi	in this work	kuyo	in it
-lungisa	prepare	de kube ngoko	until then
umhlaba	soil	ezi ngxowa	these bags
eyona ndlela ilungileyo	the best way	eniyiqokeleleyo	which you've collected
umgquba	compost	-mamela	listen
-qokelela	collect	ngenyameko	with such
inkunkuma	waste, garbage	engaka	attention
amaxolo emifuno	vegetable peels	nibe nepikiniki emnandi	have a nice picnic
amaqokobhe amaqanda	egg shells		
amagqabi	leaves	-gcina	keep
amathambo	bones	-cocekile	clean
kunye na-	together with	-chola	pick up
ingca esikiweyo	grass cuttings	phambi kokuba	before
iintyatyambo ezifileyo	dead flowers	nihambe	you leave
iintsiba	feathers	imigqomo	rubbish
uthuthu lweenkuni	ash (of wood)	yenkunkuma	bins

A traditional healer or herbalist – (ixhwele)

Examples of indigenous plants with medicinal properties used in traditional practice

*isi***cakathi**
agapanthus

Used in ante-natal and post-natal medicine

*um***hlaba**
bitter aloe

Used as a laxative but also for arthritis, eczema, conjunctivitis, hypertension and stress

*um***hlonyane**
African wormwood

One of the most widely used traditional medicines in South Africa. Used for treating coughs, colds and influenza, fever, loss of appetite, colic, headache, earache, malaria and intestinal worms

*im***phewula**
pig's ear

Another plant widely used to treat corns, warts, earache and toothache

*in***cwadi**
bushman poison bulb

Used as dressing after circumcision and for treating boils and septic wounds, to treat corns, warts, earache and toothache

*im***pepho**
everlastings

Used for wound dressings, coughs, colds, fever, infections, headache and menstrual pain

*ubu***vuma**
winter cherry

Mainly used for wound healing, abscesses, haemorrhoids and rheumatism

*um***hlabavuthwa**
thornapple

Used prolifically to relieve asthma and reduce pain

◄ *How to* ...

Introduce someone you work with

Lo nguNkosikazi _____ / **Lo** nguMnumzana _____
e**ndisebenza** na*ye*. / **Sisebenza kunye**.

Ndinga*kw*a**zisa** uNkosikazi _____ / Mnumzana _____
e**ndisebenza na***ye*.

Mandi*kw*a**zise** uNkosikazi _____ / Mnumzana _____
e**ndisebenza na***ye*.

Ndi**ngathanda** udi**bane** no_Nkosikazi ____ noMnumzana _____
e**ndisebenza na***bo*.

Point out / single out

Lo nguNkosikazi Bongela.
Le _n_**kqubo** yaqalwa ukuze si**ncede** izi**kolo**.
Le gadi idume kulo lonke *i*hlabathi.
Lo _m_**fanekiso** wa**thathwa** eChelsea Flower Show yaseLondon.

Say what a place is renowned for

Le gadi idume ngo*bu*hle.
Le gadi idume ngenxa yenkitha ye*zi*tyalo ena*zo*.
Le gadi idume nge*mi*boniso ye*zi*tyalo.

Encourage environmentally friendly practices

Tyala izi**tyalo** ezi**ngafuni** _ma_nzi _ma_ninzi.
_Wu_**lungise** _um_**hlaba** ngoku**faka** _isi_**vundiso** ukuze ukw**azi** ukuw*a*g**cina**
_ama_nzi.
_Wu_g**qume** _um_**hlaba** phakathi kwe*zi*tyalo nge*zi***nto** e*zi*g**cina** uku**fuma**
e**mhlabeni**.
Zahlule izi**tyalo** ngoku**funa** kwazo _ama_nzi.
_Yi_**tyale** _in_g**ca** kuphela apho kuy*im*funeko khona.
Nkcenkceshela ngoku**fanelekile***yo* kunjalo nje xa kuy*im*funeko.
Wenze _um_**gquba** ngoku**qokelela** _in_**kunkuma** e**khitsh***ini*.

Say what the best is

_E_**yona** _n_**dlela** i**lungile***yo* ...
_E_**yona** _n_**dawo** i**lungile***yo* ...
_E_**lona xesha** li**lungile***yo* ...

Request that appropriate etiquette is observed in a public place

Ndicela nigcine igadi icocekile.

Ningalibali ukuchola onke amaphepha phambi kokuba nihambe niwafake emigqomeni yenkunkuma.

How it works

1 Possessives of Class 1a

In **Unit 5.2**, you learnt that **possessive relationship** in Xhosa is expressed by means of a **possessive concord** (equivalent to English '*s* or *of*) for Classes 1–15, e.g.:

*um*sebenzi *w*e**ngcaphephe** ye*z*i**tyalo**
(< *um*sebenzi *wa*- + *i*ngcaphephe)

However, with nouns of **Class 1a**, i.e. proper names and kinship terms, relationships, '**ka-**' is used:

*um*sebenzi **ka**Peter　　　　　　　　Peter's job

If you look at the map of Kirstenbosch in this Unit you will find the following examples:

*I*BHAFU **KA**KOLONELI BIRD (Colonel Bird's bath)
*I*HEJI **KA**VAN RIEBEECK (van Riebeeck's hedge)

'*I*bhafu' and '*i*heji' (possessees) are Class 9 nouns. Like nouns of Classes 1, 3, 4 and 6 (*um-*, *imi-*, *ama* -) they are **weak class** nouns.

However, when the noun possessed belongs to a strong class, its subject concord is prefixed to '**ka-**'. You will also see an example of this construction on the map:

*I*SANGO *LI***KA**RYCROFT (Rycroft's entrance/gate)

'*I*sango' is a strong Class 5 noun.

2 The equivalent of English 'each'

This is formed by '**nga-**' + *adjectival concord** + '**-nye**' (one):

*um***fundi nga***m***nye**	**each** student
*um***thi nga***m***nye**	**each** tree
*isi***tyalo nga***si***nye**	**each** plant
*in***tyatyambo nga***n***nye**	**each** flower
*ulu***dwe nga***lu***nye**	**each** list
*ubu***sika nga***bu***nye**	**each** winter

→ *cf. **Unit 8.1**.

3 Emphatic pronouns referring to the 3rd person

You are already familiar with the **emphatic pronouns** referring to the 1st and 2nd persons, i.e., '*m*na,' '*thi*na,' '*we*na,' '*ni*na', (→ **Unit 3.2**).

The pronouns for the **3rd person** (Classes 1-15) usually follow the noun they emphasise:

*u*Peter	*ye*na	**Peter**, as for him
*aba*fundi	*bo*na	the **pupils**, as for them
*um*sebenzi	*wo*na	the **job**, as for it
*imi*sebenzi	*yo*na	the **jobs**, as for them,
*i*gqwetha	*lo*na	the **lawyer**, as for him / her
*ama*gqwetha	*wo*na	the **lawyers**, as for them
*isi*thethi	*so*na	the **speaker**, as for him / her
*izi*thethi	*zo*na	the **speakers**, as for them
*in*tatheli	*yo*na	the **journalist**, as for him / her
*iin*tatheli	*zo*na	the **journalists**, as for them
*u*ndwendwe	*lo*na	the **guest**, as for him / her
*iin*dwendwe	*zo*na	the **guests**, as for them
*ubu*sika	*bo*na	**winter**, as for it,
*uku*tya	*ko*na	the **food**, as for it

When the **emphatic pronoun** is used with '**na-**'= 'have' / 'with', the shortened form (i.e. without '-**na**') is used:

Una*ye* *um*ncedisi?	Do you **have** an **assistant**?
Ewe, ndina*ye*.	Yes, I **have** one.
Hayi, andina*ye*.	No, I don't **have** one.

Una*bo*	*aba*ncedisi?	Ewe, ndina*bo*.	Hayi, andina*bo*.
Una*wo*	*um*hlakulo?	Ewe, ndina*wo*.	Hayi, andina*wo*.
Una*yo*	*imi*hlakulo?	Ewe, ndina*yo*.	Hayi, andina*yo*.
Una*lo*	*i*xesha?	Ewe, ndina*lo*.	Hayi, andina*lo*.
Una*wo*	*ama*nzi?	Ewe, ndina*wo*.	Hayi, andina*wo*.
Una*so*	*isi*tyalo?	Ewe, ndina*so*.	Hayi, andina*so*.
Una*zo*	*izi*tyalo?	Ewe, ndina*zo*.	Hayi, andina*zo*.
Una*yo*	*i*gadi?	Ewe, ndina*yo*.	Hayi, andina*yo*.
Una*zo*	*iin*tyatyambo?	Ewe, ndina*zo*.	Hayi, andina*zo*.
Una*lo*	*ulu*dwe? (list)	Ewe, ndina*lo*.	Hayi, andina*lo*.
Una*ko*	*uku*tya?	Ewe, ndina*ko*.	Hayi, andina*ko*.

The **emphatic pronoun** can also be used with prepositions '**ku-**' / '**nga-**'

Kulungile ku*we*? Ewe, kulungile ku*m*. *Ndi*xelel*e* nga*we*.
Kuku*we*! (It is up **to** *you*!)

4 *Superlative pronouns* + '-lungileyo' = 'the best'

Superlative pronouns are formed by prefixing the relative elements'*o-*',
'*e-*', or '*a-*' (cf. **Unit 6.2**) to the emphatic pronoun:

*o*yena	*m*ntu	*u*lungile*yo*	the **best** person
*a*bona	*ba*ntu	*ba*lungile*yo*	the **best** people
*o*wona	*m*thi	*u*lungile*yo*	the **best** tree
*e*yona	*mi*thi	*i*lungile*yo*	the **best** trees
*e*lona	xesha	*li*lungile*yo*	the **best** time
*a*wona	*ma*nzi	*a*lungile*yo*	the **best** water
*e*sona	*si*tyalo	*si*lungile*yo*	the **best** plant
*e*zona	*zi*tyalo	*zi*lungile*yo*	the **best** plants
*e*yona	*n*to / *n*dawo	*i*lungile*yo*	the **best** thing / place
*e*zona	*n*tyatyambo	*zi*lungile*yo*	the **best** flowers
*o*kona	*ku*tya	*ku*lungile*yo*	the **best** food

Superlative pronouns can be used with any descriptive to form the
equivalent of the **English superlative**:

*e*yona *n*dlela *i*lula	the **easiest** way
*o*wona *m*buzo *u*nzima	the **most difficult** question

Note: The omission of the initial vowel of the noun after a superlative
(and a demonstrative) results in a change of the concord of descriptives
(adjectives and relatives):

Ung*um*ntu *o*lungile*yo*.	He / she is a **good** person.
*O*yena *m*ntu *u*lungile*yo*	The **very best** person

This principle also applies with **demonstratives**.

Y*i*gadi *e*ntle!	*It is* a **beautiful** garden!
Le gadi *i*ntle iseKapa.	*This* **beautiful** garden *is* in Cape Town.

To express 'it *is* / they *are*' before a **superlative**, prefix the copulative
(cf. **Unit 4.1**):

*Ii*Cycad *ze*zona *zi*tyalo *zi*dala egadini yeKirstenbosch.	Cycads **are** the **oldest plants** in Kirstenbosch gardens.

5 Demonstratives

As is the case in English, when pointing out people or objects, there are **three sets** of **demonstratives** in Xhosa corresponding to *'this'* / *'these'*; *'that'* / *'those'*; *'that over there'* / *'those over there'*.

Nouns preceded by a **demonstrative lose** their **initial vowel**:

Ngubani *lo m*ntu?	Who is *this* **person**?
Ngubani *loo m*ntu?	Who is *that* **person**?
Ngubani *laa m*ntu?	Who is *that* **person** *over there*?

As usual, each noun class has its corresponding form. It is interesting to note that the form of the **1st set** of **demonstratives** *'this'* / *'these'* corresponds to the relative concords in the 'strong' classes (cf. **Unit 6.2**) with *'l'* added in the 'weak' classes.

1st set of demonstratives

'Weak' classes

lo	*m*ntu	*this* **person**
lo	*m*thi	*this* **tree**
le	*mi*thi	*these* **trees**
la	*ma*gqabi	*these* **leaves**
le	*n*to	*this* **thing**

'Strong' classes

aba	*ba*ntu	*these* **people**
eli	**sango**	*this* **gate**
esi	*si*tyalo	*this* **plant**
ezi	*zi*tyalo	*these* **plants**
ezi	*zi*nto	*these* **things**
olu	**londolozo-manzi**	*this* **water conservation**
obu	*bu*tyebi	*this* **resource**
oku	*ku*londoloza amanzi	*this* **saving** (of) **water**

These **demonstratives** can be used **before** the noun, e.g.

Le gadi **i**dum*ile* (initial vowel of the noun omitted);

after the noun for **emphasis**, e.g. Idum*ile* **i**gadi *le* (initial vowel of the noun retained);

without a noun, e.g. *Le* **i**dum*ile*.

2nd set of demonstratives

'Weak' classes

	*m*ntu	*that* **person**
	*m*thi	*that* **tree**
loo	*mi*thi	*those* **trees**
	*ma*nzi	*that* **water**
	*n*to	*that* **thing**

Note: The full forms of the demonstratives of these nouns are *lowo* (Classes 1 and 3); *leyo* (Classes 4 and 9) and *lawo* (Class 6). They are normally used **after the noun** for emphasis:

Yinto enomdla *leyo*   It is an interesting thing *that*

'Strong' classes

ab̲o	*ba*ntu	*those* **people**
el̲o	**xesha**	*that* **time**
es̲o	*si*tyalo	*that* **plant**
ez̲o	*zi*tyalo	*those* **plants**
ez̲o	*zi*nto	*those* **things**
ol̲o	**hlobo**	*that* **way**
ob̲o	*bu*tyebi	*that* **resource**
ok̲o	*ku*tya	*that* **food**

(cf. Aph̲o = there)

3rd set of demonstratives

'Weak' classes

	*m*ntu	*that* **person** *over there*
	*m*thi	*that* **tree** *over there*
laa	*mi*thi	*those* **trees** *over there*
	*ma*phepha	*those* **papers** *over there*
	*n*dawo	*that* **place** *over there*

Note: As is the case with the 2nd set of demonstratives in the weak classes, there is a full form: *lowa* (Classes 1 and 3); *leya* (Classes 4 and 9) and *lawa* (Class 6). Like those of the 2nd set they are normally used **after the noun** for emphasis.

'Strong' classes

ab̲aa	*ba*ntu	*those* **people** *over there*
el̲aa	**sango**	*that* **gate** *over there*

es*aa*	si**tyalo**	*that* **plant** *over there*
ez*aa*	zi**tyalo**	*those* **plants** *over there*
ez*aa*	zi**nto**	*those* **things** *over there*
ol*aa*	lu**dwe**	*that* **list** *over there*
ob*aa*	bu**si**	*that* **honey** *over there*
okw*aa*	ku**tya**	*that* **food** *over there*

Note: The strong classes of the 3rd position also have full forms: *abaya* (Class 2), *eliya* (Class 5), *esiya* (Class 7), *eziya* (Classes 8 and 10), *oluya* (Class 11), *obuya* (Class 14) and *okuya* (Class 15). (Cf. 'pha*ya*' = over there).

6 Another conjunction – 'ukuze' 'in order to'

'**Ukuze**' is a **conjunction** that must be followed by a verb ending in *-e* (subjunctive) (cf. **Unit 4.5** and **Unit 8.2**):

Le nkqubo yaqalwa **ukuze** si**ncedise** izikolo ukuseka iigadi.	This project was started **to help** the schools establish gardens.
Qokelela inkunkuma yekhitshi **ukuze** wenz**e** umgquba.	Collect kitchen waste **to make** compost.

As you can see from the translations, Xhosa uses this construction where English simply uses the infinitive. However, it is interesting to note that now and again one comes across examples where the infinitive is used where one would expect the subjunctive:

'Kubaluleke kakhulu **ukunkcenkceshela** ngendlela efanelekileyo.'

It is very important **to water** in an appropriate manner.

This sentence is taken from Iigadi Ezinolondolozo-manzi ('Waterwise Gardening'), a brochure published by the Department of Water Affairs, Pretoria.

Iigadi Ezinolondolozo-Manzi

Indlela yokuyenza ntle igadi yakho.

The brochure and others can be obtained, free of charge, from Kirstenbosch, where you will also have many opportunities to test your knowledge of Xhosa by trying to read the plant information boards.

How to apply it

1 Complete the questions by filling in the appropriate link

(a) Iphi i-ofisi _____Nkosikazi Bongela?

(b) Liphi isango _____Rycroft?

(c) Abafundi _____Peter bafika nini?

(d) Umsebenzi _____Peter unomdla na?

(e) Inkqubo _____Phumla inempumelelo (success) na?

2 Give the literal translation of this idiomatic expression used to express 'hoping in vain'

Kukuza kukaNxele' _____

> **Nxele**, a Xhosa chief, is considered to be South Africa's first 'freedom fighter'. His attempt to destroy the new settlement of Grahamstown in 1819 led to his imprisonment on **Robben Island**. In 1820, when trying to escape he drowned but many of his followers did not believe that he was dead and waited in vain for his return.

3 Reading and understanding

Here is some information about *Abalimi Bezekhaya*, a community-based greening and food gardening project. Consult the Xhosa–English vocabulary list for help in understanding this extract.

Abalimi Bezekhaya yisenta yegadi yabantu. Lo mbutho wasckwa ngo-1982. Injongo yawo (its) kukwazisa, ukunceda nokucebisa abantu ngezinto zonke malunga nokulima – indlela yokulima imifuno, indlela yokutyala imithi nemithana ngokufanelekileyo. Abantu baseCape Flats banokuthenga zonke izinto zegadi ngexabiso eliphantsi kakhulu kulo mbutho.

Umzekelo_____ , _____, _____ _____ . Ungabona impumelelo yomsebenzi lo ezigadini ezininzi.

4 Ask where each garden implement is and answer appropriately

IZIXHOBO ZEGADI:

ingobozi (iin-)	basket	isikere sokuthena	pruning shears
isarha	saw	ithumbu lamanzi	hose
iharika / ireki	rake	ikani yokunkcenkceshela	watering can
ifolokhwe	fork	umhlakulo	spade
igaba	hoe	ikiriva	wheelbarrow
imbiza (iim-)	pot	i-emele	bucket
ipeki	pick	umatshini wokucheba ingca	lawn mower

Uphi umtya?	Unawo?	Ewe, nangu!
Where's the string?	Do you have it?	Yes, here it is!

(a)	___phi umhlakulo?	Una____?	Ewe, _____
(b)	___phi iimbiza?	Una____?	Ewe, _____
(c)	___phi ikiriva?	Una____?	Ewe, _____
(d)	___phi ithumbu lamanzi?	Una____?	Ewe,_____
(e)	___phi isikere sokuthena?	Una____?	Ewe,_____
(f)	___phi i-emele?	Una____?	Ewe,_____
(g)	___phi igaba?	Una____?	Ewe,_____
(h)	___phi iharika?	Una____?	Ewe, _____
(i)	___phi ifolokhwe?	Una____?	Ewe, _____
(j)	___phi umatshini wokucheba ingca?	Una____?	Ewe, _____

5 Match the instructions

Use the following phrases: (a) amanzi, (b) inkunkuma yekhitshi, (c) ingca, (d) umhlaba ngezinto ezigcina ukufuma emhlabeni, (e) inkunkuma kwimigqomo yenkunkuma, (f) umhlaba, (g) umthi and (h) amagqabi.

1	Lungisa	5	Harika
2	Tyala	6	Londoloza
3	Gquma	7	Qokelela
4	Cheba	8	Faka

6 Complete the instructions

Fill in the missing demonstratives to complete the instructions:

(a) Beka (these things) _____ _____ emgqubeni.
(b) Landa (fetch) (that wheelbarrow) _____ _____.
(c) Tyala (these trees) _____ _____ elangeni.
(d) Tyala (those trees) _____ _____ emthunzini.
(e) Nkcenkceshela (those seedlings (izithole) over there) ____ ____.
(f) Cheba (that hedge over there) _____ _____.

7 Complete the questions

Fill in the missing demonstratives to complete questions which you might ask when walking through Kirstenbosch:

(a) Ibizwa (called) njani _____ ntyatyambo?
(b) Ubizwa njani _____ mthi?
(c) Ubizwa njani _____ mthana (shrub)?
(d) Ibizwa njani _____ heji?
(e) Sibizwa njani _____ sityalo?
(f) Ubizwa njani _____ mfula (stream)?
(g) Ibizwa njani _____ ntaka (bird)?
(h) Ibizwa njani _____ ndlela?

8 Complete the information

(a) _____ ntyatyambo idumileyo yaseMzantsi Afrika yiProtea.

(b) _____ heji indala yaseKapa yatyalwa nguvan Riebeeck ngo-1660.

(c) IKirstenbosch _____ gadi idumileyo yaseMzantsiAfrika.

(d) _____ ndawo ilungileyo le yokwenza ipikiniki.

(e) Intlakohlaza _____ xesha lilungileyo lokutyelela iKirstenbosch.

(f) Ndiza kunicacisela _____ ndlela ilungileyo yokulondoloza amanzi.

9 Use the correct verb forms

Phumla goes to a school to show the pupils how to make compost and
how to water in a waterwise way. Complete the information she gives
them by filling in the correct verb forms. Consult the Xhosa–English
vocabulary for verbs you have not yet come across:

Heke, bafundi ndiyabona ukuba (a) beni_____ (have been
collecting) izinto ezininzi ukuze siqale ukwenza umgquba!
Masiwenzeni ke! Kuqala (b)_____ (separate) umhlaba
ngefolokhwe. (c)_____ (Put) uhlaza nokutya okudala nje
emgqubeni. Kufuneka ezi zinto (d) zi_____ (decay). Ukuba (e)
nizi_____ (keep) zifumile, uza kubola ngokukhawuleza umgquba.
Ukubola kuza (f) ku_____ (take) malunga neeveki ezintandathu.
Kufuneka (g) niwu_____ (water) kakuhle *rhoqo*.

Ngoku ndifuna ukunibonisa indlela efanelekileyo yokutyala imbewu.
Nantsi imbewu yemifuno. (h) Masiyi_____ (plant). Nanzi iibhokisi
ezincinci. (i) Zi_____ (fill) ngalo mhlaba. (j) *Yi*_____ (plant)
imbewu ezibhokisini ngolu hlobo (in this way). (k) *Zi*_____
(keep) iibhokisi ngaphandle okanye izityalo ziza kuba buthakathaka
(weak) (l) zi____ (die). Ngoku ndifuna uku*ni*bonisa indlela
yokunkcenkceshela izityalo ngokufanelekileyo.

(m) _____ (Remember) bafundi, amanzi (n)_____
(scarce) kakhulu eMzantsi Afrika. Kufuneka sonke sisoloko (o) si
_____ (try) (p) uku*wa*_____ (save) amanzi ngakumbi
ezigadini zethu. Ngoku, (q)_____ (water) ezi zithole
ngononophelo. Musani (r) uku_____ (water) amagqabi,
(s)_____ (water) umhlaba kuphela. (t)_____ (be careful)
(u) ningazi_____ (damage) izithole. (v)_____ (surround)
izityalo ngomgquba ukuze (w)_____ (keep) ukufuma emhlabeni.

-thatha	nkcenkceshelani	Lumkani	Jikelezani
-moshi	khumbulani	-nkcenkceshela	-tyaleni
-zaliseni	yahlukanisani	-gcine	Fakani
-zama	anqaba	-bole	-qokelela
-nkcenkceshele	-fe	-tyaleni	-gcineni
ugcine	nkcenkceshelani	-londoloza	

10 UThemba emsebenzini – udliwano-ndlebe
Themba at work – an interview

In this Unit you will learn how to:

- put an interviewee at ease
- ask questions as an employer
- talk about your education, training, previous experience
- ask for further information

Incoko

Themba interviews an applicant for a position in his company.

UThemba	Molo, Nkosazana Green. Khawungene uhlale phantsi. Ndiyavuya ukukubona. Kunjani?
UNksz Green	Molo Mnumzana Thamsanqa. Enkosi. Hayi ndiphilile ngaphandle *kokuba nentaka*!
UThemba	Hayi, nkosazana, sukuxhala! Khululeka! Ubonakala ukwazi ukusithetha kakuhle isiXhosa! Ndixelele, usazela phi?
UNksz Green	Ndaqala ukusithetha ndisemncinci kuba abazali bam babesebenza esibhedlele kufuphi nakuQoboqobo.
UThemba	Oo, uyasazi ke isiXhosa esithethwa ngamaNgqika omgquba!* Uyakwazi nokusibhala?
UNksz Green	Ewe Mnumzana Thamsanqa, ndasifunda isiXhosa esikolweni kwanaseyunivesithi.
UThemba	Uyakwazi ukuthetha nezinye iilwimi?
UNksz Green	Ewe, ndiyakwazi ukuthetha isiBhulu nesiFrentshi kancinci kodwa ke sona.
UThemba	Heke, Nkosazana, khawuthi *gqaba-gqaba* ngawe.
UNksz Green	Ndazalwa ngo-1969 eKapa. Abazali bam bafudukela kuQoboqobo ndisemncinci ngoko ke amabanga aphantsi, ukususela ku-Sub A ukuya kuStd 5, ndawenza ngakuQoboQobo.

*See Introduction.

UThemba	Amabanga aphakamileyo wawenza phi?
UNksz Green	Esinaleni ngaseMonti, iMatriki ndayiphumelela ngo-1986. Emva koko ndafundela iqondo leBA eyunivesithi yaseRhodes, eRhini.
UThemba	Wathatha ziphi izifundo eziyintloko?
UNksz Green	Ndathatha isiNgesi nesiXhosa.
UThemba	Wawufundiswa ngubani isiXhosa?
UNksz	Nguprofesa Majola. Ingaba uyamazi?
UThemba	Oo, kakhulu! Sasifunda kunye, ekrelekrele.
UNksz Green	Onjani utitshala! Wandinceda kakhulu. Ndazuza isidanga sam se-BA ngo-1989. Ndaqala ukusebenza njengotitshalakazi. Ngo-1994 ndanyuselwa ndaba lisekela-inqununu.
UThemba	Khawutsho, kutheni ufuna ukutshintsha umsebenzi?
UNksz Green	Ndinoloyiko kuza kuncitshiswa inani leetitshala. Enye into, ndingumntu wabantu. Ndithanda kakhulu ukusebenza neentlobo-ngeentlobo zabantu. Yaye ndicinga ukuba ndinganegalelo kwinkampani yakho.
UThemba	Heke, Nkosazana. Wena, unayo imibuzo?
UNksz Green	Ewe, Mnumzana Thamsanqa. Ucinga ukuba ndinethuba lokuwufumana lo msebenzi?
UThemba	Ewe, ndicinga ukuba unethuba elilungileyo kakhulu!
UNksz Green	Ndingalindela ukwaziswa nini ukuba ndiphumelele?
UThemba	Siza kukwazisa ekupheleni kweveki ezayo.
UNksz Green	Enkosi kakhulu. Ndiyabulela, Mnumzana.
UThemba	Kulungile Nkosazana Green. Bekumnandi kakhulu ukudibana nawe. Uhambe kakuhle.
UNksz Green	Kamnandi, MnumzanaThamsanqa.

Isigama

kokuba nentaka	to be nervous	-fudukela	move home
	(lit. be with a bird)	amabanga	standards
-xhala	be anxious	ukususela ku-	from
khululeka	relax i.e. be free	ukuya ku-	until
-bonakala	seem / appear	-phantsi	low(er)
-azela	know from	-phakamileyo	high(er)
kufuphi na-	near	isinala	boarding school
kuQoboqobo	to Keiskammahoek	-phumelela	succeed
kwanase-	even at	iqondo	degree
kodwa ke sona	the latter less	izifundo eziyintloko	majors

sasifunda	we studied	-tshintsha	change
kunye	together	uloyiko	fear
ekrelekrele	he being very bright	-ncitshiswa	be cut back, reduced
onjani	what	inani	the number
utitshala!	a teacher!	ngeentlobo-ntlobo	different
-zuza	graduate	igalelo	contribution
isidanga	degree (lit. necklace)	ithuba	chance
-nyuselwa	be promoted	ekupheleni kwa-	at the end of
ndaba lisekela- inqununu	I became vice-principal		

How to ...

Put an interviewee at ease

*Suku*xhala / **Khululeka**, Nkosikazi (Nkosazana, Mnumzana)

Ask questions as an employee

Wafunda phi?
Kw*esi***phi** *isi***kolo**?
Kw*eyi***phi** *iyuni***vesithi**?
Kutheni ufuna ukutshintsha *um***sebenzi**?
Wafundiswa *ng*ubani?
Waqeqeshwa *ng*ubani?
Wathatha *ezi***phi** *izi***fundo** njenge*zi***fundo** *eziyin***tloko**?
Unawo *ama***va**?
Unayo *imi***buzo**?

Talk about your education, training, experience

Nda*wenza amaba***nga** *a***phantsi** e_____
Nda*wenza amaba***nga** *a***phakamile**yo e_____
Nda**phumelela** ngo-19____ iMatriki
Nda**fundela** *iqo***ndo** leBA ngo_____
Nda**fundiswa** ngu_____
Nda**qeqeshwa** ngu_____
Nda**zuza** *isi***danga** sam se-BA

Ndasebenza njeng_____
Ndanyuselwa ndaba _____
Ndinamava ekufundiseni / ekuthengiseni / ekusebenzeni
  ngekhompyutha

Ask for further information

Uyakwazi ukuthetha isiNgesi / isiXhosa / isiBhulu / ezinye iilwimi?
Uyakwazi ukuqhuba?
Unalo iphepha lokuqhuba?
Unayo ireferensi / incwadi ekuncomayo. (lit. a letter praising you)
Wakhe wawenza lo msebenzi ngaphambili?
Wakhe wasebenza njeng _____ ngaphambili?
Uyakwazi ukusebenza ngekhompyutha?

⚙ How it works

1 The passive

The **passive** voice is a grammatical term that means exactly what it says
– something is done to somebody or something without necessarily
mentioning who is performing the action. The **passive** form is used more
extensively in everyday Xhosa speech than it is in English.

Uya**fundisa**.	He / she **teaches**.	(active)
Uya**fundiswa**.	He / she is **being taught**.	(passive)
Uya**qeqesha**.	He / she **is training**.	(active)
Uya**qeqeshwa**.	He / she is **being trained**.	(passive)

As you can see, the **passive is formed** simply by **inserting '-w-'** before
the **final -a** (cf. verbal extensions **Unit 4.6**):

Uprofesa u**fundisa** abafundi.	The professor **is teaching** (active) the students.
Abafundi ba**fundiswa** **ngu**profesa.	The students **are taught** (passive) **by** the professor.
Umqeqeshi u**qeqesha** abafundi.	The trainer **is training** (active) the apprentices.
Abafundi ba**qeqeshwa** **ngu**mqeqeshi.	The apprentices are **being** (passive) **trained by** the trainer.

Note: (1) When the agent, i.e. 'the doer of the action', is mentioned, it is prefixed by the copulative. In these examples '**ng-**' is prefixed to the agents '**u**profesa' and '**um**qeqeshi' because they belong to the '*u-*' and '*um-*' noun classes (Classes 1 and 1a).

→ cf. **Unit 4.1** for the copulatives of the other noun classes.

Note: (2) As is the case in the active voice, there is **no** '**-ya-**' when another word follows the verb (cf. **Unit 2.2**).

Noteworthy features of the passive

Some verbs which are **always used in the passive include:**

ukukholwa	to believe		
ukudinwa	to be tired	Ndidin<u>iwe</u>.	Ndidin<u>we</u> kakhulu.
ukunxanwa	to be thirsty	Ndinxan<u>iwe</u>.	Ndinxan<u>we</u> kakhulu.

→ cf. **Unit 7.3 long** and **short** form of the **recent past tense** '*-ile*' / '*-e*'.

Some expressions incorporating the **passive** are virtually untranslatable into English, e.g.:

Kuyanxanwa	(-nxanwa = be thirsty)
Kuyagodukwa*	(-goduka = go home)

*However, it is interesting to note that this construction exists in some other languages, e.g. German.

'**-w-**' can also be used in combination with other verbal extensions:

Nda**nyus**e**lwa**.	I was **promoted**.
	(lit. I **was made** to go up *for*)
Kuya ku**thethwana** ngo**mvuzo**.	**Salary** is **negotiable**.
	(lit. It will **be talked** about with *each other* about the salary.)

The infinitive form of the passive is often used in notices of **restriction**, **restraint** or **forbiddance**:

Aku**ngenwa**	*No* **entry**	(lit. *not* to **be entered**)
Aku**tshaywa**	*No* **smoking**	(lit. *not* to **be smoked**)
Aku**miswa**	*No* **stopping**	(lit. *not* to **be stopped**)
Aku**pakwa**	*No* **parking**	(lit. *not* to **be parked**)
Aku**hlalwa** engceni	*No* **sitting** on the grass	(lit. *not* to **be seated**)
Aku**tyiwa** elayibhri	*No* **eating** in the library	(lit. *not* to **be eaten**)

The **passive** form is reflected in some **common nouns**:

*isi*thand**wa**	beloved (lit. the loved one)
*um*qesh**wa**	employee (lit. hired one)
*um*phathis**wa**	cabinet minister
*u*dliwano-ndlebe	interview
< uku**dlana** *ii*n**dlebe**	'to **interview**'(lit. to **eat each other's ears**)

Note: **Consonant verbs of one syllable**, e.g. -dla > dl**iwa**; -tya > -ty**iwa** (be eaten) and **vowel verbs of two syllables**, e.g. -enz**iwa** = (been done, etc.) have **only one form** irrespective of whether they are followed by an agent or another word.

The **passive** form is also reflected in many **proper names**:

uBulel**wa**	(the one who is thanked for)
uVuyel**wa**	(the one who has been rejoiced for)
uVuyis**wa**	(the one who has been made to be joyful)
uXolis**wa**	(the one who has been made to be calm)
uZolis**wa**	(the one who has calmed)
uBong**iwe**	(the one praise has been given for)
uLind**iwe**	(the one who has been waited for)
uLiz**iwe**	(the one who has been given as a gift)
uSiph**iwe**	(the one who has been given as a gift)
uSind**iwe**	(the one who has transcended)
uThand**iwe**	(the one who is loved)

Some frequently used **idiomatic expressions** with the **passive** include:

Uphethwe *yi*ntoni?	**What**'s wrong with you? (lit. You **are ruled** *by* what?)
Ungenwe *yi*ntoni?	**What**'s got into you?
Ukhathazwa *yi*ntoni?	**What** worries you?
Ndiphelelwe *li*themba.	I've lost hope. (lit. **deprived** *of*)
Ndiphelelwe *ngum*sebenzi.	I am unemployed.
Ndibonwa *yi*ntoni?	How lucky can I be? (lit. *By* what am I **seen**?)

Many **idioms** (*iz*aci) and **proverbs** (*ama*qhalo) incorporate the **passive**:

Indlovu ayisind<u>w</u>a ngomboko wayo.	No one ever finds his natural responsibilities too burdensome. (lit. The **elephant** is not weighed down by its trunk.)

This idiom could well be said when commiserating with someone who 'has a lot on their shoulders'.

Inyathi ibuzwa kwabaphambili.	From the horse's mouth. (lit. The buffalo is asked (among the) first.)
Ukuzalwa wedwa ngumlu wanyama.	One must have family / kinship (lit. To be born alone is to be a strip of meat.)

This last concept is illustrated by Sindiwe Magona in an excerpt from her autobiography *To My Children's Children*:

'The intricate ways in which relationships are drawn among us make it almost impossible for an individual to be destitute in the sense of having connections with no living soul. One could, conceivably, be minus parent, or issue; have neither spouse nor sibling; but to be alone, with no relative, no one to care for or to lean on, is virtually unheard of except in the very rare case of an individual of such unbearable and odious disposition that no one can stand him or her or be moved to pity at the plight of such a one.'

→ See cultural background.

Some euphemistic idiomatic expressions mean 'to **be** buried':

ukufihl**wa**	lit. to **be** hidd**en**
ukugodus**wa**	lit. to **be** tak**en** home
ukusi**wa**	lit. to **be** tak**en** (to the fathers, i.e. ancestors)

When '-**w**-' occurs with the following consonants and consonant combinations certain **phonetic changes** take place. This is to **facilitate pronunciation**:

'to bury' = uku**ngcwa***b*a > uku**ngcwa***ty***wa** = to **be** buri**ed**

Some verbs frequently used which in the passive undergo this **sound change** are:

b > ty	-gqi*b*a	-gqi*ty*wa	**be** finish**ed**
	-se*b*enzisa	-se*ty*enzis**wa**	**be** used
bh > j	-bhu*bh*ela	-bhu*j*el**wa**	**be** bereaved (lit. **be died for**)
m > ny	-fu*m*ana	-fu*ny*an**wa**	**be found**
	-phu*m*a	-phu*ny*wa	lit. **be gone out**: kuphu*ny*wa apha 'exit'

mb > *nj*	-ha*mb*a	-ha*nj*wa	lit. **be gone**:
			kuha*nj*wa ngoku
	-khu*mb*ula	-khu*nj*ul*w*a	**be remembered**
ph > *tsh*	-khu*ph*a	-khu*tsh*wa	**be taken** out

Note: This **sound change** also occurs in **locatives** (cf. **Unit 4.8** and **Unit 6.7**):

*i*hlo*b*o > *e*hlo*ty*eni

The same sound change occurs with **diminutive** forms which suffix **-ana**. Look at the map of Kirstenbosch in **Unit 9** where you will find diminutives of:

*isizib*a (pool) > *isizity*ana (**small** pool)
*i*chi*b*a (pond) > *i*chi*ty*ana (**small** pond)

2 How to express 'alone' / 'by itself' / 'special' / 'exclusive' = '-odwa'

From the forms that follow you can see that for the 1st and 2nd persons '-edwa' or '-odwa' may be used:

Nd**indedwa** / Nd**indodwa** ekhaya.	I am **alone** at home.
Si**sedwa** / Si**sodwa** ekhaya.	We are **alone** at home.
U**wedwa** kowenu?	Are you **alone** at (your) home?
Ni**nedwa** / Ni**nodwa** kowenu?	Are you **alone** at (your) home?

In the 3rd person, '-odwa' is preceded by the consonant associated with the noun to which it refers, except for Class 1:

U*y*edwa kowabo.	He / she is **alone** at his / her home.
Ba*b*odwa *ab*antwana ekhaya.	The children are **alone** at home.

'-odwa' can also be used as a descriptive (relative) in which case it means 'special, exclusive' and is therefore prefixed by the relative concord:

*um*sebenzi	*ow*odwa	a **special** activity
*im*isebenzi	*ey*odwa	**special** activities
*i*yeza	*elil*odwa	**special** medicine
*ama*lungelo	*aw*odwa	**exclusive** rights
*isi*zathu	*esis*odwa	**special** reason
*izi*zathu	*eziz*odwa	**special** reasons
*in*jongo	*ey*odwa	**special** purpose
*u*dliwano-*n*dlebe	*olul*odwa	**exclusive** interview
*ubu*chule	*obub*odwa	**special** skills
*uku*tya	*okuk*odwa	**special** food

Remember: In the case of nouns prefixing '*um-*' (Class 3) the associated consonant is '*w-*' and in the case of nouns prefixing '*imi-*' / *i-*' / '*in-*' / '*im-*' the associated consonant is '*y-*'.

Note: No concord in Class 6 (*ama-*): *ama*Xhosa **odwa**, but '*-w-*' is infixed between a relative concord and '**odwa**': <u>*ama*</u>**lungelo** <u>*aw*</u>**odwa**.

3 The use of 'ukuba' = 'to be'

In the infinitive

Sonke sithanda uku**ba ne**thamsanqa. We all like *to* **be** lucky.

(lit. We all like to **be with** luck.)

In the future

Uza ku**ba ne**thuba *eli***lungile***yo*. You **will have** a good chance.

(lit. You will **be with**
a good chance.)

In the remote past

Nda**ba ne**thamsanqa. I **was** lucky.

(Lit. I **was with** luck.)

In the subjunctive

Ndinqwenela ukuba ndi**be** I wish that I **were** lucky.
nethamsanqa. (lit. I wish that I **be with** luck.)
Ndinqwenela ukuba a**be** I wish that he/she **were** lucky.
nethamsanqa. (lit. I wish that he/she
be with luck.)

U**be ne**thamsanqa! Good luck! (lit. You **be with** luck!)

Note: In the **3rd person singular**, 'he' / 'she', the subject concord changes from '**u**-' to '**a**-' (see **Exercise 6** of this Unit). This also occurs with '**-nga-**' = '**can**'/ '**may**':

<u>Anga</u>ndifowunela ngokuhlwa. He **can** phone me this evening.
(→ see **Unit 11**)

In the imperative (instructions)

*Yi***ba ne**thamsanqa! Good luck! (lit. **Be with** luck!)

Note: If a descriptive follows 'uku**ba**' = 'to **be**' it is **not** preceded by a concord:

Ndiyathemba ukuba uza ku**ba** **bhethele** kamsinya.

When a locative follows 'uku**ba**', the locative prefixes 's-':

Ndisenoku**ba** ş̱emsebenzini   I could still **be** at work

Cultural background

Quoting **idioms** and **proverbs** in Xhosa is a quintessential and much favoured way of epitomising a situation to drive home a point. They are often drawn from animal life or related to fables (*iintsomi*) (see **Unit 16**) and their meaning may be varied to suit the occasion but their application to a specific situation is rarely in doubt.

To quote Professor SC Satyo (Igrama Noncwadi LwesiXhosa ibanga le-9 nele-10, p. 215) 'Akulula ukuba ufumane umXhosa eyigqiba intetho yakhe engakhange asebenzise isaci'. (i.e. It is not easy to find a Xhosa person finishing his / her speech without using an idiom.)

This was vividly illustrated in a speech by Deputy President Mbeki on his budget vote when he said: '*Ukuthundez' ubhityo.*' (To try to do as much as possible with limited resources.) (lit. to gently coax along the most emaciated ox in order to eke out the last little reserve from it.)

☑ How to apply it

1 Match the public signs

The English equivalents are: (a) No Littering, (b) Silence, (c) No Dogs Allowed and (d) No Swimming Allowed.

1   Akuvunyelwa ukungena nezinja apha!
2   Akuthethwa
3   Akuvunyelwa ukuqubha!
4   Akungcoliswa

2 What is the literal meaning of the idioms and proverbs

(a) *Intlama idliwe yinja.*   Things have gone wrong.
    Lit.:_____

(b) *Umhlaba ubethwe lilanga.*   The soil is very dry.
    Lit.:_____

(c) *Abantwana bangenwe yintaka.*   The children are frightened.
Lit.:_____

(d) *Kuhanjwa ngesiko.*   It's done according to custom.
Lit.:_____

(e) *Le nto yaphelelwa lixesha.*   This is old fashioned.
Lit.:_____

(f) *Ubunzulu besiziba* (deep pool in river)
buviwa ngodondolo (stick)!   Look before you leap!
Lit.:_____

3 Give the English equivalent of newspaper / magazine columns

Okuxelwa ziinkwenkwezi (What is told by the stars)_____
Abakhunjulwayo (Who are remembered) _____

4 Reading, understanding and answering questions

Read the conversation between Themba and Mary at work and answer the questions that follow:

UThemba   Molo Mary, uphila njani namhlanje?

UMary   Ewe Themba. Sikhona. Wena?

UThemba   Hayi, nam ndisaphila ngaphandle komsebenzi. Kanene, uzifihle phi? *(Where have you hidden yourself?)* Andikubonanga ixesha elide.

UMary   Bendinekhefu elimnandi *(I had a nice holiday)* nosapho lwam.

UThemba   Unethamsanqa! Ndixelele ngekhefu lakho. Masiye ekhefi siphunge.

UMary   Kulungile. Andikalifumani ixesha lokuphunga. *(I have not yet found the time)* Masiye ke.

UThemba   Unjani umsebenzi wakho? Usawuvuyela? Kanene unyuselwe, ndiyavuyisana nawe! Usebenzile!

UMary   Enkosi, kodwa kunzima ngamanye amaxesha. Linqabile ixesha. Ndisoloko ndixakekile.

UThemba   Ndim lowo *(same here).* Lunjani usapho?

UMary   Sonke siphilile. Banjani abantwana nenkosikazi yakho?

UThemba   Basaphila nabo. Yho! Jonga ixesha! Mandikhawulezise *(Let me hurry)* okanye ndiza kuphoswa yintlanganiso. *(lit. I will be missed by the meeting.)*

UMary   Ewe, kufuneka nam ndihambe. Sobabini sishiywe
           lixesha.
UThemba Bekumnandi ukuphunga nawe. Sobonana kwakhona.
UMary   Kulungile. Sebenza kakuhle. Undibulisele kuThandi
           nabantwana.
UThemba Enkosi. Ube nempela-veki emnandi.

(a) UThemba noMary bancokola phi?
(b) Baphila njani?
(c) Baya phi ukuze bancokole kancinci?
(d) UThemba uvuyisana noMary. Kutheni?
(e) UThemba uza kuya phi?

5 Who's who?

Three people describe what their work entails. They are:

(a) a chef (cook)   umpheki
(b) a journalist   intatheli
(c) a receptionist in a hotel   ireceptionist yehoteli

Match the job description with the job:

1 Ininzi into ekufuneka ndiyenze! Mandinichazele ngomsebenzi wam.
Ndisebenza eFront-Office. Ndamkela iindwendwe xa zifika
ndizibonise indlela eziza kuhlala ngayo ehotele. Ndisebenza
noosomashishini beli lizwe nabamanye amazwe ngokunjalo
nabakhenkethi. Lo msebenzi unobunzima gqitha ngamanye
amaxesha. Abanye abatyeleli bakhalaza kakhulu, kufuneka ukuba
ndizisombulule kwaye zonke izikhalazo. Abanye bafuna ukwazi
iindawo ezithandwa ngabakhenkethi, imeko yelizwe njalo, njalo.
Kufuneka ukuba ndibanike iingcombolo ezichanekileyo.
Ndisenokuba semsebenzini xa abanye abantu belele okanye
bezonwabisa.

-chazela	explain (to)	imeko (ii-)	situation
undwendwe (iin-)	guest	ingcombolo (iin-)	information
-sombulula	solve	-chanekileyo	precise
kwaye	and	*xa ... belele	when ... are
isikhalazo (izi-)	complaints		asleep
*See Unit 12.1			

Ndi _____ .

2 Kuqala ndasebenza kwikhitshi lenkampani enkulu, kodwa ngoku ndisebenza ehotele enkulu. Ndilungisa imenyu. Ndi-odola ukutya ndiqeqeshe ndiphathe abasebenzi basekhitshini. Ndinomdla ebantwini nasekulungiseni izidlo. Ndithanda ukusebenza kwindawo enomdla, kodwa into endingayithandiyo ngamanye amaxesha kukusebenza iiyure ezininzi neeshifti. Ezo zinto zindenza ndizive ndicinezelekile.

-odola	order	iiyure	hours
isidlo (izi-)	meal	ezo zinto	those things
into endingayithandiyo	*what I do not like	-cinezelekile	be stressed
*See Unit 16.1			

Ndi _____ .

3 Ndithanda ukudibana nabantu nokuthetha nabo nokubaphulaphula. Ndithanda ukubhala amanqaku ngabantu nangezinto ezenzeka imihla ngemihla. Ndenza uphando ngebali lam ndilibhale kwikhompyutha yam. Ndisebenza yonke imihla iiyure ezininzi kwanangempela-veki.

-phulaphula	listen	inqaku (ama-)	article
uphando	research		

Ndi _____ .

6 Read and understand

With the help of the vocabulary you should be able to understand the following advertisements (iz**aziso**):

(a) *KUFUNWA UNONTLALO-NTLE*

Umbutho wenu ufuna inkonzo yomntu ozondelelayo onokusebenza nzima ekukhuseleni abantwana.
Izinto ezifunekayo kanye ngamava ekugcineni abantwana, iphepha lokuquhba nokukwazi ukuthetha isiXhosa.
Ukukwazi ukuthetha nesiNgesi nesiBhulu kakuhle kuyanceda kakhulu.
Kuya kuthethwana ngomvuzo ngokwamava awo omsebenzi.
Uthumele iCV neereferensi ezintathu zabantu esinokuqhagamshelana nabo, nencwadi yokucela umsebenzi ku_____. Umhla wokuvala isicelo ngu____.

umbutho (imi-)	organisation	umvuzo (imi-)	salary
inkonzo	service	-qhagamshelana na-	contact
-zondelelayo	energetic	umhla wokuvala	closing date
-thumela	send to	isicelo	application
-khusela	protect		

Note: The **non-anglisised expression** for '*i*referensi':

*in*cwadi e*ndi*ncoma*yo* = letter that praises *me*, i.e. my reference
*in*cwadi e*ku*ncoma*yo* = letter that praises *you*, i.e. your reference

(b)   *KUFUNWA IRECEPTIONIST / UNOBHALA*

Indawo enkulu ebalulekileyo ethengisa ikhande iimoto ifuna ireceptionist / unobhala okhutheleyo.
Kufuneka umceli-msebenzi abe* nobuchule obulandelayo:

- *bokusebenza ngekhompyutha*
- *bokubhala nokuthumela iincwadi zetyala*
- *bokubhala nokusabela zonke iincwadi*
- *bokuthetha nabantu*
- *bokwazi ukuthetha isiXhosa nesiNgesi nesiBhulu.*

Kufuneka kanjalo abe* namava ekusebenzeni njengereceptionist.
Umsebenzi umzekelo ngulo:
- *ukusabela ifowuni nemibuzo*
- *ukwamkela abaveleli*
- *ukubhala nokuthumela iincwadi*
- *ukugcina zonke izinto zokubhala namaphepha*
- *ukulungiselela iintlanganiso*

Thumela ngefaksi iCV neereferensi ezintathu zabantu esinokuqhagamshelana nabo ku_____.

-khanda	repair	-sabela	answer
-khutheleyo	diligent	umveleli	visitor
kufuneka abe* na-	she must have	izinto zokubhala	stationery
ubuchule	skill(s)	namaphepha	
iincwadi zetyala	accounts		
*See Unit 10.3			

7 Translate the expressions that characterise people

(a) umntu olungileyo _____

(b) umntu ombi _____

(c) umntu onomdla _____

(d) umntu onesibindi _____

(e) umntu othandayo _____

(f) umntu ozondelelayo _____

(g) umntu onolwazi _____

(h) umntu onobubele _____

(i) umntu oyedwa _____

(j) umntu onamava _____

(k) umntu ozolileyo _____

(l) umntu okhutheleyo _____

(m) umntu odumileyo _____

(n) umntu oxakekileyo _____

11 | Ndingathetha noMnumzana Thamsanqa?

May I speak to Mr Thamsanqa?

In this Unit you will learn how to:

■ communicate on the telephone
■ make arrangements to meet, including place and time

Incoko

Peter phones Themba to make arrangements to meet at the cricket.

UPeter	Hello, ndingathetha noMnumzana Thamsanqa? Ingaba ukhona?
UNobhala	Ndingabuza ukuba ngubani ofuna ukuthetha naye?
UPeter	Ewe, nguPeter Murray lo uthethayo.
UNobhala	Khawubambe njalo, Mnumzana Murray. Ndiza kubona ukuba ukhona na phaya e-ofisini yakhe.
UPeter	Kulungile.
UNobhala	Mnumzana Murray, ndilusizi, uMnumzana Thamsanqa akakho okwangoku. Usaphumile.
UPeter	Uyazi ukuba uza kufika nini na?
UNobhala	Ndilusizi, khange atsho. Ungathanda ukushiya umyalezo?
UPeter	Ewe, uze umxelele ukuba ndifuna ukuqhakamshelana naye malunga neqakamba yangomso. Mhlawumbi angandifowunela ekhaya ngokuhlwa.
UNobhala	Kulungile Mnumzana Murray. Ndiza kumxelela. Ngubani inombolo yefowuni yakho?
UPeter	Ngu 531–3767.
UNobhala	Kulungile, Mnumzana Murray.
UPeter	Ndiyabulela. Bye.
UNobhala	Bye, Mnumzana Murray.

Themba returns Peter's call that evening. David answers the phone.

UDavid	David Murray speaking.

UThemba	Hello, David. Kunjani, mfondini?
UDavid	Oo, molo Mnumzana Thamsanqa. Ndiphilile, enkosi. Wena?
UThemba	Hayi, sikhona. Ingaba utata ukhona?
UDavid	Ewe. Yima kancinci. Ndiza kumbiza.

After exchanging pleasanteries, Peter and Themba continue their conversation.

UThemba	Molo Peter. NguThemba kweli cala. Enkosi ngokufowuna. Ngelishwa bendisentlanganisweni imini yonke! Ndiwufumene umyalezo wakho sekuhlwile.
UPeter	Ayinamsebenzi loo nto. Ndiyazi ukuba uxakekile!
UThemba	Siza kudibana ngabani ixesha ngomso?
UPeter	Kunjani ngo-9.30?
UThemba	Kulungile. Phi?
UPeter	Phambi kwesango elikhulu.
UThemba	Kulungile, siza kuba lapho ngo-9.30. Sobonana!
UPeter	Sobonana!

The next morning Thandi phones Jenny.

UJenny	Hello!
UThandi	Hello, ndingathetha noNkosikazi Murray?
UJenny	Molo Thandi, ndim!
UThandi	Oo uxolo sithandwa sam, khange ndilichane ilizwi lakho! Unantoni na?
UJenny	Awu, ndinomkhuhlane kancinci phofu!
UThandi	Oo, ndiluzisi. Ndikufowunela kuba mna noThemba siya kwirestyu entsha yezakwaNtu ngokuhlwa ngoMgqibelo. Sifuna ukunimcma wena noPeter. Ningeza? Ucinga ukuba uza kuba sele ubhetele?
UJenny	Oo, ingantle loo nto. Bendifunda ngaloo restyu kwiphepha-ndaba ngempela-veki ephelileyo. Ndatsho *ndavuz' izinkcwe*! Ukutya kwayo kwandikhumbuza ubuntwana bam. Sasizitya zonke ezo zinto zakwaNtu efama!
UThandi	Heke, mandikulande ukuze sidibane noPeter noThemba erestyu emva komdlalo weqakamba.
UJenny	Ungaba undincedile, sithandwa. Sobonana!

Isigama

okwangoku	at the moment	sithandwa sam	my dear
-bamba	hold on	-chana	recognise
-shiya	leave		(lit. be accurate)
umyalezo	message	ilizwi	voice
uze	you should	phofu	though
-qhakamshelana na-	get in touch with	zakwaNtu	traditional
malunga na-	about	-mema	invite
ngokuhlwa	in the evening	bendifunda	I was reading
inombolo	number	*ndavuz' izinkcwe*	*it made my mouth water*
kweli cala	on this side	-khumbuza	remind
bendisentlanganisweni	I was at a meeting	ubuntwana	childhood
sekuhlwile	already evening	-landa	fetch
isango	gate		

CULTURE SHOCK Parliament was recently treated to a scene seldom seen in Cape Town when the Masizakhe Cultural Group of Lady Grey in the Eastern Cape, resplendent in their traditional dress, took a tour of the legislature. But the pastoral illusion was rudely shattered when this lady's cellular phone rang.

(Courtesy *Cape Times* 8/5/1996. Photo: Benny Gool)

? *How to ...*

Communicate on the telephone when you are *making* the call

*Ng*u _____ *o*thetha*yo*.
*Ng*u_____ kw*eli* cala.
Ndinga**thetha** no*M*numzana _____, nceda.
Ndi**cela** uku**thetha** no*M*numzana _____.
Oo, *u***xolo**, khange ndi*li***chane** *ili***zwi** lakho!
Ukhona *uM*numzana _____?
Ukhona *u*Nkosikazi _____?
U*m*lindele nini?
Ungan**ceda** u*n*di**fake** kwi-**ofisi** ka*M*numzana _____?
Ndinga*wu***shiya** *um*yalezo?
Ndiza ku*m***fowunela** kwakhona.

Communicate on the telephone when you are *answering* the call

Ndi**thetha** nabani?
Ndinga**buza**, *ng*ubani *o*thetha*yo*?
Ndinga*m***xelela** *ng*ubani *o***funa** uku**thetha** na*ye*?
Khawubambe njalo.
*Yi***ma** kancinci, ndiza ku*m***biza**.
*Yi***ma** kancinci, ndiza ku**khangela** ukuba u**khona** na.
Ndi**lusizi** *aka*kho okwangoku.
U**saphum**i*le*.
U**sentlanganis**weni.
U**xakek**i*le* komnye *um*nxeba. Unga**thanda** uku**bamba**?
Ndinga**thatha** *um*yalezo?
Ukhona *um*yalezo?
Unga*wu***shiya** *um*yalezo?

Make arrangements to meet

Siza ku**dibana ngabani** *i*xesha? **Phi**?
Kunjani ngo-9?
Ndiza ku**dibana** na*we* phambi kwe**sango** *eli***khulu**.
Ndiza ku**dibana** na*we* phambi kwe**restyu**.

Ndiza ku*ku*landa ngo-7.
Uze un**cede** ufi**ke** nge**xesha**.
Ungafik*i* emva kwe**xesha**!

Some idioms related to time

Ixesha lixhatshwe *(< -xhapha) yinja.*   It's late.
  (lit. time has been lapped up by the dog.)

xa kumpondo zankomo   very early in the morning
  (lit. when the horns of the cattle are just visible)

xa libantu bahle   in the early evening/twilight
  (lit. when people are beautiful, i.e. blemishes are less obvious!)

ngolwemivundla   in the early evening / dusk
  (lit. at the time that rabbits come out of their warrens)

Ask whether you may use someone's phone

Ndingasebenzisa *i*fowuni yakho, *N*kosikazi / *M*numzana?

Ask where the nearest public phone is

Iphi *i*fowuni kawonke-wonke *e*kufutshane?

Ask to borrow a telephone directory

Ndi**funa** *i*nombolo. Ndinga**boleka** *i*directory yakho ye**fowuni**?

How it works

1 More expressions incorporating 'ng-' (copulative)

'It *is* who *who*'... ? = '*N*gubani o- ...'?:

*N*gubani *o*thetha*yo*?
*N*gubani *o*funa ukuthetha na*ye*?
*N*gu**Peter Murray** *o*thetha*yo*?

'*N*gubani' with other expressions, translating 'What *is*':

*N*gubani *i*xesha?	**What** *is* the **time**?
*N*gubani *i*gama lakho?	**What** *is* your **name**?
*N*gubani *i*fani yakho?	**What** *is* your **surname**?

2 Copulatives with emphatic pronouns

ndim	It *is* me	*nguye* (*umncedisi*)	It *is* him / her
sithi	It *is* us	*ngabo* (*abancedisi*)	It *is* them
nguwe	It *is* you (s.)	*nguwo* (*umsebenzi*)	It *is* it
nini	It *is* you (pl.)	*yiyo* (*ifowuni*)	It *is* it, etc.

3 '-khona' = 'there' (be present)

Like 'apha' / 'apho' = 'here' / 'there' (cf. Unit 5.3, 'khona' can be used as an adverb:

Usebenza **khona**.	She works **there**/at that place.
Siza kuba **khona** ngo-9.30.	We'll be **there** at 9.30.

It can also be used **with a subject concord**:

U**khona** *u*Themba?	Is Themba **there**?
Ewe, u**khona**.	Yes, he (is) **there**.
I**khona** *i*fowuni?	Is **there** a phone?
Ewe, i**khona**.	Yes, it (is) **there**.
Lu**khona** *u*siba?	Is **there** a pen?
Ewe, lu**khona**.	Yes, it (is) **there**.
I**khona** *i*pensile?	Is **there** a pencil?
Ewe, i**khona**.	Yes, it (is) **there**.

'-kho' (without -na) is used in impersonal expressions – '**Ku**kho...':

Ku**kho** iphepha?	Is **there** paper?
Ewe, ku**kho** iphepha etafileni.	Yes, **there** is paper on the table.
Ku**kho** imiyalezo?	Are **there** messages?
Ewe, ku**kho** imiyalezo.	Yes, **there** are messages.

In the negative '-khona' > '-kho':

U**khona** *u*Themba?	Hayi, *aka***kho**.
U**khona** *um*sebenzi?	Hayi, *awu***kho**.
I**khona** *i*fowuni?	Hayi, *ayi***kho**.
I**khona** *i*pensile?	Hayi, *ayi***kho**.
Lu**khona** *u*siba?	Hayi, *alu***kho**.

4 Prepositions followed by 'kwa-'

The following prepositions are used before nouns expressing **place**, **time** or **manner**:

emva kwa-

behind	after
emva kwesango**emva kwe**mini	
emva komthi **emva ko**mdlalo	

ngaphandle kwa-

outside	besides
ngaphandle kwerestyu	**ngaphandle ko**kuthetha isiXhosa,
	uthetha nesiSuthu

phambi kwa-

in front	before
phambi kwerestyu	**phambi kwe**sidlo

phakathi kwa-

between	(but note **phakathi _e_bhokis_ini_**
phakathi komaleko	= **inside** the **box**)

phantsi kwa-

under	(but note Hlala **phantsi!**
phantsi kwetafile	= Sit **down**!)

phezu kwa-

on top of	(but note Jonga **phezu<u>lu</u>!**
phezu kwekhabhathini	= Look **up**!)

Note: '**phantsi kwa-**' and '**phezu kwa-**' are also used in comparatives:

Ixesha linqabe **ngaphezu kwe**mali.   Time is more scarce **than** money.
Ndinemali _e_**ngaphantsi kwe**yakho!   I have less money **than** you!

Also followed by '**kwa-**': '_e_cal_eni_ **kwa-**' = '_at_ the **side of**'.

5 Numerals

You are already familiar with the numerals 1–6 (cf. **Unit 6.2**):

*um*ntwana	*om*nye	*in*cwadi	*e*nye
*aba*ntwana	*aba*bini	*ii*ncwadi	*ezi*mbini*
*aba*ntwana	*aba*thathu	*ii*ncwadi	*ezi*ntathu†
*aba*ntwana	*aba*ne	*ii*ncwadi	*ezi*ne
*aba*ntwana	*aba*hlanu	*ii*ncwadi	*ezi*ntlanu
*aba*ntwana	*aba*thandathu	*ii*ncwadi	*ezi*ntandathu

The **sound changes** caused by 'n' in the **adjectival concord** '*ezin*'-:
*b influences a preceding 'n': n + b > **mb**, † n + th > **nt**, n + hl > **ntl**,
n + n > **n**.

Numerals 6–10 are **nouns** (not adjectival stems like 1–6):

*isi*xhenxe:	*aba*ntwana	*aba*sixhenxe	7	(lit. which are **7**)
*isi*bhozo:	*aba*ntwana	*aba*sibhozo	8	(lit. which are **8**)
*i*thoba:	*aba*ntwana	*aba*lithoba	9	(lit. which are **9**)
*i*shumi:	*aba*ntwana	*aba*lishumi	10	(lit. which are **10**)

Numerals from 11 onwards are more complex than their English equivalents, but luckily for learners, even Xhosa speakers often use the English numerals above 10.

You might like to know:

100	=	*i*khulu (*ama-*)
1,000	=	iwaka (*ama-*)
1,000,000	=	*isi*gidi

Can you work out what '*u*sozigidi' (*oo-*) means?

Ordinal numbers 1–10:

-*oku*qala	*um*ntwana *woku*qala	1st
*isi*bini	*um*ntwana *wesi*bini	2nd
*isi*thathu	*um*ntwana *wesi*thathu	3rd
*isi*ne	*um*ntwana *wesi*ne	4th
*isi*hlanu	*um*ntwana *wesi*hlanu	5th
*isi*thandathu	*um*ntwana *wesi*thandathu	6th
*isi*xhenxe	*um*ntwana *wesi*xhenxe	7th
*isi*bhozo	*um*ntwana *wesi*bhozo	8th
*isi*thoba	*um*ntwana *wesi*thoba	9th
*isi*shumi	*um*ntwana *wesi*shumi	10th

Numerals in expressions of time

Expressing the time in Xhosa is difficult. Even Xhosa mother tongue speakers often express the time in English. Especially in informal conversation. However, the time is always given in Xhosa on the radio, especially at news time.

What *is* the **time**?	
*Ng*u**bani** *i***xesha**?	(lit. **Who** is the **time**?)
Lithi**ni** *i***xesha**?	(lit. It says **what** the **time**?)
*Ng*u-1 / 2 / 3 / 4 / 5	It*'s* 1 / 2 / 3 / 4 / 5 **o'clock**.
*Y*in**tsimbi** yoku**qala** / ye*si***bini** / ye*si***thathu** / ye*si***ne** / ye*si***hlanu**.	(lit. It*'s* the **first** / **second** / **third** / **fourth** / **fifth bell**)
Nga**bani** *i***xesha**?	**At what time**?
Ngo-1 / 2 / 3 / 4 / 5.	**At** 1 / 2 / 3 / 4 / 5 **o'clock**.
Nge*n***tsimbi** yoku**qala** / ye*si***bini** / ye*si***thathu** / ye*si***ne** / ye*si***hlanu**.	**At** the **first** / **second** / **third** / **fourth** / **fifth bell**.

When it comes to expressing the time other than on the hour, the English forms are used, even in more formal situations, for example '*Y*i**kota** past **6**' is much easier and quicker to say than: '*Y*imi*z*u**zu** *eli***shumi** *eli***nantlanu** emva kwe*n***tsimbi** ye*si***thandathu**' (lit. It is **minutes** *which are* **ten** which have **five** after the **bell** of **six**); similarly '**Nge**haf past **2**' is much easier and quicker to say than '**Ngecala** emva kwe*n***tsimbi** ye*si***bini**' (lit. **At** past the **side** after the **bell** of **two**).

6 Expressions such as 'irestyu yezakwaNtu'

There are many expressions like this in Xhosa, i.e. incorporating a **double possessive**, for example 'irestyu **yeza**kwaNtu', the full form of which is irestyu **ya** + **i**zinto + **za** + kwaNtu = irestyu **ye**zinto **za**kwaNtu (a restaurant **of** things **of** tradition). However this full form is contracted to irestyu **ya** + '**i**' of **i**zinto + **za** + kwaNtu = irestyu **ye**zakwaNtu.

Here are some other examples you may come across:

Umhleli **weze**midlalo	sports editor
Umhleli **wezo**politiko	political editor
Umcebisi **wezo**mthetho	legal advisor
Umphathiswa **weze**angaphandle	minister of foreign affairs
Umphathiswa **weze**mfundo	minister of education
Umphathiswa **wezo**limo	minister of agriculture
Abalimi b**eze**khaya	home gardeners

7 '-ni?' = 'what', shortened form of 'ntoni?'

When the shortened form of '**ntoni**?' = '**-ni**?' is used it must be suffixed to the verb:

Ufuna **ntoni**?	**What** do you want?
Ufuna**ni**?	**What** do you want?
Wenza **ntoni**?	**What** are you doing?
Wenza**ni**?	**What** are you doing?

Note: With the verb '**-thi**' = '**say**' only the shortened form is used as can be seen in the following idiomatic expressions:

Lithi**ni** ixesha?	**What** is the time?
Kwenzeke**ni**? / Bekuthe**ni**?	**What** happened?
Uthe**ni** na wena?	**What**'s the matter with you?
Ndingathi**ni**?	**How** do I go about this?

How to apply it

1 Answer the questions

(a)	UThemba ukhona?	Hayi, _____.
(b)	Uza kuba khona ngo-4?	Hayi, _____.
(c)	Uza kubuya kamsinya?	Hayi, _____ namhlanje.
(d)	UPeter use-ofisini?	Hayi, _____, _____ekhaya.
(e)	Ukhona umyalezo?	Hayi, _____.
(f)	Ikhona ifowuni kawonke-wonke ekufutshane?	Hayi, _____.

2 Complete the dialogue

Hello, (a) _____ (*can I speak*) noMnumzana Thamsanqa?
(b) _____, (*I'm sorry*) uxakekile komnye umnxeba.
Khawubambe njalo.

After some minutes.

UMnu Thamsanqa (c) _____ (*is still busy*). Ungathanda ukubamba okanye ungathanda (d) _____ (*leave a message*)?

Ewe, (e) _____(*tell him that I will try to phone him again in the afternoon*).

Enkosi. Kamnandi.

3 Give the dialogue a title

UDavid	Hullo, nguDavid kweli cala. Ndingathetha noVuyo?
Ilizwi	Eh, uVuyo? Akukho Vuyo apha. Ufuna eyiphi inombolo?
UDavid	Ndifuna i-633-4253.
Ilizwi	Hayi, ndilusizi, lo ngu-633-4352.
UDavid	Khawuphinde. Yintoni inombolo yefowuni yakho?
Ilizwi	Ngu-633-4352.
UDavid	Owu, uxolo, yinombolo ewrongo.

4 Read, understand and answer the questions

See how well you have understood the dialogue by answering the questions that follow:

Bongile is looking for a job during the holidays.

UMncedisi	Molo, kukwaBizo's Takeaway. Ndingakunceda?
UBongile	Ngaba ndingamfumana uNksk. Bizo?
UMncedisi	Akakho. Usaphumile okwangoku. Ungashiya umyalezo?
UBongile	Kulungile. Ndive ukuba ufuna umntu oza kuncedisa kwishishini lakhe. Ndifuna ukwenza isicelo. Ubuya nini?
UMncedisi	Andiqinisekanga.
UBongile	Ndingaphinda ndifowune nini?
UMncedisi	Zama ukufowuna ngentsimbi yesi thandathu. Khawushiye igama lakho nenombolo.
UBongile	Igama lam nguBongile Thamsanqa. Unokunditsalela kule nombolo ithi 770555.
UMncedisi	Mandiliphinde igama. UnguBongile Thamsanqa. Inombolo ithi 770555.
UBongile	Kulungile. Enkosi. Usale kakuhle.
UMncedisi	Kamnandi.

(a) UBongile ufuna ukuthetha nabani?

(b) UNksk. Bizo ukhona?

(c) UBongile ushiya owuphi umyalezo?

(d) Uza kuzama ukufowuna ngeyiphi intsimbi?

5 Read the conversation

UVal   Molo Xoliswa.

UXoliswa Molo sisi. Nisaphila phofu?

UVal   Hayi, siphilile sonke. Ndiyakufowunela kuba ndingathanda
          ukubuza ukuba sinokudibana na kwakhona. Kunjani
          ngokuya kubukela ifilimu?

UXoliswa Eyiphi ifilimu?

UVal   Singabukela 'u*Jump the Gun*'.

UXoliswa Ngeyiphi imini?

UVal   NgoLwesine?

UXoliswa Hayi, andizi kuba kho ngoLwesine. Kunjani ngo-
          Mgqibelo?

UVal   Hayi, uMgqibelo akalungi kum. Uza kuphumelela
          ngeCawa?

UXoliswa Kulungile.

UVal   Ufuna ndikuphuthume ngabani ixesha?

UXoliswa Ngentsimbi yesihlanu.

UVal   Kulungile. Siza kubonana ke ngeCawa. Sala kakuhle.

UXoliswa Kamnandi.

Imagine that Xoliwsa tells another friend about her chat with Val:

(a) I spoke to Val today. _____.

(b) We are going to see a film on Sunday. _____.

(c) Can you come with us? _____.

(d) Val is going to fetch me at 5 o'clock. _____.

6 Say you have

(a) three children, two daughters and a son

(b) four messages

(c) two telephone numbers

(d) five tickets

(e) six letters

7 Listen to the dialogue and say whether the statements are correct or not

(a) Thandi is in a hurry.	yes	no
(b) She has to go shopping.	yes	no
(c) She prepares a party for Friday.	yes	no
(d) She only invites Nomsa and Sipho.	yes	no
(e) Nomsa has to ask Sipho first.	yes	no

8 English equivalents of newspaper / magazine section headings

Use the headings: (a) For the Children, (b) Health Matters, (c) Business, (d) Finance, (e) Sport, (f) Entertainment, (g) For Teenagers and (h) Education.

1	Ezemidlalo	5	Ezolonwabo
2	Ezempilo	6	Ezabantwana
3	Ezolutsha	7	Ezemfundo
4	Ezoshishino	8	Ezemali

9 Complete the questions

(a) Ndithetha _____?
(b) _____ othethayo?
(c) Ufuna _____?
(d) Ufuna _____ inombolo?
(e) _____ igama lakho?
(f) _____ inombolo yakho yasekhaya?
(h) _____ inombolo yakho yasemsebenzini?
(i) _____ i-adelesi yakho?
(j) Ndingakwenzela _____?
(k) Ndingakunceda _____?
(l) _____ ingxaki?
(m) Kwenzeke _____?

10 Which verb fits?

Use these verbs to fit the spaces correctly (a) -bamba, (b) -shiya, (c) -cothisisa, (d) -phinda and (e) -faka.

1 Uxolo, andiva kakuhle, unga_____ kwakhona?
2 Ungathanda uku_____ umyalezo?
3 Ungandi_____ kwi-ofisi kaMnu. Bizo?
4 Usaxakekile komnye umnxeba. Ungathanda uku_____?
5 Uthetha ngokukhawuleza kakhulu. Unga_____?

12 Kumdlalo weqakamba
At the cricket match

In this Unit you will learn how to:

■ ask about past sporting involvement and respond
■ ask about present sporting involvement and respond
■ ask what someone does to keep fit
■ say what you do to keep fit
■ ask whether someone has hobbies
■ say what your hobbies are

Incoko

During the lunch break Peter and Themba walk around the cricket ground where several mini-cricket matches are on the go and, among other things, talk about the way cricket has become so popular throughout the whole country.

UThemba	Kuhle kakhulu ukubona umdla kangaka kwiqakamba kule mihla. Jonga bonke aba **Makhaya Ntini** basakhulayo bedlala iqakamba!
UPeter	Inene. Kule mihla naphina apho ujonga khona, kukho amakhwenkwe adlala iqakamba. Wena Themba, wawuyidlala iqakamba ngeentsuku zakho usesesikolweni?
UThemba	Ewe, ndandithanda kakhulu ukudlala iqakamba. Ndandingumgcini-pali. Ndingumbethi kanjalo. Inene, ndandivula amangeno!
UPeter	Nyhani!
UThemba	Wena, mfondini, wawudlala eyiphi imidlalo?
UPeter	Heke, ndandidlala intenetya nombhoxo ngeentsuku zam. Ngelishwa, yophuka ingalo yam ndisadlala kwi-under 15. Emva koko zange ndiphinde ndidlale mbhoxo kwakhona.
UThemba	Wawudlala ndawoni?

(Courtesy United Cricket Board of South Africa)

UPeter	Ndandisisikramhafu. Nangona ndandingadlali qakamba ndithanda kakhulu ukuyibukela ngakumbi xa sidlala namaqela aphesheya. Wena, wawuwudlala umbhoxo okanye ibhola ekhatywayo?
UThemba	Ndandidlala umbhoxo.
UPeter	Kweyiphi indawo?
UThemba	Ndandiyindoda yesibhozo.
UPeter	Kunjani ngebhola ekhatywayo? Wawuyidlala?
UThemba	Ewe, ndandiyidlala kodwa ndandikhetha umbhoxo.
UPeter	Uyayibona phofu indlela umdlalo onamandla ngayo okumanya isizwe!
UThemba	Unyanisile. Khumbula ukuxhaswa kwamaBhokobhoko sisizwe sonke ngexesha lomdlalo wamanqam! Ngubani ongalibala ukuculwa kukaTshotsholoza ngelizwi elinye ngumntu wonke!
UPeter	Inene, ndiqinisekile ukuba ukucula kwesihlwele kwawanika umoya ukuze aphumelele amaBhokobhoko!
UThemba	Yho! Ingubani ongalibala igugu ebusweni bukaMongameli Mandela enxiba ijezi kaNo. 6 ephethe indebe beyithe *qhiwu* phezulu noFrancois Pienaar.*
UPeter	Ne**Bafana Bafana** yafumana kwa enjalo inkxaso, yaphumelela kwiAfrican Cup of Nations. Kanene, wenza luthambo luni kule mihla ukuzigcina uphilile?

Bafana Bafana winning the World Cup of Nations in 1996
(*Bona*, March 1996. Photos by Jacob Morake and Southlight)

UThemba   E-e ndiyazama ukubaleka kathathu ngeveki kwaye ndidlala isikhwashi *rhoqo*. Wena, mfondini?

UPeter   Mna, ndithanda ukukhwela ibhayisekile kwaye ndiyazama nokunyuka intaba ngeeCawa. Kodwa ngamanye amaxesha kunzima ukufumana ithuba lokwenza loo nto kuba umsetyenzana wam wokuzonwabisa kukuchwela.

UThemba   Owam kukufota, *qha* ke. Kodwa ke, liphi ixesha?

The cricketers come back on to the field after the lunch break.

UPeter   Jonga, abadlali babuyile; isidlo sasemini siphelile. Umdlalo uza kuqala ngoku. Masibuyele kwizihlalo zethu!

*Although President Mandela never played rugby, his interest in the game goes back to his youth. He remembers the playing days of the former Transkei homeland leader KD Matanzima with a chuckle: 'When he was tackled, the spectators would call out "help the son of a chief"' (*Cape Times* 16/3/1998. Article by Roger Friedman and Benny Gool.)

Isigama

kuhle	it's lovely
iqakamba	cricket
basakhulayo	budding (lit. still growing)
be_dlala	play_ing_
naphina	everywhere
wawudlala ...?	did you play...?
iintsuku	days
usesesikolweni	you still being at school
ndandithanda	I loved, liked
umgcini-pali	wicketkeeper
umbethi	batsman
amangeno	innings
nyhani!	really!
intenetya	tennis
umbhoxo	rugby
-ophuka	be broken
zange ndiphinde	I never again
ndawoni?	what position?
isikramhafu	scrumhalf
nangona	although
ndandingadlali	I didn't play
amaqela aphesheya	overseas teams
ibhola ekha_ty_wayo	soccer (lit. ball which is kicked < -kha_ba_ = kick)
indoda yesibhozo	8th man
phofu	in fact
-namandla	has the power
ngayo	by it
okumanya	of uniting
isizwe	nation

umdlalo wamanqam	final (game)
ukuxhaswa	support
isihlwele	crowd
kwawanika umoya	give them the impetus (lit. spirit)
igugu	pride
enxiba	wearing
ijezi	jersey
indebe (half split calabash)	trophy
beyithe *qhiwu*	*holding up high*
kwa	also, even
inkxaso	support
luthambo luni?	what sort of exercise?
-zigcina -philile	keep oneself fit
-baleka	run
isikwashi	squash
rhoqo	regularly
-khwela	ride
ibhayisekike	bicycle
-nyuka	climb
intaba	mountain
-chwela	do woodwork
umsetyenzana wokuzonwabisa	hobby (lit. a little job of making oneself happy
owam	mine
-fota	take photographs
qha ke	that's it
kodwa ke	but then
liphi ixesha?	where's the time?
-buya	return (_from_)
isidlo sasemini	lunch
-buy_ela_	return _to_
izihlalo	seats

(Sunday Times 23/11/1997,
Picture Thomas Turck Courtesy
Touchline Photo)

In 1997 a young man from **Mdingi**,
a village 15 km from King William's
Town made cricketing history by
being the first Xhosa-speaking
cricketer to be selected to represent
South Africa. In 1990 the skinny 14
year old was first spotted by Border
Cricket Development officer
Raymond Maloyi.

Makhaya Ntini was 'discovered' and
has not looked back since.

He represented Border U-15a against
a touring England team and was
considered the best fast bowler the
English team had faced. While at
school at Dale College he was chosen
for South Africa U19 to tour England
where he played at the hallowed
MCC! He also toured Australia with
the Dale College touring team. He
showed that he was not only a very
talented fast bowler but that he was
no slouch with the bat scoring 102 to
add to his bowling performance of 5
wickets for 50!

In 1998 in his debut for South Africa
against New Zealand he took 2
wickets for 30 runs.

His interest in cricket was
undoubtedly fostered by his late
father who played at club cricket
level while his uncle Lungile
Makhulu still plays in the *'Amacala
Egusha'* competition.

Cultural background

'The uncles greeted each other tumultuously. Apart from blood links
they had other ties. They had taught at Lovedale together before I
was born. In family albums I had poured over pictures of such things
as the staff cricket team in which they had both played. All my life
the men in my family were cricket mad; when they 'rooted for South
Africa' in Test Matches abroad and for provincial teams at home and
followed their fortunes in newspapers and on radio despite the
policy of apartheid in sport.' (**Noni Jabavu** *The Ochre People –
Scenes from a South African Life*, **John Murray, London, 1963**)

Tshotsholoza

(onomatopoeic – the sound of a steam train)

'Tshotsholoza! Tshotsholoza!
kwezo ntaba Stimela siphum' eRhodezhiya
Wen' uyabaleka kwezo ntaba
Wen' uyabaleka!
Stimela siphum' eRhodezhiya.'

[This is often sung by workers to give each other encouragement, hence its adoption as the unofficial anthem when *AmaBhokobhoko* needed that little extra something to win the rugby World Cup in 1995.]

Tshotsholoza, a road menders' ditty or work-song, is a popular 'train song' of which there is a whole repertoire based on the theme of railway travel. It imitated the sound of a steam engine pulling out of a station [...], and as it gathers speed and settled into a regular rhythm, the voices combine in four parts accompanied by tremendous thumps of feet stressing the beat: '*STIMela siphum' eRHODe-zhIYA!*' [...] The voices blended together exhorting the engine in the vocative, '*WEN' uya baLEka*', inflections that praised the locomotive's magnificent performance on that two-thousand mile journey across tawny *veld*, through *mopani* forest, gradations of plateaux, karoo, mountains, valleys until the coast is reached.

(Noni Jabavu, *The Ochre People*)

? *How to ...*

Ask about someone's past sporting involvement

Wawudlala *eyi***phi** *imi***dlalo** nge**entsuku** zakho u**se**se**sikolw**eni?
Wawudlala *eyi***phi** *imi***dlalo** nge**entsuku** zakho u**se**se**yunivesithi**?
Wawudlala **ndawoni**?

Respond to questions about your past sporting involvement

Ndandidlala:
  *i*qakamba
  *in*tenetya
  *um*bhoxo
  *isi*kwashi
  *i*bhola *e*kha*t*y*wa*yo
  *i*hoki
  *i*bhola yo*m*nyazi (netball)

ngee*n*tsuku zam ndis*es*esi*ko*lwen*i* / ndis*es*eyunivesithi.

Ndandidlala *isi*kramhafu / *in*doda yesibhozo / *i*phika (wing).

Ask about present sporting involvement

Uyadlala?
Udlala ntoni?
Udlala phi?
Udlala kw*eli*phi *i*qela?
Uqeqesha phi?
Uqeqesh*wa ng*ubani?

Respond to questions about your present sporting involvement

Ndidlala *i*qakamba / *in*tenetya / *um*bhoxo / *isi*kwashi / *i*bhola *e*kha*t*y*wa*yo / *i*hoki / *i*bhola yo*m*nyazi.
*An*di*dlali *m*dlalo.
*An*disadlali *m*dlalo.
*An*di*nalo *i*xesha lokudlala *i*midlalo.

Ask what someone does to keet fit

Wenza *lu*thambo *lu*ni ukuz*i*gcina uphil*ile*? (see **Unit 15.6**)

Say what you do to keep fit

Ndiyabaleka.	I run.
Ndiyaqubha.	I swim.
Ndiyahamba-hamba.	I walk.
Ndinyuka intaba / entabeni.	I do mountain climbing.
Ndikhwela ibhayisekile.	I cycle.
Ndikhwela *ama*hashe.	I do horse riding.
Ndiyadanisa.	I do ballroom dancing.
Ndiyaxhentsa.	I do traditional dancing.

Ask whether someone has hobbies

Una*yo imise*ty*enzana* yoku*z*onwabisa?

Say what your hobbies are

Ndiyachwela.	I do woodwork.
Ndiyafota.	I do photography.
Ndiya*kuthanda uku*funda.	I like reading.
Ndicula *kwi*kwayari.	I sing in a choir.
Ndiyathunga.	I sew.
Ndiyanitha.	I knit.
Ndiyazoba.	I paint.
Ndisebenza *e*gad*ini*.	I garden.
Ndiya*kuthanda uku*loba.	I like fishing.
Ndenza *izi*tya neembiza ngodongwe.	I do pottery.
Ndiqokelela *izi*tampu.	I collect stamps.
Ndiyaluka.	I do weaving.

Cultural background

Ukuxhentsa

*Um*xhentso is a traditional Xhosa dance consisting of rhythmic movements, stamping feet and various gestures accompanied by the singing and clapping of women and girls.

This dance is performed by women and men at beer drinking, by men at a wedding (*um*dudo) and by a diviner while divining.

MULTI-CULTURAL COPS These South African Police Service members spend most of their spare time dancing the traditional way. They're trying to promote cultural diversity within their service.

(Courtesy *Cape Times* 17/5/1996. Picture Alan Taylor)

Izinto zokuhambisa ixesha (*pastimes)*

uku**bukela** *u*mabona-kude / *i*TV
uku**phulaphula** *um*culo (music) ngee**teyiphu** nangee**CD**
uku**phulaphula** *u*nomathotholo

The word *u*nomathotholo = 'radio' comes from the association between the disembodied voices which certain traditional healers who may have spirits manifest in themselves – voices, whistles, etc. (regarded as both rare and singular, and an honour from the ancestors).

OONOMATHOTHOLO

'Oonomathotholo bayeza kusasa bayeza. Bayeza ekuseni Bayeza!'	The witchdoctors are coming early in morning they are coming. They are coming early in the morning They are coming!

ⓞ *How it works*

1 *The participial*

The **participial** construction, similar to the English verbal '-**ing**' form (participle), usually denotes **two simultaneous actions**. Its use is more extensive in Xhosa than it is in English. As is the case with the passive construction, you must be familiar with the **participial** should you wish to read Xhosa texts. Many examples can be found in captions under photographs in newspapers and magazines:

Ekufikeni kwakhe
evela eLusuthu,
uPrince Charles wamkelwa
eMzantsi Afrika yiNkulumbuso
yaseGauteng. (On his arrival
(coming) from Lesotho, Prince
Charles was welcomed by the
Premier of Gauteng.)

UHarry noCharles
noSekela Mongameli,
bengena kwibala lemidlalo.
(Harry and Charles and the Deputy
President entering the stadium.)

UPrince Charles
encokola nosekela Mongameli
nenkosikazi yakhe. (Prince
Charles chatting with the
Deputy President and his wife.)

Usekela Mongameli,
ebulisa isihlwele ekufikeni
kwakhe kwibala lemidlalo.
(The Deputy President greeting
the crowd on his arrival
at the stadium.)

(**BONA**, February, 1998, p.44)

Xa amaqhawe edibana ...
uNaomi Campbell uthe kudibana
nobaw' uMadiba kufana
'nokunyathelaku kukhanya
kwelanga' (When the celebrities
met, Naomi Campbell said that
to meet with 'her father' Madiba
was like stepping into the
sunshine.)
(**BONA**, October, 1997, p.36)

Amadoda axhentse imini
yonke enik' imbeko inkokeli
yawo. (The men danced the
whole day giving respect to their
leader.)
(**BONA,** November, 1997, p.21)

From these captions you can see that the subject concords referring to Classes 1/1a; 2/2a and 6 are: '-**e**'; '-**be**' ; '**e**-' respectively. The subject concords referring to all the other classes are the same as the **short forms** of the **present tense indicative** (cf. **Unit 2.2**).

The **participial** can also be translated as follows:

Waqala ukudlala ibhola ekhatywayo eseneminyaka esibhozo.	He started to play soccer **from** the age of eight.
Ukhule enomdla kakhulu kumdlalo webhola ekhatywayo.	He grew up **with** a great interest in soccer.
Bancokole bebukela iqakamba.	They chatted **while** watching cricket.

Sometimes the **participial** is **not translated** in English:

Wazalwa ngo-1970 engumntwana wesithathu kusapho lwabantwana abahlanu.	He was born in 1970, (**being**) the third child in a family of five children.
Ufotwe ekunye nabanye abadlali beqela lakhe.	He was photographed (**being**) together with other players of his team.

Note: '-*si*-' is infixed between the subject concord and a **monosyllabic verb stem**, e.g. '-**ya**' = 'to **go to**':

Ndiqhwalela ndisiya.	I am limping go**ing** along.

'-*s*-' is infixed between the SC and a **vowel verb stem**, e.g. '-**enza**':

Ungalibali ke, esenza iBA nje, ubambe mibini imisebenzi.	Don't forget then she is do**ing** her BA while holding down two jobs.

Use of the participial form

After the **conjunction** '**xa**' = 'when' / 'whenever' / 'if':

Xa esitsho uthetha inyaniso.	Say**ing** so she tells the truth.

After the **interrogative** '**kutheni**' = 'why'? (cf. Unit 8.4):

Kutheni engandixelelanga?	**Why** did she not tell me?

It is used after certain **auxiliary verbs**, e.g. '**se- / sel- / sele-**' = 'already':

Ukhona?	Is he/she there?
Hayi, **sel'**emkile.	No, he/she has **already** left.

And also after '-**soloko**' = 'always':

Wa**soloko** **e**nqwenela ukudlala iqakamba njengomkhuluwa wakhe.	He **always** wanted to play cricket like his older brother.

The participial form is also used after the adverb of time '**kudala**' = long ago:

Kudala esemtsha wayedlala *ama***nqindi**.	**Long ago** when he was still young, he used to box. (lit. used to play **fists**)

As can be seen from these examples, the **participial** occurs in the present and past tenses, both positive and negative (infix '-**nga**-').

2 The continuous recent past tense

This frequently used past tense usually covers any **continued action** or **state** during the *recent past* and is formed with '-**be**' + the **participial**.

'-**be**' = 'was' / 'were' is the recent past tense of 'uku**ba**' = 'to **be**' (cf. **Unit 10.3**):

Ndi**be** ndidlala (very rarely used in everyday speech) = I **was** I play**ing**

shortened to → **B**endidlala = I **was** play**ing**

Subject concords of the continuous recent past tense	
Ubuphi izolo?	Where **were** you yesterday?
Beniphi izolo?	Where **were** you yesterday?
Bendidlala umbhoxo.	I **was** play**ing** rugby.
Besidlala umbhoxo.	We **were** play**ing** rugby.
Ubunjani umdlalo?	How **was** the game?
Ibinomdla imidlalo.	The games **were** interest**ing**.
Ebelapho* uThemba?	**Was** Themba there?
Bebelapho ooThemba?	**Were** Themba and co. there?
Belidlala njani iqela lakho?	How did your team play?
Ebedlala kakuhle amaqela omabini.	Both teams played well.
Besidlala njani isiskramhafu?	How did the scrumhalf play?
Bezidlala kakuhle iziskramhafu zozibini!	Both scrumhalves played well!

Beziziintshatsheli!	They **were** champions!
Belunzima ukhuphiswano olo!	It **was** a tough competition.
Bebukho ubuhlobo phakathi kwamaqela?	**Was** there camaraderie among the teams?
Ibinjani inxalenye yempela-veki?	How **was** the rest of your weekend?
Bekumnandi kakhulu!	It **was** very nice.
Bekuyimini enempumelelo kwiqela lethu.	It **was** a successful day for our team.

*You may find '**ube**-' used instead of '**ebe**-'.

From these examples you can see that:

1 In the unshaded examples 'be-' is simply prefixed to the subject concords. However, in the shaded examples where the **subject concords** consist of **a vowel only**, the subject concords and / or '**be**-' are slightly modified.

2 The **continuous recent past tense** is also used to describe an action or process taking place **at a certain point in time in the near past** where English would simply use the past tense:

Belidlala njani iqela lakho?   How **did** your team play (at the time)?

3 The **continuous recent past tense** is used not only with **verbs** but with **copulatives, interrogatives, locatives** and **descriptives** as well. These descriptives also include **stative verbs**:

Stative verbs **present tense**	**Stative verbs** **past tense**
Ndi**xakek**ile. I **am** busy.	**Be**ndi**xakek**ile. I **was** busy.
Si**thabathek**ile. We **are** impressed.	**Be**si**thabathek**ile. We **were** impressed.
Ndi**ngxam**ile. I **am** in a hurry.	**Be**ndi**ngxam**ile. I **was** in a hurry.
B**onwab**ile abaxhasi! The supporters **are** happy!	**Be**b**onwab**ile abaxhasi! The supporters **were** happy!

Note: As is the case with the **participial**, the **two infixes** '-*si*-' and '-*s*-' also occur in the **continuous recent past tense**.

'-*si*-' with **verbs of one syllable**:

Bebe_si_thini?   What **were** they saying?

'-*s*-' with **vowel verbs**:

Ubu_senza_ ntoni izolo?   What **were** you doing yesterday?

The **negative** of the **continuous past tense** is formed by:
infixing '-**nga**-' and changing the final vowel to '-**i**' with **consonant verbs**:

Bendi_nga_sebenzi.   I **wasn't** working.

Use '-**ng**-' and change the final vowel to '-**i**' with **vowel verbs**:

Bendi_ng_enzi nto izolo.   I **wasn't** doing anything yesterday.

Use '-**nga**-' and suffix '-**anga**' with a stative verb:

Bendi_nga_xakeke_nga_.   I **wasn't** busy.

Use '-**nge**-' with non-verbal predicates:

Ebeng_e_kho uThemba?   **Wasn't** Themba there?
Belung_e_nzima ukhuphiswano olo! **Wasn't** that a difficult competition!

3 The continuous remote past tense

This past tense usually covers any continued action or state during the *remote past*. It is frequently used in biographies and reports of past events. (cf. **Units 3.4** and **7.4**).

It is formed with: SC of remote past tense + '-**be**' or '-**ye**' + the **participial**

'-**be**' = 'was' / 'were' – the recent past tense of 'uku**ba**' = 'to **be**'
'-**ye**' = 'went' – the recent past tense of 'uku**ya**'   = 'to **go to**'

Ndabe ndidlala. I **used to** play (long ago). (lit. I **was** I̲ play**ing**)
shortened to: **Ndandi**dlala.

Waya edlala.   He **was** play**ing** (long ago)
shortened to: **Waye**dlala.

Note: As is the case with the continuous recent past tense, the full form is very rarely used in everyday speech.

This tense often has the connotation of '**used to**', which can be expressed explicitly by adding '-**kade**':

Ndandikade ndi**dlala**. = lit. I was **long ago** I playing.

Wawudlala ntoni ngelaa xesha?	What **were you** playing **at** that time?
Ndandidlala iqakamba.	**I was** playing cricket.
Ndandingum**gcini-pali**.	**I was** a wicket-keeper.
Nanidlala ntoni ngelaa xesha?	What **were you** playing at that time?
Sasidlala umbhoxo.	**We were** playing rugby.
Wayezigcina **e**philile ngokuhamba.	**He used to** keep himself fit by walking.
Babezigcina **be**philile ngokubaleka.	**They used to** keep themselves fit by running.
Wawunjani umdlalo wombhoxo ngelaa xesha?	What **was** the game of rugby like at that time?
Yayino**m**dla imidlalo.	**They were** interesting games.
Lalidlala njani iqela lakho?	How **did** your team **play**?
Ayelung**ile** amaqela ngelaa xesha.	The teams **were** good at that time.
Kwakumnandi ngoko.	It **was** (very) nice then.

As you can see from these examples, '-**be**' or '-**ye**' is omitted except for Classes 1/1a, 4, 6 and 9.

Note: As is the case with the **participial** and the **continuous recent past tense**, the infixes '-*si*-' / '-*s*-' also occur in the **continuous remote past tense** with **verbs** of **one syllable** and **vowel verbs** respectively, while '-**nga**-' is infixed in the negative.

How to apply it

1 Listen to the Xhosalised English words on tape and write down the English equivalents

(a) _____

(b) _____

(c) _____

(d) _____

(e) _____

(f) _____

(g) _____
(h) _____
(i) _____
(j) _____

2 Okunokwenziwa ngebhola

Unokuyikhaba.	You can kick it.
Unokuyibamba.	You can catch (hold) it.
Unokuyiphosa.	You can throw it.
Unokuyigqithisela.	You can pass it.
Unokuyibetha.	You can hit it.

Now instruct somebody to:

(a) kick it! _____
(b) catch (hold) it! _____
(c) throw it! _____
(d) pass it! _____
(e) hit it! _____

3 Complete the questions with the appropriate interrogative

(a) Uqala _____ umdlalo weqakamba?
(b) Kudlala ___ amaqela namhlanje?
(c) Ngu_____ usompempe?
(d) Ngu_____ ophume phambili?
(e) Umdlalo udlalwa _____?
(f) Kuphumelele _____?
(g) Kuphumelele _____ iqela?

4 Complete the statements

(a)	Ndi_____dlala iqakamba.	I **still** play cricket.
(b)	_____dlal_____ bhola ikhatywayo.	I **don't** play soccer.
(c)	___ndi____dlal___ ntenetya.	I **don't** play tennis **any longer**.
(d)	_____ndikade _____dlala intenetya.	I **used to** play tennis.
(e)	_____ ndiwudlal___ umbhoxo.	I **never** played rugby.

5 Sports preferences

You express your preferences for certain sports. Ask somebody why he/she prefers a certain sport:

(a) Andithandi mbhoxo. Ndiyacinga ukuba undlongo-ndlongo (*rough*) ungaba nengozi.
Why do <u>you</u> like rugby? _____

(b) Andithandi kuqubha. Ndiyawoyika amanzi.
Why do <u>you</u> like it? _____

(c) Ndithanda intenetya kakhulu.
Why don't <u>you</u> like it? _____

(d) Ndithanda ukunyuka intaba kakhulu. Indalo (*nature*) intle gqitha!
Why don't <u>you</u> like it? _____

6 Past hobbies

Somebody tells you about past hobbies and you ask questions about them:

(a) Ndandikade ndithunga kakhulu.
What did you use to sew? _____

(b) Ndandikade ndinitha yonke imihla.
What did you use to knit? _____

(c) Ndandikade ndicula.
What did you use to sing? _____

(d) Ndandikade ndidanisa kakhulu.
Which dances? _____

(e) Ndandikade ndiloba kakhulu.
Where? _____

7 Meeting somebody for the first time

You meet someone for the first time. Ask them these questions:

(a) Do you like sport?
(b) Which team do you support?
(c) Do you watch sport on TV?
(d) Do you have hobbies?
(e) Do you like music?

8 Complete appropriately.

Fill in the correct subject concord to complete the following particulars about past soccer personalities:

(a) UJomo Sono _____mele ibhola yaseMzantsi-Afrika phesheya.
(b) UGeorge Thebe ____yintloko yeSANFA.
(c) UMbanya ____dlalela iMorokaSwallows.
(d) UKaizer Motaung ____ngomnye wabadlali abaphambili
     beOrlandoPirates.

9 Read the dialogue and answer the questions

USIPHO NOVUYANI BADIBANA BANCOKOLE

USipho	Molo, bhuti. Uzifihle phi? Ubuphi? Khange ndikubone ixesha elide.
UVuyani	Mfondini, bendigula inyanga yonke.
USipho	Awu! Ndilusizi. Ubhetele ngoku?
UVuyani	Ewe, ndiphilile kwakhona kangangokuba ndiqale ukuphangela kwakhona namhlanje. Ukhe wambona uNomsa kutshanje? (*recently*)
USipho	Hayi. Ndiva ukuba usesibhedlele.
UVuyani	Uphethwe yintoni?
USipho	Andiqinisekanga. Ingathi waba kwingozi. (*she was in an accident*)
UVuyani	Awu! Ingozi enjani?
USipho	Uyazi, uNomsa udla ngokubaleka. (*usually runs*) Ebeziqeqeshela iTwo Oceans. Ngoku, kuthiwa wawa. Wophuka umlenze.
UVuyani	Torhwana! Imbaleki enje ukuqaqamba. (*she's an outstanding athlete*) Ukwesiphi isibhedlele?
USipho	Andazi.
UVuyani	Ndiza kufowunela umyeni wakhe ukufumanisa (*find out about*) ngesibhedlele.

(a) USipho udibana nabani?
(b) Kutheni engambonanga uVuyani ixesha elide?
(c) Akasebenzanga ixesha elingakanani uVuyani?
(d) Abahlobo bathetha ngabani?

(e) UNomsa udla ngokwenza ntoni?

(f) Kutheni uNomsa esesibhedlele?

(g) Kutheni uVuyani efuna ukufowunela umyeni kaNomsa?

10 Fill in the appropriate missing elements

(a) UVuyani __funa ukufowunela umyeni __mhlobo ___khe.

(b) UVuyani __funa ukufowunela inkosikazi __mhlobo ___khe.

(c) UVuyani __funa ukufowunela abazali ___mhlobo ___khe.

11 Hobbies and pastimes

Read the following about hobbies and pastimes. Fill in the appropriate words and phrases from the list:

(a) inabo nobuchule bokwenza izinto ngezandla, (b) abadlala imidlalo, (c) Luphulaphula lubukele, (d) ukuphulaphula, (e) ubomi bangaphandle, (f) abaphila, ngomculo, (g) ukuqokelela, (h) nokubukela, (i) baqokelela and (j) ukufunda.

Bakho abantu abathanda (1) _____ izinto, umzekelo izitampu. Baneencwadi ekuthiwa zii-album, apho kukho izitampu ezininzi ezikhoyo ehlabathini. *(from all over the world).* Abantu abambalwa (2) _____ izinto zakudala, umzekelo ifanitsha *(furniture)* okanye imizobo *(paintings).*

Baninzi abantu abathanda (3) _____. Ngempela-veki banyuka iintaba, bayabaleka, bakhwela ibhayisekile, baqubha elwandle okanye emilanjeni okanye bayaloba kuba bathanda ukutya iintlanzi.

Inkoliso *(most)* yabantu (4) _____ umzekelo initha iijezi, yaluka imilengalenga yodonga, ithunga iilokhwe, iyachwela, yenza izitya ngodongwe okanye isebenza egadini.

Uninzi *(many)* lwabantu luthanda (5) _____kunomathotholo (6) _____ kumabona-kude imini yonke. (7) _____ _____ iindaba, umculo, imidlalo eqhutywayo, *(serials, lit. plays which are continued)* iifilim, imidlalo enjengombhoxo, iqakamba, isoka njalo, njalo.

Baninzi abantu (8) _____, ngakumbi isoka, umbhoxo, neqakamba ezithandwa kakhulu.

Abanye abantu bathanda (9) _____ amaphephandaba neencwadi.
Bathenga iincwadi okanye baboleka kwithala leencwadi *(from the library)*.

CAPE TOWN CITY LIBRARIES

The holder of this card is responsible for items issued on it.
Loss of this card must be reported immediately.

KAAPSE STADSBIBLIOTEKE

Houer van hierdie kaartjie is verantwoordelik vir items hierop
uitgeleen. Meld verlies van hierdie kaartjie sonder
versuim aan.

ITHALA LEENCWADI LESIXEKO SASEKAPA

Umnikazi weli cwecwe uyakuphendula ngazo zonke izinto
eziphume ngalo. Ukuba lithe lalahleka masaziswe kwangoko.

Kukho abantu (10) _____. Bacula ekwayarini, badlala
izikhaliso *(musical instruments)* umzekelo ipiyano okanye
bayadanisa.

13 | Masiye kulaa restyu intsha!
Let's go to that new restaurant!

In this Unit you will learn how to:

ask for a table for the appropriate number in your party

ask for a particular table

ask for a menu

ask what dishes are recommended

excuse yourself from the table

comment on your food

ask for the bill

Incoko

After the cricket, Peter and Themba, Jenny and Thandi go to a recently opened restaurant specialising in traditional Xhosa fare.

Umphathi-werestyu	Molweni. Namkelekile kwi*Ziko Lethu*. Siyavuya kakhulu ukunibona! Ninjani?
UThemba	Hayi, siphilile ngaphandle kokulamba! Ingaba unayo itafile yabantu abane?
Umphathi-werestyu	Ngokuqinisekileyo! Ndilandeleni.
UThandi	Ingaba singafumana itafile ngasefestileni?
Umphathi-werestyu	Nantsi. Injani le?
UThandi	Ilungile! Siyabulela.

They sit down.

Umphathi-werestyu	Nalu uluhlu lokutya.
UThemba	Ucebisa sithathe ntoni na? Yintoni isipeshali sanamhlanje?
Umphathi-werestyu	Heke, kwizidlo zokuqala sine*sonka samanzi*.

UJenny	Oo! loo nto indikhumbuza ubuntwana bam efama! Ndiyasithanda kakhulu *isonka samanzi*!
Umphathi-werestyu	Nyhani, Nkosikazi! Nisuka phi?
UJenny	Ndakhulela efama emaXhoseni.
Umphathi-werestyu	Ndawoni?
UJenny	NgaseKomani.
Umphathi-werestyu	Oo, andiwazi loo mhlaba. Mna ndikhulele phesheya kweNciba. Heke, mandibalule n*omphokoqo*, *umngqusho*, *umfino*, *imutton stew nolusu*.
UPeter	Ndilibele, yintoni *umphokoqo* kanye?
Umphathi-werestyu	Ngumgubo wombona ophekiweyo.
UPeter	Oo, ewe, ndiyakhumbula ngoku.
UJenny	Ngowuphi *umfino* wakho?
Umphathi-werestyu	Sisipinatshi netswele. Ndinganizisela into yokusela elixa nikhetha into yokutya? Kunjani ng*omqombothi*, *amarhewu* okanye *utywala*.
UThemba	Masingcamleni zonke! Sizisele nebhotile yewayini. Ungayivula?
Umphathi	Ngokuqinisekileyo!

The restaurant owner comes back with the open bottle of wine and asks whether they are ready to order.

Umphathi-werestyu	Nilungele uku-odola? Senikhethile?
UThemba	Hayi, asikakhethi. Sisacinga.
Umphathi-werestyu	Kulungile, ndiza kubuya emva kwexeshana.
UJenny	Kanene, Mnumzana, liphi igumbi lokuhlambela?
Umphathi-wesrestyu	Ndilandele, ndiza kukubonisa.
UJenny	Enkosi. Ndixoleleni kancinci.
Abanye	Kulungile.

When Jenny comes back they order and after a while their meal arrives.

Umphathi-werestyu	Naku ukutya!
UJenny	Mm, kunuka mnandi! Kujongeka mnandi kanjalo!
Umphathi-werestyu	Heke, ndiyathemba ukuba niza konwabela ukutya kwenu!

They finish the meal.

Umphathi-werestyu	Ingaba nitye kamnandi?
Abahlobo	Kakhulu!
UJenny	Ndingathanda ukufumana iresiphi yakho yo*mngqusho* ukuba asilohlebo?
Umphathi-werestyu	Ndiza kukucelela kumpheki.
UJenny	Ndiyabuyela.
Umphathi-werestyu	Heke, kunjani ngesimuncumuncu?
Abahlobo	Enkosi kakhulu kodwa sonke sanele!
UThemba	Singayifumana i-bill ngoku?
Umphathi-werestyu	*Utsho endodeni!*

Isigama

iziko	hearth
itafile	table
ngokuqinisekileyo	certainly
-landela	follow someone
uluhlu	menu
-cebisa	advise, recommend
isipeshali	speciality
-suka	come from (lit. to go out from)
phesheya	on the other side of / beyond
kweNciba	the Kei River, i.e. Transkei
-balula	select, pick out
umgubo	flour
umbona	maize
-phekiweyo	cooked
isipinatshi	spinach
itswele	onion
elixa	while
-ngcamla	taste
-odola	order
asikakhethi	we haven't chosen yet
-cinga	think
igumbi lokuhlambela	bathroom
ndixoleleni	would you excuse me?
-onwabela	enjoy something
asilohlebo	it isn't a secret
ihlebo	a secret
isimuncumuncu	dessert (lit. something sweet)
-anele / -onele	enough

IZIKO

ULUHLU LOKUTYA

Izidlo zokuqala

Inkozo zethanga ezojiwe
namandongomane

Isigezenga

Isonka samanzi

Umphokoqo

Isipheko Esikhulu

Idubhayi

Imithwane

Umngqusho

Umfino

Ithanga

Imifino

Ulusu

Umkhupha

Isimuncumuncu

Isaladi yeziqhamo
ne-ayisikhrim

Starters

Roasted pumpkin pips
and roasted groundnuts

Steamed green mealie balls

Soft freshly steamed bread

Crumbly mealie meal
porridge with sour milk

Main Course

Bean & Mealie Stew

Pumpkin Runner Stew

Samp & beans

Spinach & Onion Stew

Boiled Pumpkin

Stewed Greens

Tripe

Porridge of Maize & Beans
with Meat

Dessert

Fruit salad & ice cream

Cultural background

'I am very fond of this sour milk, which is known as *amasi* among the Xhosa people and is greatly prized as a healthy and nourishing food. It is very simple to make and merely involves letting the milk stand in the open air and curdle. It then becomes thick and sour rather like yogurt.'

(Nelson Rolihlahla Mandela, *Long walk to Freedom*, p. 266,
Randburg MacDonald Purnell, 1994)

Some traditional dishes (Izidlo zakwaNtu)

The most popular dish, in its numerous forms, is porridge: porridge made of sorghum – *ama*zimba – (indigenous to Africa) and maize / mealie – *u*mbona- (pl. *imi*mbona) which was introduced to Southern Africa via Western and Central Africa from South America by Portuguese navigators. The word 'mealie' is derived from the Portuguese word for sorghum, 'milho' (cf. Renata Coetzee, *Funa*, Heinemann, Johannesburg, p. 66).

*isi*dudu

thin mealie meal porridge (2,5 parts of water, 1 part of meal)

or

sweet milk porridge (1 part ground green mealies, 6 parts fresh sweet milk)

*um*qa

thick mealie meal porridge mixed with pumpkin (2 parts meal, 1 part water)

*um*phokoqo

crumbly mealie meal porridge (4 parts of meal, 1-2 parts of water)

CEREAL AND VEGETABLE MIXES

*um*qa we**thanga** / *in*gubela

1 medium pumpkin, 250 ml mealie meal

*um*xhaxha

5 parts pumpkin, 2 parts green mealies

*um*fino / *um*qubela / *isi*gibane

greens and mealie meal

LEGUME DISHES

*Um*ngqusho

samp (crushed maize) and beans

Umngqusho

Ingredients

125 g beans, soaked overnight
125 g samp, soaked overnight
500 g brisket, cut into cubes
1 onion, chopped
2 tomatoes, chopped
1 green pepper, chopped
salt, pepper, lemon juice to taste

Method

Cook the beans and samp for approx. 3 hours. Brown meat and onion, add salt, pepper and water to cover and simmer until almost done. Add onion, tomato and green pepper and simmer till the ingredients are cooked. Mix with the *um*ngqusho, add lemon juice to taste, heat through and serve.

(**Renata Coetzee**, Funa, p. 159)

'Ukutya kwethu thina maXhosa ngumbona esithi siwenze umngqusho, isidudu, isonka, amarhewu, utywala ukanti abakwaZulu bathanda irayisi kakhulu. [...] Kwezinye indawo yenziwa ngumgubo wamazimba.'

(**K.S. Bongela**; *IPhulo*, Maskew Miller Longman, 1977)

ooo0ooo

'This same veld offered grazing for our livestock and yielded *umfino*, wild spinach, to our mothers, in rich variety [. . .]

I do not remember ever being desperately hungry as a child. No. There was always more than enough to eat. New mealies cooked on the cob, dry mealies cooked with beans, mealies roasted, mealies stamped and broken into bits, mealies crushed and ground to powder; pumpkin as vegetable, pumpkin mixed with mealie-meal, other squash, eggs, fruit, sour milk, milk fresh foamy warm, straight from the udder; garden vegetable, wild vegetable, *amazimba*, and a host of other delectable eatables. Such variety; such ready availability.'

(**Sindiwe Magona**, *To My Children's Children*,
David Philip Publishers, 1990)

? How to ...

Ask for a table for the appropriate number in your party

Unayo *i*tafile ya*ba*ntu a*ba*bini / a*ba*thathu / a*ba*ne / a*ba*hlanu?
Singafumana *i*tafile ya*ba*ntu a*ba*ne?

Ask for a particular table

Singafumana *i*tafile ngas*e*festil*eni*?

Ask for a menu

Singafumana *ulu*hlu loku*tya* / *i*menyu?
Singafumana *ulu*hlu loku*sela*?

Ask what is recommended / special

Ubalula ntoni?
Ucebisa ntoni?
Ucebisa sikhethe ntoni na?
*Y*intoni *isi*peshali sanamhlanje?
Une*si*dlo *esi*sodwa namhlanje?

Excuse yourself from the table

*Ndi*xolele kancinci.

Comment on your food

Kujongeka mnandi.
Kunuka mnandi.
Kumnandi.

Ask for the bill

Singayi**fumana** *i*-bill?

🎞 How it works

1 Two nouns in possessive relationship in many words to do with food, having meals, etc.

*in*yama *ye*nkomo	beef (lit. **meat** *of* **cow**)
*in*yama *ye*gusha	mutton / lamb (lit. **meat** *of* **sheep**)
*in*yama *ye*nkuku	chicken (lit. **meat** *of* **chicken**)
*in*yama *ye*hagu	pork (lit. **meat** *of* **hog**)
*uku*tya *kwase*lwandle	sea food (lit. **food** *of* **the sea**)
*i*suphu *ye*nkuku	chicken soup
*i*suphu *ye*tumato	tomato soup
*i*sonka *sa*masi	cheese (lit. **bread** *of* **sour milk**)
*i*sidlo *sa*kusasa	breakfast (lit. **meal** *of* **early morning**)
*i*sidlo *sase*mini	lunch (lit. **meal** *of* **midday**)
*i*sidlo *sa*ngokuhlwa	dinner, supper (lit. **meal** *of* **the evening**)
*i*gumbi *lo*kutyela	dining room (lit. **room** *of* **eating (for)**)
(*in*dlu *yo*kutyela)	
*i*tafile *yo*kutyela	dinner table
*i*laphu *le*tafile	tablecloth
*ulu*hlu *lwezi*selo	beverages
*ulu*hlu *lwe*wayini	wine list

2 More about verbal extensions

The causative infix '**-z-**' instead of '**-is-**' (cf. **Unit 4.6**) is used in the following verbs ending in '**-la**':

Ndiyakhumbu**la** ngoku.	I **remember** now.
I*ndi*khumbu**z**a ubuntwana bam.	It **reminds** *me* of my childhood. (lit. it **makes me remember**)
Khathale**la** impilo yakho.	**Care for** your health.
Musa uku*zi*khatha**z**a.	You must not **worry** (*yourself*).
Ndiza kuphum**la** ixeshana.	I'm going to **rest** for a while.
Ziphum**z**e ixeshana.	**Rest** (*yourself*) for a while.

The stative or neuter infix '-ek-'

This infix indicates a state or condition without referring to the agent causing that condition similar to the passive voice. The English equivalent would be '**be** (do) -**able**' or 'can **be**' (**done**):

Iyavul**ek**a le festile?	Is this window open**able**?
	Can this window **be** open**ed**?
Ifuman**ek**a lula inyama?	Is meat readily obtain**able**?

-thanda	love	-tya	eat
-thand**wa**	**be** lov**ed**	-ty**iw**a	**be** eat**en**
-thand**ek**a	**be** lov**able**	-ty**ek**a	**be** ed**ible**
-funda	read	-funa	need / want
-fund**wa**	**be** read	-fun**wa**	**be** want**ed**
-fund**ek**a	**be** leg**ible**	-fun**ek**a	**be** desir**able**

There are a number of verbal forms ending in -'**ek***ile*' which correspond to English 'to be' + adjectives (cf. **Unit 5.6**):

Ndiqinis**ek***ile*.	I am **certain**.
Ndixak**ek***ile*.	I am **busy**.
Sikhulul**ek***ile*.	We are **free**.
Kubalul**ek***ile*.	It is **important**.

In some instances, verbs with '-**ek** (*ile*)' or '-**w**-' seem to be interchangeable:

Kushiy**ek**a ukutya okuninzi.
Kushiy**w**e ukutya okuninzi.
(Much food is **left over**.)

'-jong**ek**a' < '-jonga' (< 'look') is literally translated as '**looked at as**':

Kujong**ek**a mnandi.

3 Infix -'ka'- with verb in the negative = 'not yet'

*Asi***ka**kheth*i*.	We have**n't** chosen **yet**.
*Andi***k**azi.	I do**n't** know **yet**.
*Asi*ty*i i*langa linge**katsh**on*i*.	We **don't** eat before sunset.
	(lit. before the sun has not **yet** gone down)
*Andi***ka***li*fuman*i i*xesha loku**phumla**.	I have *not* **yet** found time to **rest**.

'Ukuba *akukayi*
emaMpondomis*eni*
m**fundi**, *aku*k*a*wa**boni**
*ama***Afrikakazi** *ama***hle**.'
(A.C. Jordan)

If you **have** *not* <u>yet</u> been to the
land of the Mpondomise,
reader, you have **not** <u>yet</u> seen
beautiful African women.

☑ *How to apply it*

1 Give the negative

(a) Ukutya kumnandi.
(b) Ndinambitha (*enjoy*) ukutya.
(c) Isonka sinencasa.
(d) Ndithanda inyama.

2 Answer the question 'How are you?' in a typical Xhosa way

Remember, this involves saying something along the lines of '*I am
well except for ...*'.

(a) Ndiphilile ngaphandle _____ (being very hungry).
(b) _____ (being very thirsty).
(c) _____ (the work).
(d) _____ (the weather).
(e) _____ (too much studying).

3 Give the opposite description

(a) Imifuno mitsha kakhulu: _____
(b) Ii-apile zimuncu (sour): _____
(c) Isuphu inetyuwa kakhulu: _____
(d) Ndithanda isonka esimdaka: _____
(e) Ndikhetha ukusela iwayini ebomvu: _____
(f) Iitapile zishushu: _____

4 Ask

(a) Do you have a table for two? _____
(b) Do you have a table for three? _____
(c) Do you have a table for four? _____
(d) Do you have a table for five? _____

5 Ask the waiter

(a) whether you can sit outside _____

(b) to bring the menu _____

(c) whether you can order now _____

(d) whether you can have red wine _____

(e) whether you can have vegetables / fruit _____

6 Ask the waiter for something

(Start the sentence off by saying 'Ndingafumana':)

(a) another slice of bread _____

(b) another beer _____

(c) another fork _____

(d) another knife (imela) _____

(e) another spoon _____

(f) another teaspoon _____

(g) another plate (ipleyiti) _____

(h) another cup of tea _____

7 English equivalents

You know that 'igumbi lokutyela' means 'dining room'. Can you guess the English equivalent of:

(a) igumbi lokulala _____

(b) igumbi lokuhlala _____

(c) igumbi lokufundela _____

8 Match these Xhosalised words with the original Xhosa

1	ibhlakfesi	(a)	isonka samasi
2	ilantshi	(b)	uluhlu lokutya
3	idinala	(c)	indlu yangasese (lit. house of privacy)
4	imenyu	(d)	igumbi lokuhlambela
5	itshizi	(e)	isidlo sakusasa
6	ibhafrum	(f)	isidlo sangokuhlwa
7	ithoyilethi	(g)	isidlo sasemini

9 You are asked what you would like

(a) **for breakfast**. Say that you would like:
porridge; two slices of brown (lit. dark) bread; a soft-boiled
(-thambileyo) egg; butter and jam (ijam).

_____

_____

(b) **for lunch**. Say that you would like:
cold meat , salad (isaladi), a slice of white bread and a slice of
cheese.

_____

_____

(c) **for supper**. Say that you would like:
lamb, potatoes, vegetables, fruit.

_____

_____

10 List all the vegetables you will need to make the soup

Izithako zokupheka

500g yesuphu yenyama
  yenkomo
1 itswele elikhulu
3 iikomityi zeminqathe
1 ikomityi yeembotyi ezintsha
1 icephe letyuwa
½ itispuni yepepile
1 ikomityi yee-ertyisi

1 ikomityi yeembotyi zeswekile
1 itoti yesuphu yetumato okanye
  isuphu yemifuno
½ ikomityi yerhasi
intwana yetyuwa yegaliki
2 iitispuni zepasili
3 iitapile

| imifuno | vegetables | iimbotyi ezintsha | green beans | irhasi | barley |
| iminqathe | carrots | iiertyisi | peas | | |

11 Read the dialogue and answer the questions

Umncedisi   Molo, ndingakunceda ngantoni?
UThandi   Mm, iziqhamo zakho zijongeka zintle.
Umncedisi   Zitsha _krebhe_, Nkosikazi, ndiziphuthume ngokwam
          namhlanje ekuseni. Enye into, zitshiphu _bhe_!

UThandi	Ndiza kwenza isaladi yeziqhamo. Ndifuna ama-apile, amapere, ipayina, ii-orenji, iipesika neebhanana. Ezi bhanana ziseluhlaza. Unazo ezivuthiweyo?
UThandi	
Umncedisi	Nazi ezivuthiweyo, Nkosikazi.
UThandi	Enkosi. Iivatala zijongeka mnandi. Zidla malini?
Umncedisi	Zidla R7.00 Zimnandi zinamanzi kakhulu. Kunjani ngokungcamla?
UThandi	Enkosi. Ingantle loo nto. Mm, imnandi kakhulu. Ndiphe enkulu leya.
Umncedisi	Kunjani ngamakhiwane neediliya?
UThandi	Hayi, Mnumzana. Ezi ziqhamo zanele.
Umncedisi	Kulungile.

(a) Kutheni uThandi efuna ukuthenga iziqhamo?

(b) Uthenga eziphi iziqhamo?

(c) Zinjani iibhanana?

(d) Injani ivatala?

(e) Idla malini ivatala?

(f) UThandi akathengi ziphi ziqhamo?

iziqhamo	fruit	ipere (ama-)	pear
ivatala (ii-)	watermelon	-tsha *krebhe*	*very* fresh
i-apile (ama-)	apple	-ngokwam	myself
idiliya (ii-)	grape	-phuthuma	fetch
ikhiwane (ama-)	fig	-tshiphu *bhe*	*very* cheap
ipayina (ii-)	pineapple	-vuthiweyo	ripe
i-orenji (ii-)	orange	-dla malini?	cost how much?
ipesika (ii-)	peach	-namanzi	juicy

12 A friend is helping you prepare a meal. Tell her/him what to do:

(a) Please wash (-hlamba) the potatoes.

(b) Don't take the big potatoes, take the small ones.

(c) Peel (-chuba) two onions and an apple.

(d) Chop (-nqunqa) the onions and the pumpkin.

(e) Grate (-tshweza) the carrots.

(f) Wash the lettuce (iletisi) leaves and the tomatoes.

(g) Bring some dishes (izitya).

(h)   They are in the cupboard (ikhabhathi) above the sink (isinki).
(i)   Open the tin.
(j)   Open this one as well.
(k)   Please set (-lungisa) the table.

13 Writing an invitation

Try to write the appropriate invitation that would have elicited the following answer:

Nomsa othandekayo,

> Ndiyabulela kakhulu ngencwadi yakho nangokundimema.
> Kuza kuba mnandi ukutya isidlo sangokuhlwa nawe. Ndiyazi
> ukuba ungumpheki wenene ngakumbi kwizidlo zakwaNtu.

> Sobonana ngoMgqibelo ke. Undibulisele kubazali bakho.

> Bayeza na nabo ekhayeni lakho ngoMgqibelo?

> Ngolukhulu uthando Nomvuyo.

NEW AFRICAN CUISINE. Traditional dishes with a modern twist is what party people get when they hire the catering services of **Ubusuku Be-Afrika!** If you are planning a real African party, they will bring along a praise singer, sangoma, artists and a township band to dinner. *Cape Times*, 23/10/98.

14 | Ukuthenga impahla nezinto yinto zakwaNtu zesiNtu

Buying clothes and various African arts and crafts

In this unit you will learn how to:

marvel at something

discuss size

ask about colour preference

compliment someone on their appearance

discuss price

say something fits well

offer a discount

ask what payment is acceptable

make more comparisons

Incoko

Peter and Jenny want to buy some Xhosa handicrafts and traditional clothes.

UJenny	Tyhini! Khawujonge nje zonke ezi zinto zintle! Iinkukho ezolukiweyo, imilengalenga yodonga, izinto zodongwe, iingobozi nenye impahla. Kuza kuba nzima ukukhetha!
UMncedisi	Molweni, ndinganinceda?
UJenny	Inene, ivenkile yakho intle kakhulu!
	Ndiyazi, ndiza kuchitha imali eninzi namhlanje!
UMncedisi	Enkosi kakhulu. Ningathanda ukujonga kuqala?
UJenny	Ingantle loo.
UMncedisi	Ndibizeni ukuba nifuna uncedo okanye nifuna ukwazi nto.
UJenny	Kulungile, Nkosikazi. Mna, ndingathanda ukuqala ngokujonga iilokhwe nemibhinqo.
UPeter	Lo ngumlengalenga wodonga phaya koluya donga, mhle, Nkosikazi.
UMncedisi	Owuphi, Mnumzana?

UPeter	Lo ubonisa umfazi otshaya inqawa. Wenziwa phi?
UMncedisi	Wenziwa ngabafazi bale ndawo.
UPeter	Yimalini, nkosikazi?
UMncedisi	Ngelishwa le milengalenga yodonga idla imali eninzi kule mihla kuba kaloku yolukwe ngesandla yaye yeyoboya beseyibhokwe.
UPeter	Ndiyeva.

Jenny emerges from the changing room.

Umncedisi	Mm! Ufanelekile, Nkosikazi! Intle kakhulu loo lokhwe! Iyakufanela kunjalo nje!
UJenny	Ewe, kodwa ngathi inobuncinci. Nceda, Nkosikazi, ndiphathele enye enkulu kunale.
UMncedisi	Kulungile, ndiza kubona. Eyiphi isayizi?
UJenny	U36.
UMsebenzi	Ungathanda owuphi umbala?
UJenny	Yiza nelubhelu okanye ebomvu.

The assistant returns with a bigger size.

UMncedisi	Ngelishwa sinemhlophe nentsundu neluhlaza kuphela kwisayizi yakho, Nkosikazi.
UJenny	Kulungile ke, ndiza kulinganisa le intsundu.
UJenny	Heke, indilingana *twatse*! Ndiza kuyithenga! Idla malini, Nkosikazi?
UMncedisi	Ukuba uthenga ilokhwe nombhinqo ndingalihlisa ixabiso. Ziza kudla R225 zombini.
UJenny	Kulungile. Ndiza kuzithenga zombini kodwa andiqinisekanga ukuba ndinemali eyaneleyo. Uyalamkela ikhadi?
UMncedisi	Sukuxhala, Nkosikazi. Samkela imali, itsheki nekhadi.
UJenny	Kulungile kuba ndisafuna ukuthenga nezinye izinto njengezodongwe neengobozi, ngakumbi namaso.
UMncedisi	Utsho ukuthi izihombiso-mzimba ezenziwe ngeentsimbi. Amaso makhulu kuneentsimbi, Nkosikazi!
UJenny	Kakade! Ndilibele!
UMncedisi	Ufuna ntsimbi zini? Ezomqala okanye ezengalo? Uyazithanda zona ezamaqatha?
UJenny	Yho! Zonke zintle kakhulu! Kwakhona kuza kuba nzima kum ukukhetha! Jonga yonke le mibala ngemibala!
UMncedisi	Kulungile, Nkosikazi, thatha ixesha lakho!

Isigama

tyhini!	gosh!	ufanelekile	you look very smart
iinkukho	mats		(lit. it becomes you)
-olukiweyo	woven	iyakufanela	it suits you
imilengalenga	hangings	inobuncinci	it's small
udonga	wall	-phathela	bring (for)
izinto zodongwe	pottery	eyiphi isayizi?	which size?
	(lit.things of clay)	owuphi umbala?	which colour?
iingobozi	baskets	-linganisa	try on
nenye impahla	and other goods	lingana twatse	fit *perfectly*
-chitha	spend (also, waste)	-hlisa / -ehlisa	reduce
uncedo	help	ixabiso	price
iilokhwe	dresses	zombini	both
imibhinqo	skirts	-amkela	accept
owuphi?	which one?	itsheki	cheque
umfazi	woman	amaso	big beads
-tshaya	smoke	utsho ukuthi	you mean
inqawa	pipe	izihombiso-mzimba	jewellery made from
yimalini?	how much is it? (lit.	ezenziwe ngeentsimbi	beads
	it is what money?)	-khulu ku-	bigger than
-dla	cost (lit. eat)	iintsimbi	smaller beads
uboya	wool	ntsimbi zini?	what kind of beads
yeyoboya	it is of the wool	ezomqala (of the neck)	necklace
beseyibhokhwe	being of goats,	ezengalo (of the arm)	bracelet
	i.e. mohair	ezamaqatha (of the ankles)	anklets
ibhokhwe	goat		

How to ...

Marvel at something

Tyhini! **Khawu**jonge nje zonke *ezi zinto zintle*!
Jonga yonke *le mi*bala nge*mi*bala!

Discuss size

Eyiphi isayizi?
Ngathi inobuncinci / inobukhulu.
Ndiphathele enye enkulu kunale / enye encinci kunale.

Ask about colour preference

*Owu*phi *um*bala?
*Eli*phi *i*bala?

Compliment someone on their appearance

Ufanelek*ile*!
*In*tle kakhulu loo **lokhwe**! Iya*ku*fanela kunjalo nje!

Say something fits well

Ilingana *twatse* leyo!

Offer a discount

Ndinga*li*hlisa *i*xabiso.

Ask what payment is acceptable

Uya*l*amkela *i*khadi?

How it works

1 Superlative and comparison

In **Unit 9.4,** you were introduced to the **superlative pronoun**:

*o*yena *m*ntu *u*lungile*yo*	the **best** person
*e*lona xesha *li*lungile*yo*	the **best** time
*e*yona *n*to / *n*dawo *i*lungile*yo*	the **best** thing / place, etc.

Another way of expressing the **superlative** is by using **kuna- +** emphatic pronoun **+ -onke**:

Ukhuthele **kuna**bo **bonke**.	He / she is the **most diligent of** them **all**.
Intle le lokhwe **kuna**zo **zonke**.	This is the **nicest** dress **of** them **all**.

You can also express it with **ngaphezu kwa- + -onke**:

Ndithanda le milengalenga yodonga **ngaphezu kwe**nto **yonke**.	I like these wall hangings **best of all** (things).

You can make **comparisons** by using '**kuna-**' = ' ... **than**':

Ilokhwe ebomvu *in*kulu **kune**lokhwe emhlophe.	The red dress is **bigger than** the white one.
Loo lokhwe *in*kulu **kuna**le.	That dress is **bigger than** this.
Iingxowa yakho *in*kulu **kune**ngxowa yam.	Your bag is **bigger than** my bag.
Eyakho *in*kulu **kune**yam.	Yours is **bigger than** mine.
Wena unemali *e*ninzi **kuna**m.	You have **more** money **than** me (I do).
UJenny unemali *e*ninzi **kuno**Peter.	Jenny has **more** money **than** Peter.
Uchitha imali *e*ninzi **kuna**ye.	She spends **more** money **than** he does.

Another way of expressing comparison is by using '**ngaphezu kwa-**' = '**more** ... **than**':

Ilokhwe entsundu *i*dulu **ngaphezu kwe**lokhwe ebomvu.	The brown dress is **more expensive than** the red one.
UJenny uchithe imali eninzi **ngaphezu ko**Peter.	Jenny spends **more** money **than** Peter.

Sahamba **ngaphezu kwee**veki ezimbini.	We travelled for **more than** two weeks.

You can also use '**-ngcono kuna-**' = '**better than**':

Lo mgaqo u**ngcono kuna**lowo.	This road is **better than** that (road).

'**njenga-**' is used for an **equal** comparison '**as ... as**':

Ilokhwe ebomvu *i*dulu **njenge**mhlophe.	The red dress is **as expensive as** the white one.
Loo lokhwe *i*dulu **njenga**le.	That dress is **as expensive as** this (one).
Ixesha lam linexabiso **njenge**xesha lakho.	My time is **as** precious **as** your time.
Ixesha lam linexabiso **njenge**lakho.	My time is **as** precious **as yours**.
Unemali *e*ninzi **njenga**m.	You have **as much** money **as** me (I do).
UJenny unomsebenzi *om*ninzi **njengo**Peter.	Jenny has **as much** work **as** Peter.
Usebenza kakhulu **njenga**ye.	She works **as much as** he does.

To express '**a few more**' you can use '**-nye**':

Kufuneka ndithenge *ezi*nye *izi*pho.	I need to buy **a few more** gifts.

To express '**as soon as**' '**-kangangoko**' is used:

Yiza kamsinya **kangangoko** unakho.	Come **as soon as** you can.

2 *Various ways of expressing 'much'*

kakhulu (adverb)	**very / much / very much**
Ndiyayithanda **kakhulu**.	I like it **very much**.
gqitha	**very / too much / so**
Inencasa **gqitha**!	It's **too** delicious!
kangaka / kangako	**so much**
Hayi sukuthetha **kangaka**!	Don't talk **so much**!
kangangoko	**as much as**
Thenga **kangangoko** unakho	Buy **as much as** you can.

-ngakanani na?	**how much**?
Ufuna imali **engakanani**?	How **much** money do you need?
kangangokuba (conjunction)	**so much so that**
Usithetha njengomXhosa	She speaks it (Xhosa) like a Xhosa
isiXhosa **kangangokuba**	**so much so that** she teaches *it*.
uya*si*fundisa.	
-ninzi (adjective)	**much**
Ufuna imali e**ninzi**?	Do you need **much** money?

3 The Xhosa equivalent of English 'both' (of)

The corresponding forms for the 1st and 2nd person plural are:

so*ba*bini	**both** of us
no*ba*bini	**both** of you
bo*ba*bini	**both** of them

The corresponding forms for the noun classes (obviously only the plural classes) are:

yo*mi*bini i*mi*lengalenga	**both** curtains
o*ma*bini a*ma*cici	**both** earrings
zo*zi*bini i*za*ndla	**both** hands
zo*m*bini i*zi*nto	**both** things

Note: An expression often heard when saying thank you: Ndibamba nga*zo* zo*zi*bini. (lit. I hold with **both** (hands).)

From the last set of examples you will see that these forms consist of class concord + **o** + adjectival concord + numeral stem **-bini**:

s-	+	o-	+	*ba*-	+	-bini:	so*ba*bini
b-	+	o	+	*ba*-	+	-bini:	bo*ba*bini

To express, for example, 'the **three of us**, the **four of you**, the **five of them**', etc., **numeral stems 3–6** (adjectives) are used in the same way:

so*ba*thathu	the **three** of us	no*ba*ne	the **four** of you
bo*ba*hlanu	the **five** of them	o*ma*thandathu	the **six** of them
(*aba*ntwana)		(*ama*doda)	

4 More possessive adjectives

In **Unit 2.8**, you learnt that the **possessive adjectives** of the **1st** and **2nd persons** (s. and pl.), i.e. '**my**'; '**our**'; '**your**' **follow the nouns** to which they refer and consist of **two parts** (**possessive concord** representing '*of*' which changes according to the noun possessed and a **second element** which does not change):

*um*sebenzi *wa*m	*i*khaya *la*m	*i*mali *ya*m
*um*sebenzi *we*thu	*i*khaya *le*thu	*i*mali *ye*thu
*um*sebenzi *wa*kho	*i*khaya *la*kho	*i*mali *ya*kho
*um*sebenzi *we*nu	*i*khaya *le*nu	*i*mali *ye*nu

The formation of **possessive adjectives** of the **3rd person** (s. and pl.) '**his**'/ '**her**' '**its**' / '**their**' is quite simple when '**his**'/ '**her**' '**its**' refer to nouns of Classes **1/1a** and '**their**' refers to nouns of Classes **2/2a**:

'his / her / its'

*um*sebenzi *wa*khe	*i*khaya *la*khe	*ubu*so *ba*khe
(**her** work e.g. *um*ongikazi)	(**his** home e.g. *U*Themba)	(its face e.g. *u*nopopi)

'their'

Kulunge kakhulu ukufunda	It is very good to learn
iilwimi zabanye *aba*ntu	the languages of other **people**
kuba ngaloo ndlela	because in that way
umntu uzuza ulwazi	a person gains knowledge
ngemo-ntlalo *ya*bo*	of **their** way of life
nezithethe *za*bo* nokuba	and **their** customs and what
bangabantu abaluhlobo luni na.	sort of people they are.

*< emphatic pronoun '*bo*na' minus '**na**' referring to '*aba*ntu'.

→ cf. **Unit 9.3**.

However, when it comes to formulating the **possessive adjective** referring to nouns of **other classes** it is a little more challenging because of the many possible combinations of **possessive concord** and **emphatic pronoun**.

Do you remember the idiom '*I*ndlovu ayisindwa ng*um*boko *wa*yo'. (lit. The **elephant** is not burdened by **its** trunk) i.e. No-one ever finds his natural responsibilites too burdensome:

wa-	is the **possessive concord** of '*um*boko' (Class 3)
-*yo*	< **emphatic pronoun** referring to '*i*ndlovu' (Class 9)

5 Possessive pronouns 'mine', 'yours', etc.

The **possessive pronouns** are formed by prefixing *a-*, *e-* or *o-* to the **possessive adjectives** (cf. Unit 2.8):

Mine	Yours	Ours	(Referring to)
*o*wam	*o*wakho	*o*wethu	(*u*nyana / *um*bhinqo)
*a*bam	*a*bakho	*a*bethu	(*aba*ntwana)
*e*yam	*e*yam	*e*yethu	(*imi*bhinqo)
*e*lam	*e*lakho	*e*lethu	(*i*khadi)
*a*wam	*a*wakho	*a*wethu	(*ama*khadi)
*e*sam	*e*sakho	*e*sethu	(*isa*ndla)
*e*zam	*e*zakho	*e*zethu	(*iza*ndla)
*e*yam	*e*yakho	*e*yethu	(*i*lokhwe)
*e*zam	*e*zakho	*e*zethu	(*ii*lokhwe)

In the same way you can form:

*o*wenu	yours (pl.)
*o*wakhe	his / hers
*o*wabo	theirs

6 More about ideophones (izifanekisozwi)

You were first introduced to this distinctive feature of the Xhosa language in Unit 5. **Ideophones** occur not only in the spoken but also in the written language. They can be used to emphasise intensity of colour and are often onomatopoeic to indicate movement, action, state, sound, etc. They are mainly used with the verb 'uku**thi**' which has no meaning of its own but simply marks the mood (i.e. indicative, imperative, subjunctive, participial), tense, person, class, number, positive or negative of the predicate, while the **ideophone** carries the **meaning**:

uku**thi** *tu*	be silent	Yi**thi** *tu*!
uku**thi** *shwaka*	disappear	Ilanga li**the** *shwaka*!
uku**thi** *cwaka*	calm down	Umoya wa**thi** *cwaka*.
uku**thi** *thu*	appear suddenly	Kwa**thi** *thu* amafu.
uku**thi** *hlasi*	grab	Wajika wam**thi** *hlasi*.
uku**thi** *vu*	sit down	Ndixakeke andinaxesha lo̱ku**thi** *vu*.
uku**thi** *ncwaba*	lie very still	Lala u**thi** *ncwaba*.

Ideophones also occur with other verbs in which case the verb retains its original meaning while the **ideophone** functions as an **adverb**:

-**bheka** *ngqo*	go straight	**Bheka** *ngqo* endleleni.
-**buya** *ngqo*	come straight back	*Aba***buya***nga ngqo.*
-**thetha** *ngqo*	talk straight out	**Thetha**ni *ngqo.*
-**ma** *nkqo*	stand up straight	*Yi***ma** *nkqo*!
-**funda** *nkqi*	learn quickly	Abantwana ba**funda** *nkqi.*
-**lala** *yoyi*	fall fast asleep	**Walala** *yoyi.*
-**phila** *qete*	completely well	Ndi**phile** *qete* ngoku.

Ideophones also occur with **descriptives** other than colours:

Iziqhamo zi**tsha** *krebhe*!
Iziqhamo zi**tshiphu** *bhe*!

→ cf. **Unit 13**.

Some **ideophones** function as adverbs:

gqitha	very / too much	*In***tle** *qgitha* le lokhwe!
mpela	at all	*Andi***phila***nga mpela.*
qha	only	Ndifuna ilokhwe **enye** *qha.*
qho	continually	Imvula i**na** *qho* namhlanje.
tu	at all	*Andi***lala***nga tu* phezolo (last night).
	absolutely	Kuthe *cwaka tu.*
		(It is *absolutely* silent.)
	completely	I-emele i**zele** ithi *tu* ngamanzi.
		(The bucket is *completely* full of water.)

Another **ideophone** for expressing 'completely' is '**s***hici*' used mostly in the sense of 'to forget *completely*':

Ithe *shici* kum.	I had *completely* forgotten.
Enkosi ngoku*ndi***khumbuza** sendi**libele** *shici.*	Thanks for **reminding** *me*, I had *completely* **forgotten**.

Ideophones can be used in many contexts to express:

temperature

futhu	very warm / excited
Lithi *futhu* kwelanga!	It is very *warm!*
ceke	icy (cold)
La manzi a**banda** *ceke*!	This water is *icy!*

state of mind

nqa	astonishment
Ndithe *nqa*!	I was *astonished*!
qabu	be relieved
Ndithe *qabu*!	I was very *relieved*!

sudden appearance / disappearance

gqi	sudden appearance
Uthe *gqi*!	He appeared *unexpectedly*!
shwaka	sudden disappearance
Ilanga lithe *shwaka*.	The sun *suddenly disappeared*.
thu	sudden appearance
Wathi *thu*!	He *suddenly appeared*!

positions and directions

zwi	stretched out
Naba *zwi*!	**Lie** *stretched out*!
nkqo	straight up
Yima *nkqo*!	**Stand** up *straight*!

The vividness of **ideophones** is well illustrated when you compare the following two sentences. They describe someone running into a house, grabbing a child, running out to a car, getting into it and leaving:

Wabaleka wangena endlwini wathatha umntwana waphuma ebaleka wangena emotweni wahamba.	Wabaleka *dyulukudu* endlwini, *hlasi* umntwana, *gqi* phandle, *ngqe*, *khatha* emotweni, *watsala*!

Some **ideophones** taken from **Sindiwe Magona's** autobiography *Kubantwana Babantwana Bam* (Cape Town, David Philip, 1995):

'UMhla weNkosi yayingumhla onocoselelo; uthe *tse* yaya ungakhululanga konke. (p.26) Thina babengazange baya *nkqu* kuTsolo.' (p.28)	The Day of the Lord was a careful day; *correct* (straight) and thoroughly ill at ease. We had not *even* been to Tsolo.
'Ngomhla weKrisimesi wonk' umntwana wayenxiba impahla yeKrisimesi, intsha *kraca* ...' (p.75)	On Christmas Day every child wore *brand* new 'Christmas clothes'.

'Wandithela *thsuphe* ubawo ngonobangela wengxaki endandikuyo.' (p. 8)

Father began *hinting* at what was at the root of my problem.

'*Hebhu hebhu* uThembeka, kungekudala *phekhethe*. [...] Naba bantwana basekhaya *yoyi, yoyi, yoyi, cum.*' (p. 236)

'Lee *thaa* kum ithamsanqa elikhulu elilelam.' (p. 237)

Thembeka *slowly dozed* off till finally she was out like a candle One by one, off, off, off they went until they too were out. My exceeding good fortune began to *dawn* on me. (lit. It *became clear* to me the great fortune which was mine.)

Cultural background

Beadwork

Beadwork is an integral part of traditional Nguni dress. Before the introduction of glass beads (probably first obtained from Portuguese explorers and traders) natural material was used (and still is): ostrich egg shells, seeds, horn, etc. Decorating with beads has a purpose far beyond mere ornamentation and 'dressing up'. It is also the outward sign of relationships between people, their status in society, their age group as well as the ritual status or spiritual power of the wearer. Messages were often transmitted through the use of various colours, colour combinations and motifs, (peculiar to different regions), e.g. the small rectangular 'love letters' (ama**phico**) made by teenage girls to indicate their love for a young man.

Traditionally, young girls and women made beadwork with a particular wearer in mind, but also for themselves and other women. Highly prized items of beadwork were handed down from mother to daughter or were made by mothers for daughters. Apart from necklaces, bracelets and anklets they also made aprons, collars, headbands and belts.

Necklaces with many strings of beads, izid**anga**, were usually worn by chiefs and senior men on ceremonial occasions. The beaded collar worn by Nelson Mandela in this famous picture and the one worn by US vice-president Al Gore when he was granted the honorary mayorship of Crossroads, Cape Town in June 1997, are called ama**thumbu** or ama**cangqi**.

Nelson Mandela
(Courtesy: Mayibuye Centre)

izidanga
(National Gallery)

Al Gore (Cape Times
09/06/98)

Much of the beadwork produced today caters for the tourist trade. This market has lead to changes in design, colours and colour combinations. 'The sale of beadwork to strangers has meant that a greater emphasis is placed on its commercial value than on its symbolic meaning.' (*Cape Times*, 15/01/97)

Beads are also an integral part of the traditional healer's dress.
(*Cape Angus*, 15/01/97)

How to apply it

1 Complete questions appropriately.

Complete the following questions which you might ask a shopkeeper by filling in the missing object concords:

(a) Ndinga____fumana phi amacici?

(b) Ndinga____fumana phi iingobozi?

(c) Ndinga____fumana phi imibhinqo?

(d) Uya____thengisa iminqwazi? (*hats*)

(e) Uya____thengisa izinxibo zakwaNtu?

2 A shop assistant needs to know 'which'

(a) Ufuna _____ umbala?
(b) Ufuna _____ isayizi?
(c) Ufuna _____ izihombiso-mzimba?
(d) Ufuna _____ ingobozi?
(e) Ufuna _____ amacici?

3 Read the text and answer the questions

EZAKWANTU
Nantoni na eyenziwe ngeentsimbi
Siziincutshe zezakwaNtu

Sithengisa iimpahla, oonopopi, iinqawa, iingxowa, imilengalenga yodonga, iimagi ezihonjiswe ngeentsimbi, amatsheyini eendondo, iintsimbi zomqala, ezengalo, ezamaqatha njalo, njalo.

Kuphela sifowunele: Siza kukwenzela zonke izinto ngakumbi ezeentsimbi okanye ke ngaphandle kweentsimbi!

(a) What kind of text is it?
(b) What is the active form of '-honjiswa'?
(c) Fill in the correct form of the possessives:
    ixabiso ____nopopi; ixabiso ___nqawa (pl.);
    ixabiso ____ngxowa
(d) There are two nouns adopted from English. What are they?

4 Read the dialogue and answer the questions

(You might need to consult the Xhosa–English vocabulary.)

A Molo, Nkosikazi. Uthengise izinxibo zakwaNtu na?
B Hayi, ndilusizi, ziphelile. Ndizithengise kakhulu. Zifunwa gqitha kule mihla.
A Uyazi uza kuzifumana nini kwakhona?
B Ngelishwa andazi. Mhlawumbi kule nyanga izayo.
A Andizi kuba kho kule nyanga izayo. Ndiza kubuyela apha kulo nyaka uzayo. Andihlali apha.
B Uvela phi?
A Ndivela eKapa.
B Oo ndiyabona. Mhlawumbi kukho enye into oyinqwenelayo? Sinazo izihombiso-mzimba ezihle zakwaNtu. Sikwanazo neentlobo ngeentlobo zeengobozi ezintle.
A Ndifuna iingobozi, enye enkulu nenye encinci noko.

B   Yiza ngapha ukhethe.

A   Ndiyasithanda kakhulu isihombo sale, kodwa inzima inkulu gqitha. Andinakuyiphatha.

B   Uyithanda njani le?

A   Intle. Ikhaphukhaphu. Ndifuna le. Yimalini?

B   Yi-R250.00.

A   Yhu, idulu kakhulu. Undibiza ixabiso eliqhelekileyo?

B   Kakade. Zonke izinto zidulu kule mihla.

A   Ungandibonisa le isekoneni. Ndiyayithanda. Ilula kunale. Isihombo sayo sihle kanjalo.

B   Le itshiphu kunale inzima.

A   Ndiza kuyithenga nale incinane. Ukuba ndithenga ezimbini uza kulihlisa ixabiso kancinci?

B   Ewe, Nkosikazi, ndiza kulihlisa nge 10%.

A   Ndiyabulela. Athini amaxabiso azo?

B   R280.00. Nantoni enye?

A   Hayi, kulungile.

B   Hamba kakuhle Nkosikazi. Sobonana kulo nyaka uzayo.

A   Kulungile.

(a)   Uvela phi umthengi?

(b)   Kutheni zingekho izinxibo zakwaNtu?

(c)   Umthengi uthenga ntoni endaweni yezinxibo?

(d)   Umthengisi ulihlisa ixabiso ngepesenti engakanani?

(e)   Umthengi ufuna ukubuyela nini evenkileni yezakwaNtu?

5   List the clothes usually worn by men and women

Use the following words: (a) ilokhwe, (b) iikawusi, (c) ibhatyi, (d) ibhatyi yemvula, (e) umnqwazi, (f) ihempe, (g) iqhina, (h) izihlangu, (i) ibhulukhwe,   (j) ibhlawuzi, (k) isuti and (i) iqhiya.

1   Anxiba iimpahla eziphi
     amadoda?

     _____

     _____

     _____

     _____

     _____

     _____

2   Kunxitywa ntoni ngabafazi?

      _____

      _____

      _____

      _____

      _____

6 Buying a skirt

Fill in the missing relative concords to describe what kind of skirt you want to buy:

(a) Ndifuna umbhinqo ____namabala _____ninzi.

(b) Ndithanda amabala ____qaqambileyo.

(c) Andithandi mibhinqo ____futshane gqitha.

(d) Zange ndithenge mbhinqo ____dulu gqitha, kodwa andithengi mibhinqa ____tshiphu kanjalo. Ndithanda iimpahla zeempawu _____ (-hle; of good quality).

7 What goes with what?

Fill in the relative concords:

(a) Ndicinga ukuba iblawuzi ___mhlophe ihamba kakuhle nombhinqo ____mnyama okanye ____luhlaza?

(b) Ucinga ukuba le lokhwe ____bomvu ihamba kakuhle nebhatyi ____ntsundu?

(c) Andicingi ukuba ezi zihlangu ____lubhelu ·___kho (your) ziyahamba nebhulukhwe _____pinki!

8 Use the comparative or superlative and say

(a) Ndithanda iintsimbi zomqala nga_____
    kwazo __onke izihombiso-mzimba.

(b) Ndicinga ukuba le yeyona ngobozi __lungileyo.

(c) Zihle ezi zihlangu kuna__ __onke.

(d) Le lokhwe __ntle __luhlaza njengengca idulu kuna__
    __luhlaza njengesibhakabhaka.

9 Characterise people by comparing them to certain animals

Use this list: ihlosi (leopard), inyosi (bee), ingonyama (lion), indlovu (elephant), undlebende < indlebe = ear + de = long (donkey).

(a) Unamandla kuna- _____

(b) Unamendu kuna- _____

(c) Unenkani kuna- _____

(d) Ukhuthele kuna- _____

(e) Unzima kuna- _____

10 Change the above comparisons in Exercise 9 using 'njenga-'

(a) _____

(b) _____

(c) _____

(d) _____

(e) _____

11 Read the text and answer the questions

ULindiwe Mabuza ngomnye (a) wamabhinqa anempumelelo (b) ebomini. Ungumyili nomthungi weempahla ophambili. Ungumnini we*Fashion Design Studio*. Igama lakhe laziwa gqitha kwezefashoni kweli (c) naphesheya. Ngo-1995 (d) wamenywa ukuba amele uMzantsi-Afrika Kwi'*Sun Europa Fashion Show*' eParis. Abantu baseFrance bazithanda gqitha iimpahla zakhe. Ungumlawuli nenqununu ye*Lindiwe Academy of Fashion Design*. Ufundisa abathungi abakhasayo (who are still novices Lit. still crawling). ULindiwe uthi (e) uyifumene impumelelo ngenxa yabantwana bakhe ebebesoloko bemkhuthaza. Ukholelwa ukuba 'Xa ufundisa umntwana, ufundisa ilizwe, xa utyebisa ibhinqa, utyebisa ihlabathi.'

(a) What is another word for *i*bhinqa? You should know its derivation.

(b) ebomini is a **locative**. What is the basic noun?

(c) Which word could you insert here?

(d) What is the **active** of this **passive** form?

(e) What is the **infinitive**?

(f) Find the four **copulative forms** and the three **object concords** in the text.

15 | Iinkathazo zohamho
Travel woes

In this Unit you will learn how to:

- ask for and give directions
- ask about and describe road conditions
- offer someone a lift
- express irritation at oneself
- express gratitude at someone's fortuitous arrival / presence
- say what is wrong with your car
- make arrangements for car repairs

Incoko

After making their purchases Jenny and Peter resume their journey but get lost and ask a passerby for directions.

UPeter	Molo tata, kunjani?
Umhambi	Molweni. Hayi, ndisatotoba, mfo wam!
UPeter	Ungasinceda, bawo? Silahlekile. Ingaba le yindlela eya engcwabeni lika**Sandile**?
Umhambi	Hayi, nihamba ngendlela engeyiyo.
UPeter	Siza kuyibamba phi ke ngoku eyiyo?
Umhambi	Buyani umva ngalo mgaqo nize ngawo. Nakufika kwisiphambuka sokuqala, nilandele indlela yasekhohlo. Emva koko, hambani *ngqo*. Emva kwekhilomitha niza kubona isalathiso esithi '*Engcwabeni likaSandile*'.
UPeter	Injani indlela? Yindlela yetha?
Umhambi	Hayi, yindlela yegrabile. Enye into, ilisongololo! Kukho enye indlela apha ngasekunene ekufutshane kunayo. Ngelishwa ayilunganga.
UPeter	Enkosi kakhulu, tata, usincedile. Kanene, uya phi, tata? Ingaba singakukhwelisa?
Umhambi	Hayi enkosi, ndilinde intombi yam apha.

They follow the shorter road and have a puncture!

UPeter	Nx! Ivili ngebe lingagqabhukanga ukuba bendithathe umgaqo wetha!
UJenny	Kusoloko kulula ukuqonda emva kwesithonga!

Luckily a passing motorist stops to give assistance.

Umqhubi	Molweni, yintoni umonakalo? Ndinganinceda?
UPeter	Molo Mnumzana. Ngathi ivili lam ligqabhukile. Ungandiboleka ujack? Ngelishwa owam uthe *shwaka!*
Umqhubi	Hayi, ilishwa! Linda umzuzwana, ndiza kumkhupha ujack ebhuthini. Linomoya ivili lolaleliso?
UPeter	Ngethamsanqa ndilimpompe izolo!

The good Samaritan helps Peter change the tyre.

UJenny	*Kwekhu, tshotsho ufike,* Mnumzana!
UPeter	Inene! Kambe ke, Mnumzana, ingaba ikhona igaraji ekufutshane? Ndiyoyika ngathi siza kuphelelwa yipetroli kamsinyane. Andiyiqondi le nto kuba ndiyizalise izolo itanki!
Umqhubi	Ingaba kukho umngxuma etankini? Uyazi, yenzeka lula loo nto ezindleleni zasemaphandleni! Masikhangele!
UPeter	Oo! ilishwa! Unyanisile! Inene, kukho umngxunyana ongange-ertyisi! Siza kuthini?
Umqhubi	Hayi, mfondini, sukuxhala. Ukuba unayo isepha, ndiza kuwuvingca. Emva koko, ungaqhuba uye egaraji.
UPeter	Igaraji ikude kangakanani?
Umqhubi	Ikufuphi, ndilandele.
UPeter	*Nangamso,* Mnumzana. Inene usincedile!

When they reach the garage Peter expresses his gratitude again. They exchange names and addresses before taking leave of each other. Peter then arranges for the petrol tank to be repaired.

Umkhandi	Molo, ndingakunceda ngantoni, Mnumzana?
UPeter	Molo, Mnumzana. Ngelishwa kukho umngxunyana kwitanki yepetroli yam. Ungayilungisa kwangoku?
Umkhandi	Eh, ndinomsebenzi omninzi kodwa ndiza kuzama.
UPeter	Oo ndiyabulela. Kuza kuthatha ixesha elingakanani ukwenza loo nto?
Umkhandi	Mm, mandibone, malunga neeyure ezimbini.

UPeter	Ungandixelela, uza kubiza malini lo msebenzi?
UMkhandi	Kunzima ukutsho kanye, Mnumzana. Malunga neR350
UPeter	Kulungile, Mnumzana. Masiyishiye ke imoto. Sobonana mva!

Isigama

-totoba	totter along	-boleka	borrow / also lend
-lahleka	be lost	ujack	jack
ingcwaba	grave	umzuzwana	moment
indlela engeyiyo	the wrong road (lit. the road which is not)	-khupha	take out
		ibhuthi	boot
-buya umva	turn back	ivili lolaleliso	spare wheel
umgaqo	road	*kwekhu, tshotsho ufike!*	*thank goodness you arrived*
nakufika	when you arrive at		
isiphambuka	intersection	-phelelwa	used up completely
isalathiso	sign	umngxu**ma**	hole
itha	tar	umngxu**ny**ana	small hole
igrabile	gravel	amaphandle	countryside, rural areas
ilisongololo	it's winding like a millipede	siza kuthini?	what are we going to do?
-khwelisa	give a lift	-ngange-ertyisi	like a pea
nx!	damn!	isepha	soap
-gqabhuka	burst	-vingca	close up
ukuqonda	to be wise	kangakanani?	how far?
emva kwesithonga	after an event	-lungisa	repair
isithonga	loud bang / report	-ngakanani?	how long?
umonakalo	trouble / damage	mva	later

❓ *How to ...*

Ask for and give directions

Ingaba le y*in*dlela *e*ya *e*_____?
Siza kuy*i*bamba phi ke *in*dlela *e*ya *e*_____?
*U*xolo ndinga*fikelela njani e*_____?

Hambani *ngqo*.
Nihamb*e* kw*isi*phambuka so*ku*qala, nilandel*e in*dlela yase**kunene**.
Buyani umva **nga**lo *m*gaqo.
Uphantse ufik*e*! (You're nearly there!)

Ask about and describe road conditions

Injani *in*dlela?

Ilung*ile*.
Im**bi**.
Ayi**lung***anga*.
*Yin*dlela yetha.
*Yin*dlela yegrabile.
*In*dlela i*li*songololo.
*Yin*dlela *e*kufutshane.
*Yin*dlela *e*kude kakhulu.

Offer someone a lift

Singa*ku*khwelisa?

Express irritation at oneself

Nx! Nxa!

Express gratitude at someone's fortuitous arrival/ presence

Kwekhu, tshotsho ufike!
Kwekhu, tshotsho ube kho!

Say what is wrong with your car

Ingathi kukho *um*ngxuma *e*tanki ye**petroli**.
*I*moto yam y**aphuk***ile*.
*I*moto yam i**xing***ile* (stuck).
*I*moto yam *ayiqhwith*i (won't start).
*I*moto yam i**funa** *ama*nzi.
*I*moto yam i**phelelwe** *yi***petroli**.
*Izi*bane *azi*sebenz*i*.
*I*bhetri yemoto yam i**flethi**.

Make arrangements about car repairs

Ungayi**lungisa** kwangoku?
Kuza ku**thatha** i*xesha* e*li*ngakanani ukuyi**lungisa**?
Ungayi**tsala** *i*moto yam? (tow)
Uza ku**dla malini** lo *m*sebenzi?
Uza ku**xabisa malini** lo *m*sebenzi?

How it works

1 Conditional constructions

Simple conditional clause:

You are already familiar with the **simple conditional clause** introduced by '**ukuba**' = 'if':

Siza konga (sokonga) ixesha
  ukuba sithatha lo mgaqo
  wegrabile.

We'll save time **if** we take this
  gravel road.

Unfulfilled past condition

In order to express '... **would** (**not**) **have** ..., **if** ...' you use **ngebe** (past tense of **nga-** and **ba-**) + **ukuba** followed by the **participial ending in -e**:

Ivili **ngebe** li**nga**gqabhuk**anga**
  ukuba b**e**ndithath**e** indlela yetha.

I **wouldn't have had** a puncture
  if I had taken the tar road.

Ngebe si**ahlek***ile* **ukuba**
  ubu**nga***si*bonis**anga** indlela.

We **would have** got lost **if**
  you had**n't** shown *us* the way.

These forms can be contracted to:

Ngeli**nga**gqabhuk**anga** . . .
Ngesi**ahlek***ile* . . .

2 Negative forms with '-nga-' and '-nge-'

Summary of where '**-nga-**' is used to form the **negative**:

Infinitive   Zama uku**nga**qhubi ebusuku. Try **not to drive** at night.

Subjunctive U**nga***wu*thathi *u*mgaqo wegrabile. You should **not** take the
                 gravel road.

Participial Wahamba e**nga**thathi ndlela yetha. (lit. He left **not** taking
                 the tar road.)

Relative   Nceda ulungise *izi***bane** *ezi***nga**sebenzi*yo*. Please repair the
                 lights that are **not** working.

→ See **Unit 6.3**, **Unit 6.5** and **Unit 7.3** for revision of **other negative constructions**.

The negative infix '**-nge-**' is used with **relative stems**:

*i*vili *eli*ngenamoya   (lit. wheel *that* has **no** pressure) = **flat** tyre
*in*dlela *e*ngeyiyo   (lit. the road *that* is **not** it) = **wrong** road

→ cf. **Unit 11.2** – copulative of shortened **emphatic pronoun**.

3   How to express: 'I am not', 'you are not', 'we are not', 'he / she is not', 'they are not' + noun (copulative)

The **negative** of the **copulative construction** is formed from the **negative SC** + copulative '**-ng-**' + <u>o</u> + **prefix minus initial vowel**:

*Andingo*mqhubi unamava.	I am <u>not</u> an experienced **driver**.
*Asingo*baqhubi banamava.	We are <u>not</u> experienced **drivers**.
*Akungo*mqhubi mbi.	You are <u>not</u> a bad **driver**.
*Aningo*baqhubi banamava.	You are <u>not</u> experienced **drivers**.
*Akango*mqhubi ulungileyo.	He /she is <u>not</u> a good **driver**.
*Abango*baqhubi balungileyo.	They are <u>not</u> good **drivers**.

'*Asi-*'can replace the negative SC in an impersonal statement:

*Asingo*mgaqo u*lungileyo*.	It *is not* a good road.
*Asiyo*migaqo i*lungileyo* .	They *are not* good roads.
*Asilo*cebo lihle elo.	It *is not* a good idea.
*Asiso*sibhedlele sikhulu.	It *is not* a big hospital.
*Asiyo*ndlela i*lungileyo*.	It *is not* a good road.

4   How to express 'it is not me' / 'you' / 'us', etc.

'**Asi**'- is also prefixed to the copulative of **emphatic pronouns** to form the negative (cf. **Unit 11.2**). Look at these positives and negatives:

*Ndi*m.	It is me.
*Asindi*m.	It *is not* me.
*Si*thi.	It *is* us.
*Asisi*thi.	It *is not* us.
*Ngu*we.	It *is* you (s.).
*Asingu*we.	It *is not* you (s.).

*Ni*ni.	It *is* **you**. (pl.)
*Asini*ni.	It *is not* **you**. (pl.)
*Ngu*ye. (*umqhubi*)	It *is* **him / her**.
*Asingu*ye.	It *is not* **him / her**.
*Nga*bo. (*abaqhubi*)	It *is* **them**.
*Asinga*bo.	It *is not* **them**.
*Nga*wo. (*umgaqo*)	It *is* **it**.
*Asinga*wo.	It *is not* **it**, etc.
*Yi*yo. (*indlela*)	It *is* **it**, etc.
*Asiyi*yo.	It *is not* **it**, etc.

5 Negative forms of descriptives

In **Unit 8.1**, you saw that simply prefixing the subject concord to the relative stem forms the predicate:

Ndilusizi, *i*moto yam **i**mdaka.   I **am** sorry, my car **is** dirty.

To form the negative, simply prefix the **negative subject concord**:

*Umgaqo awu*banzi.	The road *is not* **wide**.
*Imigaqo ayi*banzi.	The roads *are not* **wide**.
*Indlela ayi*banzi.	The road *is not* **wide**.
*Iindlela azi*banzi.	The roads *are not* **wide**.

Negative forms of **adjectival stems** (cf. **Unit 8.1**), however, must **infix** the **AC** between the **negative subject concord** and the **adjectival stem**:

*Um*gaqo *m*hle.	The road *is* **good**.
*Um*gaqo *awumu*hle.	The road *is not* **good**.
*Imi*gaqo *mi*tsha.	The roads *are* **new**.
*Imi*gaqo *ayimi*tsha.	The roads *are not* **new**.
*In*dlela *im*bi.	The road *is* **bad**.
*In*dlela *ayim*bi.	The road *is not* **bad**.
*Iin*dlela *zim*bi.	The roads *are* **bad**.
*Iin*dlela *azim*bi.	The roads *are not* **bad**.
*Is*alathiso *si*ncinci.	The sign *is* **small**.
*Is*alathiso *asisi*ncinci.	The sign *is not* **small**.

Note: In colloquial speech the **negative** form of descriptives (adjectives and relatives) will often be heard ending in '-anga':

*Um*gaqo *awum*hlanga.	The road *is not* **good**.
*Imi*gaqo *ayimi*tshanga.	The roads *are not* **new**.
*In*dlela *ayim*banga.	The road *is not* **bad**.
*Iin*dlela *azim*banga.	The roads *are not* **bad**.
*Aku*shushwanga namhlanje.	It *is not* **hot** today.

6 Interrogative adjective '-ni?' = 'of what sort / kind?'

This construction may be used with reference to new-born babies and animals to find out whether they are male or female:

Ufuna **m***ntwana* **mni?**   Inkwenkwe okanye intombazana?

Uthanda	*m*ntu	*m*ni?	Uthanda	*ba*ntu	*ba*ni?
Ukhetha	*m*sebenzi	*m*ni?	Ukhetha	*mi*funo	*mi*ni?
Ufuna	**phepha**	*li*ni?	Ufuna	*ma*so	*ma*ni?
Ukhetha	*si*qhamo	*si*ni?	Ufuna	*zi*qhamo	*zi*ni?
Ukhetha	*n*ja	ni?	Uthanda	*zi*ngobozi*	*zi*ni?
	Wenza	*lu*thambo* (exercise) *lu*ni?			
	Ukhetha	*bu*tywala* (alcohol) *bu*ni?			
	Ukhetha	*ku*tya	*ku*ni?		

As you can see the **initial vowel** of the **prefix** of the noun has been omitted and its corresponding adjectival concord is prefixed to '-**ni**'.

*****Note:** the reappearance of the consonant associated with nouns of **Class 10** (*z*), **Class 11** (*l*) and **Class 14** (*b*).

Note also: This occurs in the **locative** in **Classes 10** and **11**:

*ii*ntaba	> e*zi*ntabeni	*on / at* the **mountains**
*ii*ndlela	> e*zi*ndleleni	*on* the **roads**
*ii*ndawo	> e*zi*ndaweni	*at* **places**
*ii*nxweme	> e*zi*nxwemeni	*at* the **coasts**
*ii*ndonga	> e*zi*ndongeni	*at / on* the **walls**
*u*nxweme	> e*lu*nxwemeni	*at / on* the **coast**
*u*donga	> e*lu*dongeni	*at / on* the **wall**

7 Exclamations

There are a number of frequently used exclamations in Xhosa which add 'spice' to the language. Here are some examples:

Annoyance

I-i...! / ish!	Go away! You tire me out!
Nxa!	Damn!
Nx!	Damn!

Assertion

Nako ke!	There you are!

Comfort

Ngxesiii!	Let me kiss it better! (to a child)

Compassion

Mawo-o-o!	I'm sorry!
Yeha!	Oh dear!
Torho! / Torhwana	Shame! (cf. Afrikaans 'tog')

Congratulations

Halala!	Hurrah!
Huntshu!	Hurrah!

Emphatic affirmation

E-e!	Yes!
Hayi ke!	Sure!
Heke!	Well then!
Ngxatsho ke!	Excellent! / To the point!

Emphatic negation

Hayi bo!	No way!
Hayi khona!	Absolutely not!

Pain

Shu!	Ouch!

Regret

Owu!	Alas!
Ngxe!	Sorry!
Hayi ilishwa!	Oh dear!

Relief

Qabu!

Kwekhu, tshotsho ufike!

Surprise, astonishment

(Oo / Awu) Nkosi yam!	Dear Lord!
Yho! / Yhu!	Gee whizz!
Tyhini!	Gosh!
Tyho! Tyhu!	Good heavens!
Kwowu!	Oh!
Mawo!	My! / Wonderful!
Nyhani!	Really!
Kazi!	I wonder!

Warning

Heyi ... heyi ... heyi	(accompanying gesture of
(andifuni loo nto)	shaking one's finger at a person)

⁊ *How to apply it*

1 Match the road signs with the English equivalent

The equivalents are: (a) Dangerous curve, (b) Dead end, (c) Caution, (d) Road closed, (e) No overtaking, (f) Do not enter, (g) Roadworks ahead, (h) Road flooded, (i) Emergency exit and (j) Drive carefully.

1 Indlela iyaphela
2 Indlela ivaliwe
3 Indlela iyalungiswa phambili
4 Igophe eliyingozi
5 Qhuba kakuhle
6 Eyakuphuma ngesiquphe
7 Lumka
8 Ungangeni
9 Indlela igqunywe ngamanzi
10 Ungayigqithi enye imoto

2   Ask the condition of the road

(a) Is the road good? Ingaba _____

(b) Is the road safe? _____

(c) Is it a tar road? _____

(d) Is it a gravel road? _____

(e) Is the road still under construction?_____

(f) Is the road already open to traffic? Ingaba _____

    _____kwizithuthu?

3   You are lost in a town and ask a passerby for directions

(a) *Excuse me sir. Could you help me? I am lost.*
     Ufuna ukuya phi?

(b) *I want to go to a shop called Kwantu Crafts. Do you know it*?
     Ewe, ndiyayazi. Ikufutshane kakhulu xa ulapha. Ndiza
     kukucacisela indlela. Hamba *ngqo*. Ekoneni yokuqala ujike
     ngasekunene. Uza kudlula ezinye iivenkile. Ekoneni elandelayo
     ecaleni lasekhohlo uza kubona ivenkile yezaKwantu.
     Ungathanda ukuba ndikukhaphe?

(c) *No, thank you, I understand where to find the shop. It seems
     very near indeed. First I go straight, then right and then I must
     turn left.*
     Kulungile. Hamba kakuhle.

(d) *Thank you very much, sir. Goodbye.*

4   Complete the questions

(a) ___ma phi iiteksi?

(b) ___khona iibhasi ___ya eRhini?

(c) Kukho ibhasi __ya eRhini namhlanje?

(d) ___phi isikhululo ____bhasi?

(e) __ma phi ibhasi ___ya esitishini?

(f) Iiteksi ___nqabile na ku___ ndawo?

5   Ask

(a) ___khona _____ (a garage) endleleni?

(b) _____ _____ (a shop) endleleni?

(c) _____ isikhululo samapolisa endleleni?

6 Ask for the nearest

(a) shop   Indawoni _____ _kufutshane?
(b) hospital   Sindawoni _____ _kufutshane?
(c) police station   Sindawoni _____ _kufutshane?
(d) phone   Indawoni _____ _kufutshane?
(e) doctor   Undawoni _____ _kufutshane?
(f) petrol station   Indawoni _____ _kufutshane?
(g) place ('dorp')   Indawoni _____ _kufutshane?

7 Ask somebody

(a) to give you a lift   Unga_____?
(b) to help you   Unga_____?
(c) to lend you a jack   Unga_____?
(d) to show you the way to
     Grahamstown   Unga_____?

8 Tell the mechanic what's wrong with your car

(a) The lights are not working.   Izibane _____sebenzi.
(b) The hooter is not working.   Uphondo ____sebenzi.
(c) The handbrake is not working.   Ibhreki ___sandla ____sebenzi.
(d) The fan belt is broken.   Ifenibelti ____sebenzi.
(e) The windscreen wiper is   Isihlambi ___festile
     not working.   ____ngaphambili ____sebenzi.
(f) My left rear light is not working. Isibane sam ___ngasemva

     __sekhohlo ___sebenzi.

9 What can be wrong with your car?

(a) I have a flat tyre.   Ndin__vili _____ngen__moya.
(b) My right front tyre is flat.   __vili ___m ___ngaphambili
                                      __sekunene __flethi.
(c) My car has broken down.   Imoto __m __aphukile.
(d) My car is stuck.   Imoto __m __xingile.
(e) My car won't start.   Imoto __m ___qhwithi.
(f) It needs water.   __funa amanzi.
(g) It has run out of petrol.   __phelelwe ___petroli.
(h) My car battery is flat.   Ibhetri __moto __m __file.
(i) My car must be towed.   Kufuneka imoto __m _tsalwe.

10 What has been stolen?

(a) Imoto yam ___biwe.

(b) Ujack __m ___biwe.

(c) Ivili __m lolaleliso __biwe.

(d) Isipaji (wallet) __m __biwe.

(e) Ingxowa ___nkosikazi __m __biwe.

11 Read the dialogue and answer the questions

A Uxolo, Mnumzana, ungandixelela ukuba kukude kangakanani ukusuka apha ukuya eCala? Kukude kakhulu?

B Hayi, akukude. Kukufuphi.

A Ziikhilometha ezingaphi?

B Ndicinga ukuba malunga neekhilometha ezilishumi.

A Ingaba indlela intle?

B Ayimbi gqitha, kodwa ayintle kanjalo.

A Asiyondlela yetha?

B Hayi, asingomgaqo wetha, ngumgaqo wegrabile kodwa ngethamsanqa awumxinwa, ubanzi noko.

A Kulungile. Phambi kokuya eCala singathanda ukubuka idolophu yakho kancinci. Unokusixelela apho kukho indawo ekhuselekile yokumisa imoto?

B Ewe ikhona. Hamba *ngqo*, kwisiphambuka esilandelayo ujike ngasekhohlo uza kubona ibala lokupaka elikhulu elikhuselekileyo ecaleni lasekunene.

A Enkosi kakhulu, Mnumzana.

B Ndlela ntle.

(a) Umqhubi ufuna ukuya phi?

(b) Ziikhilomitha ezingaphi ukuya apho?

(c) Injani indlela?

(d) Yindlela ni?

(e) Kutheni umqhubi efuna indawo yokumisa imoto yakhe?

(f) Ufuna ukupaka imoto yakhe ndawoni?

16 | Umzila welifa likaXhosa
Xhosa heritage trail

In this Unit you will learn how to:

- ask about someone's holiday
- ask where someone went
- describe travel route
- express delight

Incoko

The Murrays discuss their recent trip with the Thamsanqas.

UThemba	Belinjani ikhefu lenu emaXhoseni? Nibe nohambo olumyoli?
UPeter	Belungummangaliso nangona besineenkathazo zemoto ezimbalwa kodwa ngethamsanqa sancedwa ngabantu abanobubele gqitha!
UThandi	Heke, ngesiqhelo kunjalo ke emaphandleni. Kanene, beniye phi kanye?
UJenny	Siluqale ukhenketho lwethu e**Peddie**. Ukususela kwiintsuku zam zokufunda isiXhosa eyunivesithi, soloko ndafuna ukutyelela iindawo zembali yamaXhosa eMpuma-Koloni. Kanene, yintoni 'iPeddie' ngesiXhosa? Ndilibele.
UThandi	Yi**Ngqushwa**, wethu!
UJenny	Oo, ewe, kanene. Heke, siye e**Ngqushwa** kuba besifuna ukubuka laa mthi wodumo – umthi wo*mqwashu*. Emva koko, sasinga e**Qonce** kwimyuziyam yeKaffrarian apho kukho khona inkitha yezinto zakwaNtu ezidala umdla kakhulu. Emva kwemini saya kwikhaya lika**Steve Biko**. Sabona kwanendawo apho wafihlwa kuyo.
UPeter	Ngemini elandelayo, yekoko ukusinga ku**Belekazana**; sihambe ngokugwegweleza sadlula ku**Qoboqobo** saya kutsho kummandla w**Amalinde**.

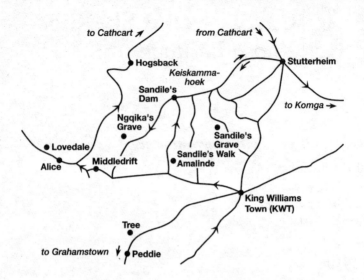

UThemba	Oo **Amalinde**! Niyazi, kulapho kwaliwa khona elinye lamadabi amabi kwimbali yamaXhosa.*
UJenny	Kakade! Lidabi elo elixelwa kumbongo kaJolobe '*UThuthula*', *omnye wemibongo yethu eyunivesithi.
UThemba	Wonke ummandla lowa ngasezintabeni z**Amathole** uzele ziindawo zembali yamaXhosa. Kukho iindawo ezininzi ezithiywe ngamakhosi ama**Rharhabe**.
UPeter	Unyanisile. Sidlule idama lika**Sandile** kwaye sibone nengcwaba lika**Ngqika** endleleni eya *e***Dikeni**.
UPeter	E**Dikeni** sibe nomdla kakhulu ukutyelela i**Lovedale College** ne**Yunivesithi yaseFort Hare** apho uNelson Mandela wayengumfundi khona kunye nezinye iinkokeli zanamhlanje.
UJenny	Mna, ndisand' ukufunda incwadi *The Ochre People* ebhalwe ngu**Noni Jabavu**. Ngoko ke bendifuna kakhulu ukufumana umzi kayise, u**Profesa Jabavu,** owayehlala e**Xesi** xa wayenguprofesa weelwimi zakwaNtu e**Fort Hare**. Ingaba nina nakhe nay*i*funda le ncwadi?
UThandi	Ewe. U**Noni Jabavu** ubhala kakuhle kakhulu, atsho ububone ubuhle balo mmandla. Enye into uzoba umfanekiso omhle

*See p.254 for historical context

ngemo-ntlalo nezithethe zamaXhosa ngaloo maxesha. Niyifundile kanjalo enye incwadi yakhe u*Drawn in Colour*?

UJenny   Ewe, andithi kanene waqala ngayo?

UThemba   Nawufumana ke umzi ka**Jabavu**?

UJenny   Hayi, ngelishwa asibanga nampumelelo!

UThandi   Nasinga phi emva koko?

UPeter   Sahlala ku**Belekazana** iintsuku ezimbalwa. Yho! Ubuhle baloo mmandla buqaqambile. Uxolo olulapho! Nokuzola! Amahlathi elo zwe neengxangxasi *ezixhomis' amehlo*, neentaka ezintlobo-ntlobo nentsholo yazo zizinto ezingummangaliso ukuzibona!

UThemba   *Bekuxhelw' eXhukwana* kuwe, Peter, wena mntu wendalo!

UPeter   Yitsho uphinde! Yiyo loo nto sigqibe sihlala phaya zonke ezo ntsuku.

UJenny   Indawo elandelayo esityelela kuyo ibiyi**Cumakala**. Besifuna ukubona ingcwaba lika**Sandile** kodwa salahleka sancama. Sathi masilande kumkhondo wakhe kodwa saphelelwa lixesha.

UPeter   Ngemini elandelayo, sasinga e**Mtata**. Endleleni, sicande amadlelo amahle, iinkomo neegusha zithe *gqa gqa gqa* emathambekeni ukudlula kooma**Qumrha**, nooma**Gcuwa**, nooma**Dytuwa**. Sinjani ukunqwenela ukutyelela i**Qunu** apho wazalelwa khona u**Nelson Mandela**. Ngelishwa, ikhaya elo lakhe lobuntwana alisekho kodwa sisekho sona isikolo sakhe.

UThemba	Nibe nalo ixesha lokuya elunxwemeni?
UPeter	Kakade! Sihlale e**Mzimvubu** iintsuku zantathu. Indalo apho! Iinduli ezihla ukuya elunxwemeni, amanqugwala namasimi ombona! Inene *ilizwe liyintombazana* kwelo!

Courtesy T.V. Bulpin

UThemba	Hayi, mfowethu, utsho ndanekhwele!
UJenny	Endleleni eya e**Mzimvubu** sidlule ivenkile yangaphandle yakudala e**Libode**. Yandikhumbuza isincoko sika**Jolobe** '*Ivenkile Yangaphandle*'. Kodwa eyona ndawo ebesifuna ukuya kuyo kuse**Cala**.
UThandi	Nibizwa yintoni e**Cala**?
UJenny	Besimenywe ngabahlobo bethu.
UThandi	Nenza ntoni ke apho?
UJenny	Sithabathe inxaxheba ebomini bemihla ngemihla. Yaye, ububele esibufumene kubantu balapho buyamangalisa. Ngorhatya singqonge umlilo siphulaphule iintsomi njengemihla yakudala!

Isigama

uhambo	trip	eXesi	at Middledrift
nangona	although	atsho ububone	so that you see
ummangaliso	a delight	imo-ntlalo	way of life
ububele	kindness	isithethe	custom
ukhenketho	trip	andithi kanene?	aren't I right
ukususela kwa-	since		in saying?
imbali	history	-qaqambile	stunning
udumo	fame	ukuzola	tranquillity
umthi womqwashu	milkwood tree	amahlathi elo zwe	indigenous forests
-singa e- / ku-	head for	ingxangxasi	waterfall
eQonce	to KWT	ezixhomis' amehlo	sight for sore eyes
imyuziyam	museum	izintlobo-ntlobo	different kinds
-fihlwa	be hidden,	intsholo	singing
	i.e. buried	-xhelw' eXhukwana*	be delighted
apha wafihlwa	where he	umntu wendalo	nature lover
	was buried	yitsho uphinde!	say that again!
kuyo	at it	eCumakala	at Stutterheim
yekoko ukusinga	and off we went	salahleka	we got lost
kuBelekazana	to Hogsback	sancama	we gave up
-gwegweleza	make a detour	sathi	we wanted
-dlula	pass	masilande	to follow
ummandla	region	umkhondo	track
idabi	battle	-canda	cut through
umbongo	poem	amadlelo	pastures
-zele + cop.	filled with	iinkomo	cattle
-thiywa	be named	iigusha	sheep
idama	dam	-thi gqa gqa gqa	dotted
eDikeni	to Alice	amathambeka	slopes
inkokeli	leader	iGcuwa	Butterworth
ndisand' ukufunda	I've just read	unxweme	coast
umzi kayise	her father's home		

*lit. An animal has been slaughtered at **Xhukane**.

Xhukwane in the **Middledrift** district was known as a residential area where the people lived in dire poverty and where meat was a rarity. When, therefore, anyone slaughtered a beast it was cause for rejoicing for all the inhabitants. This saying was coined by **A.C. Jordan** in *Ingqumbo Yeminyanya (The Wrath of the Ancestors)*: 'Kwaku**xhelwe eXhukwane** kuDingindawo asakubona ngathi zimbi ngakuZwelinzima.' (Dingindawo was **delighted** to see that the tables were turning on Zwelinzima.)

eMzumvubu	at Port St John	isincoko	essay
induli	hill	-me*ny*wa (<me*m*a)	be invited
inqugwala	round hut	-ngqonga	sit around
amasimi	fields	umlilo	fire
ilizwe liyintombazana	*the country is*	intsomi	folktale
	beautiful (lit. the	njengemihla	like days
	country is a young girl)	yakudala	of old
ndanekhwele	you've made me		
	quite jealous!		
ivenkile yangaphandle	country store		

? *How to ...*

Ask about someone's holiday

Belinjani *i*khefu <u>l</u>akho / <u>l</u>enu?
Ibinjani *i*holide <u>y</u>akho / <u>y</u>enu?
Benibe no**hambo** *olu*myoli?

Ask where someone went

<u>Ubu</u>ye phi kanye?
Beniye phi kanye?
Nibe na*lo* i*x*esha lo*ku*ya e*l*unxwem*eni*?
Nen*ze* ntoni ke apho?

Say how and where you went

Si*lu*qale *u*khenketho lwethu -e-... / *ku-*...
Besifuna ukubukela ...
Emva koko sa*singa* e-... / *ku-*...
Nge**mini** *e*landela*yo*, yekoko uku*singa* e-... / *ku-*...
Nge**mini** *e*landela*yo* sa*singa* e-... / *ku-*...
Si**hambe** ngoku*gwegweleza* sa*dlula* e-... / *ku-*...
Sa**hlala** e-... / *ku-*... ii*n*tsuku e*z*imbalwa.
*I*ndawo *e*landela*yo* e*sit*yelele ku*yo*<u>i</u>bi*y*i...
*E*ndleleni si*cande amadlelo ama*hle.

Express delight

Belu_ngum_**mangaliso**!
Ubu**hle** baloo _m_**mandla** bu**qaqamb**_ile_!
_In_**dalo** apho!
Bekuxhelw' eXhukwana kum!
Ilizwe yintombazana!
Ama**hlathi** elo **zwe** nee**ngxangxasi** _ezixhomis' amehlo_!
_Ii_**ntaka** _ezin_**tlobo-ntlobo** ne**ntsholo** yazo **zizin**to _ezingum_**mangaliso**
ukuz_i_**bona**!
Ubu**bele** _esibu_**fumane** ku_ba_**ntu** balapho buya**mangalisa**.

How it works

1 How to express 'who' / 'whom' in relative clauses

Look at this verse from **'Umfo Endimthandayo'** a poem by Samuel
Edward Krune Mqhayi from the anthology _Indyebo Yesihobe_.

'UMFO ENDIMTHANDAYO	A FELLOW **WHOM I** LIKE (_HIM_)
Ndithand' umf' _o_hlamba futhi,	I like a fellow **who** washes often,
Ndithand' umf' _o_funda futhi,	I like a fellow **who** studies often,
Ndithand' umf' _o_lima futhi,	I like a fellow **who** cultivates often,
Ndithand' umf' _o_guqa futhi,	I like a fellow **who** kneels often,
Nanko k'umf' _e_ndi_m_thanda_yo_.'	That's the fellow **whom** I like.

Note the difference between 'Ndithand'umfo _o_hlamba futhi.' (I like the
man **_who_** washes often.) and 'Nanko k' umf' _e_ndi_m_**thanda**_yo_.' (That's the
man **_whom_ I** like. (_him_))

_um_**fo** _o_- ... = lit. a fellow **who** ...

Here the **relative concord** _o_- connects the noun '_um_**fo**' to the predicate '-
hlamba' of the **relative clause**. umf' _e_ndi_m_**thanda**_yo_ = lit. **whom** I **like** _him_.

Here the **relative concord** _e_- prefixed to '-ndi-' = '**whom** I' introduces the
relative clause which is completed by the object concord '-_m_-' = '_him_'.

Here are some other examples of **relatives clauses** _with_ **object concords**
which you have met in the preceding units:

Ningafaka yonke into	You can put everything
_e_ni_yi_**qokelel**_eyo_	_that_ you have **collected** (_it_)
kwezi ngxowa.	into these bags. (Unit 9)

Into *e*ndingay*i*thandi*yo*
kukusebenza iiyure ezininzi.

The thing *that* I do not **like** (*it*)
is to work many hours. (Unit 10)

Enye into *oyi*nqwenela*yo*?

Something else *that* you
want (*it*)? (Unit 14)

As you can see the **relative concord** is '*e-*' or '*o-*':

*e*ndi- whom I / that I   *e*si- whom we / that we
o- whom you / that you (s.)   *e*ni- whom you / that you (pl.)

'*-yo*' marks a relative clause (cf. **Unit 6.2**).

If the verb is followed by '**na-**'/ '**nga-**' or '**ku-**' the **shortened emphatic pronoun** is added in which case there is **no object concord**:

Lo nguPhumla *e*ndisebenza **na**ye. (Unit 9)
Ndizibonise indlela eziza kuhlala **nga**yo ehotele. (Unit 10)
Thumela iireferensi ezintathu abantu esinokuqhakamshelana **na**bo
ku ... (Unit 10)

2 How to express 'anybody', 'anything', 'any time', 'anywhere', etc.

nabani (na) = *anybody*

Nabani angakuxelela apho
igaraji ikhona.

Anybody can tell you where the
garage is.

nayiphina = *anything*

Unokwenza **nayiphina** into.   He/she can do **anything**.

naninina = *any time*

Ungasityelela **naninina**.   You can visit us **any time**.

naphina = *anywhere*

Unokupaka imoto yakho **naphina**   You can park your car **anywhere**
apha.   here.

3 Summary of the ways of expressing 'and'

With **nouns**: '**na**'- (with vowel coalescence taking place, cf. **Unit 2.9**).

amanqugwala **na**masimi ombona   huts **and** maize fields
isikolo **ne**yunivesithi   school **and** university
iinduli **no**nxweme   the hills **and** the coast

Remember: -_s_- is infixed in locatives:

_ezi_ndul_eni_ **na_sema_**thambek_eni_   on the hills **and** slopes

With **verbs**: second verb ends in -**e** (cf. **Unit 8.2**).

Connecting **clauses**: **yaye** or **kwaye**:

Kungenwa simahla **yaye** kuhanjwa simahla.	Free entrance **and** free transport. (lit. It is freely entered **and** freely gone.)

4 Summary of the use of the emphatic pronoun

			copula + Abs. pr.	na- + Abs. pr.	nga- + Abs. pr.	ku- + Abs. pr.
		As for me etc.	**It is** me etc.	**and/with** me etc.	**about** me etc.	**to** me etc.
1st		mna	**ndi**m	**na**m	**nga**m	**ku**m
		thina	**si**thi	**na**thi	**nga**thi	**ku**thi
2nd		wena	**ngu**we	**na**we	**nga**we	**ku**we
		nina	**ni**ni	**na**ni	**nga**ni	**ku**ni
Noun Classes						
3rd	1/a	yena	**ngu**ye	**na**ye	**nga**ye	**ku**ye
	2/2a	bona	**nga**bo	**na**bo	**nga**bo	**ku**bo
P	3	wona	**ngu**wo	**na**wo	**nga**wo	**ku**wo
	4	yona	**yi**yo	**na**yo	**nga**yo	**ku**yo
e	5	lona	**li**lo	**na**lo	**nga**lo	**ku**lo
	6	wona	**nga**wo	**na**wo	**nga**wo	**ku**wo
r	7	sona	**si**so	**na**so	**nga**so	**ku**so
	8	zona	**zi**zo	**na**zo	**nga**zo	**ku**zo
s	9	yona	**yi**yo	**na**yo	**nga**yo	**ku**yo
	10	zona	**zi**zo	**na**zo	**nga**zo	**ku**zo
o	11	lona	**lu**lo	**na**lo	**nga**lo	**ku**lo
	10	zona	**zi**zo	**na**zo	**nga**zo	**ku**zo
n	14	bona	**bu**bo	**na**bo	**nga**bo	**ku**bo
	15	kona	**ku**ko	**na**ko	**nga**ko	**ku**ko

5 Place names

Many Xhosa place names derive from geographical features such as rivers, ponds, cliffs, mountains, plants and even animals found in a particular area. **Lusikisiki** takes its pleasant name from the sound of the reeds rustling in a nearby marsh, **Gonubie** (< *i*Qunube) from the wild bramble berries which grow along the banks of the river. **Keiskamma**, shining water, **Tsitsikamma** clear water, are derived from the Khoi languages as are many other place names recognisable by their clicks. A number of Xhosa place names, especially the cities, have been adopted from English and Afrikaans:

■ **Major cities**	**Izixeko ezikhulu**	**Known derivations**
Cape Town	*i*Kapa (*e*Kapa)	< Xhosalised '**Cape**'
East London	*i*Monti (*e*Monti)	< Afrikaans '**mond**' i.e. the mouth of the Buffalo River
Durban	*i*Theku (*e*Thek*wini*)	< Xhosa '**itheku**' = 'bay'
Johannesburg	*i*Goli (*e*Goli)	< English '**gold**'
	*i*Rhawuti (*e*Rhawut*ini*)	< Afrikaans '**goud**'
Port Elizabeth	*i*Bhayi (*e*Bhayi)	< Xhosalised '**bay**'
Pietermaritzburg	*um*Gungundlovu (*e*Mgungundlovu)	= place of the elephant
Pretoria	*i*Pitoli (*e*Pitoli)	< Xhosalised 'Pretoria'
■ **Some Towns in the Eastern Cape**	**Ezinye Iidolophu zaseMpuma-Koloni**	
Alice	*i*Dike (*e*Dik*eni*)	< Xhosa '*i*dike' = pool
Butterworth	*i*Gcuwa (*e*Gcuwa)	
Fort Beaufort	*i*Bhofolo (*e*Bhofolo)	(< English Beaufort)
Grahamstown	*i*Rhini (*e*Rhini)	
Healdtown	*i*Nxukhwebe (*e*Nxukhwebe)	
Keiskammahoek	*u*Qoboqobo (*ku*Qoboqobo)	
King Williams Town	*i*Qonce (*e*Qonce)	
Lady Frere	*i*Cacadu (*e*Cacadu)	
Middledrift	*i*Xesi (*e*Xesi)	
Peddie	*i*Ngqushwa (*e*Ngqushwa)	
Port St. Johns	*u*Mzimvubu (*e*Mzimvubu)	(at the home of the hippos)
Queenstown	*u*Komani (*ku*Komani)	
Somerset East	*u*Nojoli (*kwa*Nojoli)	(< *i*joni = English soldier)
Stutterheim	*i*Cumakala (*e*Cumakala)	
Uitenhage	*i*Tinarha (*e*Tinarha)	

Terminology related to administrative divisions

location, settlement, village	*i*lali (< Afrikaans 'laager')
village	*i*dolophana
town	*i*dolophu (< Afrikaans 'dorp')
city	*isi*xeko
capital	*i*komkhulu
district	*isi*thili
area, constituency	*in*gingqi
region	*um*mandla
province	*i*phondo

6 Word adaptations

'Xhosa has manifested itself as a dynamic, vibrant, virile language adaptable to, and developing in harmony with, the changing environment.' → see Introduction p.6

Here are a number of examples of this aspect of the Xhosa language some of which you have come across in this book:

■ **confer degrees, cap** = uku**thwesa** *isi***danga** – original meaning of 'uku**thwesa**' = to **crown**, put something on the head; original meaning of '*isi***danga**' = necklace of many strings of beads

'Waye**thweswa** *isi***danga** sembeko sobugqirha boncwadi (iD Litt) yiyunivesithi yaseFort Hare ngowe-1974 yokumbulela ngokubhala kwakhe isiXhosa.'

■ **capital** i.e. money = *in***kunzi** – original meaning of '*in***kunzi**' = 'a bull'. Cattle (*iin***komo**) have always been the centre and pride of Xhosa life, representing wealth and respect. Apart from supplying milk, meat and leather for clothing, they play a very important part in ancestral sacrifice and in bridal payment (*i***lobolo**). In urban life money, '**capital**', has largely replaced cattle as a symbol of wealth.

■ **way, road**   = *um***gaqo** –
                        original meaning **animal track**

     rules, regulations = *imi***gaqo**
     grammar = *imi***gaqo**-*n***tetho**
     constitution = *imi***gaqo**-*si***seko**

■ **headquarters, depot** = *i*ziko –
                                    original meaning **hearth**
                                    in centre of **hut**

   polling **booth**   = *i*ziko lo**voto**
   civic **centre**   = *i*ziko lo**luntu**

■ **electricity**   = *um***bane** –
                                    original meaning
                                    lightning

■ **telephone**   = *um***nxeba** –
                                    original meaning
                                    rope

■ **library**   = *i*thala len**cwadi** –
                                    original meaning **shelf in a hut**

■ **book**, letter   = *in***cwadi** original meaning thin
                                    transparent **coat of the poisonous**
                                    bulb *buphane disticha': 'in***cwadi***'

■ **page**   = *i***khasi** – original meaning
                                    ensheathing leaf of mealie cob

■ **source**, channel   = *i***jelo** – original meaning **tube**, **reed**
                                    to spurt water through when smoking

   news **channels**   = *ama***jelo** een**daba**
   reliable **sources** = *ama***jelo** *a***thembekile***yo*

■ weather **forecaster** = *is***anuse** semo**zulu** – original meaning
                                    '*is***anuse**' = diviner (< **-nuka** = to smell).

How to apply it

In this unit, instead of the usual variety of exercises, you will find a
number of Xhosa texts where you can exercise your **reading skill**. Some
English texts are also included and these together, with the ones in Xhosa,
should whet your appetite to learn more about Xhosa literature, history,
culture and tradition.

JAMES JAMES RANISI JOLOBE (1902–1976) Ulibone ilanga ngowa-25 Julayi ngonyaka we-1902 e**Ndwe** ngase**Cala** apho uyise wayengumfundisi khona. Wafumana imfundo yokuqala e**Ndwe** nase**Matatiele**. Ngo1916 wathunyelwa e**Mthwaku**. Ukususela ngo-1919 ufundise kwizikolo ngezikolo.

Ngelo xesha wayehlala ngase**Mt.Frere** apho kuthethwa isiBhaca, isiHlubi nesiSuthu khona. Ngoko ke isiXhosa sakhe sasibuthathaka. Incwadi yakhe yokuqala *UZagula* yalungiswa kunene ngu**S.E.K. Mqhayi**, Imbongi yeSizwe. Phofu, xa wayengutitshala e**Bhobhotyane** nase**Mankazana**, wafunda isiXhosa esithethwa ngamaNgqika omgquba. (→ See next page) Ngo-1926 uye e**Fort Hare** e**Dikeni**. Apho waqeqeshwa kwimfundo yobufundisi waza waphumelela neB.A. Ukususela ngelo xesha upapashe iincwadi ezininzi – umzekelo *Umyezo, Amavo, Elundini loThukela* nezinye. *UThuthula* yimbalasane kwizibongo zikaJolobe ngakumbi ezothando. Ngumbongo-mbaliso osikhumbuza ngoHelen of Troy.

Wahlela iincwadi ezininzi. Kananjalo ukwaguqulele ezinye esiXhoseni. Ngo-1952 wathiwa *jize* ngeMbasa kaVilakazi* yiYunivesithi yaseWitwatersrand. Wayethweswa isidanga sembeko sobugqirha boncwadi (iD.Litt.) yiyunivesithi yase**Fort Hare** ngowe-1974 yokumbulela ngokubhala kwakhe isiXhosa.

UGqirha Jolobe usweleke ngomhla we-16 Meyi ngo-1976.

UJolobe akasayi kulityalwa kwimbali yolwimi lwamaXhosa kuba ulutyebisile watyebisa *nkqu* isithethe sawo.

wathunyelwa	was sent	umbongo-mbaliso	narrative poem
izikolo ngezikolo	different schools	wahlela	he edited
iindawo ngeendawo	different places	wathiwa *jize*	he was awarded
sasibuthathaka	was weak	iMbasa kaVilakazi*	the Vilakazi Medal
yalungiswa kunene	was extensively corrected	yokumbulela	in acknowledgement
		usweleke	he died
Imbongi yeSizwe	Poet Laureate	akasayi	he will never
upapashe	he published	kulityalwa	be forgotten
yimbalasane	is the outstanding	ulutyebisile	he has enriched it
kwizibongo	among the poems	watyebisa *nkqu*	(the language)
ezothando	lit. of things of love	isithethe sawo	and even Xhosa culture

*Prof. BW Vilakazi was the first black lecturer to be appointed at the University of Witwatersrand. This award, in his name, is given to scholars who have made significant contributions to African languages.

HISTORICAL CONTEXT OF THE BATTLE OF AMALINDE

At the beginning of the 18th century there was a great deal of fighting between **Ngqika** (1778–1829), and his uncle **Ndlambe**, son of **Rharhabe** and brother of **Mlawu (Ngqika's** father), who died, together with his father **Rharhabe**, in a battle against **abaThembu** in 1782. **Ngqika** was only four years old when his father died. **Ndlambe**, therefore, ruled as regent for **Ngqika**. He handed over power before **Ngqika** reached his 20th birthday but continued to try to exercise power which angered **Ngqika** whose ambition it was to rule all ama**Xhosa**. With the help of alliances with other Xhosa chiefs and with the Boers and the British of the Cape Colony, **Ngqika** and **Ndlambe** were engaged in bitter battles. One of the reasons for such bitterness and hostility was **Ngqika**'s abduction of the beautiful **Thuthula**, one of **Ndlambe**'s wives. This action resulted in widespread rebellion. Eventually peace was restored through an agreement whereby **Ndlambe** recognised **Ngqika** as his senior. However, in the great battle of **Amalinde**, fought in 1818, **Ngqika** was defeated by **Ndlambe** but soon after that he secured a victory over his uncle with the help of the British troops. (c.f. Peires)

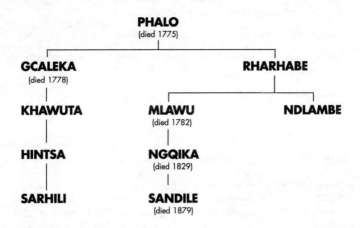

PHALO
(died 1775)

GCALEKA
(died 1778)

RHARHABE

KHAWUTA

MLAWU
(died 1782)

NDLAMBE

HINTSA

NGQIKA
(died 1829)

SARHILI

SANDILE
(died 1879)

UNontando – Noni Jabavu was born on August 20, 1919 at Middledrift in the Eastern Cape Province. At the age of 14 she was sent to England in the care of English friends and went to school in York. Her studies at the Royal Academy of Music were interrupted by the Second World War when she joined the first group of women trained as semi-skilled workers and became an oxy-acetylene welder in the aircraft industry. She met her husband Michael Cadbury Crosfield, a film director, while still at school. Their families had first became associated when her grandfather, **John Tengo Jabavu**, politician and journalist who founded and was the first editor of *Imvo Zabantsundu*, led a deputation to the Houses of Parliament to protest against the policies to be implemented in South Africa. It was during this time that he met George Cadbury of the chocolate firm and Joseph Crosfield, Noni's husband's grandfathers.

Scenes from a South African life

The hum of conversation was deafening. Every buyer was helped to make his or her choice by the others standing about and who all spoke in the usual terrific tones as if addressing people far off up mountains. From time to time, someone would turn aside, remove his or her pipe that was as long as your arm from the mouth and indulge in a splendid hard jet-like spit on to the floor boards. You had to keep a sharp look-out and leap out of the way.

The Europeans spoke Xhosa, and as locals usually were, seemed relaxed, unhurried, like their customers. I pushed my way through and stood at the counter next to a woman in the act of announcing that she had at last reached 'the moment of being about to buy'. She shouted, 'Come, European, I am ready for you.'

Her shoulders were bare, for she had wound her shawl under her armpits and over the married woman's modesty bib in order to free her hands. She now lifted them to her huge turban. The brass bangles from wrist to forearm gleamed. She felt in the folds of the turban, patting the folds back into place – all the while keeping up a powerful running commentary on the reasons why she had decided on the goods she had picked in preference to other specimens of the same, interrupting it to repeat, 'Come, European.'

Then she began to untie the knotted rag. She took out of it some pound and ten-shilling notes. They were grubby, and wrapped around coins: half-crowns, florins, shillings, sixpences, even 'tickeys' – the tiny silver threepenny bits.

'Come, man! What is the matter with this European – is he pretending not to want money?' Her every move was watched, men and women sucking their long pipes, eyes glued on her fingers as she fumbled. One man called out after the last tickey had been unwrapped, 'Where are the pennies and halfpennies?'

'Oh, I keep those in my purse', she said. That in turn was inside a twill bag decorated with black piping and suspended from her waist. She counted out the money. One of the Europeans now sauntered up and joined in the watching. She counted the money a second time, and a third time through, then paused. She raised her face to the ceiling and burst out in loud lament, 'Oh God, these Europeans are killing me! Why do you kill me, European, taking all my money?'

I leapt back a step for she 'threw' her voice like an actress, within inches of my ear. You could have heard her from the back row of a theatre, yet the shopkeeper was only across the counter. He was not disturbed but replied quietly, blandly, in Xhosa, his brown eyes scanning the money spread out in front of him, 'Have you not come of your own volition then, to be killed?'

(**Noni Jabavu**, *The Ochre People*, **pages 64-5, John Murray, London, 1963**)

Cape Times, 18/3/98

Jean Morris (from Abantu)

IVENKILE YANGAPHANDLE

Courtesy: T.V. Bulpin

Nokuba ungumhambi akunzima ezilalini zethu ukwazi ukuba ivenkile yiyiphi na kuba iba nguwona mzi uzindlu zibalulekileyo umzi kananjalo ojikelezwe yimithi. (p.69) Abantu abaNtsundu abaninzi bayoyiswa kukubiza amagama abantu abaMhlophe kwaye nangaphandle koko bathanda ukumnika igama lentetho yabo umntu oMhlophe osebenza phakathi kwabo – igama elidla ngokulandela izimbo zomninilo lowo. Ngenxa yezi ndawo wofumana ukuba abeLungu beevenkile bonke ezilalini phaya banamagama esiNtu. Okuya bezingekandi kakhulu iintsimbi zamehlo phakathi kwabaNtsundu ubesakuthi Mhlophe ofike enxiba zona kwa-oko kube sekuthiwa nguMehlomane ukubizwa kwakhe. Umfo osisiqololwane enengxeba isiqingqi sendodana ebenganyali ukuzizuzela igama lokuba nguMafutha. Umfo oyindlezane ububele ubesele eya kubizwa ngokuba nguThandabantu. (p.70–71) Mhlawumbi wena uba kule venkile kuthengwa ngemali ngabo bonke abantu ukanti akunjalo. Le venkile ifana nendawo yentengiso ngezinye iindawo. Abanye ukuze bathenge kufuneka bona ngokwabo bathengise kwakumnini-venkile. Omnye uza namaqanda kwakunye nodaba olubangela ukuba ananise ngawo. (p.71) Lo mzi uyivenkile akwanele ukuba kuthengwe kuthengiswe kuwo kuphela, neposi yesithili esi iphuma kwakuwo apha. Yinto leyo oya kufika iincwadi ziyimfumba kwityeyana ebethelelwe eludongeni phaya. (p.72) Ngaphandle kwezi ndawo sezikhankanyiwe, ivenkile yangaphandle, ivala nelinye ikroba entlalweni yabantu bengingqi leyo ikuyo. Ifana nendawo yembutho, indawo yokubonana kwabantu neyokuthululwa kwemiyalezo eya kumacala abengenakufikelela kuwo lula umntu. Evenkileni uyazi ukuba uya kumbona nokuba mnye umntu oya ngakwelo cala. Andithethi ngolutsha lona kuba luse lusazi ukuba apho lungabonana khona kusevenkileni. (p.72–73)

(J.J.R. Jolobe, *Amavo*, Witwatersrand University Press, Johannesburg, 1973)

SAMUEL EDWARD KRUNE MQHAYI (1875 – 1945)

Courtesy: Imvo

IKHULU

LEMINYAKA

KWILITYE lengcwaba likaSamuel Edward Krune Mqhayi kubhalwe kwathiwa "Apha kulele imbongi yesizwe nombhali wencwadi, iphakathi lesizwe sakwaXhosa siphela, inkokheli ekwangumKrestu wenene, makaphumle ngoxolo, umoya wakhe mawuhlale usikhokela isizwe".

'In my final year at Healdtown, an event occurred that for me was like a comet streaking across the night sky. Towards the end of the year, we were informed that the great Xhosa poet, **Krune Mqhayi**, was going to visit the school.'

*(See pages 38–40 in **Long Walk to Freedom**, McDonald Purnell, 1994, for the full account of this momentous occasion in the life of the young Nelson Mandela.)*

This editorial in **Imvo** was written on the occasion of the centenary of the birth of '**Imbongi** ye**Sizwe Jikelele**' – **The Poet of the Nation**, **Samuel Edward Krune Mqhayi. Mqhayi** , playwright, poet and praise singer extraordinaire, was born at Tyhume near Alice. His formative years were spent at the Great Place of his uncle Chief Nzanzana where he remained for six years absorbing the traditional atmosphere and studying the customs and traditions of the Xhosa. He listened attentively to the discussions on customary law grasping the intricacies of legal procedure which he would later use as the basis for his chef d'oeuvre *Ityala Lamawele*. He received his education at Lovedale and became a teacher and wrote *Ityala Lamawele* in 1914 while teaching at Macleantown. He was a prolific writer producing many books including poetry, plays and biographies.

After teaching for a year in East London he became assistant editor of *Izwe Labantu* and edited *Imvo Zabantsundu* from 1920–1921, during the last months of Jabavu's life.

In 1927 he wrote 7 additional stanzas of *Nkosi Sikelel' iAfrika* and in 1939 he published his autobiography. Among his well-known publications are *Don Jadu, Imihobe nemibongo* and *Inzuzo.*

The editor of *Abantu Batho*, the official organ of the African National Congress named him *iMbongi yeSizwe Jikelele* – the Poet of the Nation. On his retirement he went to Ntab' oZuko near Berlin, where he died in 1945.

The Telling of Folktales (Ukwenziwa Kweentsomi)

It was, and is still to some extent, a Xhosa custom for grandmothers to tell their grandchildren **iintsomi** – folktales. Their purpose was to enforce and support some point of family discipline or custom. They upheld conduct that was for the good of society or the welfare of the community.

Folktales always start with: *Kwathi ke kaloku ngantsomi* (Once upon a time) while the grandchildren usually respond by saying *Chosi!* (Hush!).

'Always, however, there was at least one adult, usually grandmama, sitting with us around the fire. To keep us children awake, she would tell *iintsomi*, the fairy-tale of amaXhosa.

There were tales about ogres and giants, about animals of the forests, great beasts, and about little hopping creatures of the veld. There were tales about animals of the river, huge scale-covered reptiles that could swallow people and animals whole, crushing them to death as they did so. And later on, when hungry, bring them up and chew them as cud.

There were happy tales also; princes and princesses, kings and queens, and chiefs and chieftainesses: stories that we listened to and believed. Stories that were told with such vivid detail and in such modulation of voice that we children saw them in our minds and lived them in our feelings; crying when a little orphaned girl, on her way to her uncle or her grandparents who would look after her (this would-be guardian angel always lived far, far away) fell into the hands of an ogre disguised as a kindly little old lady, with designs to have her for his dinner. We roared with laughter – the kind of laughter that leaves you feeling weak in your belly, tears streaming down your face; honest no-nonsense and no-decorum laughter – whenever cruel giants and cannibals came to grief, usually by inadvertently falling prey to the very traps intended for their victims.

Oh, no doubt, we were blood-thirsty little people ourselves, but we felt self-righteous about it as long as it was the bad, terrible, cruel, ugly ogre, or some such, who thus met his demise.

Some of these stories told us of the origin of man, others were about natural phenomena, and others still were designed to teach us, the unwary audience, some aspect of morality. Looking back now, I see clearly how *iintsomi* are an essential and integral part of the socialisation of the child among amaXhosa.'

(Sindiwe Magona, *To My Children's Children*), David Philip Publishers (Pty) Ltd, Cape Town 1990

Imbangi yokuba imbila iswele umsila

Kwathi ke kaloku ngantsomi ebutsheni belizwe zonke izilwanyana zazingenamsila. Zonke zazonwabile ngaphandle kokumkani wezilo, *iNgonyama*.

Ithe ke ngenye imini yagqiba ukuba zonke zamkele izipho ukuze zijongeke zintle kakhulu. Yazimema zonke ukuba zize enkundleni. Izilo zaphambana luvuyo ngaphandle kwee*mbila*.

Endaweni yokuya enkundleni zona zakhetha ukuhlala zigcakamele ilanga. Zazisonqena kakhulu kodwa zazizifuna zona izipho. Ngoko ke, zacela *iinkawu* ukuba zize zizamkele izipho ezo. *Iinkawu* zavuma zaya enkundleni

apho zonke izilo zazihlangene khona. *INgonyama* yazibulisa yazamkelisa izipho zonke. Ngasinye samkela umsila! Noko ke ukumkani lo wayesel' emdala kakhulu namehlo emadala waza ke ngoko wenza iimpazamo ezininzi. Umzekelo, wanika *indlovu*, isilo esikhulu kakhulu umsilana omncinane kodwa *unomatse*, emncinci enjalo, wamnika umsila omkhulukazi. *Iinkawu* ke zanikwa imisila yazo zanikwa neyee*mbila* imisila. Zahamba zonwabile. Zadlula ekhayeni leembila ezo. Zabuza *iimbila* ngetheko. *Iinkawu* zahleka zaveza imisila yazo emitsha ngokuzidla okukhulu zatsho zisithi: 'Zizipho zokumkani ezi.' Zabongoza zathi *iimbila*:

'Sinikeni imisila yethu! Ncedani nisinike imisila yethu!' Kodwa *iinkawu* zahleka zagigitheka zalatha isihlomelo

ngaphantsi koboya emsileni zathi: 'Khangelani. Nantsi imisila yenu. Anizikhathazanga ngokuya kuyamkela, saza ke thina sayihlomela kweyethu.' Zatsho zathi *shwaka iinkawu*. Zaqumba kakhulu *iimbila* kodwa azaba nakwenza nto. Zisayiswele imisila *iimbila* kude kube nanamhla oko. Kodwa ke, azonqeni njengoko zazinjalo ebutsheni belizwe.

Phela phela ngantsomi!

(**Note**: The proverb closely related to this intsomi is '*Imbila yaswela umsila ngokuyalezela*'.)

Why the rock rabbit has no tail

Once upon a time when the world was young (lit. at the newness of the land) all animals did not have tails. All were happy except for the king of the beasts, the ***Lion***.

So one day he decided that all the animals should receive presents so that they should look beautiful. He invited all to come to his court. The animals were overjoyed (lit. mad with joy) except for the ***rock rabbits***.

Instead of going to the court they preferred to bask in the sun. They were very lazy but they still wanted to receive their presents. Therefore they asked the ***monkeys*** to go and get their presents. The ***monkeys*** agreed and went to the court where all the animals were gathered. The ***Lion*** greeted

them and gave out their presents. Each one received a tail. It happened that this king was already very old and his eyes, too, were old with the result that he made many mistakes. For example, he gave the ***elephant***, a very big animal,

a very small tail but to the ***squirrel*** which is very small, he gave a huge tail. The ***monkeys*** were then given their tails and were also given those of the ***rock rabbits***. They left happy. They passed by the home of those ***rock rabbits***. The ***rock rabbits*** asked them about the party. The ***monkeys*** laughed and proudly showed off their tails and said: 'These are the gifts from the King.' The ***rock rabbits*** pleaded saying: 'Give us our tails. Please give us our tails'. But the ***monkeys*** laughed and giggled and pointed to a joint under the fur on the tail:

'Look, here are your tails. You couldn't be bothered to go and get them yourselves, so we joined them onto ours!' Having said so the ***monkeys*** disappeared. The ***rock rabbits*** were very angry but they could not do anything. So they are tailless till this day, but they are not nearly as lazy as they were when the world was young!

That is the end of the story!

(lit. The dassie has no tail because he sent someone on his behalf, i.e. don't rely on others to do your bidding!)

Translations of dialogues

It goes without saying that word-for-word translations from one language to another are virtually impossible. For literal translations consult the vocabulary boxes in each unit.

Unit 1 Getting acquainted on the aeroplane

Stewardess	Good day, ladies and gentlemen. Welcome to flight 301 going to Cape Town.

oooOooo

Thandi	Hello, how are you today?
Jenny	I am well.
Thandi	Oh! You speak Xhosa well! I am Thandi Thamsanqa.
Jenny	I am Jenny Murray. I am glad to meet you. How are you?
Thandi	(No), I am well, thanks. I'm also glad to meet you.
Jenny	Do you live in Cape Town, Thandi?
Thandi	Yes, we live in Pinelands.
Jenny	Oh! I also live in Pinelands.
Thandi	Where exactly?
Jenny	Near Forest Drive. Where do you live exactly?
Thandi	Near Pinelands High School.

oooOooo

Stewardess	Excuse me, ladies and gentlemen. Fasten your seat belts. We'll shortly be arriving in Cape Town. Thank you for choosing Rainbow Airlines. I hope we'll see each other again soon! Welcome to Cape Town! Goodbye.

oooOooo

Jenny	Goodbye, Thandi. It was nice to speak to you.
Thandi	We'll see each other again!

Unit 2 Meeting again at the Murrays' home

Jenny	Hello, come in!
Thandi	How are you?
Jenny	We are well. It's nice to see you again.
Thandi	This is my husband, Themba.
Jenny	Hello, Themba. I'm very glad to meet you. This is my husband Peter.
Themba	I'm glad to meet you.
Peter	We are also glad to meet you. Welcome to our home. This is our son.
Thandi	Hello, my child. What's your name?
David	I am David.
Themba	Do you go to school, David?
David	Yes, I go to Grove.
Thandi	Where are you learning to speak Xhosa?
David	I'm learning it at school (*Nkosikazi*).
Peter	Do you have children?
Themba	Yes, we have, a son and a daughter.
Peter	Do they go to school?
Themba	Yes, they do. They go to Westerford.
Jenny	What about something to drink? Would you prefer tea or coffee or something cold?
Thamsanqas	Whatever. Yes, whatever.
Peter	Would you like to sit inside or outside?
Thandi	Let's sit outside. It's beautiful. May I help you Jenny?
Jenny	Thank you Peter and Themba. You can chat (in the meantime).
Peter	Okay!

Unit 3 Knowing how to speak Xhosa

Themba	Peter, you speak Xhosa well. Tell me, where did you learn to speak it so well?
Peter	I grew up on a farm near Grahamstown. Then I continued to learn it at school. Unfortunately, I've forgotten a lot. Also, I know that I make a lot of mistakes, but I'm trying (my best).
Themba	That doesn't matter, making mistakes. What is important is that you try to speak it every day.
Peter	You're right. You must tell me though when I make mistakes.

Themba	Fine, but you do follow (understand) well.
Peter	Yes, if one speaks slowly.
Themba	Well then, I'll also try to speak slowly.
Peter	Thanks, because I don't speak as well as Jenny. She also grew up on a farm in the Eastern Cape. She learnt it at school and university. She speaks as well as a Xhosa-speaking person – so much so that she teaches it now.
Themba	That's lovely! You know, the Dutch saying: *'So veel tale as jij kan, so veel male is jij man.'*
Peter	That's so true!

Unit 4 Speaking about work

Peter	Tell me, Themba, what's your line of work?
Themba	I work for an airline as a personnel manager.
Peter	Oh, (that's) personnel manager in English?
Themba	You're spot on!
Peter	You obviously communicate and work well with people.
Themba	Yes, I like to work with people very much. You know the Xhosa idiom: *A person is a person through other persons.*
Peter	You are so right!
Themba	What's your work, Peter?
Peter	I am a horticulturist at Kirstenbosch.
Themba	Mm, that's interesting!
Peter	Yes, it's interesting work. It is such a beautiful place to work at. Does Thandi also work?
Themba	Yes, she also likes to work with people. She is a doctor. She works at the Red Cross Children's Hospital. She goes there in the mornings only. In the afternoon she works at a Primary Health Care clinic.
Peter	She also works very hard then.
Themba	At which school does Jenny teach?
Peter	She doesn't teach at a school. She teaches adults who want to learn to speak Xhosa. You know, there are many people who want to learn to speak Xhosa now, especially business people and staff of companies, housewives, doctors and nurses, etc., etc.
Themba	Well, as they say in English: *'Better late than never!'*
Peter	How do you say that in Xhosa?
Themba	I don't know. Language is like that. It is not always easy to translate, especially when it comes to idioms.

Unit 5 How do you like your coffee?

Peter	At last! Let's quench (our) thirst!
Jenny	Sorry for letting you wait (such) a long time. We were chatting! I'm sure that you must be thirsty.
Peter	Yes, we are very thirsty. We are also hungry.
Themba	No, that's okay, we were also chatting.
Jenny	Thandi, how do you like your coffee? Do you want milk and sugar?
Thandi	Milk only, thanks.
Jenny	And you, Themba, do you want coffee with milk?
Themba	Yes, thanks, and two teaspoons of sugar.
Jenny	Here is the sugar. Help yourself.
Peter	How about some cake and sandwiches, Thandi?
Thandi	Thanks, Peter. May I have a small slice of cake? It looks lovely!
Peter	Indeed, it is delicious. Here's a slice!
Thandi	Thanks. Mm! This cake is delicious, Jenny, may I have the recipe?
Jenny	Sure! Just remind me. Themba, can I also give you a slice of cake?
Themba	Thanks Jenny. I love sweet things very much!
Jenny	Peter, please pass Themba the cake (while) I pour your coffee.
Peter	Okay. Thandi, what about another cup of coffee?
Thandi	No, thanks. One cup of coffee is enough for me.
Peter	Gosh, the sun has disappeared. It's getting cool now. Shouldn't we go inside?
Jenny	Yes, it's suddenly got cold. I am cold. Aren't you cold too?
Thandi	A little.
Jenny	Well, let's go inside then! Peter, please close the door.

oooOooo

Thandi	Jenny, don't forget to give me the recipe for the cake.
Jenny	I haven't forgotten. Here it is. If you prefer chocolate icing you can dissolve a spoon of cocoa powder in a spoon of boiling water and beat well into the icing.

Unit 6 Are you warm enough?

Peter	Are you warm enough or should I switch on the heater?
Themba	No thanks, we don't need a heater. It's not that cold.

Jenny	The Cape weather is like that. One minute the sun is shining, the next (minute) it is raining.
Thandi	No man, don't exaggerate. And don't complain about the Cape weather! The rain is better than drought. We need rain in South Africa. It's scarce.
Peter	Jenny, you sound like the Gautengers! They don't like our weather; they complain about the rain in winter and about the wind in summer!
Themba	But let's be honest, the weather is beautiful in Gauteng in winter. It's dry, it doesn't rain.
Thandi	But the thunderstorms and lightning there in summer!
Jenny	No, let's admit, every place has its advantages and disadvantages.
Thandi	You're right. For instance, in Durban, the winter is pleasant, but the humidity there in summer is intolerable.
Jenny	Yes, it's exactly like that.
Peter	I hope that the weather will be fine this coming weekend because there is a big cricket match at Newlands. Do you like cricket, Themba?
Themba	Very much! Like Makhaya Ntini says on TV: *'I don't like cricket, I love it!'*
Peter	Well, I'm going on Saturday with David. Would you and your son like to come with us?
Themba	Yes, I would like that very much.
Peter	Okay, I'll phone you on Friday so that we can arrange where and when to meet.

Unit 7   Jenny at work – 'Let's speak Xhosa'

Jenny	Hello, students! Today **you** are going to speak Xhosa, and **I** am going to listen! Who wants to start?
Mark and Paul	We'll start, Jenny.
Mark	I'll be the petrol attendant, Paul will be the motorist.
Jenny	All right, students, talk!

At the garage

Attendant	Good day, sir. How are you, today? How can I help you?
Motorist	Good day, *Mnumzana*. How are you?
Attendant	No, nothing wrong. I'm okay despite the problems. And you?

Motorist	I'm also fine, thanks.
Attendant	Should I fill the tank today?
Motorist	No, give me only 50 rands' worth today.
Attendant	All right sir. How are the tyres?
Motorist	It seems the left front tyre needs a little air. Please check all round.
Attendant	All right, sir. How much air?
Motorist	Pump them to 210 all round. Please don't forget to check the water and oil.
Attendant	No sooner said than done, sir!

oooOooo

Attendant	Well, everything is okay in front. Should I also wipe the windows?
Motorist	That would be helpful!
Attendant	Well, I've finished, sir.
Motorist	I am grateful. Thank you. Here's the money for the petrol. Here's also something for tobacco (tip).
Attendant	Thank you. Goodbye, sir.
Motorist	Goodbye, *Mnumzana*. We'll see each other again.
Jenny	Mark and Paul, you've done well. Congratulations!
	Well, Val and Sally, let's hear your conversation!
Val and Sally	All right.

At the supermarket

Val	Sorry, *Nkosikazi*! Did I hurt you?
Lady	No, it's nothing. Oh! You speak Xhosa?
Val	I'm trying.
Lady	No, you're not just trying, you speak it! Where do you know Xhosa from?
Val	Sorry, I didn't understand. Please say that again.
Lady	I said, where did you learn it?
Val	Oh now I understand! I attend Xhosa classes.
Lady	Who is teaching you? (By whom are you being taught?)
Val	A Mrs Murray. She grew up with Xhosa-speaking people, *emaXhoseni*.
Lady	I too am from *emaXhoseni*.
Val	Where is your home?
Lady	In Cacadu.

Val	Oh, isn't that Lady Frere in English?
Lady	Gosh! You're right. Indeed, you do know Xhosa!
Val	Where do you live, *Nkosikazi*?
Lady	In Claremont. Where do you live?
Val	In Kenilworth, but I work here in Claremont.
Lady	I also work here in Claremont. I have a restaurant in Fir Avenue called *'Ningene'* (*Come in*).
Val	Really! Perhaps I'll visit you there. Gosh, I nearly forgot, my name is Val Todd.
Lady	I'm pleased to meet you, Val. I am Xoliswa Silinga.
Val	I'm also glad to meet you, Xoliswa. It was very nice to talk to you. I hope we'll see each other again. I'm going to tell my teacher and the class about your restaurant. Perhaps we'll all visit you there soon.
Xoliswa	That would be nice. Goodbye.
Val	Goodbye Xoliswa. I'm sure we'll see each other again at the restaurant.

oooOooo

Jenny	You also did very well, Val and Sally. I'm happy. I'm very happy with your progress! Congratulations! Now let me wish you all a pleasant holiday.

Unit 8 Thandi at work – 'I am Dr Thamsanqa'

Thandi	Good morning, *Nkosikazi*. Hello, my child. Please come in. I am Dr Thamsanqa. Sit down. Here's a chair. What's your name, *Nkosikazi*?
Mother	I am Nonceba Majola.
Thandi	And you, my child, what's your name?
Child	Lindiwe.
Thandi	No, don't cry my child. Don't worry. I won't hurt you. Here's a doll. Do you want to hold it? Well then, *Nkosikazi*, tell me, why have you come to see us here at the hospital?
Mother	It's this little one, doctor.
Thandi	What is the matter (with her)?
Mother	She's complaining of a bad headache, doctor. Another thing, she is coughing. She is coughing a lot.
Thandi	How old is she?
Mother	Five, doctor.

Thandi	Did you bring her *Road to Health* Card?
Mother	Yes, here it is.
Thandi	That's fine. Well then, my child, show me, where exactly is your head sore? Can you point to where your head is sore?
ULindiwe	It's sore here.
UThandi	Is your throat sore?
ULindiwe	No.
UThandi	Are your ears sore?
ULindiwe	Yes.
UThandi	Is there any discharge from her ears, *Nkosikazi*?
UMama	Yes. there is.
Thandi	Since when has your child been ill, Mrs Majola?
Mother	This is the third day.
Thandi	Tell me, have you given her something to alleviate the pain?
Mother	Yes, I gave her Panado, but it didn't help at all.
Thandi	Has she (this child) ever hurt her head before?
Mother	No, doctor.
Thandi	Has she ever been sick before?
Mother	No, doctor.
Thandi	Has she (this child) any other problems?
Mother	Yes, doctor, she is not eating well.
Thandi	All right, Mrs Majola. I would like to examine her now. Please undress her and lie her down here on the bed.

Unit 9 Peter at work at Kirstenbosch

Peter	Good morning, pupils. Welcome to Kirstenbosch! My name is Peter Murray. This is my colleague Mrs Phumla Bongela. We both are horticulturists here at Kirstenbosch. Mrs Bongela will tell you about the waterwise gardens and the Outreach Gardening Project. This project was started to help schools to establish gardens suitable to your area. But first, I'm going to tell you a little about Kirstenbosch (itself). This garden, famous all over the world for its beauty, was founded in 1913. It is much acclaimed for its collection of South African plants. Look at these pictures taken at the Chelsea Flower Show in London where year after year Kirstenbosch has won many medals.

oooOooo

Phumla	Well then, pupils, I'm going to visit you at your school so that

we can start a waterwise garden. I'll bring plants and garden tools, but I also want you to participate in this exercise by trying to prepare the soil at the school.

Pupils   How can we do that, *Nkosikazi*?

Phumla   The best way to start is to make compost. You can start by collecting kitchen waste. For instance, vegetable peels, egg shells, leaves, bones together with grass cuttings, dead flowers, feathers and ash. But don't put in tins, plastic or paper. I'll visit your school next week. We'll choose a suitable spot to make a compost heap. Until then, you can put everything you have collected into these bags. Well then, pupils, I am grateful to you for listening so attentively. Have a nice picnic now but I ask you please to keep the garden clean. Don't forget to pick up all your papers before you leave and put them into the rubbish bins. Goodbye. We'll see each other next week.

Unit 10 Themba at work – an interview

Themba   Good morning, Miss Green. Please sit down. I'm glad to see you. How are you?

Miss Green   Good morning, Mr Thamsanqa. Thank you. I'm fine except for feeling a little nervous.

Themba   No, Miss Green, don't be anxious. Relax! It seems that you speak Xhosa well. Tell me, where do you know it from?

Miss Green   I started to speak it when I was still small because my parents worked at a hospital near Keiskammahoek.

Themba   Oh, then you know the pure Xhosa! Can you also write it?

Miss Green   Yes, Mr Thamsanqa, I learned Xhosa at school and also at university.

Themba   Do you know any other languages as well?

Miss Green   Yes, I speak Afrikaans and a little French but the latter less.

Themba   Well then, Miss Green, please tell me a little about yourself.

Miss Green   I was born in 1969 in Cape Town. My parents moved to Keiskammahoek when I was still small, therefore I did the lower standards from Sub A to Std 5 at Keiskammahoek.

Themba   Where did you do your higher standards?

Miss Green   At boarding school in Port Elizabeth. I passed Matric in 1986. After that I studied for a BA degree at Rhodes University in Grahamstown.

Themba	What were your majors?
Miss Green	English and Xhosa.
Themba	Who taught you Xhosa?
Miss Green	Professor Majola. Do you perhaps know him?
Themba	Oh, very well! We studied together. He is a very bright man.
Miss Green	What a teacher! He helped me a lot. Well, I graduated in 1989. I started to work as a teacher. In 1994 I was promoted and became vice-principal.
Themba	Please tell me, why do you want to change jobs now?
Miss Green	I'm afraid many teachers are going to be retrenched. Besides, I am a 'people person'. I would very much like to work with different people. And I think I can make a contribution to your company.
Themba	Well then, Miss Green, do **you** have questions?
Miss Green	Yes, Mr Thamsanqa. Do you think that I have a chance of being appointed?
Themba	Yes, I think that you have a very good chance!
Miss Green	When can I expect to hear whether I have been successful?
Themba	We'll let you know at the end of next week.
Miss Green	Thank you very much, Mr Thamsanqa.
Themba	All right, Miss Green. It was nice to meet you. Goodbye.
Miss Green	Goodbye, Mr Thamsanqa.

Unit 11 May I speak to Mr Thamsanqa?

Peter	Hello, may I speak to Mr Thamsanqa? Is he perhaps there?
Secretary	May I ask who would like to speak to him?
Peter	Yes, this is Peter Murray speaking.
Secretary	Please hold on, Mr Murray. I'll just look and see whether he is in his office.
Peter	Okay.

oooOooo

Secretary	Mr Murray, I'm sorry, Mr Thamsanqa is not here at the moment. He went out.
Peter	Do you know when he'll be back?
Secretary	I'm sorry, he didn't say. Would you like to leave a message?
Peter	Yes, please tell him that I wanted to get in touch with him about the cricket tomorrow. Perhaps he can phone me at home this evening.

Secretary	All right Mr Murray. I'll tell him. What's your telephone number?
Peter	It's 531-3767.
Secretary	All right, Mr Murray.
Peter	Thank you. Goodbye.
Secretary	Goodbye, Mr Murray.

oooOooo

David	David Murray speaking.
Themba	Hello, David. How are you, my boy?
David	Oh, hello, Mr Thamsanqa. I'm fine thanks. And you?
Themba	No, I'm fine. Is your father perhaps there, David?
David	Yes. Wait a moment. I'll call him.

oooOooo

Themba	Hello, Peter. It's Themba here. Thanks for phoning. Unfortunately I was at a meeting the whole day. I got your message when it was already late (evening).
Peter	It doesn't matter. I know you are busy.
Themba	What time shall we meet tomorrow?
Peter	What about 9.30?
Themba	That's fine. Where?
Peter	In front of the main gate.
Themba	Okay, we'll be there at 9.30. We'll see each other then.
Peter	We'll see each other.

oooOooo

Jenny	Hello!
Thandi	Hello, may I speak to Mrs Murray?
Jenny	Hello, Thandi, it's me!
Thandi	Oh, sorry, my dear, I didn't recognise your voice. What's wrong?
Jenny	Oh, I've just got a little cold.
Thandi	Oh, I'm sorry. I'm phoning you because Themba and I are going to that new Xhosa restaurant on Saturday evening. We would like to invite you and Peter to join us. Can you come? Do you think you will be better by then?
Jenny	Oh, that would be lovely. I read about that restaurant in the paper last weekend. My mouth was watering. The (description of the) food brought back childhood memories. We used to eat all those traditional dishes on the farm!

Thandi   Well then, let me fetch you so that we can meet Peter and
          Themba after the cricket game.
Jenny   Thank you, my dear. We'll see each other.

Unit 12 At the cricket match

Themba   It's lovely to see so much interest in cricket these days.
          Look at all these budding Makhaya Ntinis playing cricket.
Peter   Indeed. Wherever you look these days there are boys playing
          cricket. Did you play cricket when you were at school,
          Themba?
Themba   Yes, I liked playing cricket very much. I was a wicket-
          keeper–batsman. In fact, I opened the innings!
Peter   Really!
Themba   And you, mate, which sports did you play?
Peter   Well, I played tennis and rugby at school. Unfortunately, I
          broke my arm when I was still playing under 15. After that I
          never played rugby again.
Themba   What position did you play?
Peter   I was a scrumhalf. Though I didn't play cricket I like to watch
          it very much especially when we play overseas teams. Did you
          play rugby or soccer?
Themba   I played rugby.
Peter   What position?
Themba   I was 8th man.
Peter   What about soccer? Did you play it?
Themba   Yes, I played, it but I preferred rugby.
Peter   It is very interesting how sport has the power to unite
          a nation.
Themba   You're right. Remember the support the whole country gave
          AmaBhokobhoko at the world cup final! Who can forget how
          everyone sang, *Tshotsholoza*, as if in one voice.
Peter   Indeed, I'm sure that the way the crowd sang gave
          AmaBhokobhoko the impetus that they needed to win the
          world cup!
Themba   Wow! Who could forget the pride on President Mandela's face
          when he wore the No.6 jersey and held the trophy aloft together
          with François Pienaar.

Peter	*Bafana Bafana* also got support like that when they won the African Cup of Nations. By the way, what do you do these days to keep yourself fit?
Themba	E-e, I try to run three times a week, and I play squash regularly. And you?
Peter	I cycle, and I try to walk up the mountain on Sundays. But sometimes it's difficult to find the time because my hobby is woodwork.
Themba	Mine is photography. But the problem is just to find the time!
Peter	Look, the players have come back. Lunch is finished. The game is going to start now. Let's go back to our seats.

Unit 13 Let's go to that new restaurant

Restauranteur	Good evening. Welcome to *iZiko Lethu*. We are very glad to see you. How are you?
Themba	No, we are fine except that we are hungry! Do you perhaps have a table for four?
Restauranteur	Of course! Follow me.
Thandi	Can we perhaps have a table near the window?
Restauranteur	Here it is. How is this?
Thandi	It's fine! Thank you.
Restauranteur	Here is the menu.
Themba	What do you recommend? What are the specials today?
Restauranteur	Well, to start with we have *isonka samanzi*.
Jenny	Oh! That reminds me of my childhood on the farm. I really loved *isonka samanzi*.
Restauranteur	Is that so, *Nkosikazi*! Where do you come from?
Jenny	I grew up on a farm e*maXhoseni*.
Restauranteur	Where exactly?
Jenny	Near Queenstown.
Restauranteur	Oh, I don't know that region. I grew up in Transkei. Well, let me also recommend *umphokoqo*, *umngqusho*, *umfino*, mutton stew and tripe.
Peter	I have forgotten, what exactly is *umphokoqo*?
Restauranteur	It's cooked mealie meal.
Peter	Oh yes, I remember now.
Jenny	How is your *umfino* (made)?
Restauranteur	It's with spinach and onion. May I bring you something

	to drink while you are deciding. How about *umqombothi*, *amarhewu* or beer?
Themba	Let's taste all! We have brought a bottle of wine. Can you open it?
Restauranteur	Of course!

oooOooo

Restauranteur	Are you ready to order?
Themba	No, we haven't chosen yet.
Restauranteur	Fine, I'll come back in a little while.
Jenny	By the way, *Mnumzana*, where is the cloakroom?
Restauranteur	Follow me, I'll show you.
Jenny	Thank you. Excuse me for a little.
The others	That's fine.

oooOooo

Restauranteur	Here's the meal!
Jenny	Mm, it smells delicious! It also looks delicious!
Restauranteur	Well then, I hope that you'll enjoy your meal!

oooOooo

Restauranteur	Have you eaten well?
The friends	Very much so!
Jenny	I would like to get your recipe of *umngqusho* if it is not a secret?
Restauranteur	I'll ask the cook for it.
Jenny	I would be grateful.
Restauranteur	What about (some) dessert?
The friends	Thanks very much but we've all had enough (to eat).
Themba	May we have the bill now?
Restauranteur	No sooner said than done!

Unit 14 Buying clothes and various African arts and crafts

Jenny	Gosh! Please just look at all these beautiful things! Woven mats, wall hangings, pottery, baskets and clothing. It's going to be difficult to choose!
Assistant	Good day, may I help you?
Jenny	Your shop is really very beautiful! I know I'm going to spend a lot of money today!
Assistant	Thanks very much. Would you like to look around first?

Jenny	That would be nice.
Assistant	Call me if you need help or you want to know anything.
Jenny	Okay, *Nkosikazi*. I would like to start looking at dresses and skirts.
Peter	That wall hanging on that wall over there is beautiful, *Nkosikazi*.
Assistant	Which one, sir?
Peter	That one with the woman smoking a pipe. Where was it made?
Assistant	It was made by the local women.
Peter	How much does it cost, *Nkosikazi*?
Assistant	Unfortunately these wall hangings cost a lot of money nowadays because they are made by hand and are of mohair.
Peter	I understand.

oooOooo

Assistant	Oo! You look very smart, *Nkosikazi*! That dress is very beautiful! It really suits you!
Jenny	Yes, but it's a bit small. Have you got it in a bigger size?
Assistant	I'll look for a bigger size. What size?
Jenny	36.
Assistant	What colour would you like?
Jenny	Yellow or red.
Assistant	Unfortunately we only have white, brown and green in your size.
Jenny	That's fine, I'll try on the brown one.

oooOooo

Jenny	It fits me perfectly. I'll take it! How much is it?
Assistant	If you buy the dress and the skirt I can reduce the price. They'll cost R225 together.
Jenny	Fine. I'll buy both but I don't have enough money. Do you accept credit cards?
Assistant	Don't worry, *Nkosikazi*. We accept cash, cheques and credit cards.
Jenny	That's good, because I still want to buy other things like pottery, basketware, and especially (jewellery) beads. (*amaso*)
Assistant	You mean '*iintsimbi*'. '*Amaso*' are bigger than *iintsimbi*.
Jenny	Of course! Now I remember!
Assistant	What sort of beads do you want? Necklaces, bracelets? Do you like these anklets?

Jenny	Gosh! Everything is very beautiful. Again it's going to be very difficult for me to choose! Look at all the colours!
Assistant	That's OK, *Nkosikazi*, take your time!

Unit 15 Travel woes

Peter	Good day, *tata*, how are you?
Passerby	Good day. No, I am still tottering along, my chap.
Peter	Can you help us, *bawo*? We are lost. Is this perhaps the road leading to *Sandile*'s grave?
Passerby	No, you are on the wrong road.
Peter	Where do we get (on) the right road then?
Passerby	Turn back on the road you are on now. When you come to the first intersection follow the road to the left. After that, go straight. After one kilometre you'll see the sign 'To Sandile's Grave'.
Peter	What is the road like? Is it a tarred road?
Passerby	No, it's a gravel road. It is also rather winding like a millipede! There is another road to the right which is shorter. Unfortunately it is not good.
Peter	Thank you very much, *tata*. By the way, where are you going? Can we give you a lift?
Passerby	No, thank you, I'm waiting here for my daughter.

oooOooo

Peter	Damn! The tyre wouldn't have burst if we had taken the tarred road!
Jenny	One is always wise after an event!

oooOooo

Motorist	Hello, What's the trouble? Can I help you?
Peter	Hello, *Mnumzana*. My tyre seems to have burst. Can you lend me your jack? Unfortunately mine has disappeared.
Motorist	What a shame! Wait a minute, I'll get the jack out of my boot. Has your spare got air?
Peter	Fortunately I pumped it up yesterday.
Jenny	Thank goodness, you arrived, *Mnumzana*!
Peter	Indeed! By the way, is there a garage nearby? I'm afraid we are soon going to run out of petrol. I can't understand it because I filled the tank yesterday!

Motorist   Perhaps there is a hole in the tank? You know, that happens quite easily on country roads. Let's have a look!

Peter   Oh, heavens! You are right. Indeed, there is a little hole the size of a pea. What are we going to do now?

Motorist   No, don't worry. If you have some soap I'll close it up. After that you will be able to drive to the garage.

Peter   How far is the garage?

Motorist   It's nearby, follow me.

Peter   Thank you, *Mnumzana*. You've really helped us.

oooOooo

Mechanic   Good day, can I help you, sir?

Peter   Good day, *Mnumzana*. Unfortunately, there is a little hole in my petrol tank. Can you repair it immediately?

Mechanic   Eh, I have a lot of work but I'll try.

Peter   Oh I thank you. How long will it take?

Mechanic   Mm, let me see, perhaps two hours.

Peter   Can you tell me how much it will cost?

Mechanic   It's difficult to tell exactly. About R350.

Peter   Fine, *Mnumzana*. Let's leave the car. We'll see each other later.

Unit 16 Xhosa heritage trail

Themba   How was your holiday *emaXhoseni*? Did you have a pleasant trip?

Peter   It was wonderful, though we had some problems with the car but luckily we were helped by some very kind people.

Thandi   Well, it's usually like that in the rural areas. But where exactly did you go?

Jenny   We started our trip in **Peddie**. Since my university days when I was studying Xhosa, I've always wanted to visit the historical places of the Eastern Cape. By the way, what is **Peddie** in Xhosa? I've forgotten.

Thandi   It's *Ngqushwa*.

Jenny   Oh, yes, of course. Well, we went to **Peddie** because we wanted to see that famous tree, the white milkwood tree. After that we headed for **King William's Town** to visit the **Kaffrarian Museum** where there is a very interesting collection of traditional artifacts. In the afternoon we went to **Steve Biko**'s house. We also visited his grave.

Peter	The following day, we went off to **Hogsback** making a detour and passing through **Keiskammahoek** into the *Amalinde* region.
Themba	Oh *Amalinde*! You know, it was in that region that one of the bloodiest battles in Xhosa history was fought.
Jenny	Of course! That's the battle that is described in the poem *UThuthula* by **Jolobe**, which was one of our (prescribed) poems at university.
Themba	The whole region near the *Amathole* Mountains is full of Xhosa history. There are many places which are named after *Rharhabe* chiefs.
Peter	Yes, we passed *Sandile*'s Dam and also saw *Ngqika's* grave on the way to **Alice**. In **Alice** we were very interested to visit Lovedale College and **Fort Hare University** where **Nelson Mandela** was a student together with many other present-day leaders.
Jenny	I had just finished reading *The Ochre People* written by **Noni Jabavu**. I therefore very much wanted to find the house in **Middledrift** where her father, Professor Jabavu, lived when he was professor of African languages at **Fort Hare**. Have you ever read this book?
Thandi	Yes, **Noni Jabavu** writes very well so much so that one can actually see the beauty of this region. She describes so beautifully the way of life and customs of the Xhosa people of that time. Have you also read her other book *Drawn in Colour*?
Jenny	Yes, am I not right in saying that that was her first book?
Themba	Did you find **Jabavu**'s house after all?
Jenny	No, unfortunately we didn't.
Thandi	Where did you head for after that?
Peter	We stayed at **Hogsback** for a few days. Gosh! The beauty of that region is breathtaking. The peace! And the tranquillity! The indigenous forests and the waterfalls are quite stunning, and the many species of birds and their singing are just too wonderful to experience.
Themba	You must have been in your element, Peter, person of nature that you are!
Peter	You can say that again! Therefore we decided to stay there several days.

Jenny   The next place we visited was **Stutterheim**. We wanted to see *Sandile's* grave but we got lost and gave up. We wanted to follow *Sandile's* walk but we had no time.

Peter   The following day we headed for **Umtata**. On the way, we cut through beautiful pastures, with cattle and sheep dotting the slopes, passing through **Komga**, **Butterworth** and **Idyutywa**. We wanted to visit **Qunu** where **Nelson Mandela** was born. Unfortunately, his childhood home is not there any more but his school is still there.

Themba   Did you have time to go to the coast?

Peter   Of course! We stayed at **Port St Johns** for three days.
The nature there! The hills descending to the coast, the round huts and the maize fields! Indeed, the country is still so unspoilt (it is like a young maiden!).

Themba   No, you've made me quite jealous!

Jenny   On the way to **Umtata**, at **Libode**, we passed by an old country store. It reminded me of **Jolobe**'s essay *Ivenkile Yangaphandle*. We actually wanted to go to **Cala**.

Thandi   What attracted you to **Cala**?

Jenny   We were invited there by friends.

Thandi   What did you do there?

Jenny   We took part in the daily activities. And the kindness we found there was so heartwarming. In the evenings, we even sat around the fire and listened to folktales like days of old!

Key to exercises

Unit 1

1 (a) Molo Thandi. (b) Molo mama.
(c) Molo tata. (d) Molo sisi. (e) Molo
bhuti. (f) Molo nkosikazi. (g) Molo
mnumzana/ mhlekazi. (h) Molo
nkosazana. (i) Molo mntwan'am.
(j) Molweni manene namanenekazi.
(k) Ndingu... (l) Ndiyavuya ukukwazi.
2 (a) Unjani (namhlanje)? (b) Uhlala
eKapa? (c) Ndawoni kanye?
3 (a) Namkelekile eKapa, manene
namanenekazi. (b) Ndiyaphila, enkosi.
(c) Ndiyavuya ukukwazi. (d) Ndihlala
eKapa. (e) Bekumnandi ukuthetha
nawe. (f) Bekumnandi ukudibana
nawe. (g) Sobonana kwakhona
kamsinya. (h) Sala kakuhle. (i) Salani
kakuhle. (j) Hamba kakuhle.
(k) Hambani kakuhle. **4** (a) Uphila
njani? / Unjani namhlanje? (b) Uhlala
phi? (c) Ndawoni kanye? **5** Nam
ndiyavuya ukukwazi Jenny.
6 knowledgeable person; news/affair;
danger; opportunity/chance; try, strive.
7 (a) ibhafrum – bathroom (b) ibhedi –
bed (c) ikhabhathi – cupboard
(d) idrowa – drawer (e) iwodrophu –
wardrobe (f) ishelefu – shelf
(g) ibhokisi – box (h) itipoti – teapot
(i) ifolokhwe – fork (j) iwotshi – watch
(k) ipensile – pencil (l) irediyo – radio
(m) iheji – hedge (n) igaraji – garage
(o) ibhayisikile – bicycle (p) imoto –
motor(car) (q) ilori – lorry (r) iteksi –
taxi (s) ifomu – form (t) imali – money.

Unit 2

1 (a) Ngubani igama lakho? /
Ùngubani? (b) Ùnjani namhlanje?
(c) Uyafunda? (d) Ufunda phi
ukusithetha isiXhosa? **2** <u>wakho</u>; <u>wam</u>;
<u>wakho</u>; <u>wam</u>. **3** (a) Ngena.
(b) Kumnandi kakhulu ukudibana
nawe. (c) Hlala phantsi. (d) Kunjani
ngokuphunga okanye ngokusela?
(e) Hamba kakuhle. **4** (a) Ùfuna
(ukuphunga) ikofu? (b) Ùfuna
(ukuphunga) iti? (c) Ùfuna ukudibana
noPeter? (d) Ùfuna ukuthetha
noThemba? (e) Ufuna ukuthetha
isiXhosa? (f) Ufuna ukuhlala
ngaphandle? (g) Ufuna ukuhlala
ngaphakathi? (h) Ufuna ukuhamba
ngoku? **5** (a) Nifuna (ukuphunga)
ikofu? (b) Nifuna (ukuphunga) iti?
(c) Nifuna ukudibana noPeter?
(d) Nifuna ukuthetha noThemba?
(e) Nifuna ukuthetha isiXhosa?
(f) Nifuna ukuhlala ngaphandle?
(g) Nifuna ukuhlala ngaphakathi?
(h) Nifuna ukuhamba ngoku?
6 (a) Ukhetha iti okanye ikofu?
(b) Ukhetha ukuhlala ngaphakathi
okanye ngaphandle? (c) Ukhetha
ukuthetha isiXhosa okanye isiNgesi?
7 (a) Masingene!

(b) Masihlale phantsi! (c) Masithethe isiXhosa! (d) Masiphunge ikofu! (e) Masiphunge iti! (f) Masisele into ebandayo! (g) Masihlale ngaphandle! (h) Masincokole! (i) Masisale! (j) Masiye / Masihambe. **8** (a) Ḇahlala; eKapa / ePinelands. (b) Ùfunda; esikolweni. (c) Úfunda; esikolweni. (d) Ḇahlala; ePinelands. **9** (a) Nguḇani igama lakho? (b) Ùhlala phi? (c) Ùphila njani namhlanje? Possible answers: (a) NdinguJohn Smith. (b) Ndihlala eKapa. (c) Ndiphila kakuhle. **10** UJenny: Molo Thandi, wamkelekile. UThandi: Molo, sisi. UJenny: Ngena. Kunjani namhlanje? UThandi: Ndisaphila. Unjani wena? UJenny: Ndikhona, sisi. Ufuna into yokusela? UThandi: Hayi, Jenny, ndikhetha ikofu. UJenny: Kulungile. Masiphunge. Ufuna ukuhlala ngaphakathi? UThandi: Hayi, sisi. Masihlale ngaphandle. Lihle namhlanje. Ndingakuncedisa? UJenny: Ewe, ungandincedisa, enkosi. (a) yes (b) no (c) no (d) yes.

Unit 3

1 (a) Ndifuna ukuthetha isiXhosa. (b) Ndingathetha isiNgesi? (c) Ndithanda ukuthetha isiXhosa. (d) Ndizama ukuthetha isiXhosa. (e) Ndithetha isiXhosa kancinci nje. (f) Ndisafunda. (g) Ndisaphazama kakhulu xa ndithetha isiXhosa. (h) Nceda ndilungise. **2** (a) Andiqondi. (b) Nceda uphinde kwakhona. (c) Andilandeli. (d) Uxolo, ùthini? **3** (a) Hayi, andikwazi. (b) Hayi, andisithethi kakuhle. (c) Hayi, andiqondi. (d) Hayi,

andiphilanga. (e) Hayi, andikhumbuli. (f) Hayi, andifuni (kuphunga) kofu. (g) Hayi, andifuni manzi. (water) **4** (a) Nceda uthethe isiXhosa / Ndicela uthethe isiXhosa. (b) Nceda uzekelele / Ndicela uzekelele. (c) Nceda uphinde kwakhona / Ndicela uphinde kwakhona. (d) Nceda uzame kwakhona / Ndicela uzame kwakhona. (e) Nceda undixelele / Ndicela undixelele. **5** (a) When was President Nelson Mandela born? (b) He was born on July 18, 1918. (a) Where did he grow up? (b) He grew up in Qunu in the Eastern Cape Province. (a) Where did he go to school? (b) He went to a Weslyan school. After that he went to the University of Fort Hare. (a) What did he do after that? (b) He worked as a policeman on the mines but he carried on with his law studies. **6** (a) Kuthethwa isiNgesi, isiBhulu nesiXhosa. (b) Kuthethwa isiXhosa, isiNgesi nesiBhulu. (c) Kuthethwa isiTswana nesiBhulu. (d) Kuthethwa isiSuthu nesiBhulu. (e) Zonke iilwimi zithethwa eGauteng. (f) Kuthethwa isiSwati, isiTsonga, isiZulu, isiNdebele nesiBhulu. (g) Kuthethwa isiZulu nesiNgesi. (h) Kuthethwa isiTswana, nesiBhulu. (i) Kuthethwa isiVenda, isiPedi nesiBhulu. (j) Kuthethwa isiXhosa eMpuma-Koloni naseNtshona-Koloni. (k) Kuthethwa isiZulu kwaZulu-Natal eMpumalanga naseGoli. (l) Kuthethwa isiTswana eMntla-Ntshona naseMntla-Koloni. (m) Kuthethwa isiSuthu eFreyistata. **7** (a) AmaZulu athetha isiZulu. (b) AmaSwati athetha isiSwati. (c) AmaNdebele athetha isiNdebele. (d) AmaBhulu athetha isiBhulu.

(e) AmaVenda athetha isiVenda.
(f) AmaNgesi athetha isiNgesi.
(g) Abe̲Tswana bathetha isiTswana.
(h) Abe̲Suthu bathetha isiSuthu.

Unit 4

1 (a) o̲o̲titshala (b) ba̲lungile (c) ntoni?
(d) Ungumfundi (e) ntoni? (f) abazali
bakho? (g) Uyingcaphephe yezityalo
(h) ungutitshalakazi (i) ntoni?
(j) isiXhosa (k) nesiNgesi (l) abazali
(m) ungumphathi (n) ungugqirha.
2 umakhi̲, umbhali̲, umcoci̲, umculi̲,
umfoti, umguquli̲, umlawuli̲, umlimi̲,
umphathi̲, umqeqeshi̲, umsasazi̲,
umthengisi̲, umthwali (*porter),
umzobi̲. 3 (a) UThemba
ungumphathi. (b) USipho ungumakhi.
(c) ULinda ungumcoci.
(d) UNozipho ungumsasazi.
(e) USindi ungumbhali. (f) ULumkile
ungumlimi. (g) UThandeka
ungumculi. (h) UXoliswa
ungumguquli. (i) UYizani
ungumthengisi. (j) UThandi
ungugqirha. 4 Ngabantwana;
ngabazukulwana; y̲intombi: ngutata;
ngumama; ngutat'omkhulu;
ngumakhulu. 5 (a) Lo ngunyana wam.
(b) Ngabazali bam. (c) Yintombi yam.
(d) Lo ngutat'omkhulu wam. (e) Lo
ngumama wam. (f) Yinkosikazi yam.
(g) Ngabantwana bam. (h) Lo
ngumyeni wam. 6 (a) Uvela efama
ngaseRhini. (b) Uhlala eKapa ngoku.
(c) Uya eKirstenbosch yonke imihla.
(d) Uvela eMpuma-Koloni.
(e) Ufundisa abantu abafuna ukufunda
ukuthetha isiXhosa, oosomashishini,

abasebenzi beenkampani njalo, njalo.
(f) Usebenza kwisibhedlele
sabantwana iRed Cross. (g) Uya
kwikliniki yePrimary Health Care.
(h) Usebenzela inkampani yeenqwelo-
moya. 7 (a) Ndivela e__; (b) Ndihlala
e___ ngoku; (c) Nding___ / Ndil___;
Ndiy___; (d) Ndisebenza e___ /
Ndisebenzela ___ 8 (a) ndisebenze̲la
(b) iphekela (c) uyandifundi̲sa (d)
ufunde̲la (e) bayathanda̲na.
9 (a) Masifundi̲sane! (b) Masidibane!
(c) Masincedi̲sane! (d) Masakhane!
10 (a) ndihambe ngoku (b) ndiye
emsebenzini (c) ndisebenze ngoku
(d) ndiye esibhedlele (e) ndigoduke
(f) ndithethe isiXhosa yonke imihla
(g) ndihlawule ngekhadi.

11 (a) ngebhasi; nge-eropleni (b) nge-
eropleni; ngemoto (c) ngokomsebenzi;
ndingumphathi (d) kwishishini;
e-ofisi̲ni (e) nangokuhlwa; ngamanye
(f) ngento. 12 Ba̲ngumthi; Ba̲yinyoka;
Uyinyoka; Ungumkhombe;
Uyindlovu. 13 UJenny: Thandi,
usebenza kwesiphi isibhedlele?
UThandi: Ndisebenza kwisibhedlele
sabantwana iRed Cross. UJenny: Oo,
wenza umsebenzi omkhulu. Usebenza
khona imini yonke? UThandi: Hayi,
ndisebenza esibhedlele kusasa
kuphela. Emva kwemini ndisebenza
kwikliniki yePrimary Health Care.
UJenny: Ngumsebenzi onzima
kanjalo. UThandi: Nawe usebenza
kakhulu, Jenny. UJenny: Masiye
ngaphandle ngoku. Nantsi ikofu
nekeyiki. Ndigqibile ekhitshini.
(a) Jenny and Thandi (b) about their
work (c) in the kitchen.

Unit 5

1 (a) Iphi iswekile? (b) Luphi ubisi?
(c) Iphi ikeyiki? (d) Liphi icephe?
(e) Iphi ikofu? (f) Iphi iti? (g) Iphi
itispuni? 2 (a) Nantsi iswekile.
(b) Nalu ubisi. (c) Nantsi ikeyiki.
(d) Nali icephe. (e) Nantsi ikofu.
(f) Nantsi iti. (g) Nantsi itispuni.
3 (a) Ndi_yayi_thanda.
(b)Ndi_yawa_thanda. (c) Ndi_yazi_thanda.
(d) Ndi_yazi_thanda. (e) Ndi_yayi_thanda.
4 (a) _Yi_zalise. (b) _Wa_bilise. (c) _Lu_zise.
(d) _Yi_gqithise. (e) _Zi_ncede.
5 (a) Unjani namhlanje? (b) Banjani
abantwana? (c) Unjani umyeni
wakho? (d) Injani inkosikazi yakho?
(e) Banjani abazali bakho? (f) Unjani
umsebenzi? (g) Linjani izulu?
(h) Injani ikeyeki? (i) Zinjani
iisengwitshi? 6 (a) (Ionti) _y_enze
shushu; (_u_bisi) unga_lu_bilisi; (umxube)
_wu_zamisele (b)1¼ iikomityi _ze_castor
sugar; 2 iikomityi _ze_flawa; ikomity
_y_obisi; 90gm _ye_majarini; 1½ iitispuni
_ze_vanilla essence; indlela _y_okwenza;
umxube _wo_bisi; iitin _ze_keyiki;
ipakethe _ye_-icing sugar; 250 gm
_ye_majarini; icephe lecocoa powder;
icephc _la_manzi. 7 Amaqanda; iflawa;
ibhotholo; iswekile; ubisi; imajarini;
i-icing sugar. 8 ikofu; amanzi; ikofu;
ubisi; ubisi; ubisi; ubisi; ubisi.
9 1(c) 2(d) 3(g) 4(a) 5(e) 6(h) 7(b) 8(f).

Unit 6

1 1(b) 2(d) 3(a) 4(e) 5(c) 6(f).
2 (a) Ndiyagodola; kuyabanda
(b) Ndifudumele; kufudumele
(c) Kuyaphola; kupholile (d) Kuza
kuna ngomso; akuzi kuna namhlanje.

3 (a) Yimini _entle_ (b) embi
(c) _epholileyo_ (d) _eshushu_
(e) Bubusuku _obupholileyo_.
4 (a) _Si_za (b) _ni_ngathanda
(c) _Si_namanye (d) _nd_ingathanda
(e) _ku_xhomekeke (f) _u_vuthuza
(g) _lu_za kulwa (h) _N_diyoyika
(i) _a_sizi kuya (j) _ku_vuthuza gqitha
(k) _N_iza kuya (l) _ku_yanetha?
(m) _an_doyiki (n) _N_iza kuya
(o) _ku_shushu (p) _an_dikhathazeki /
_a_sikhathazeki.
5 **Weather forecast**: (a) winter
(b) summer
Makhe sikhangele ukuba imozulu
yangomso iza kuba njani na. Liza
kusibekela libanda linentshizane
eNtshona-Koloni kodwa
liqhaqhazelise amazinyo embindini
emva kwemini kude kuwe nekhephu
kwimimandla ephakamileyo
nasezintabeni. Siya phaya **eMpuma-
Koloni**. Gqaba amafu lipholile
linemvulana. Iimvula ziza
kunwenwela ngasempuma ngomso.
Ziya kuphela emva kwemini. (_Let's
just have a look at what the weather
will be tomorrow. It will be overcast
and cold with drizzle in the **Western
Cape** but in the interior it will be so
cold as to make your teeth chatter and
even snow falling in the high regions
and on the mountains. We go over to
the **Eastern Cape**. Scattered clouds,
cool with light rain. The rain will
spread towards the east tomorrow in
the afternoon._) Izanuse zemo-zulu
zilumkise ukuba liza kuzola de ilanga
ligqatse ubhobhoyi eNtshona-Koloni
ngomso. Kanti kuza kubhudla umoya
ongephi kodwa uza kutsho ngamandla
kufutshane nomxweme ngokuhlwa.

EMpuma-Koloni liya kuzola lithe gqaba amafu, kanti kungakho neendudumo mva. (*The weather forecasters warn that it will be fine becoming so hot that the sun will scorch even the African hoopoe bird in the* **Western Cape** *tomorrow. Whereas there will be a slight wind but it will be stronger near the coast towards evening. In the* **Eastern Cape** *it will be fine with a few scattered clouds and there could even be thunder later.*)
6 (a) Uyakwazi ukuthetha isiXhosa? Hayi, ndikwazi ukuthetha isiZulu kancinci kuphela / qha. (b) Uyakwazi ukuthetha isiNgesi? Ewe, ndisifunda esikolweni. (c) Ungandinceda? Kakade, ndiza kukunceda. Ndilusizi, andinakho ukukunceda / andinakukunceda. (d) Unokuza ngoLwesihlanu? Ndilusizi, andinakuza. Ndixakekile gqitha. (e) Ndingakufowunela ngomso? Kulungile. (f) Ndingakugalelela enye ikomityi yekofu? Hayi, enkosi. Ikomityi enye yanelekum. (g) Ndingangena? Ewe, ndicela ungene. **7** (a) Ndikhetha izinto ezimnandi. (b) Ndikhetha ikofu enobisi neswekile. (c) Ndikhetha iisengwitshi. (d) Ndikhetha imajarini. (e) Ndikhetha iwayini emhlophe.
8 (1) imnyama (2) ilubhelu (3) iluhlaza (4) imhlophe (5) ibomvu (6) iblawu / iluhlaza.
9 'Now we (have) hope for peace, Now we (have) hope for happiness / Through the coming of the summer rains / Because summer has now come.' From a summer rain region, i.e. Eastern Cape.

Unit 7

1 (a) Uxolo, ndikwenzakalisile? (b) Uxolo ngokukuphazamisa. (c) Ndilusizi, ndileyithi. (d) Uxolo, ndilibele. (e) Uxolo ngokukulindisa. (f) Uxolo, andisithethi kakuhle isiXhosa. **2** 1(c) 2(a) 3(e) 4(b) 5(d). **3** (a) Yiza apha. Kulungile, ndiyeza. (b) Yima! Kulungile, ndiyema. (c) Yenza iti ngoku. Kulungile, ndiza kuyenza ngoku. **4** / Ewe, ndifuna ipetroli. / (u-97) Ndifuna u-97/ Nceda ugalele u-97. / Hayi, ndiphe nge-50 rand qha namhlanje. / Nazi. / Hayi, kodwa unokukhangela amavili. / Faka 210. / Ewe. Musa ukulibala ukukhangela amanzi. / Enkosi. Nali icuba. **5** (a) Wazalelwa (b) ndazalelwa (c) bafudukela (d) Ndakhulela (e) wazalelwa (f) ndazalelwa (g) ndahlala (h) Utshatile? (i) sisebenza (j) Utshatile wena? (k) ndineentombi (l) unabantwana? (m) sinabantwana / ndinabantwana (n) isencinci (o) Kufuneka (p) Ndileyithi / Kuleyelithi (q) Bekumnandi. **6** (a) Ube nempela veki emnandi eRhini. (b) Ube neholide emnandi. (c) Ndikunqwenela impumelelo emsebenzini wakho. (d) Ubhale kakuhle. (e) Ube neKresmesi emyoli nonyak' omtsha omnandi. (f) On birthdays. At weddings. (On the occasion of President Mandela's marriage to Graca Machel, family members sang this song which is traditionally only sung at weddings.
7 1(i) 2(j) 3(b) 4(h) 5(g) 6(d) 7(c) 8(e) 9(f) 10(a). **8** Title.

Unit 8

1 amehlo; iindlebe; iingalo, izandla; iminwe; imilenze; iinyawo; iinzwane; amazinyo; amadolo. **2** (a) Unjani umntwana wakho? Usesesibhedlele? (b) Ndilusizi ukuba ubhetele kancinci kuphela/qha kodwa ndonwabile ukuba usekhaya kwakhona. (c) Utheni ugqirha? (d) Masithembe ukuba uza kuphila kamsinyane kwakhona. **3** (a) iflu (b) ifiva (c) ibhedi (d) usisi. **4** (a) Molo mama. (b) Unjani namhlanje? (c) Ndilusizi ukuba usesibhedlele ugula. (d) Ndingakunceda ngantoni? (e) Uneentlungu? (f) Ndithemba / ndinqwenela ukuba uya kuchacha ngokukhawuleza. (g) Sala kakuhle, mama. **5** 1(f) 2(d) 3(b) 4(c) 5(a) 6(e). **6** (c) (a) (d) (f) (b) (e). **7** (a) Unesibindi. (b) Unentliziyo kakhulu. (c) Banomqolo kakhulu. (d) Unomlomo. (e) Unesandla. **8** He/she has a cold hand. (b) He/she has a hot hand. (c) He/she gives with a beautiful heart. (d) He/she has a white heart. (e) Do you have heavy knees? **9** (a) My heart is sore. (b) He/she has a dark/black heart. (c) He/she has a pure heart. **10** (a) oluphi ulwimi (b) eziphi iilwimi (c) nezinye iilwimi ... kwelinye ilizwe? (d) oluphi ulwimi? (e) ngowuphi unyaka? (f) ngeyiphi inyanga? (g) Ngeyiphi imini? (h) kweliphi ilizwe? (i) Kweyiphi idolophu? (j) kwesiphi isikolo? (k) kweliphi ibanga? (l) kweyiphi iyunivesithi?

Unit 9

1 (a) kaNkosikazi Bongela (b) likaRycroft (c) bakaPeter (d) kaPeter (e) kaPhumla. **2** It is the coming of Nxele. **3** Umgquba, imbewu, imithi, izixhobo. **4** (a) Uphi – Unaye? nangu. (b) Ziphi – Unazo? nanzi. (c) Iphi – Unayo? Nantsi. (d) Liphi – Unalo? Nali. (e) Siphi – Unaso? Nasi. (f) Iphi – Unayo? Nantsi. (g) Liphi – Unalo? Nali. (h) Iphi – Unayo? Nantsi. (i) Iphi – Unayo? Nantsi. (j) Uphi – Unawo? Nanku. **5** 1(f) 2(g) 3(d) 4(c) 5(h) 6(a) 7(b) 8(e). **6** (a) ezi zinto (b) loo kiriva (c) le mithi (d) loo mithi (e) ezaa zithole (f) laa heji. **7** (a) le (b) lo (c) lo (d) le (e) esi (f) lo (g) le (h) le. **8** (a) Eyona (b) Eyona; (c) yeyona (d) Yeyona (e) lelona (f) eyona. **9** (a) -qokelela (b) yahlukanisani (c) Fakani (d) -bole (e) -gcine (f) -thatha (g) -nkcenkceshele (h) -tyaleni (i) -zaliseni (j) -tyaleni (k) -gcineni (l) -fe (m) Khumbulani (n) nqabe (o) -zama (p) -londoloza (q) nkcenkceshelani (r) -nkcenkceshela (s) nkcenkceshelani (t) Lumkani (u) -moshi (v) Jikelezani (w) -gcine.

Unit 10

1 1(c) 2(b) 3(d) 4(a). **2** (a) The dough is eaten by the dog. (b) The soil is beaten by the sun. (c) The children were entered by a bird. (d) It was gone by the custom. (e) This thing is deprived of time. (f) The depth of a pool is felt by a stick. **3** Horoscope; obituary. **4** (a) Bancokola e-ofisini / emsebenzini. (b) Kakuhle. (c) Baya ekhefi baphunge. (d) Ngoba/Kuba

uMary unyuselwe emsebenzini.
(e) Entlanganisweni.

5 1 (c) Ndiyireceptionist;
2 (a) Ndingumpheki; 3 (b) Ndiyintatheli.

6 (a) **Social worker** (wanted). *Our company is looking for the service of an energetic hard-working person (who can work hard) in child protection. A driver's licence and knowledge of Xhosa are essential. Experience in child care and speaking English and Afrikaans well is of advantage. Salary is negotiable according to work experience. Send your CV and references of three people who can be contacted and the job application to _____. Closing date is ____.* (b) **Receptionist / secretary** (wanted). *A well-known garage (place that repairs and sells cars) is looking for a receptionist / secretary. The applicant must have the following skills: be computer literate; able to write and send accounts; write and answer all letters; communicate with people; speak Xhosa, English and Afrikaans well. Experience in secretarial work is also required. This includes: answering calls and enquiries; dealing with visitors; writing letters and posting outgoing mail; looking after all stationery; preparing meetings. Fax CV and three contactable references to __.*

7 (a) good (b) bad (c) interesting
(d) brave (e) popular (beloved)
(f) energetic (g) knowledgeable
(h) kind (i) lonely (j) experienced
(k) calm (l) diligent (m) famous
(n) busy.

Unit 11

1 (a) akakho (b) akazi kuba kho (na)
(c) akazi kubuya (d) akakho,
usekhaya. (e) awukho (f) ayikho.

2 (a) ndingathetha (b) Ndilusizi
(c) usaxakekile (d) ukushiya umyalezo
(e) Mxelele ukuba ndiza kuzama
ukumfowunela kwakhona emva
kwemini. **3** For example, Wrong
number. (Inombolo ewrongo)

4 (a) Ufuna ukuthetha noNksk. Bizo.
(b) Hayi, akakho. (c) Uvile ukuba
uNksk. Bizo ufuna umntu oza
kumncedisa kwishishini lakhe. Ufuna
ukwenza isicelo. (d) Uza kuzama
ukufowuna ngentsimbi yesithandathu.

5 (a) Ndithethe noVal namhlanje.
(b) Siza kuya kubukela ifilim ngeCawa.
(c) Ungahamba nathi? (d) UVal uza
kundiphuthuma ngentsimbi yesihlanu.

6 (a) Ndinabantwana abathathu,
iintombi ezimbini nonyana omnye.
(b) imiyalezo emine (c) iinombolo
zefowuni ezimbini (d) amatikiti
amahlanu (e) iincwadi ezintandathu.

7 UThandi: Molo sisi. UNomsa: Ewe
ke, sisi. Kunjani? UThandi: Ndikhona,
sisi, ngaphandle nje komsebenzi.
Unjani wena? UNomsa: Ndiphilile,
enkosi. Uxakekile? UThandi: Ewe,
kufuneka ndiye evenkileni. Sifuna
ukulungiselela itheko ngoMgqibelo.
Ukuba lihle singenza ibrayi
ngokuhlwa. Singathanda ukuba nize
wena noSipho? Siza kumema nabanye
abahlobo. UNomsa: Enkosi
ngokusimema. Ndingathanda ukuza
kodwa ndiza kuthetha noSipho kuqala.
Ndiza kukufowunela ngokuhlwa
okanye ngomso. UThandi:
Ndiyathemba ukuba uSipho unokuza.

UNomsa: Nam ndiyathemba.
UThandi: Awu, nkosi yam, seyi-5
o'clock. Kufuneka ndikhawuleze
ndiye evenkileni. Sobonana
ngoMgqibelo mhlawumbi. UNomsa:
Kamnandi. (a) yes (b) yes (c) no
(d) no (e) yes. **8** 1(e) 2(b) 3(g) 4(c)
5(f) 6(a) 7(h) 8(d).
9 (a) nabani? (b) Ngubani (c) bani?
(d) eyiphi (e) Ngubani (f) Ithini (h)
Ithini (i) Ithini (j) ntoni? (k) ngantoni?
(l) Yintoni (m) ntoni? **10** 1(d) 2(b) 3(e)
4(a) 5(c).

Unit 12

1 (a) isenta – centre (b) iflenki – flank
(c) iflyhafu – flyhalf (d) ihoka –
hooker (e) ilokhu – lock (f) isikramhafu
– scrumhalf (g) irenka / front rank
(h) isikoro – score (i) isoka – soccer
(j) amatikiti – tickets. **2** (a) Yikhabe!
(b) Yibambe! (c) Yiphose! (d) Yigqithise!
(e) Yibethe! **3** (a) nini (b) awaphi
(c) ngubani (d) ngubani (e) njani /
ngubani (f) bani (g) eliphi.
4 (a) Ndi<u>s</u>adlala (b) <u>Andidlali</u>
(c) <u>Andis</u>adlali (d) <u>Nd</u>andikade
<u>nd</u>idlala (e) (Andi)zange ndiwudlal<u>e</u>.
5 (a) Kutheni wena uw<u>u</u>thanda
umbhoxo? (b) Kutheni wena
ukuthanda? (c) Kutheni wena
ungayithandi? (d) Kutheni wena
ungakuthandi? **6** (a) Wawukade
uthunga / Wawuthunga ntoni?
(b) Wawukade unitha / Wawunitha
ntoni? (c) Wawukade ucula /
Wawucula / ntoni? (d) Wawukade
udanisa yeyiphi imidaniso?
(e) Wawukade uloba phi? **7**
(a) Uyayithanda imidlalo?
(b) Uxhasa eliphi iqela?

(c) Uyayibukela imidlalo kumabona-
kude? (d) Unemisetyenzana
yokuzonwabisa? (e) Uyawuthanda
umculo? **8** (a) <u>waye</u>mele
(b) <u>waye</u>yintloko (c) <u>waye</u>dlalela
(d) <u>waye</u>ngomnye. **9** (a) USipho
udibana noVuyani. (b) Ebegula.
(c) Ebegula inyanga yonke.
(d) Bathetha ngoNomsa. (e) Udla
ngokubaleka. (f) Wawa, wophuka
umlenze. (g) Ufuna ukufowunela
umyeni wakhe kuba ufuna ukufumana
isibhedlele. **10** (a) UVuyani <u>u</u>funa
ukufowunela umyeni wo<u>m</u>hlobo
<u>wa</u>khe. (b) UVuyani <u>u</u>funa
ukufowunela inkosikazi <u>y</u>omhlobo
<u>wa</u>khe. (c) UVuyani <u>u</u>funa
ukufowunela abazali <u>b</u>omhlobo
<u>wa</u>khe. **11** 1(g) 2(i) 3(e) 4(a) 5(d) 6(h)
7(c) 8(b) 9(j) 10(f).

Unit 13

1 (a) Ukutya akumnandi.
(b) Andinambithi kutya. (c) Isonka
asinancasa. (d) Andithandi nyama.
2 (a) kokulamba (b) kokunxanwa
(c) komsebenzi (d) kwezulu
(e) kokufunda gqitha. **3** (a) Imifuno
midala kakhulu. (b) Ama-apile
amnandi. (c) Isuphu ayinatyuwa
(konke). (d) Ndithanda isonka
esimhlophe. (e) iwayini ebomvu.
(f) Iitapile azishushu / ziyabanda.
4 (a) Unayo itafile yabantu ababini
(b) abathathu (c) abane (d) abahlanu?
5 (a) Ndingahlala ngaphandle?
(b) Nceda / Ndicela uzise uluhlu
lokutya / imenyu. (c) Ndingaodola
ngoku? (d) Ndingafumana iwayini
ebomvu? (e) Ndingafumana imifuno /
iziqhamo? **6** Ndingafumana (a) esinye

isilayi sesonka (b) obunye utywala
(c) enye ifolokhwe (d) enye imela
(e) elinye icephe (f) enye itispuni
(g) enye ipleyiti (h) enye ikomityi yeti.
7 (a) bedroom (b) sitting room /
lounge (c) study. **8** 1(e) 2(g) 3(f) 4(b)
5(a) 6(d) 7(c). **9** (a) Ndingathanda
isidudu, izilayi ezibini zesonka
esimdaka, iqanda elithambileyo,
ibhotolo nejam. (b) Ndingathanda
inyama ebandayo, isaladi, isilayi
esinye sesonka esimhlophe nesilayi
esinye sesonka samasi (setshizi).
(c) Ndingathanda inyama yegusha,
iitapile, imifuno neziqhamo.
10 itswele elikhulu, iminqathe,
iimbotyi ezintsha, iiphizi, iimbotyi
zeswekile, igaliki, ipasili, iitapile.
11 (a) (Kuba) ufuna ukwenza isaladi
yeziqhamo. (b) Ama-apile, amapere,
ipayina, ii-orenji, iipesika, iibhanana
nevatala. (c) Ezinye ziluhlaza, ezinye
zivuthiwe. (d) Ivatala imnandi
inamanzi kakhulu. (e) Idla R7.
(f) Akathengi makhiwane neediliya.
12 (a) Nceda uhlambe iitapile.
(b) Musa ukuthatha iitapile ezinkulu,
thatha ezi ezincinci. (c) Chuba
amatswele amabini ne-apile (elinye).
(d) Nqunqa amatswele (kunye)
nethanga. (e) Tshweza iminqathe.
(f) Hlamba amagqabi eletisi
neetumato. (g) Zisa ezinye izitya.
(h) Zisekhabhathini phezu kwesinki.
(i) Vula itoti. (j) Vula nale.
(k) Khawulungise itafile. **13** Nomvuyo
othandekayo, Ndingathanda
ukukumema kwisidlo sangokuhlwa
ngoMgqibelo. Asibonananga ixesha
elide ngoko ke kungamnandi
ukuncokola kwakhona. Ndithemba

ukuba uMgqibelo ngokuhlwa ulungile
kuwe. Ngothando Nomsa.

Unit 14

1 (a) Ndingawafumana
(b) Ndingazifumana
(c) Ndingayifumana (d) Uyayithengisa
(e) Uyazithengisa. **2** (a) owuphi
(b) eyiphi (c) eziphi (d) eyiphi
(e) awaphi. **3** (a) advertisement
(b) ukuhombisa (c) likanopopi;
leenqawa; lengxowa (d) iimagi
< mug(s); iitsheyini < chain(s).
4 (a) Uvela eKapa (b) Ziphelile
(c) Uthenga iingobozi ezimbini
(d) Ulihlisa nge-10% (e) Kulo nyaka
uzayo. **5** 1 (b) (c) (d) (e) (f) (g) (h) (i)
(k); 2 (a) (b) (c) (d) (e) (h) (i) (j) (l).
6 (a) onamabala amaninzi
(b) aqaqambileyo (c) mifutshane
(d) udulu; itshipu; ezintle.
7 (a) emhlophe; omnyama; oluhlaza
(b) ibomvu; entsundu (c) zilubhelu
zakho; epinki. **8** (a) ngaphezu; zonke
(b) ilungileyo (c) kunazo zonke
(d) intle iluhlaza; kunayo iluhlaza.
9 (a) kunengonyama (b) kunehlosi
(c) kunondlebende (d) kunenyosi
(e) kunendlovu.
10 (a) njengonyama (b) njengehlosi
(c) njengondlebende (d) njengenyosi
(e) njengendlovu.
11 (a) inkosikazi / umfazi; from
umbhinqo 'skirt' (b) ubomi (c) lizwe
(d) wamema (e) ukufumana (f)
ngomnye; ungumyili; ungumnini;
ungumlawuli; bazithanda; uyifumene
bemkhuthaza.

Unit 15

1 1(b) 2(d) 3(g) 4(a) 5(j) 6(i) 7(c) 8(f)
9(h) 10(e). **2** (a) indlela ilungile?
(b) ayinangozi? (c) yindlela yetha?
(d) yindlela yegrabile? (e) indlela
isakhiwa (f) indlela sel' ivuliwe na.
3 (a) Uxolo Mnumzana. Ungandinceda
na? Ndilahlekile. (b) Ndifuna ukuya
kwivenkile ingu*Kwantu Crafts*/
evenkileni egama lingu*Kwantu Crafts*.
Uyayazi? (c) Hayi enkosi. Ndiyaqonda
apho ndiyifumana khona ivenkile.
Ngathi ikufutshane nam. Kuqala ndiza
kuhamba ngqo, emva koko ndijike
ngasekunene, emva koko kufuneka
ndijike ngasekhohlo. (d) Enkosi
kakhulu, Mnumzana. Kamnandi /
Hamba kakuhle. **4** (a) Zima
(b) Zikhona iibhasi eziya (c) eya
(d) Siphi isikhululo seebhasi (e) Ima
phi ibhasi eya (f) zinqabile kule.
5 (a) Ikhona igaraji (b) Ikhona
ivenkile (c) Sikhona. **6** (a) ivenkile e-
(b) isibhedlele esi- (c) isikhululo
samapolisa esi- (d) ifowuni e-
(e) ugqirha o- (f) igaraji e- (g)
idolophu e-. **7** (a) Ungandikhwelisa
na? (b) Ungandinceda na?
(c) Ungandiboleka ujack?
(d) Ungandibonisa indlela eya eRhini?
8 (a) azisebenzi (b) alusebenzi
(c) Ibhreki yesandla ayisebenzi
(d) ayisebenzi (e) Isihlambi sefestile
yangaphambili asisebenzi (f) Isibane
sangasemva sasekhohlo asisebenzi.
9 (a) Ndinevili elingenamoya. (b) Ivili
lam langaphambili lasekunene lifleti.
(c) Imoto yam yaphukile. (d) Imoto
yam ixingile. (e) Imoto yam
ayiqhwithi. (f) Ifuna amanzi.
(g) Iphelelwe yipretoli. (h) Ibhetri

yemoto yam ifile. (i) imoto yam
itsalwe. **10** (a) Imoto yam ibiwe
(b) Ujack wam ubiwe (c) Ivili lam
lolaleliso libiwe (d) Isipaji sam sibiwe
(e) Ingxowa yenkosikazi yam ibiwe.
11 (a) eCala. (b) Malunga
neekhilometha ezilishumi. (c) Ayintle
kangako. (d) Ngumgaqo wegrabile.
(e) Ungathanda ukubuka idolophu.
(f) Apho kukho indawo ekhuselekileyo
khona.

Unit 16

JJR Jolobe was born on July 25 1902
at Indwe near Cala where his father
was a minister. He first went to
schools at Indwe and Matatiele. In
1916 he was sent to St Matthews.
From 1916 onwards he taught at
different schools. At that time he lived
near Mt Frere where the Xhosa
dialects 'isiBhaca' and 'isiHlubi' and
Sotho are spoken. Therefore, his
Xhosa was weak. His first book,
UZagula, was extensively corrected by
SEK **Mqhayi**, Poet Laureate.
However, when he was a teacher in
Bhobhotyane and Mankazane he
learned pure Xhosa (lit. which is
spoken by the amaNgqika). In 1926 he
went to Fort Hare in Alice. There he
trained as a minister and received a
BA degree. From that time onwards he
published many books: *Umyezo*
('Orchard'), *Amavo* ('Stories'),
Elundini lo Thukela ('On the banks of
the Thukela') and others. *UThuthula* is
the most outstanding among **Jolobe**'s
poems especially his love poems. It is
a narrative poem which reminds us of

Helen of Troy. He edited many books. He also translated others into Xhosa. In 1952 he was awarded the **Vilakazi** medal by the University of the Witwatersrand. In 1973 he received a DLitt in acknowledgement of his Xhosa writing from the University of Fort Hare. **Dr Jolobe** died on May 16, 1976. He will never be forgotten in the history of the Xhosa language because he enriched it and its culture.

The Country Store

Even if you are a stranger it is not difficult to recognise a country store in our villages because it is the homestead with the most prominent buildings and which is also surrounded by trees. [...] Many black people are uneasy about calling white people by their names, and moreover, they like to give the white person who works among them a name in their language – a name that usually refers to the pecularities of its owner. Therefore, you will find that all the white shopkeepers in the villages have Xhosa names. As spectacles were not very common among blacks a white who arrived wearing them was immediately called '*Four Eyes*'. A short, chubby person would earn himself the name of '*Fatty*'. A chap oozing human kindness would be called '*Lover of the People*'. [...] Perhaps you may assume that at that store trade was conducted with money only, but this is not so. This store resembles a market place in other respects. For some to buy goods it is necessary that they themselves sell

goods to the shopkeeper. One brings eggs together with the sad news behind what necessitates their sale. [...] At this store it is not enough that only buying and selling takes place, it is also where the mail of the area comes. Thus you will find a pile of letters in the little chest nailed to the wall over there. [...] Apart from the points already mentioned, the country store fills another gap in the lives of the people of the area. It is also a gathering place where people meet one another and where messages going to areas not easily accessible are disseminated. At the store, you know that you'll meet at least one person who is going that way. To say nothing of the youth because the young people already enjoy the certainty of knowing that the store is the place to meet. [...]

Xhosa–English vocabulary

Nouns and verbs are listed in alphabetical order according to the **first letter of** the stem, e.g. *u*hambo, *uku*hamba, *ukw*azi, *ub*omi, *is*onka.

However, the question of where the division between prefix and stem in many **Class 9 and 10 nouns** 'presents an insoluble problem' (Pahl, H.W. (ed.) p. xxxv), e.g.:

| ingozi: | *in*gozi | or | *i*ngozi |
| incwadi: | *in*cwadi | or | *i*ncwadi |

To avoid possible confusion between these nouns and those that belong to **Class 5**, which also prefix 'i-' (but '*ama-*' in the plural), the **Class 9** prefix throughout this book is '*in-*' e.g. *in*gozi, *in*cwadi.

Nouns where '*g*' or '<u>k</u>' is inserted for reasons of pronunciation, e.g.:

> *in*gqokelela (< *uku*qokelela)
> *in*<u>k</u>xaso (< *uku*xhasa)

are listed according to the s**tem of the verb** from which they are derived. The bold numbers indicate the unit in which the word first appears or is explained.

A

*is*aci (*iz-*) *saying, idiom* **4**
*ukw*ahlula *to separate* **9**
-**ahlukene** *be divorced* **7**
*ukw*akha *to build* **4**
*um*akhi (*ab-*) *builder* **4**
*is*akhiwo (*iz-*) *building* **16**
*is*alathiso (*iz-*) *sign* **15**
*ukw*aluka *to weave* **12**
*am*andla *strength, power* **12**
*um*andlalo (*im-*) *mat, bed* **8**
*ukw*amkela *to welcome* **1**; *accept* **14**
*is*andla (*iz-*) *hand* **8**
-**anele** *be enough* **5**
apha *here* **6**

apho *there* **6**
apho ... khona *where ...* **8**
*ukw*aphuka *to break* **8**
*i-*apile (*ama-*) *apple* **13**
-**asekhohlo** *left* **15**
-**asekunene** *right* **15**
*ukw*azana *to get acquainted* **1**
*ukw*azela *to know from* **7**
*ukw*azi *to know* **1**; *knowledge* **3**
*ukw*azisa *to introduce* **2**
*is*aziso *advertisement* **10**

B

*uku*ba *to be, become* **10**
*uku*ba *to steal* **15**

*uku*balisa to *relate* 4
umbala (*imi-*) *colour* 5 / *i*bala
   (*ama-*) 14
*i*bala *open space* 15
imbalela *drought* 6
-balele *be intensely hot* 6
*uku*baleka *to run* 12
imbaleki (*iim-*) *athlete, runner* 12
imbalisi (*iim-*) *historian* 4
imbali *history* 16
*uku*balula *to recommend* 13
-balulek*ile be important* 3
*uku*bamba *to hold on* 11; *catch* 15
*uku*banda *to be cold* 5
*i*banga (*ama-*) *standard* (at school) 8
umbane (*imi-*) *lightning* 6;
   electricity 16
*isi*bane (*izi-*) *light* 15
-bani? *who?* 2
-banzi *wide* 8
*u*bawo (*oo-*) (*my*) *father* 1
*u*bawokazi (*oo-*) (*my*) *paternal
   uncle* 2
*uku*baxa *to exaggerate* 6
*uku*beka *to put, place, lay* 9
ububele *kindness* 10
imbewu *seed(s)* 9
*i*bhafrum (*ii-*) *bathroom* 1
*uku*bhaka *to bake* 5
*isi*bhakabhaka *sky* 14
*uku*bhala *to write* 4
umbhali (*aba-*) *writer* 4
*i*bhanti (*ama-*)(*seat*) *belt* 1
*i*bhasi (*ii-*) *bus* 4
*i*bhatyi (*ii-*) *jacket, coat* 14
*i*bhayisekile / *i*bhayisikile (*ii-*)
   bicycle 1
*i*bhedi (*ii-*) *bed* 1
*isi*bhedlele (*izi-*) *hospital* 4
-bhethele *better* 5
*i*bhetri (*ii-*) *battery* 7
umbhinqo (*imi-*) *skirt* 14
*i*bhinqa (*ama-*) *woman* 14
*uku*bhitya *to lose weight* 8
-bhity*ile thin* 5
*i*bhlawuzi (*ii-*) *blouse* 14

*i*bhokisi (*ii-*) *box* 1
*i*bhokhwe (*ii-*) *goat* 16
*i*bhola ekha*t*y*w*ayo *football* 12
*i*bhola yom*nyazi netball* 12
*i*bhotolo *butter* 5
umbhoxo *rugby* 12
*i*bhreki (*ii-*) *brake* 15
*uku*bhubha *to die* 10
*uku*bhudla *to blow* (wind) 6
*isi*Bhulu *Afrikaans* 3
ubhuti (*oo-*) *brother* 1
*i*bhulukhwe (*ii-*) *trousers* 14
*i*bhuthi *boot of car* 15
-bi *bad, ugly* 6
-bila*yo boiled* 5
*uku*bilisa *to boil* (something) 5
*isi*bindi *liver* 8
-bini *two* 5
ubisi *milk* 5
imbiza (*iim-*) *pot* 9
*uku*biza *to call* 7
*i*blekfesi (*ii-*) *breakfast* 13
-blowu *blue* 6
*uku*bola *to decay, rot* 9
*uku*boleka *to borrow* 11; also *lend*
-bomvu *red* 6
*uku*bona *to see* 2
*uku*bonakala *to seem* 10
*uku*bonisana *to discuss* 4
*uku*bonana *to see each other* 1
imbongi (*iim-*) *poet* 16
umbongo (*imi-*) *poem* 7
*uku*bonisa *to show* 4
umboniso (*imi-*) *exhibition* 9
imbotyi (*iim-*) *green beans* 13
-buhlungu *painful, sore* 8
*uku*bukela *to watch* 6
-bukhali *sharp* 8
*uku*bulela *to be grateful* 7
*uku*bulisela *to greet from* 8
-buthakathaka *weak* 9
umbutho (*imi-*) *organisation* 9
*uku*buya *to go back, return from* 8
*uku*buyela *to return to* 12
*uku*buza *to ask* 11
umbuzo (*imi-*) *question* 9

C

icala (*ama-*) *side* 11
ukucanda *to traverse* 16
ucango (*iing*cango) *door* 5
icawa *religious service; church* 6
ukucebisa *to advise* 7
ukucela *to ask, beg for* 3
umceli-**msebenzi** (*aba-*) *job applicant* 10
isicelo (*izi-*) *application, request* 5
icephe (*ama-*) *spoon* 5
ukuchacha *to recover* 8
ukuchana *to aim, hit* 4
-chanekileyo *precise* 10
ukuchazela *to explain to* 10
ukucheba *to trim* 9
ichiba (*ama-*) *pond* 9
ukuchitha *to spend* 14
ichityana *little pond* 9
ukuchola *to pick up* 9
ukuchopha *to sit down, perch* 7
ukuchuba *to peel* 13
ubuchule *skill* 10
ukuchwela *to do woodwork* 12
amacici *earrings* 14
ukucinga *to think* 4
ukucingisisa *to think carefully* 4
ukucoca *to clean* 4
-cocekile *clean* 9
umcoci (*aba-*) *cleaner* 4
incoko (*ii-*) *conversation; dialogue* 1
ukucothisisa *to speak very slowly* 3
isichotho *hail* 6
icuba *tobacco* 7
ukucula *to sing* 4
umculi (*aba-*) *singer* 4
umculo *music* 12
incutshe (*iin-*) *specialist* 14
incwadi (*iin-*) *book, letter* 8
ucwethe (*oo-*) *shrew* 4

D

idabi (*ama-*) *battle* 16
udadewabo *his / her /their sister* 2
udadewethu *my sister* 2
udadewenu *your sister* 2
udad'**o**bawo (*oo-*) *paternal aunt* 2
-dala *old, stale* 6
ukudala *to create* 16
indalo *nature* 12
idama (*ama-*) *dam* 16
ukudambisa *to alleviate* 8
isidanga *degree, necklace* 10
ukudanisa *to dance* 12
umdaniso (*imi-*) *dance* 12
indawo (*iin-*) *place* 4
ndawoni *whereabouts?* 1
-de *long* 5; *tall*
indebe (*iin-*) *trophy* 12
ukudibana **na-** *to meet (with)* 1
udidi *quality* 14
-dikidiki *lukewarm* 8
idilesi (*ii-*) *address* 7
iidiliya *grapes* 13
idinala *dinner* 13
umdla *interest* 4
ukudla *to eat* 10; *to cost* 14
-dla ngoku- *usually* 8
ukudlala *to play* 12
ukudlala **ama**nqindi *to box* 12
umdlalo (*imi-*) *game* 6; *play* 12
umdlali (*aba-*) *player* 12
umdlalo oqhutywayo *serial* 12
umdlalo wamanqindi *boxing* 12
indlebe (*iin-*) *ear* 8
indleko (*iin-*) *expense* 10
idlelo (*ama-*) *pasture* 16
indlela (*iin-*) *way, road* 14
udliwano-**ndlebe** *interview* 10
isidlo (*izi-*) *meal* 10
isidlo sakusasa *breakfast* 13
isidlo sangokuhlwa *supper* 13
isidlo sasemini *lunch* 12
izidlo zakwaNtu *traditional fare* 13
ukudlokova *to roll (ship)* 6
indlovu (*iin-*) *elephant* 4
indlu (*izin-*) *house* 13
indlu yangasese *toilet* 13
ukudlula *to pass by* 15
indoda (*ama-*) *man* 3
idolo (*ama-*) *knee* 8
idolophu (*ii-*) *town* 15

i*indondo* *spectacles / glasses* 14
u*donga* (*iin-*) *wall* 14
u*dongwe* *clay* 14
i*drowa* (*ii-*) *drawer* 1
isi*dudu* *porridge* 13
iin*dudumo* *thunder* 6
in*duli* (*iin-*) *hill* 16
-*dulu* *expensive* 8
uku*duma* *to become famous* 9
-*dumile* *be famous*
u*dumo* *fame* 16
ulu*dwe* (*izin-*) *list* 9; *menu* 13

E

ekugqibeleni *at last* 5
ekupheleni kwa- *at the end of* 10
i-emele (*ii-*) *bucket* 9
emva kwa- *after / behind* 4
emva kwemini *in the afternoon* 4
amendo *speed* 14
enkosi *thank you* 1
ukwenza *to do, make* 4
ukwenzalisa *to hurt* 6
ukwenzeka *to happen* 5
i-eropleni (*ii-*) *aeroplane* 1
i-ertyisi (*ii-*) *pea* 13
ewe *yes* 1

F

uku*fa* *to die* 9
uku*faka* *to put in* 9
i*fama* (*ii-*) *farm* 3
um*fana* (*aba-*) *young man* 1
uku*fana na-* *to be like* 6
uku*fanela* *to suit* 14
-*fanele* *ought* 5
-*fanelekileyo* *appropriate* 9
i*fani* (*ii-*) *surname* 2
i*fanitsha* (*ii-*) *furniture* 12
um*fazi* (*aba-*) *woman* 8
i*fenibelti*(*ii-*) *fanbelt* 15
i*festile* (*ii-*) *window* 7
uku*zifihla* *to hide oneself* 10
uku*fihlwa* *to be buried* 16
uku*fika* *to arrive* 1
um*fino* *wild spinach* 13

i*flawa* *flour* 5
um*fo* (*aba-*) *fellow* 1
i*folokhwe* (*ii-*) *fork* 1
i*fomu* (*ii-*) *form* 1
m*fondini*! (*my*) *fellow*!
uku*fota* *to take photographs* 4
um*foti* (*aba-*) *photographer* 4
uku*fowun(el)a* *to phone (for)* 6
i*fowuni / *i*foni* *telephone* 5
isi*Frentshi* *French* (language*)* 3
i*friji* (*ii-*) *fridge* 5
isi*fuba* (*izi-*) *chest* 8
uku*fudukela* *to move to* 7
uku*fudumala* *to become warm* 6
-*fudumele* *be warm* 6
isi*fudumezi* (*izi-*) *heater* 6
um*fula* (*imi-*) *stream* 9
uku*fuma* *humidity* 6
uku*fumana* (-*fumene*) *to get, find* 5
uku*fumaneka* *to be obtainable* 13
uku*fumanisa* nga- *to find out about* 12
uku*funa* *to want* 2
uku*funda* *to learn* 2
uku*fundela* *to study (for)* 3
um*fundi* (*aba-*) *student, pupil* 4
uku*fundisa* *to teach* 3
uku*fundisisa* *to read carefully* 4
isi*fundo* *lesson* 10
isi*fundo* esiyintloko *major subject* 10
ku*funeka* *it is necessary, must* 3
-*funeka*yo *necessary* 5
im*funeko* *necessity* 9
imi*funo* *vegetables* 9
-*fuphi* *near* 6
futhi *often* 6
-*futshane* *short* 6

G

i*gaba* (*ama-*) *hoe* 9
i*gadi* (*ii-*) *garden* 9
uku*galela* *to pour* 5
i*galelo* (*ama-*) *contribution* 10
i*ngalo* (*iin-*) *arm* 8
isi*gama* *vocabulary* 1
i*gama* (*ama-*) *name* 2; *word*
um*gaqo* (*imi-*) *road* 15

igaraji (ii-) *garage* 1
ingca *grass* 9
-thi **gca gca gca** *dotted* 16
ingcaphephe yezityalo *horticulturist* 4
uku**g**cina *to look after* 8; *keep* 9
uku̱zi̱gcina -phili̱le *to keep* <u>oneself</u> *fit* 12
ingobozi (iin-) *basket* 9
uku**g**odola *to be cold (humans)* 5
uku**g**oduka *to go home* 4
igophe (ama-) *curve / bend* 15
ingozi *danger, accident* 12
igqabi (ama-) *leaf* 9
uku**gq**abhuka *to burst (of a tyre)* 15
uku**gq**iba *to decide* 13
-**gq**ibi̱le *have finished something* 4
ingqiniba (iin-) *elbow* 8
ugqirha (oo-) *doctor* (medical) 4
igqirha (ama-) *traditional healer* 4
gqitha *very, too much* 5
uku**gq**ithis(el)a *to pass (for)* 5
umgqomo (imi-) *bin* 9
umgquba *compost* 9
uku**g**quma *to cover* 9
igqwetha (ama-) *lawyer* 4
ubugqwetha *legal profession* 3
igrabile *gravel* 15
umgubo *flour* 5
ingubo (iin-) *blanket* 6
igugu *pride* 12
uku**g**ula *to be ill* 6
igumbi (ama-) *room* 5
igumbi loku**f**undela *study* 13
igumbi loku**h**lala *lounge* 13
igumbi loku**h**lambela *kitchen* 13
igumbi loku**l**ala *bedroom* 13
igumbi loku**p**hekela *kitchen* 5
igumbi loku**t**yela *diningroom* 13
uku**g**uqula *to translate* 4
umguquli (aba-) *translator* 4
igusha (ii-) *sheep* 13
uku**g**wegweleza *to make a detour* 16
ingxangxasi (ii-) *waterfall* 16
igxalaba (ama-) *shoulder* 8
igxobha *marsh* 9
ingxowa (ii̱n-) *bag* 9

H

i̱hagu (ii-) *pig, hog* 13
halala! *hurray!* 7
uku**h**amba *to go, walk* 1
uku**h**amba na- *to go with* 14
uku**h**amba **ngqo** *to walk straight
   along* 5
uku**h**ambisa *to continue* 4
uhambo *trip* 16
i̱harika (ii-) *rake* 9
i̱hashe (ama-) *horse* 12
hayi *no* 1
i̱heji (ii-) *hedge* 1
heke *well then* 3
i̱hempe (ii-) *shirt* 14
umhla (imi-) *day* 3; *date* 10
umhla woku**z**alwa *birthday* 7
injingalwazi (iin-) *professor* 4
yonke imi**h**la *every day* 3
uku**h**la *to come down* 7
umhlaba *soil* 9
uku**h**laba *to stab* 8
i̱hlabathi *world* 9
umhlakulo (imi-) *spade* 9
uku**h**lala *to stay, live, sit* 1
-**h**leli *be seated* 7
uku**h**lamba *to wash* 8
isi**h**lambi se**f**estile *windscreen
   wiper* 15
umhlangala (imi-) *mongoose* 9
isi̱hlangu (izi-) *shoe* 14
i̱hlathi lelo **zwe** (ama-) *indigenous
   forest* 16
uku**h**lawula *to pay* 4
-hle (-ntle) *beautiful* 2
ubuhle *beauty* 9
i̱hlebo (ama-) *secret* 13
umhlekazi (aba-) *sir* 1
uku**h**lisa *to reduce, bring down* 14
umhlobo (aba-) *friend* 1
i̱hlobo *summer* 6
uhlobo (iintlobo) *kind / sort / way* 10
ubuhlobo *friendship* 12
i̱hlosi (ama-) *leopard* 14
ulu**h**lu *list* 5
ulu**h**lu loku**t**ya *menu* 13

*ulu*hlu lweziselo *beverages* 13
*isi*hlwele *crowd* 12
*i*hoki *hockey* 12
*i*holide *holiday* 7
*uku*hombisa *to adorn, decorate* 14
*izi*hombiso-*m*zimba *jewellery* 14
*isi*hombo (*izi-*) *pattern* 14
*i*hotele (*ii-*) *hotel* 10
huntshu! *hurray!* 5

J

*in*ja (*izin-*) *dog* 10
*isi*Jamani *German* (language) 3
*isi*Japani *Japanese* (language) 3
*i*jezi (*ii-*) *jersey* 12
jikelele (*all*) *round* 7
*uku*jikeleza *to surround* 9
*in*jineli (*iin-*) *engineer* 4
*uku*jonga *to look at* 6
*uku*jongeka *to look as if* 5
*in*jongo (*iin-*) *aim* 9
*i*joni (*ama-*) *soldier* 4

K

kabini *twice* 6
kahle! *hold on!* (exclamation) 6
kakubi *badly* 6
kakhulu *very* 1
kakuhle *well* 1
kamnandi *nicely/goodbye* 6
*in*kampani (*iin-*) *company* 4
kamsinya(ne) *soon, shortly* 1
kananjalo *also* 4
kancinci *a little* 3
kanene *indeed* 4
*in*kani *obstinacy* 14
kanjalo *also, as well* 3
kanjalo *like this* 6
kangaka *so (much)* 3
kangako *so* 6
kangangokuba *so much so* 3
*u*kanina (*oo-*) *cousin* 2
kaninzi *often* 6
kanye *once, exactly* 4
*i*kawusi (*ii-*) *sock* 14
*u*kayise (*oo-*) *cousin* 2

ke *then* 3
*isi*kere sok*u*thena *pruning shears* 9
*i*ketile (*ii-*) *kettle* 5
*i*keyiki (*ii-*) *cake* 5
*i*khabathi (*ii-*) *cupboard* 1
*i*khadi (*ama-*) *card* 4
*uku*khala *to cry, complain* 8
*uku*khalaza (nga-) *to complain*
  (about) 6
*isi*khaliso (*izi-*) *musical instrument* 12
*uku*khanda *to repair (car)* 10
*uku*khangela *to look, check* 7
*uku*khapha *to accompany* 6
*uku*khanya *to shine* 6
-khaphukhaphu *light and fluffy* 5
*um*khasayo (*aba-*) *novice* 14
*uku*khathazeka *to mind, worry* 6
*uku*z*i*khathaza *to worry (oneself)* 8
*i*khaya (*ama-*) *home* 2
*uku*khawuleza *to hurry* 10
*i*khefi *café* 10
*i*khefu *holiday* 10
*u*khenketho *trip* 16
*uku*khetha *to choose* 1; *prefer* 2
*i*khitshi (*ama-*) *kitchen* 5
*i*khiwane (*ama-*) *fig* 13
*uku*khohlela *to cough* 7
*uku*kholwa *to believe* 10
*um*khombe (*imi-*) *rhino* 4
*uku*khombisa *to point* 8
khona *there* 4
-khona *here, present* 1
*um*khondo *track* 16
*um*khuhlane *cold, flu* 8
*uku*khula *to grow* 12
*uku*khulela *to grow up at* 3
-khulu *big* 6
*uku*khulula *to undress* 8
*uku*khululeka *to free, be comfortable*
  7; *relax* 10
*isi*khululo (*izi-*) sama*polisa* *police*
  station 15
*isi*khululo se*bhasi* *bus stop* 15
*um*khuluwa (*aba-*) *elder brother* 2
*uku*khumbula *to remember* 7
*uku*khumbuza *to remind* 5

*uku*khupha *to take out* (also *vomit*) 15
*u*khuphiswano *match, competition* 6
*uku*khusela *to protect* 10
-khusel*ekile be safe* 15
*uku*khuthaza *to encourage* 14
-khuthele *be diligent* 10
*uku*khwela *i*bhayisekile *to ride a bike* 12
*uku*khwela *i*hashe *to ride a horse* 12
*uku*khwelisa *to give a lift* 15
*i*kiriva (*ii*-) *wheelbarrow* 9
*in*kitho (*iin*-) *collection* 9
*i*kliniki (*ii*-) *clinic* 4
kodwa *but* 3
*i*kofu *coffee* 2
*in*kokeli (*iin*-) *leader* 16
*in*koliso *majority, many* 12
*isi*kolo (*izi*-) *school* 2
*i*komityi (*ii*-) *cup* 5
*in*komo *cow* 13
*iin*komo *cattle* 6
*i*kona (*ii*-) *corner* 15
*in*konzo *service* 10
*in*kosazana (*ama*khosazana) *miss* 1
*in*kosi (*ama*khosi) *chief* 4
*in*kosikazi (*ama*khosikazi) *madam* 1
*uN*kosikazi *Mrs* 1
-krakra *bitter* 8
-krelekrele *sharp, bright* 10
kuba *because* 3
kudala *long ago* 6
kude *far* 15
kufuphi na- *near to* 10
-kufutshane *near* 11
*in*kukho (*iin*-) *mat* 14
kulung*ile very well, all right; OK* 2
kungekudala *shortly* 6
*in*kungu *mist* 6
*in*kunkuma *rubbish, waste, garbage* 9
kunye na- *together with* 9
kuphela *only* 4
kusasa *in the morning, early* 4
*in*kuthalo *diligence* 14
kutheni? (+ participial) *why?* 8
kutshanje *recently* 6
kwakhona *again* 1
*isi*kwashi *squash* 12

*i*kwayari *choir* 12
kwaye *and* 10
kwedini! *little chap*! 1
*in*kwenkwe (*ama*khwenkwe) *boy* 1
*in*kwenkwezi (*iin*-) *star* 10
*in*kwenkwana *little boy* 1
*u*kwindla *autumn* (Class 14) 6
*in*kuku (*iin*-) *chicken* 13

L

*uku*lahleka *to be lost* 15
*uku*lala (-lele) *to sleep* 7
*i*lali (*ii*-) *settlement* 7
*uku*lalisa *to make someone lie down* 8
-lamb*ile be hungry* 5
*um*lambo (*imi*-) *river* 4
*um*lambokazi *large river* 4
*uku*landa *to fetch* 9
*uku*landela *to follow* 3
-landela*yo next, following* 6
*i*langa (*ama*-) *sun* 5
*i*lantshi *lunch* 13
*i*laphu (*ii*-) *cloth* 13
*uku*lawula *to direct, rule* 4
*um*lawuli (*aba*-) *director* 4
*isi*layi (*izi*-) *slice* 5
*i*layibhri (*ii*-) 10
*uku*layita *to switch on* 5
*um*lengalenga (*imi*-) *hangings, curtains* 14
*ii*lekese *sweets* 7
*um*lcnze (*imi*-) *leg* 8
*i*letisi *lettuce* 13
-leyithi *late* 7
*uku*libala (-libele) *to forget* 3
*uku*lila *to weep / cry* 8
*uku*lima *to farm, cultivate* 4
*um*limi (*aba*-) *farmer* 4
*uku*lindela *to wait for* 11
*uku*lindisa *to keep someone waiting* 5
*uku*lingana *to try on* 14
*uku*loba *to fish* 12
*u*loliwe (*oo*-) *train* 3
*i*lokhwe (*ii*-) *dress* 14
*um*lomo (*imi*-) *mouth* 8
*uku*londoloza *to save* 9

*i*lori, also *i*loli (*ii-*) *lorry* 1
-lubhelu *yellow* 5
-luhlaza *green, blue* 6
-lula *easy* 4; *light* 6
uku*luma to bite* 8
uku*lumka to be careful* 9
uku*lungisa to prepare* 9; *set the table* 13; *repair* 15
-lusizi *sorry, sad* 6
uku*lwa to fight* 6
u*lwandle* (*ii-*) *sea* 6
u*lwimi* (*ii-*) *tongue, language* 3

M
uku*ma to stop, stand* 7
u*mabona-kude TV* 12
*oo*mabonwakude *TV* 12
u*mafungwashe eldest sister* 2
*i*magi (*ii-*) *mug* 14
u*makazi* (*oo-*) (*my*) *maternal aunt* 4
u*makhulu* (*oo-*) *grandmother* 1
u*maleko* (*oo-*) *layer* 5
*i*mali *money* 1
u*malume* (*oo-*) *maternal uncle* 2
u*mama* (*oo-*) *mother* 1
uku*mamela to listen* 9
malunga na- *concerning* 9
u*mmandla* (*imi-*) *region* 16
u*mmangaliso* (*imi-*) *delight, wonder* 16
u*mantyi* (*oo-*) *magistrate* 4
*i*maphu (*ii-*) *map* 9
u*matshini* wou*cheba* *ingca lawn mower* 9
*oo*mawokhulu *grandparents* 2
uku*mba to dig* 7
u*mbona* (*imi-*) *maize* 13
-mdaka *dirty* 8
*i*meko (*ii-*) *situation* 10
*i*mela (*ii-*) *knife* 13
uku*mela to represent* 12
uku*mema to invite* (passive -me*ny*a) 11
*i*menyu (*ii-*) *menu* 13
mhlawumbi *perhaps* 7
-mhlophe *white* 6
*i*mini *day* 4

emva kwe*mini in the afternoon* 4
uku*mka to go away* 6
mna *as for me* 4
-mnandi *nice, pleasant* 1; *sweet, delicious* 5
-mnyama *black* 6
*i*mo-ntlalo *way of life* 16
molo / molweni *hello* 1
uku*mosha to damage* 9
*i*moto (*ii-*) (*motor*)*car* 1
u*moya* (*imi-*) *wind* 6; *air* 7
uku*mpompa to pump* 7
-msulwa *pure, innocent* 8
-muncu *sour* 6
*isi*muncumuncu *dessert* 13
-mxinwa *narrow* 8
-myoli *lovely* 16

N
uku*na to rain* 6
na- *and* / *with*; (*to*) *have* 2
... na? *to denote a question* 1
uku*naba to stretch* 14
nabani *anybody* 16
u*mnakwabo his/her/their brother* 2
u*mnakwethu my/our brother* 2
u*mnakwenu your brother* 2
nam *me too* / *and* / *with me* 1
-namandla *strong* 6
-namanzi *wet* 6; *juicy* 13
-namava *experienced* 15
uku*nambitha to enjoy, relish* 13
-namendu *speedy* 14
namhlanje *today* 1
nangona *although* 16
*i*nani (*ii-*) *number* 10
nanini na *any time* 16
nantsi (*i*kofu) *here it is* 4
naphina *anywhere* 16
na*se*- *and in* 3
nawe *with* / *and you* 1
nayiphina *into anything* 16
uku*nceda to help someone* 5
uku*zi*nceda *to help* <u>oneself</u> 5
uku*ncedisa to help someone with something* 2

um**ncedisi** (*aba-*) *assistant* 9
u**ncedo** *help* 14
-**ncinane** *small, little* 6
-**ncinci** *small, little* 5
uku**nci**_phi_**sa** *reduce* (passive
  -**nci**_tshis_**wa**) 10
uku**ncokola** *to chat* 2
isi**ncoko** (*izi-*) *essay* 16
ndawonye *together* 5
isi**Ndebele** *Ndebele* (language) 3
-**ndlongo-ndlongo** *rough* 12
u**ndwendwe** (*iin-*) *guest, visitor* 9
-**nencasa** *delicious* 5
i**nene** *truth* 5; *indeed* 5
i**nene** (*ama-*) *gentleman* 1
i**nenekazi** (*ama-*) *lady* 1
-**nenkani** *stubborn* 14
uku**netha** *to rain* 6
-**nga-** *may, can* 2
(i)**ngaba** *perhaps* 11
-**ngakanani**? *how much?* 7
ngakumbi *especially* 3
nga_ma_**nye** *ama*xesha *sometimes* 4
ngaphakathi *inside* 2
ngaphambili *in front* 7; *before* 8
ngaphandle *outside* 2
ngaphandle kwa- *outside of /
  besides* 11
-**ngaphi**? *how many?* 6
ngase- *in the vicinity of* 1
(i)**ngathi** (*it*) *seems* 5
uku**ngcamla** *to taste* 13
-**ngcono** (*kuna-*) *better* (*than*) 8
i**ngcwaba** (*ama-*) *grave* 15
ngelishwa *unfortunately* 3
uku**ngena** *to come in* 2
ngenene *indeed* 5
ngenxa *ya- because of* 6
ngesaquphe *suddenly* 5
isi**Ngesi** *English* (language) 2
ngethamsanqa *luckily* 4
ngoku *now* 2
ngokufanelekile_yo_ *properly* 9
ngokuhlwa *in the evening* 4
ngokukhawuleza *quickly* 6

ngokuqinisekile_yo_ *certainly* 5
ngokwanele_yo_ *enough, sufficiently* 6
ngomso *tomorrow* 6
ngononophelo *carefully* 9
uku**ngqonga** *to sit around
  something* 16
-**ngqukuva** *round* 5; *blunt* 8
ngubani? / **ngoobani**? *who is/are?* 2
-**ngxam**_ile_ *be in a hurry* 5
um**ngxuma** (*imi-*) *hole* 15
um**ngxun**_yana_ *little hole* 15
uku**nika** *to give* 5
uku**nika** u**moya** *to give spirit, i.e.
  support* 12
um**nikazi-khaya** (*aba-*) *housewife* 4
nina *as for you* (pl.) 2
um**ninawa** (*aba-*) *younger brother* 2
nini? *when?* 3
um**nini(kazi)** (*aba-*) *owner* 4
-**ninzi** *many* 4
u**ninzi** *majority, many* 12
uku**nitha** *to knit* 12
njalo *like that* 6
njalo njalo *and so on, etc.* 4
njani? *how?* 1
nje *just* 3
njenga- *like, as* 3
u**njingalwazi** (*oo-*) *professor + name* 4
uku**nkcenkceshela** *to water* 9
u**nobhala** (*oo-*) *secretary* 4
u**nogadi** (*oo-*) *guard* 4
noko *in a small way* 3; *though* 14
nokuba **yintoni** *whatever* 2
u**nomathotholo** (*oo-*) *radio* 12
i**nombolo** **yefoni** *telephone number* 7
-**nomdla** *interesting* 4
u**noncwadi** (*oo-*) *librarian* 4
u**nondyebo** (*oo-*) *treasurer* 4
u**nongendi** (*oo-*) *nun* 4
nonke *you all* 1
u**nontlalo-ntle** (*oo-*) *social worker* 4
u**nopopi** (*oo-*) *doll* 8
u**noposi** (*oo-*) *postman* 4
u**nosilarha** (*oo-*) *butcher* 4
u**novenkile** (*oo-*) *shopkeeper* 4

-the **nqa** *be surprised* **5**
-**nqab***ile be scarce* **6**
i**nqaku** (*ama-*) *written article* **10**
um**nqathe** (*imi-*) *carrot* **13**
i**nqindi** (*ama-*) *fist* **12**
uku**nqunqa** *to chop* **13**
i**nqugwala** (*ama-*) *round hut* **16**
um**nqwazi** (*imi-*) *hat* **14**
uku**nqwenela** *to wish* **7**
aba**ntakwethu** *my/our siblings* **2**
aba**ntakwenu** *your siblings* **2**
aba**ntakwabo** *his/her siblings* **2**
u**Mntla** *north* **3**
e**ntla** *in the north* **3**
ntoni? *what?* **4**
-**ntsundu** *brown* **6**
um**ntu** (*aba-*) *person* **3**
aba**ntu** aba**dala** *adults* **4**
ubu**ntu**   *human decency* **3**
um**ntwana** (*aba-*) *child* **1**
ubu**ntwana** *childhood* **11**
uku**nuka** *to smell* **13**
um**numzana**   *gentleman* **1**
Mnumzana! *Sir!* **1**
u**Mnumzana** (*uMnu.*) … *Mr* … **10**
um**nwe** (*imi-*) *finger* **8**
-**nxan***iwe be thirsty* **5**
u**nxano** *thirst* **5**
um**nxeba** (*imi-*) *a phone* **5**; *rope*
uku**nxiba** *to dress* **12**
isi**nxibo** (*izi-*) *dress* **14**
u**nxweme** (*ii-*) *coast* **16**
u(m)**nyaka** (*imi-*) **6**
u**nyana** (*oo-*) *son* **2**
-**nyanis***ile be right* **3**
u**nyawo** (*iin-*) *foot* **8**
-**nye** (after noun) *one* **5**
-**nye** (before noun) *another* **5**
aba**nye** *some, others* **4**
nyhani! *really!* **12**
uku**nyibilikisa** *dissolve* **5**
uku**nyuka** *to climb* **12**
uku**nyuselwa** *to be promoted* **10**
ama**nzi** *water* **3**
-**nzima** *difficult, heavy* **6**
ubu**nzima** *heaviness* **14**

-**nzulu** *deep* **8**
ubu**nzulu** *depth* **10**

O

uku-**odola** *to order* **10**
-**odwa** *special* **10**
i-**ofisi** (*ii-*) *office* **4**
okanye *or* **2**
-**okuqala** *first* **11**
okwangoku *at present* **11**
-**olukiwe***yo woven* **14**
u**bomi** *life* **16**
-**omil***e be dry* **6**
um**onakala** (*im-*) *trouble, damage* **15**
uk**ongamela** *to rule over* **4**
um**ongameli** (*ab-*) *president* **3**
um**ongi**(**kazi**) (*ab-*) *nurse* **4**
is**onka** (*iz-*) *bread* **13**
is**onka** sa**masi** *cheese* **13**
-**onke** *all* **3**
onke ama**xesha** *always* **6**
i-**onti** (*ii-*) *oven* **5**
uk**onwaba** *become happy, happiness* **6**
uk**onwabela** *to enjoy something* **13**
uku**z**onwabisa *to enjoy* _oneself_ **7**
uk**ophuka** *to break* **12**
u**boya** *wool* **14**
uk**oyika** *to be afraid of* **6**
ul**oyiko** *fear* **10**
i-**oyile** *oil* **7**

P

i**mpahla** *goods*; ii**mpahla** *clothes* **14**
isi**paji** (*izi-*) *wallet* **15**
uku**paka** *to park* **10**
i**pakethe** (*ii-*) *packet* **5**
i**palamente** *parliament* **4**
uku**papasha** *to publish* **7**
i**payina** (*ii-*) *pineapple* **13**
isi**Pedi** *Northern Sotho* **3**
i**mpela**-**veki** (iim-) *weekend* **6**
i**pensile** (*ii-*) *pencil* **1**
i**pere** (*ama-*) *pear* **13**
isi**peshali** *special* **13**
i**petroli** *petrol* **7**
uku**pha** *to give* **5**

phakathi *kwa- between* **5**; *inside* **11**
-phambili *outstanding* **12**
*isi***phambuka** *(izi-) intersection* **15**
*uku***phangela** *to work* **4**
phantse *nearly* **15**
phantsi *down* **1**
phantsi *kwa- under* **11**
*uku***phatha** *to manage, rule* **4**; *to hold / bring* **7**
*uku***phathela** *to bring for* **14**
*um***phathi** *(aba-) manager* **4**
*um***phathi**-*ba*sebenzi *personnel manager* **4**
*um***phathiswa** *(aba-) Cabinet minister* **10**
phaya *over there* **6**
*uku***phazama** *to make mistakes* **3**
*uku***phazamisa** *to interrupt* **4**
*uku***pheka** *to cook* **4**
*um***pheki** *(aba-) cook* **4**, *chef* **10**
*uku***phela** *to come to an end* **6**
*uku***phelelwa** *to be used up completely* **15**
*i***phepha** *(ama-) paper* **5**
*i***phepha**-*n*daba *(ama-) newspaper* **7**
*i***phepha** lo*ku*qhuba *driver's licence* **10**
-phesheya *overseas* **12**
phesheya *kwa- on the other side of* **13**
phezulu *up* **11**
phezu kwa- *on top of, above* **5**
phi? *where?* **1**
*uku***phila** *be well, be alive* **1**
*uku***phila** *qete to be completely well* **5**
*uku***phinda** *repeat* **3**
*isi***pho** *(izi-) gift* **14**
phofu *then* **12**
*um***phokoqo** *mealie meal porridge* **13**
*uku***phola** *to become cool* **5**
-pholile *be cool* **5**
*u***phondo** *hooter* **15**
*uku***phosa** *to miss* **10**
*uku***phulaphula** *to listen* **7**
*uku***phuma** *to go out* **7**
*uku***phumelela** *manage, succeed* **4**
*uku***phumla** *to rest, relax* **5**
*uku*zi**phumza** *to rest oneself* **13**

*uku***phunga** *to drink (hot liquid)* **2**
*isi***Phutukezi** *Portuguese* (language) **3**
*uku***phuthuma** *to fetch* **11**
*isi***pili** *(izi-) mirror* **3**
*i***pilisi** *(ii-) pill* **8**
*isi***pinatshi** *spinach* **13**
*i***pleyiti** *(ii-) plate* **13**
*i***polisa** *(ama-) policeman* **4**
*u***profesa** *(oo-) professor* **4**
*iM***pumalanga** *east* **3**
*i***mpumelelo** *success* **7**

Q

qabu! *relief!* **5**
*um***qa** *thick maize porridge* **13**
*uku***qabula** *to quench (thirst)* **5**
*um***qala** *(imi-) throat* **8**
*uku***qala** *to begin* **8**
*i***qakamba** *cricket* **6**
*um***qamelo** *(imi-) pillow* **5**
*i***nqanawa** *(ii-) ship* **6**
*i***qanda** *(ama-) egg* **5**
*uku***qaqamba** *to shine* **6**; *to throb* **8**
-qaqambile *bright* **14**; *stunning* **16**
*i***nqawa** *(iin-) pipe* **14**
*i***qela** *(ama-) team* **12**
*uku***qeqesha** *to train* **4**
*um***qeqeshi** *(aba-) trainer* **4**
*um***qeshwa** *(aba-) employee* **10**
qha *only* **5**
*uku***qhagamshelana** *na- to contact* **10**; also -**qhakamshelana** *na-*
*i***qhalo** *(ama-) proverb* **10**
*isi***qhamo** *(izi-) fruit* **13**
-qhelekile *normal, usual* **14**
*i***qhina** *(ama-) tie* **14**
-thi qhiwu *hold up* **12**
*i***qhiya** *(ii-) head covering* **14**
qho *always* **6**
*uku***qhobosha** *to fasten* **1**
*uku***qhuba** *to continue* **3**; *to drive* **4**
*uku***qhubela phambili** *to progress* **7**
*um***qhubi** *(aba-) driver* **4**
*uku***qhuqha** *to beat* **5**
*uku***qhuqhisisa** *to beat very well* **4**
*uku***qhwitha** *to start (car)* **15**

*uku*qina *to become stiff* 5
-qinisek*ile be sure* 5
*uku*qokelela *to collect* 9
*in*gqokelela *(iin-) collection* 7
*i*qokobhe *(ama-) shell* 9
*um*qolo *spine, back* 8
*uku*qonda *to understand* 3
*i*qondo *(ama-) degree* 10
*i*qondo lo*bu*shushu *temperature* 6
*uku*qubha *to swim* 10
*i*qunube *(ama-) berry* 7
*in*qununu *(iin-) principal* 10
*um*ququzelelikazi *(aba-) stewardess* 1
*in*qwelo-moya *(iin-) aeroplane* 1

R

*i*rediyo *(ii-) radio* 1
*i*resiphi *(ii-) recipe* 5
*i*restyu *(ii-) restaurant* 7
*i*rhasi *barley* 13
*u*rhatya *dusk* 16
rhoqo regularly 9

S

-sa- *still* 2
*um*sakwethu *my / our sister* 2
*uku*sala *to stay, remain* 1
*i*saladi *(ii-) salad* 13
*u*sana *(iint-) baby* 8
*i*sengwitshi *(ii-) sandwich* 5
*i*sango *(ama-) entrance, gate* 9
*u*sapho *(iint-) family* 4
*i*sarha *(ii-) saw* 9
*uku*sasaza *to broadcast* 4
*um*sasazi *(aba-) broadcaster* 4
*uku*sebenza *to work* 4
*uku*sebenzela *to work for* 4
*um*sebenzi *(aba-) employee* 4
*aba*sebenzi *staff* 4
*um*sebenzi *(imi-) work* 4
*uku*sebenzisa *to use* 5
*i*sekela-*in*qununu *vice-principal* 10
*uku*sela *to drink (cold liquid)* 2
*i*sele *(ama-) frog* 4
*i*sepha *soap* 15
*um*setyenzana *(imi-)* wo*ku*zonwabisa

hobby 10
*i*shelefu *(ii-) shelf* 1
*i*shishini *(ii-) factory* 4
*i*shishini lee*n*cwadi *publishing house* 4
*i*shishini lem*pahla clothing factory* 4
*uku*shiya *to leave* 11
*uku*shiyeka *to be left over* 13
-shushu *hot* 3
*ubu*shushu *heat* 6; *fever* 8
shwaka (-thi) disappear 5
*ama*si *sour milk* 13
*ubu*si *honey* 5
*u*siba *(iint-) feather, pen* 8
-sibekele *be overcast* 6
*i*siko *(ama-) custom* 10
*uku*sika *to cut* 9
*ubu*sika *winter* 3
simahla free, gratis 16
*i*sinala *(ii-) boarding school* 10
*uku*singa *to head for* 16
*i*sinki *sink* 13
*u*sisi *sister* 1
*i*liso *(ame*hlo) *eye* 8
*ama*so *big beads* 14
-soloko *always* 4
*u*Somandla *the Almighty* 4
*u*somashishini *(oo-) businessman* 4
*uku*sombulula *to solve* 10
*u*sompempe *(oo-) referee* 4
*i*songololo *(ama-) millipede* 15
*so*ze *never will* 8
*i*sisu *stomach, abdomen* 8
*uku*suka *to come from* 13
*u*suku *(iint-) 24-hour day* 6
*uku*sula *to wipe* 7
*i*suphu *(ii-) soup*
*i*suti *(ii-) suit* 14
*isi*Suthu *Sotho* (language) 3
*isi*Swati *Swati* (language) 3
*i*swekile *sugar* 5

T

*in*taba *(iin-) mountain* 4
*in*tabakazi *high mountain* 4
*i*tafile *(ii-) table* 13
*in*taka *(iin-) bird* 9

*in*tamo (*iin*-) *neck* 8
*isi*tampu (*izi*-) *stamp* 12
*i*tanki *tank* 7
*i*tapile (*ii*-) *potato* 13
*uku*thunga *to sew* 4
*um*thungi(kazi) (*aba*-) *tailor,*
  seamstress 4
*um*thunzi *shade* 9
*u*tata (*oo*-) *father* 1
*in*tatheli (*iin*-) *journalist* 9
*u*tatomkhulu (*oo*-) *grandfather* 1
*i*teksi (*ii*-) *taxi* 1
*in*tenetya *tennis* 12
*izi*teps *steps* 8
*in*tetho (*iin*-) *saying* 4
*i*tha *tar* 15
*uku*thabatha inxaxheba *to take part* 9
-thabathe*ile* *be impressed* 7
*izi*thako *ingredients* 5
*i*thala (*ama*-) leencwadi *library* 12
*i*thambeko (*ama*-) *slope* 16
-thambile*yo* *soft* 5
*i*thambo (*ama*-) *bone* 9
*u*thambo *exercise* 12
*um*thana (*imi*-) *shrub (small tree)* 9
*uku*thanda *to love, like* 4
-thandeka*yo* *dear* 13
*u*thando *love* 13
*isi*thandwa *dear, darling* 11
*i*thanga (*ama*-) *pumpkin* 13
*uku*thatha *to take* 5
*uku*thathela *to take for* 4
*uku*themba *to hope* 1
*uku*thenga *to buy* 4
*uku*thengisa *to sell* 4
*um*thengisi (*aba*-) *shop assistant* 4
*uku*thetha *to speak* 1
*isi*thethe (*izi*-) *custom* 16
*isi*thethi (*izi*-) *speaker* 4
*um*thetho (*imi*-) *law* 3
*i*theyiphu (*ii*-) *tape* 12
*um*thi (*imi*-) *tree* 4
*ulu*thi (*izin*ti) *stick* 3
*uku*thi *to say* 2
-thile *certain* 8
*uku*thiywa *to be named* 16

*izi*thole *seedlings* 9
*i*thoyilethi *toilet* 13
*i*thuba (*ama*-) *chance* 10
*i*thumbu lamanzi *hose* 9
*i*thumbu *beaded collared necklace* 14
*uku*thumela *to send to* 8
*izi*thuthu *traffic* 15
*u*thuthu lweenkuni *ash* 9
*uku*thwala *to carry* 4
*um*thwali (*aba*-) *porter* 4
*i*ti *tea* 2
*i*tikiti (*ama*-) *ticket* 5
*in*tini *Cape otter* 9
*i*tipoti (*ii*-) *teapot* 1
*i*tispuni (*ii*-) *teaspoon* 5
*in*tlakohlaza *spring* 6
*u*titshala(kazi) (*oo*-) *teacher* 4
*i*titshala(kazi) (*ii*-) *teacher* 4
*in*tlama (*iin*-) *batter, dough* 5
*in*tlanganiso (*iin*-) *meeting* 10
*in*tliziyo *heart* 8
*in*tloko *head* 8
*iin*tlungu (pl.) *pain* 8
*in*to (*izin*to) *thing* 3
*in*to eninzi *a lot* 3
enye *in*to *another thing* 3
*in*to yoku*sela *something cold to drink* 2
*uku*tolika *to translate* 4
*i*toliki (*ii*-) *translator / interpreter* 4
*in*tombi (*iin*-) *girl, daughter* 1
*in*tombazana *little girl* 1
ama*n*tombazana *little girls* 1
torho! *shame!* 7
torhwana! *shame!* 12
*i*toti (*ii*-) *tin* 9
*isi*tovu (*izi*-) *stove* 3
*uku*tsala *to tow* 15
*uku*tsalela *to phone someone* 11
-tsha *young, fresh* 6
-tsha *krebhe* *very fresh* 13
*um*tshana (*aba*-) *niece / nephew* 2
-tshate*ile* *be married* 5
*in*tshatsheli (*iin*-) *champion* 12
*uku*tshaya *to smoke* 7
*i*tsheki (*ii*-) *cheque* 14
*i*tsheyini (*ii*-) *chain* 14

-tshiphu *cheap* 8
-tshiphu *bhe very cheap* 13
uku*tshintsha to change* 10
uku*tshisa to burn something* 6
isi*tshixo (izi-) key* 7
i*tshizi cheese* 13
uku*tsho to say so* 2
uku*tshona to go down (sun)* 5
i*Ntshonalanga west* 3
uku*tshweza to grate* 13
intsimbi *(iin-) small beads* 14
intsimbi ya*maqatha anklet* 14
intsimbi ye*ngalo bracelet* 14
intsimbi yo*mqala necklace* 14
intsimbi *clock* 11; also *bell, iron*
nge*ntsimbi ya- at ... o'clock* 11
-tsolo *pointed* 8
intsomi *(iin-) folktale* 16
isi*Tsonga Tsonga language* 3
isi*Tswana Tswana language* 3
i*tswele (ama-) onion* 13
isi*tulo (izi-) chair* 8
intwasahlobo *early summer* 6
twatse*(ukuthi) fit perfectly* 14
um*tya (imi-) string* 9
ili*tya (ama-) stone* 9
isi*tya (izi-) dish* 12
uku*tya to eat, food* 5
i*tyala (ama-) debt* 10
uku*tyala to plant* 9
isi*tyalo (izi-) plant* 9
in*tyatyambo (iin-) flower* 9
uku*tyebisa to enrich* 14
ubu*tyebi resource* 9
uku*tyelela to visit* 7
tyhini*! gosh!* 14
i*tyuwa salt* 13
u*tywala (Class 14) beer, alcohol* 5

U

ukuba *that; if* 3
ukususela *kwa- since* 16
ukususela *ku- ... ukuya ku- from ... until / to* 16
ukuze *(so) that + subjunctive* 6

V

ama*va experience* 10
um*va / mva back* 15
uku*va to hear, understand* 3
uku*vala to close* 5
i*vatala (ii-) watermelon* 13
uku*vela to come from* 4
um*veleli (aba-) visitor* 10
isi*Venda Venda language* 3
i*venkile (ii-) shop, store* 16
i*venkile yangaphandle country store* 16
i*vili (ama-) wheel, tyre* 5
i*vili lolaleliso spare wheel* 15
uku*vingca to close up* 15
uku*vuka to wake up* 7
i*mvula (imi-) rain* 6
uku*vula to open* 12
uku*vuma agree, admit* 6
i*vumba (ama-) fragrance* 9
uku*vumela to allow (for)* 10
    (passive -vu*nyelwa allowed* 10)
uku*vumelana to be in harmony* 7
isi*vundiso fertiliser* 9
-vuthiwe*yo ripe* 13
uku*vuthuza (komoya) to blow* 6
uku*vuya to be glad* 1
uku*vuyisana na- to rejoice with* 7
uku*vuza to leak, discharge* 8
um*vuzo (imi-) salary* 10

W

uku*wa to fall* 8
i*wayini wine* 5
wena *as for you* 1
i*wodrophu (ii-) wardrobe* 1
-wonke-wonke *public* 11
i*wotshi (ii-) watch* 1

X

xa *when(ever)* 3
eli*xa (<ixesha) while* 13
i*xabiso price* 9
i*xabiso eliphantsi low price* 9
-xakek*ile busy* 5

*ing***x***aki* (*iin-*) *problem* 8
*in***x***alenye* *rest* 12
*in***k***x***aso* (*iin-*) *support* 12
*uku***x***ela* *to tell* 4
*uku***x***elela* *to tell to* 3
*i***x***esha* (*ama-*) *time* 5
*i***x***eshana* *a little while* 13
*uku***x***hala* *to be anxious* 10
*uku***x***hasa* *to support* 12
*um***x***hasi* (*aba-*) *supporter* 12
*i***x***hego* (*ama-*) *old man*
*i***x***hegokazi* (*ama-*) *old woman* 8
*uku***x***hentsa* *to dance (traditional)* 12
*um***x***hentso* (*imi-*) *traditional dance*12
*izi***x***hobo* *tools* 9
*-***x***homekeke* *ku- depend on* 6
*isi***X***hosa* *Xhosa* (language) 1
*i***x***hwele* (*ama-*) *herbalist* 4
*uku***x***ilonga* *to examine* (medically) 8
*-***x***ing*ile* *be stuck* 15
*uku***x***olela* *to forgive* 13
*i***x***olo* (*ama-*) *peel* 9
*u***x***olo* *peace; pardon / excuse me* 1
*uku***x***uba* *to mix* 5
*um***x***ube* (*imi-*) *mixture* 5
*uku***x***ubisisa* *to mix very well* 4

Y

*uku***y***a* *to go to* 1
*um***y***alezo* (*imi-*) *message* 11
*in***y***ama* *meat* 13
*in***y***ameko* *attention* 9
*in***y***anga* (*ii-*) *month, moon* 8
*in***y***ani* *truth* 6
*in***y***aniso* *truth* 3
*y***aye** *and* 6
*uku***y***eka* *to stop* 6
*um***y***eni* (*aba-*) *husband* 2
*i***y***eza* (*ama-*) *medicine* 8
*um***y***ili* (*aba-*) *designer* 14
*u***y***ise* (*oo-*) *her / his father* 16
*in***y***oka* (*iin-*) *snake* 4
*i***y***univesithi* (*ii-*) *university* 2
*i***y***ure* (*ii-*) *hour* 10

Z

*uku***z***a* *to come*
*-***z***ayo* *coming, next* 6
*z***akwaNtu** *traditional* 13
*aba***z***ali* *parents* 2
*um***z***a / *um***z***ala* (*aba-*) *cousin* 2
*uku***z***alisa* *to fill* 5
*uku***z***alelwa* *to be born in / at* 3
*uku***z***alwa* *to be born* 3
*uku***z***ama* *to try* 3
*uku***z***amisela* *to stir* 5
*uM***z***antsi* *south* 3
*isi***z***athu* (*izi-*) *reason* 10
*uku***z***ekelela* *to speak slowly* 3
*um***z***ekelo* (*imi-*) *example* 6
*-***z***ele** + copulative *full of* 16
*-***z***i-* *myself, yourself, etc.* 5
*i***z***iko* (*ama-*) *hearth* 13
*um***z***i* (*imi-*) *homestead* 16
*isi***z***iba* (*izi-*) *deep pool in a river* 10
*um***z***imba* (*imi-*) *body* 8
*i***z***inyo* (*ama-*) *tooth* 8
*uku***z***isa* *to fetch, bring* 5
*uku***z***oba* *to paint, draw* 4
*um***z***obi* (*aba-*) *artist* 4
*um***z***obo* (*imi-*) *illustration* 5;
    painting 12
*uku***z***ola* *tranquillity* 16
*-***z***olile** *be calm* 6
*i***z***olo* *yesterday* 6
*-***z***ondelelayo** *energetic* 10
*um***z***ukulwana* (*aba-*) *grandchild* 2
*i***z***ulu / *i***moz***ulu* *weather* 5
*isi***Z***ulu* *Zulu* (language) 3
*uku***z***uza* *to win* 9; *obtain* 10
*um***z***uzu* (*imi-*) *minute* 6
*um***z***uzwana* (*imi-*) *moment* 5
*u***z***wane* (*iin-*) *toe* 8
*i***liz***we* (*ama-*) *country* 3
*i***liz***wekazi* (*ama-*) *continent* 4
*isi***z***we* *nation* 12
*i***liz***wi* (*ama-*) *voice* 11 (also *spoken
    word*)

English–Xhosa vocabulary

above **phezulu**
accept, to *ukw*amkela
accident *in*gozi
accompany, to *uku*khapha
acquainted, to get *ukw*azana
address *i*-adelesi (*ii-*)
adult *um*ntu *om*dala
advertise, to *ukw*azisa; *uku*bhengeza
advertisement *isa*ziso (*iz-*); *isi*bhengezo
   (*izi-*)
advice *i*cebiso, *in*gcebiso
advise, to *uku*cebisa
aeroplane *in*qwelo-moya (*iin-*);
   i-eropleni (*ii-*)
afraid, to be *uko*yika
after emva **kwa-**
after that emva **koko**
afternoon emva **kwemini**
again **kwakhona**
age *ubu*dala
agree, to *uku*vuma
air *u*moya
all **-onke**
allow, to *uku*vumela
alone **-odwa**
also **kanjalo, kananjalo**
animal *isi*lo; *isi*lwanyana (domestic)
   (*izi-*)
ankle *i*qatha (*ama-*)
answer, an *im*pendulo (*iim-*)
answer, to *uku*phendula
applicant *um*celi-msebenzi (*aba-*)
arm *in*galo (*iin-*)
arrive, to *uku*fika
ask, to *uku*buza
assist, to *uku*ncedisa
assistant *um*necedisi (*aba-*)
at last **ekugqibeleni**
autumn *u*kwindla

baby *u*sana (*iint-*)
bad **-bi**
bag *in*gxowa (*iin-*)
basket *in*gobozi (*iin-*)
beach *u*nxweme (*ii-*)
beautiful **-hle**; beauty *ubu*hle
because **kuba**
because of **ngenxa ya-**
bed *um*andlalo (*im-*); *i*bhedi (*ii-*)
bedroom *i*gumbi lokulala
beer *u*tywala
before **phambi kwa-**
begin, to *uku*qala
behind emva **kwa-**
better **-bhetele**
better than **ngcono kuna-**
between **phakathi kwa-**
bin *um*gqoma (*imi-*)
birthday *um*hla wokuzalwa
black **-mnyama**
blanket *in*gubo (*iin-*)
blue **-luhlaza okwesibhakabhaka**;
   -blowu
boat *i*phenyane (*ama-*); *in*qanawa (*iin-*)
boil something, to *uku*bilisa
book *in*cwadi (*iin-*)
born, to be(at) *uku*zal(el)wa
borrow, to *uku*boleka
boy *in*kwenkwe (*ama*khwenkwe)
bread *i*sonka
break, to *ukw*aphuka
breakfast *isi*dlo *sa*kusasa; *i*blakfesi
bring, to *uku*zisa
brown **-ntsundu**
bucket *i*-emele (*ii-*)
build, to *ukw*akha; builder *um*akhi (*ab-*)
building *isa*khiwo (*iz-*)
bus *i*bhasi (*ii-*)
bus stop *isi*tishi *se*bhasi (*izi-*)

busy, be -**xakek**_ile_
but **kodwa**
butter _i_**bhotolo**
buy, to _uku_**thenga**

call, to _uku_**biza**
calm, be -**zol**_ile_
car _i_**moto** (_ii_-)
careful, to be _uku_**lumka**
carefully **ngononophelo**
carry, to _uku_**phatha**
catch, to _uku_**bamba**
celebrate, to _uku_**bhiyoza**
certainly **ngokuqinisekileyo**
chair _isi_**tulo** (_izi_-)
chance _i_**thuba** (_ama_-)
change, to _uku_**tshintsha**
chat, to _uku_**ncokola**
cheap -**tshiphu**
check, look at, to _uku_**khangela**
child _um_**ntwana** (_aba_-)
childhood _ubu_**ntwana**
choose, to _uku_**khetha**
church _i_**cawa** (_ii_-)
city _isi_**xeko** (_izi_-)
clean, be -**cocek**_ile_
close, to _uku_**vala**
clothes (also goods, luggage) _ii_**mpahla**
coast _u_**nxweme** (_ii_-)
coat _i_**bhatyi** (_ii_-)
cold, to be _uku_**banda**
cold, to feel _uku_**godola**
colour _um_**bala** (_imi_-); _i_**bala** (_ama_-)
come, to _uku_**za**
come from, to _uku_**vela**
come in, to _uku_**ngena**
come to an end, to _uku_**phela**
comfortable, be -**khululek**_ile_
competition _u_**khuphiswano**
complain, to _uku_**khalaza**
concerning **malunga na-**
congratulate, to _uku_**vuyisana na-**
conserve, to _uku_**londoloza**
contact to, _uku_**qhagamshelana na-**
continue, to _uku_**hambisa**
conversation _in_**coko** (_iin_-)
cook, to _uku_**pheka**
cool, be -**phol**_ile_

count, to _uku_**bala**
country _i_**lizwe** (_ama_-)
cover, to _uku_**gquma**
cow _in_**komo** (_iin_-)
cultivate, to _uku_**lima**
cup _i_**komityi** (_ii_-)
custom _isi_**ko** (_ama_-); _isi_**thethe** (_izi_-)
customer _um_**thengi** (_aba_-)
cut, to _uku_**sika**

damage _umo_**nakalo**
danger _in_**gozi**
date, day _um_**hla** (_imi_-)
daughter _in_**tombi** (_iin_-)
decrease, to _uku_**hlisa**
deep -**nzulu**; depth _ubu_**nzulu**
delicious -**mnandi** / -**nencasa**
depend on -**xhomekeke ku-**
die, to _uku_**bhubha** (humans)
   uku**fa** (animals)
difficult -**nzima**; difficulty _ubu_**nzima**
dig, to _uku_**mba**
diningroom _i_**gumbi lokutyela**
discuss, to _uku_**bonisana**; _uku_**xoxa**
dish _isi_**tya** (_izi_-)
divorced, be -**ahlukene**
do, to _ukw_**enza**
doctor _u_**gqirha** (_oo_-)
dog _in_**ja** (_izin_-)
door _u_**cango** (_iing_-)
doorway _um_**nyango**
down **phantsi**
dress _i_**lokhwe** (_ii_-)
dress, to (also wear) _uku_**nxiba**
drink, to _uku_**sela** (cold) _uku_**phunga**
   (hot)
drive, to _uku_**qhuba**
driver's licence _i_**phepha(-mvume)**
   lokuqhuba
drought _im_**balela**
dry, be -**om**_ile_

ear _in_**dlebe** (_iin_-)
early **kusasa**
easy -**lula**
eat, to _uku_**tya**
egg _i_**qanda** (_ama_-)
electricity _um_**bane**
enough, be -**anele**

enter, to *uku*ngena
especially **ngakumbi**
evening, in the **ngokuhlwa**
every **-onke**; everyday **yonke** *imi*hla
exactly **kanye**
example *um*zekelo (*imi-*)
excuse (me)! *u*xolo!
exhibition *um*boniso (*imi-*)
expensive **-dulu**
experience *ama*va; experienced
  -namava
expert *in*cutshe (*iin-*)
explain, to *uku*chaza
eye *ili*so (*ame*hlo)

fall, to *uku*wa
fame *u*dumo; famous, be **-dum**ile
family *u*sapho (*iint̲-*)
famous, bec. *uku*duma
far **kude**
fast **ngokukhawuleza**
fat, be **-tyeb**ile
father *u*tata (*oo-*); my father *u*bawo
  (*oo-*)
fetch, to *uku*landa
few **-mbalwa**
fight, to *uku*lwa
fill, to *uku*zalisa
find, (get, obtain), to *uku*fumana
fine **-hle**
finger *um*nwe (*imi-*)
finish, to *uku*gqiba; finished **-gqib**ile
fire *um*lilo (*imi-*)
first **-oku**qala; firstly *ku*qala
fish *in*tlanzi (*iin-*)
flag *in*dwe (*izin-*); *i*flegi (*ii-*)
flour *in*gubo
flower *in*tyatyambo (*iin-*)
follow, to *uku*landela
food *uku*tya
foot *u*nyawo (*ii-*)
forest (indigenous) *i*hlathi (**lelo zwe**)
  (*ama-*)
forget, to *uku*libala
forgive, to *uku*xolela
fork *i*folokhwe (*ii-*)
fresh **-tsha**
friend *um*hlobo (*aba-*)

fruit *izi*qhamo
full **-zele**

garbage *in*kunkuma
gate *i*sango (*ama-*)
gentleman *i*nene (*ama-*)
get, to *uku*fumana
gift *isi*pho (*izi-*)
girl *in*tombi (*iin-*)
give, to *uku*nika; *uku*pha
give a lift, to *uku*khwelisa
glad, to be *uku*vuya
go, to (with) *uku*hamba (na-)
go home, to *uku*goduka
go out, to *uku*phuma
go to, to *uku*ya
good **-lung**ile
goodbye **hamba**(ni) / **sala**(ni) **kakuhle**
grandchild *um*zukulwana (*aba-*)
grandfather *u*tat'omkhulu (*oo-*)
grandmother *u*makhulu (*oo-*)
grateful, to be *uku*bulela
gratis **simahla**
great **-khulu**
green **-luhlaza okwengca**
greet, to (for) *uku*bulis(**el**)a
grow, to *uku*khula
grow up at, **uku**khul̲el̲a
guest *u*ndwendwe (*ii-*)

hand *is*andla (*iz-*)
happen, to *uku*wenzeka
happy, be **-onwab**ile
hat *um*nqwazi (*imi-*)
head *in*tloko (*iin-*); headache **-nentloko**
hear, to *uku*va
heart *in*tliziyo (*iin-*)
heat *ubu*shushu
heavy **-nzima**
help, to *uku*nceda; help *u*ncedo
help oneself, to *uku*zinceda
help someone with something, to
  *uku*ncedisa
here **apha**
high **-phakamile**yo
hold, to *uku*phatha
hold on, to *uku*bamba
hole *um*ngxuma (*imi-*)

holiday *i*holide; *i*khefu (a breather)
home *i*khaya; at home *e*khaya
homestead *umzi* (*imi-*)
hope *i*themba (*ama-*)
horse *i*hashe (*ama-*)
hospital *isi*bhedlele (*izi-*)
hot **-shushu**
house *in*dlu (*izin-*)
how? **njani?**
how big, much? **-ngakanani?**
how many? **-ngaphi?**
hungry, be **-lamb***ile*
hurt, be **-enzakalis***ile*
hurry, to *uku*khawuleza
hurry, be in a **-ngxam***ile*
husband *umyeni* (*aba-*)

if **ukuba**
ill, to be *uku*gula
immediately **kwangoko**
important, it is **kubalulek***ile*
in front of **phambi kwa-**
indeed **inene**
information *ukw*azisa
injured, be **-enzakalis***ile*
inside **phakathi kwa-**
instead of **endaweni ya-**
interest *um*dla; interesting -nom**dla**
intersection *isi*phambuka (*izi-*)
introduce, to *ukw*azisa
invite, to *uku*mema

keep, to *uku*gcina
keep s.o. waiting, to *uku*lindisa
key *isi*tshixo (*izi-*)
kindness *ubu*bele
kitchen *i*khitshi (*ama-*); *i*gumbi
*loku*phekela
knee *i*dolo (*ama-*)
knife *i*mela (*ii-*)
know, to *ukw*azi, knowledge *ulw*azi

lady *in*kosikazi (*amak*hosikazi)
language *ulw*imi (*ii-*)
large **-khulu**
last **-okugqibela**
late **-leyiti, emva kwexesha**
learn, to *uku*funda
leave, to *uku*hamba, *uku*mka

left **-asekhohlo**
leg *um*lenze (*imi-*)
lend, to *uku*boleka
lesson *isi*fundo (*izi-*)
letter *in*cwadi (*iin-*); *i*leta (*ii-*)
lie down, to *uku*lala **phantsi**
light *isi*bane (*izi-*)
lightning *um*bane
life *ubo*mi
like, to *uku*thanda
listen, to *uku*mamela; *uku*phulaphula
little **-ncinci; -ncinane**
live, to (= reside) *uku*hlala
long **-de**
long ago **kudala**
look, to *uku*jonga
look after, to *uku*gcina
look as if, to *uku*jongeka
look for, to *uku*funa
lost, be **-lahlek***ile*
lounge *i*gumbi *loku*hlala
love, to *uku*thanda
lovely **-myoli**
luck *i*thamsanqa; luckily
ngethamsanqa
lunch *isi*dlo sas*e*mini

make, to *ukw*enza
man *in*doda (*ama-*)
manage, to *uku*phatha
manager *um*phathi (*aba-*)
many **-ninzi**
marry, to *uku*tshata, married, be
-tshat*ile*
meal *isi*dlo (*izi-*)
meat *in*yama
medicine *i*yeza (*ama-*)
meet with, to *uku*dibana **na-**
meeting *in*tlanganiso (*iin-*)
menu *i*menyu; *ulu*hlu *loku*tya
message *um*yalezo (*imi-*)
milk *u*bisi
mistake, to make a *uku*phazama
moment *um*zuzwana (*imi-*)
money *i*mali
month; moon *in*yanga (*iin-*)
morning, in the **kusasa**
mother *u*mama (*oo-*)

motorcycle *isi*thuthuthu (*izi-*)
mountain *in*taba (*iin-*)
music *um*culo

name *i*gama (*ama-*)
narrow -mxinwa
nation *isi*zwe (*izi-*)
nature *in*dalo
near (to) -kufuphi na-
necessary, it is kufuneka ...
need, to *uku*funa
new -tsha
news *ii*ndaba
newspaper *i*phepha-*n*daba (*ama-*)
next (coming) -landela*yo* (-za*yo*)
nice -mnandi
night *ubu*suku; *at* night *e*busuku
nose *im*pumlo (*iim-*)
now ngoku
nurse *um*ongi(kazi) (*ab-*)

often futhi, *ama*xesha *ama*ninzi, kaninzi
old -dala
once kanye
only kuphela, qha
open, to *uku*vula, be open -vul*ile*
opportunity *i*thuba (*ama-*)
or okanye
organisation *um*butho (*imi-*)
outside ngaphandle
over there phaya
overseas -phesheya

pain *ii*ntlungu; painful -buhlungu
paper *i*phepha (*ama-*)
parent *um*zali (*aba-*)
passenger *um*hambi (*aba-*)
patient *um*guli (*aba-*)
pay, to *uku*hlawula
peace *u*xolo
peel, to *uku*chuba
pen *u*siba (*iin*tsiba)
perhaps mhlawumbi; (i)ngaba
person *um*ntu (*aba-*)
pick up, to *uku*chola
place *in*dawo (*iin-*)
place, to *uku*beka
play, to *uku*dlala, a play *um*dlalo (*imi-*)
pleasant -mnandi

please! nceda!
point, to *uku*khombisa
policeman *i*polisa (*ama-*)
police station *isi*khululo *sama*polisa
   (*izi*khululo *zama*polisa)
pot *im*biza (*iim-*)
pour, to *uku*galela
prefer, to *uku*khetha
prepare, to *uku*lungisa
president *um*ongameli (*ab-*)
price *i*xabiso (*ama-*) (low *eli*phantsi)
problem *in*gxaki (*iin-*)
properly ngokufanelekileyo
protect, to *uku*khusela
power *ama*ndla
public phone *i*fowuni kawonke-wonke
put (on), to *uku*beka
put into, to *uku*faka

question *um*buzo (*imi-*)
quickly ngokukhawuleza
quiet, to be *uku*thula

rain *im*vula (*iim-*)
rain, to *uku*na; *uku*netha
read, to *uku*funda
ready, be (finished) -gqib*ile*
receive, to *uku*fumana
recently kutshanje
recommend, to *uku*cebisa, *uku*balula
recover, to *uku*chacha
red -bomvu
region *um*mandla (*imi-*)
relax, to *uku*khululeka
remember, to *uku*khumbula
remind, to *uku*khumbuza
repair, to *uku*lungisa; *uku*khanda (car)
repeat, to *uku*phinda
reply, to *uku*phendula
request, to *uku*cela
request *isi*celo (*izi-*)
resemble, to *uku*fana na-
rest, to *uku*phumla
restaurant *i*restyu (*ii-*)
return from *uku*buya
return to *uku*buyela
ride, to *uku*khwela (car, horse)
right -asekunene
right, be -nyanis*ile*

river *um*lambo (*imi-*)
road *in*dlela (*iin-*); *um*gaqo (*imi-*)
room *i*gumbi (*ama-*)
rubbish *in*kunkuma
run, to *uku*baleka

sad -lusizi
safe -khuselekile*yo*
salary *um*vuzo (*imi-*)
save, to *uku*londoloza
say, to *uku*thi; say so *uku*tsho
school *isi*kolo (*izi-*)
sea *u*lwandle
see, to *uku*bona
sell, to *uku*thengisa
send to *uku*thumela
separate, to *ukw*ahlula
settlement *i*lali (*ii-*)
shoe *isi*hlangu (*izi-*)
shop *i*venkile (*ii-*)
short -futshane
show, to *uku*bonisa
side *i*cala (*ama-*)
sign *i*salathiso (*iz-*)
sit (down), to *uku*hlala (**phantsi**)
skill *ubu*chule
skirt *um*bhinqo (*imi-*)
sky *isi*bhakabhaka
sleep (well), to *uku*lala (**kakuhle**)
slowly **kade**; **ngokucothayo**
small -ncinci, -ncinane
smell, to *uku*nuka
sock *i*kawusi (*ii-*)
soil *um*hlaba
sometimes *ama*nye *ama*xesha
son *u*nyana (*oo-*)
soon **kamsinya(ne)**
sore -buhlungu
sorry, be -lusizi, sorry! **uxolo!**
sort (type) *u*hlobo (*iint-*)
speak, to *uku*thetha
speak slowly, to *uku*cothisisa;
    *uku*zekelela
specialist *in*cutshe (*iin-*)
spoon *i*cephe (*ama-*)
sport *um*dlalo (*imi-*)
staff *aba*sebenzi
stand, to *uku*ma
star *in*kwenkwezi (*iin-*)

start, to *uku*qala
station *isi*tishi (*izi-*)
stay, to (= reside) *uku*hlala; *uku*sala
    (= remain)
steal, to *uku*ba
still -sa- (ndisafunda); -se- (usemtsha)
stone *i*litya (*ama-*)
stop, to *uku*ma; *uku*misa; *uku*yeka
story *i*bali (*ama-*); *in*tsomi (*iin-*)
street *isi*talato (*izi-*)
strong -namandla
student *um*fundi (*aba-*)
study (for), to *uku*fund(el)a
study *i*gumbi lokufundela
succeed, to *uku*phumelela
success *im*pumelelo
suddenly **ngesaquphe**
sufficiently **ngokwaneleyo**
summer *i*hlobo
sun *i*langa
supper *isi*dlo sangokuhlwa; *i*dinala
sure, be -qinisek*ile*
surname *i*fani (*ii-*)
sweet -mnandi
swim, to *uku*qubha

table *i*tafile (*ii-*)
take, to *uku*thatha; *uku*thabatha
take out, to *uku*khupha
take part in, to *uku*thabatha *in*xaxheba
talk, to *uku*thetha
tall -de
taste, to *uku*ngcamla
taxi *i*teksi (*ii-*); by taxi **ngeteksi**
teach, to *uku*fundisa
team *i*qela (*ama-*)
telephone, to *uku*fowun(el)a,
    telephone *i*fowuni / *i*foni; *um*nxeba
tell (to), to -xel(el)a
thank, to *uku*bulela; thanks **enkosi**
that (conj) **ukuba**
there **apho, khona**
thing *i*nto (*izin-*)
think, to *uku*cinga
thirsty -nxaniwe; thirst *u*nxano
thunder *ii*ndudumo
ticket *i*tikiti (*ama-*)
time *i*xesha (*ama-*); on time **ngexesha**
tired, be -diniwe

tobacco *i*cuba
today **namhlanje**
together (with) **kunye na-**, **ndawonye**
toilet *in*dlu yangasese; *i*thoyilethi
tomorrow **ngomso**
too (much) **gqitha**
tools *izi*xhobo
tooth *i*zinyo (*ama-*)
town *i*dolophu (*ii-*)
traditional -zakwaNtu
traditional fare *izi*dlo zakwaNtu
traditional healer *i*gqirha (*ama-*)
train *u*loliwe (*oo-*); *i*treyini (*ii-*)
train, to *uku*qeqesha
traffic *izi*thuthu
translate, to *uku*guqula; *uku*tolika
travel, to *uku*hamba
tree *um*thi (*imi-*)
trip *u*hambo; *u*khenketho
trouble *umo*nakala (*im-*)
trousers *i*bhulukhwe (*ii-*)
try, to *uku*zama
turn towards, to *uku*jika nga-

ugly **-bi**
under **phantsi kwa-**
understand, to *uku*qonda; *uku*va
undress, to *uku*khulula
unfortunately **ngelishwa**
up **phezulu**
use, to *uku*sebenzisa
usually **ngesiqhelo**

very **kakhulu**
vicinity, in the **ngase-**
village *i*lali; *i*dolophana (*ii-*)
visit, to *uku*tyelela; *uku*hambela
visitor *u*ndwendwe (*ii-*)
voice *ili*zwi (*ama-*)

wait (for), to *uku*linda
wake up, to *uku*vuka
walk, to (straight) *uku*hamba (*ngqo*)
wall *u*donga (*iin-*)
wallet *isi*paji (*izi-*)
want, to *uku*funa

warm, be **-fudumele**
wash, to *uku*hlamba
waste, to *uku*chitha
watch, to (e.g. TV) *uku*bukela
water *ama*nzi
way *in*dlela (*iin-*)
weak **-buthathaka**
wear, to *uku*nxiba
weather *i*zulu; *imo*zulu
weather forecast *u*qikelelo lwemozulu
week *i*veki (*ii-*)
weekend *im*pela-veki (*iim-*)
weight *ubu*nzima
welcome! **wamkelek***ile*/**namkelek***ile*!
welcome, to *ukw*amkela
well **kakuhle**
well, to be *uku*phila
wet **-manzi**
what? **ntoni?**
whatever **nokuba yintoni**
when **xa**, when? **nini?**
where? **phi?** whereabouts? **ndawoni?**
white **-mhlophe**
who? **-bani?**
why? **kutheni?**
wide **-banzi**
wife *in*kosikazi (*ama*khosikazi)
wind *u*moya (*imi-*)
window *i*festile (*ii-*)
wipe, to *uku*sula
wish, to *uku*nqwenela
woman *um*fazi (*aba-*); *i*bhinqa (*ama-*)
word *i*gama (*ama-*)
work *um*sebenzi (*imi-*)
work, to *uku*sebenza; *uku*phangela
world *i*hlabathi
worry, to *uku*khathazeka
worry oneself, to *uku*zikhathaza
write, to *uku*bhala

year *u*nyaka (*imi-*)
yellow **-lubhelu**
yesterday *i*zolo
young **-tsha**

Bibliography

Xhosa language

Kirsch, B. and **Skorge**, S., *Masithethe isiXhosa*, Cape Town, Juta & Co. 1995.

Lanham, L.W., **Riordan**, J., **Mathiso**, M., **Davey**, A.S., **Bentele**, S.V. and **Mahlasela**, B. *Lumko Self-instruction Course in Xhosa*, Grahamstown, Institute of Social and Economical Research, Rhodes University, 1969.

McLaren, J., *A Xhosa Grammar* 4th edn., Cape Town, Longman, 1955.

Pahl, H.W., *IsiXhosa* 3rd edn., Johannesburg, Educum, 1985.

Satyo, S.C., *Igrama Noncwadi LwesiXhosa Ibanga 10*, Via Afrika, 1992.

Zotwana, Z. S., *Xhosa in Context – from Novice to Intermediate*, Cape Town, Perskor, 1991.

Dictionaries

Fischer, A., **Weiss**, E., **Mdala**, E. and **Tshabe**, S., *English–Xhosa Dictionary*, Cape Town, Oxford University Press, 1985.

Godfrey, R., *A Xhosa–English Dictionary* 2nd edn., Lovedale Mission Press, 1918.

McLaren, J., *A New Concise Xhosa–English Dictionary* 2nd edn., Cape Town, Longmans, 1963.

Pahl, H.W. (ed.) *The Greater Dictionary of Xhosa* vol. 3. Alice, University of Fort Hare, 1989.

South African *Multi-Language Dictionary and Phrase Book*, The Reader's Digest Association, Cape Town, 1991.

Literature and Further Reading

Bongela, K.S., *IPhulo*, Cape Town, Maskew Miller Longman, 1977.

Jabavu, N., *The Ochre People*, London, John Murray, 1963.

Jolobe, J.J.R., *Amavo*, Johannesburg, Witwatersrand UP, 1973.

Jolobe, J.J.R. (ed), *Indyebo Yesihobe*, Johannesburg, Educum, 1970.

Jordan, A.C., *Towards an African Literature – The Emergence of Literary Form in Xhosa*, Berkeley and Los Angeles, University of California Press, 1973.

Magona, S., *To My Children's Children*, Cape Town, David Philip, 1990.

Magona, S., *Kubantwana Babantwana Bam*, Cape Town, David Philip, 1995.

Mandela, N.R., *Long Walk to Freedom*, Randburg, Purnell, 1994.

Mesatywa, E.W.M., *Izaci namaQhalo EsiXhosa*, Cape Town, Longman Southern Africa (Pty) Ltd, 1954.

Peires, J.B., *The House of Phalo*, Johannesburg, Ravan Press, 1981.

Index